PIANO • VOCAL • GUITAR

INSPIRATIONAL BALLADS

26 SONGS OF FAITH, HOPE & LOVE

2 ALWAYS THERE
SECRET GARDEN

7 BLESS THE BROKEN ROAD
RASCAL FLATTS

14 BRAID MY HAIR
RANDY OWEN

22 FRIENDS
MICHAEL W. SMITH

28 FROM A DISTANCE
BETTE MIDLER

33 GOD BLESS THE U.S.A.
LEE GREENWOOD

38 HERO
MARIAH CAREY

42 I BELIEVE I CAN FLY
R. KELLY

48 I CAN ONLY IMAGINE
MERCYME

66 I HOPE YOU DANCE
LEE ANN WOMACK WITH SONS OF THE DESERT

74 I WILL BE HERE FOR YOU
MICHAEL W. SMITH

80 I'M ALREADY THERE
LONESTAR

88 JESUS TAKE THE WHEEL
CARRIE UNDERWOOD

55 LIVE LIKE YOU WERE DYING
TIM MCGRAW

94 LOVE OF MY LIFE
MICHAEL W. SMITH

98 A MOMENT LIKE THIS
KELLY CLARKSON

106 MY HEART WILL GO ON (LOVE THEME FROM 'TITANIC')
CELINE DION

112 ONLY HOPE
MANDY MOORE

118 SOMEWHERE OUT THERE
LINDA RONSTADT & JAMES INGRAM

123 THAT'S WHAT LOVE IS FOR
AMY GRANT

133 THERE YOU'LL BE
FAITH HILL

128 UP TO THE MOUNTAIN
PATTY GRIFFIN

138 WAY UP THERE
PATTI LABELLE

154 WHEN YOU BELIEVE (FROM THE PRINCE OF EGYPT)
WHITNEY HOUSTON & MARIAH CAREY

144 YOU LIGHT UP MY LIFE
DEBBY BOONE

148 YOU RAISE ME UP
JOSH GROBAN

ISBN 978-1-4234-3830-4

7777 W. BLUEMOUND RD. P.O. BOX 13819 MILWAUKEE, WI 53213

Visit Hal Leonard Online at
www.halleonard.com

ALWAYS THERE

Words and Music by BRENDAN GRAHAM
and ROLF LOVLAND

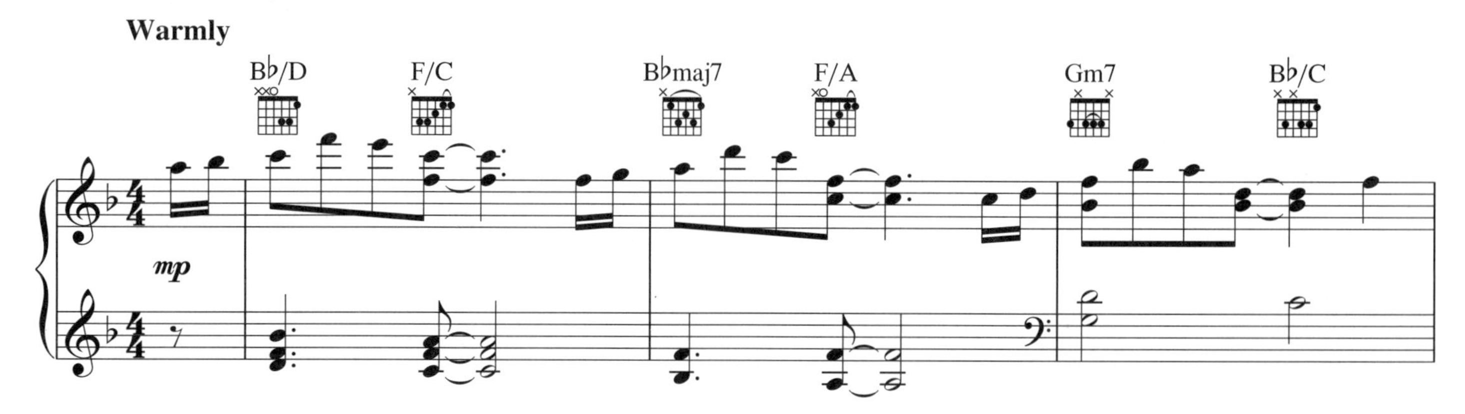

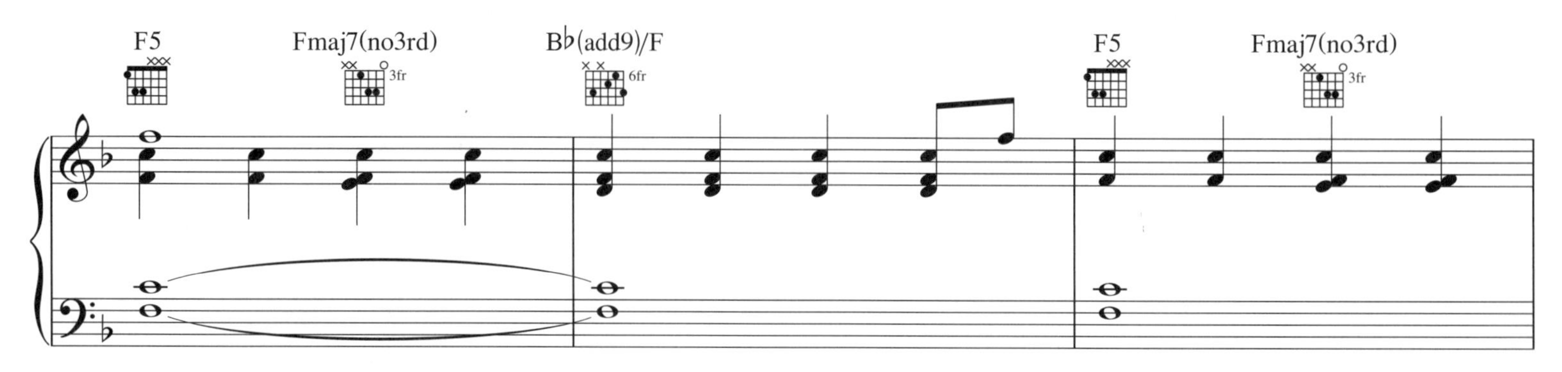

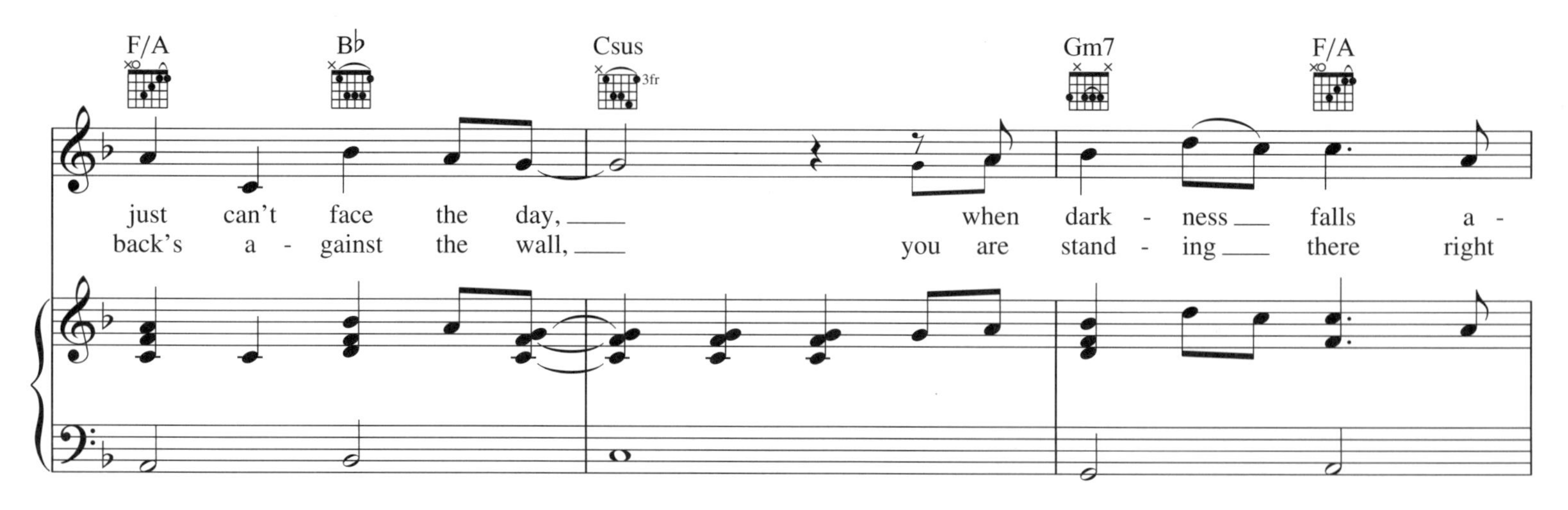

B♭
Dm
B♭6
Csus
3fr
B♭/D
C/E
round me, and I just can't find my way. When my
with me, just to keep me stand - ing tall. Though a

F
Gm/F
F
F/A
B♭
eyes don't clear - ly see, when I stum - ble through it all,
bur - den I may be, you don't wea - ry, you don't rest.

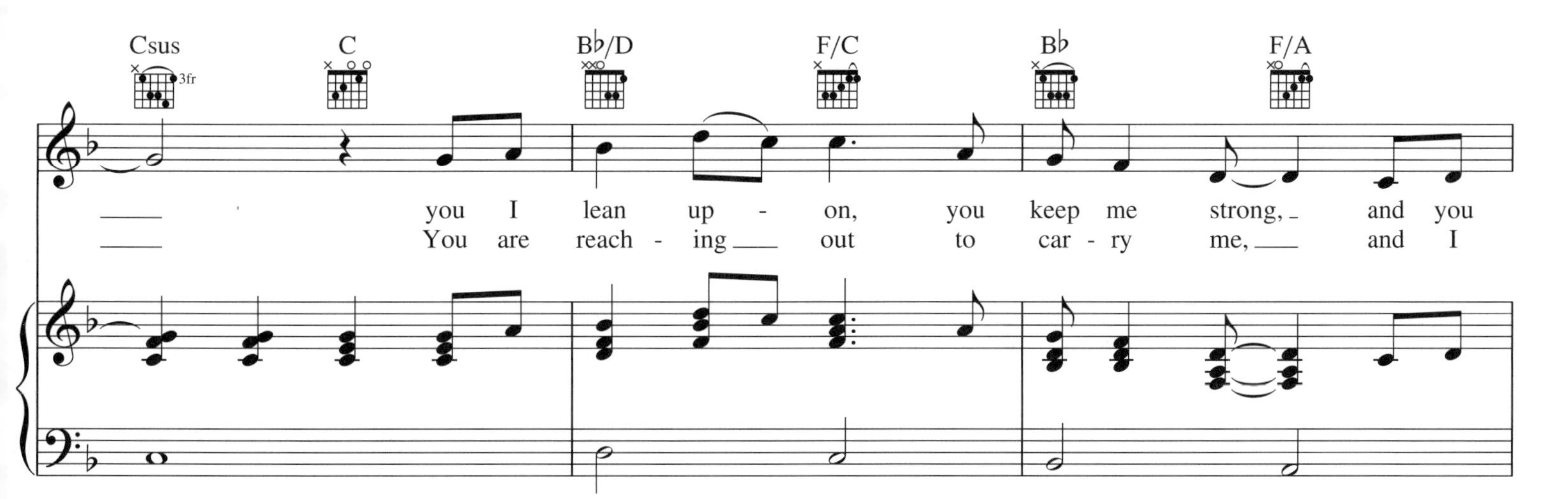
Csus
3fr
C
B♭/D
F/C
B♭
F/A
you I lean up - on, you keep me strong, and you
You are reach - ing out to car - ry me, and I

Gm7
C7
F
C/E
Dm
Dm/C
rise me when I fall.
know I'm heav - en - blest.
You are there when I most

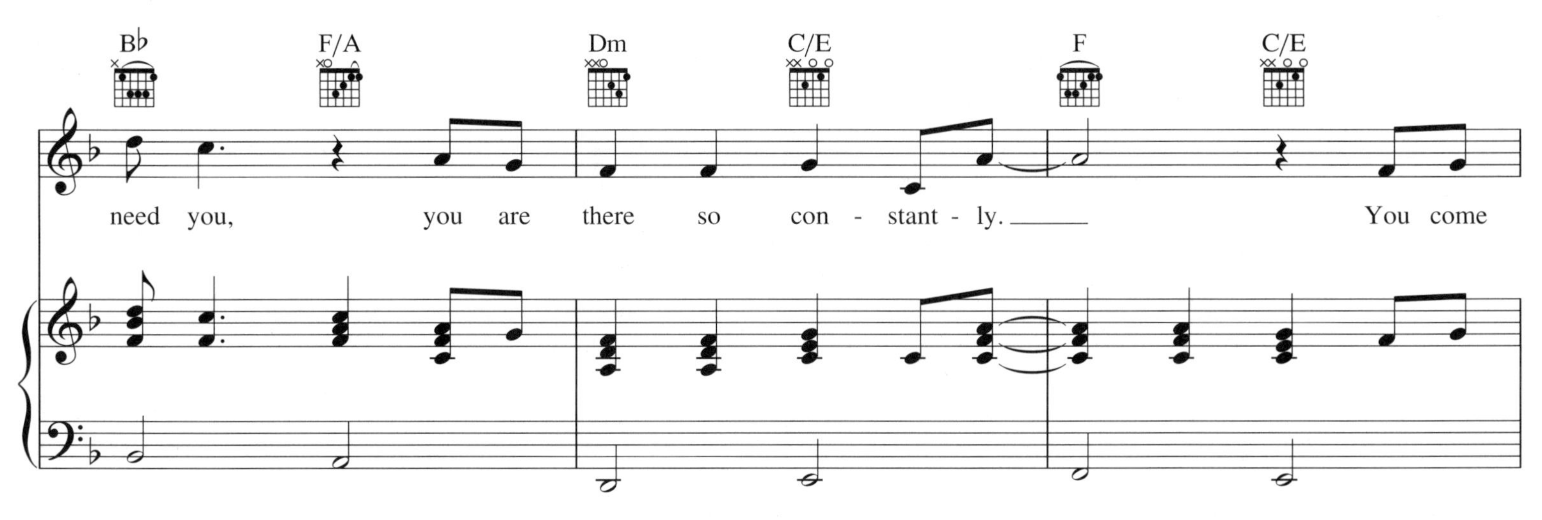
Bb
F/A
Dm
C/E
F
C/E
need you, you are there so con - stant - ly.
You come

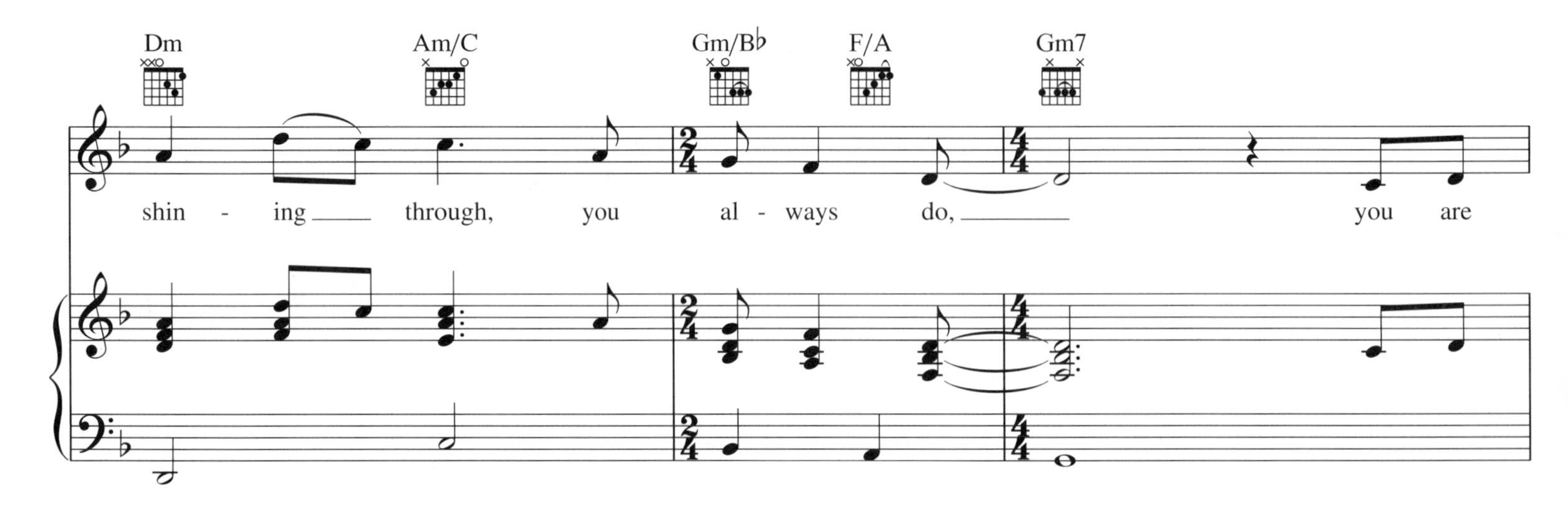
Dm
Am/C
Gm/Bb
F/A
Gm7
shin - ing through, you al - ways do,
you are

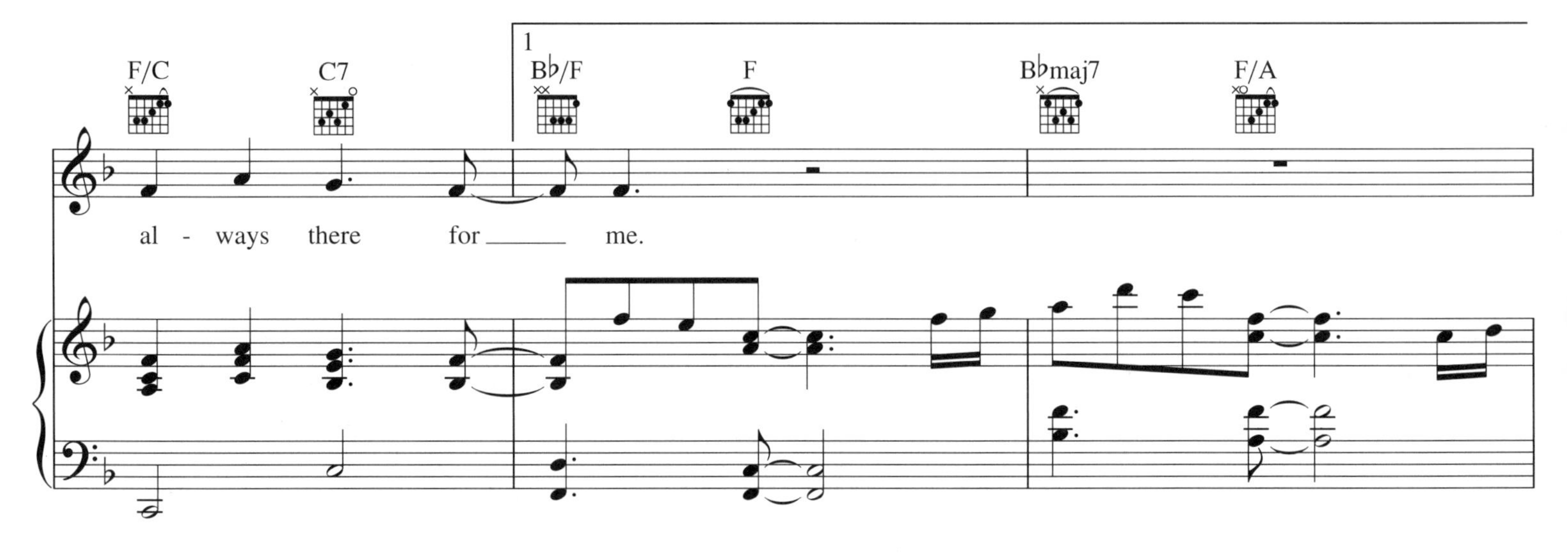
F/C
C7
1
Bb/F
F
Bbmaj7
F/A
al - ways there for me.

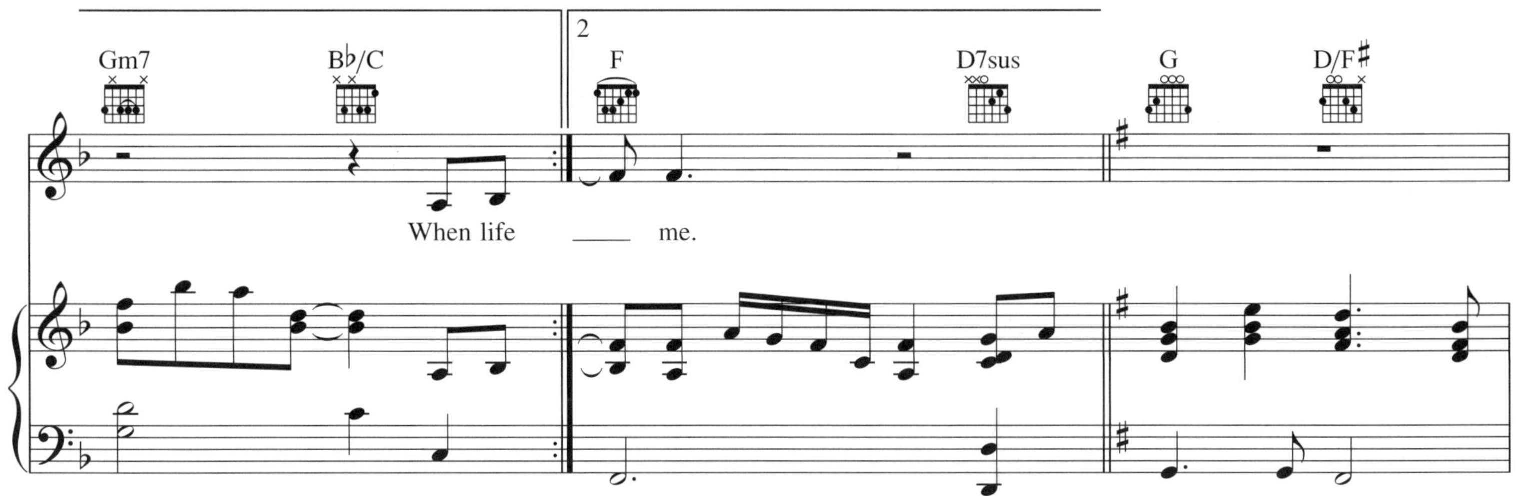
Gm7
Bb/C
2
F
D7sus
G
D/F#
When life me.

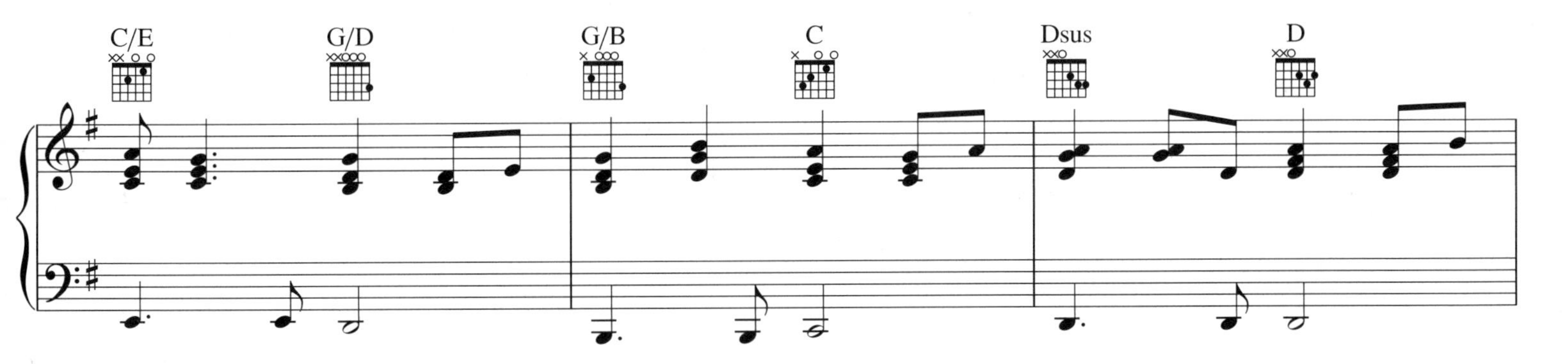
C/E
G/D
G/B
C
Dsus
D

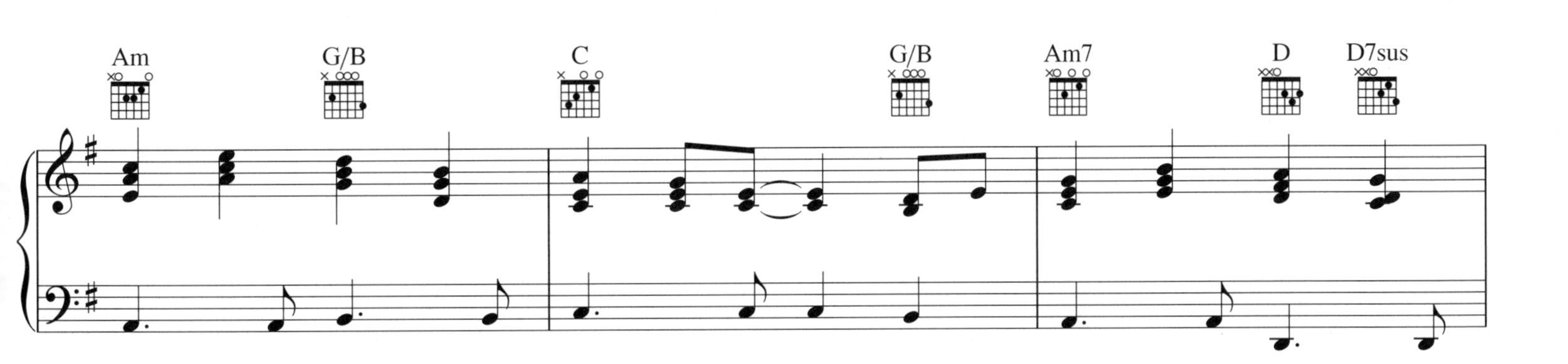
Am
G/B
C
G/B
Am7
D
D7sus

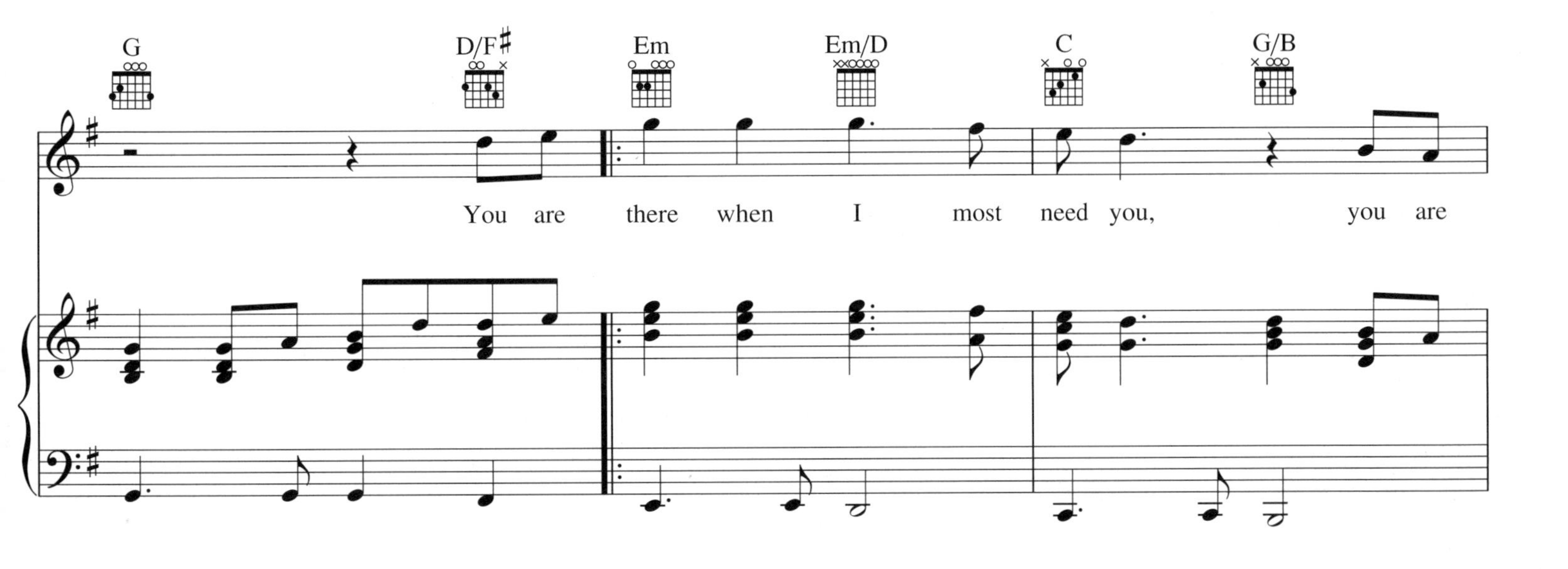
G
D/F#
Em
Em/D
C
G/B
You are there when I most need you, you are

Em
D/F#
G
D/F#
Em
Bm/D
there so con - stant - ly. And you come shin - ing through, you

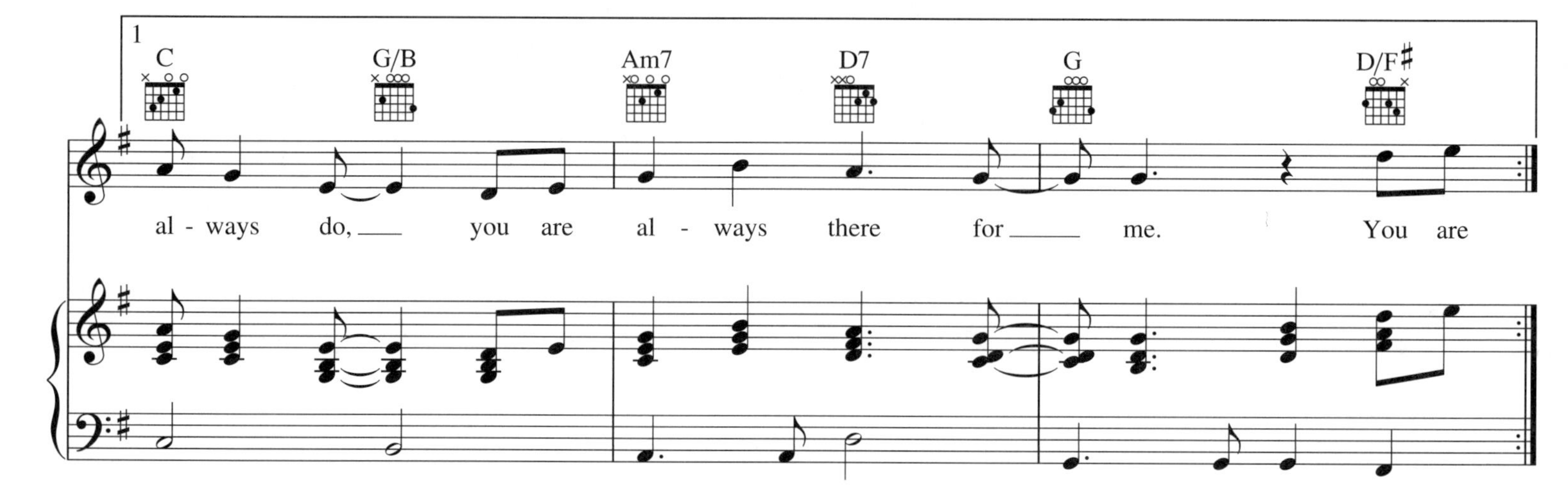
1
C
G/B
Am7
D7
G
D/F♯
al - ways do, you are al - ways there for me. You are

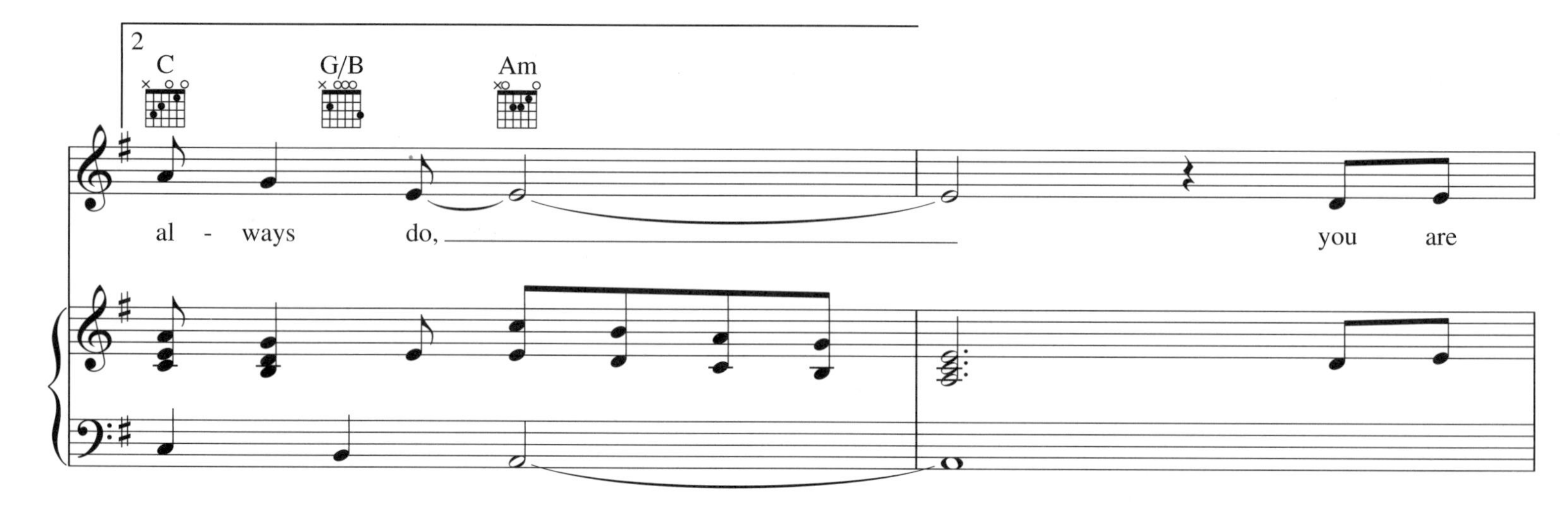
2
C
G/B
Am
al - ways do, you are

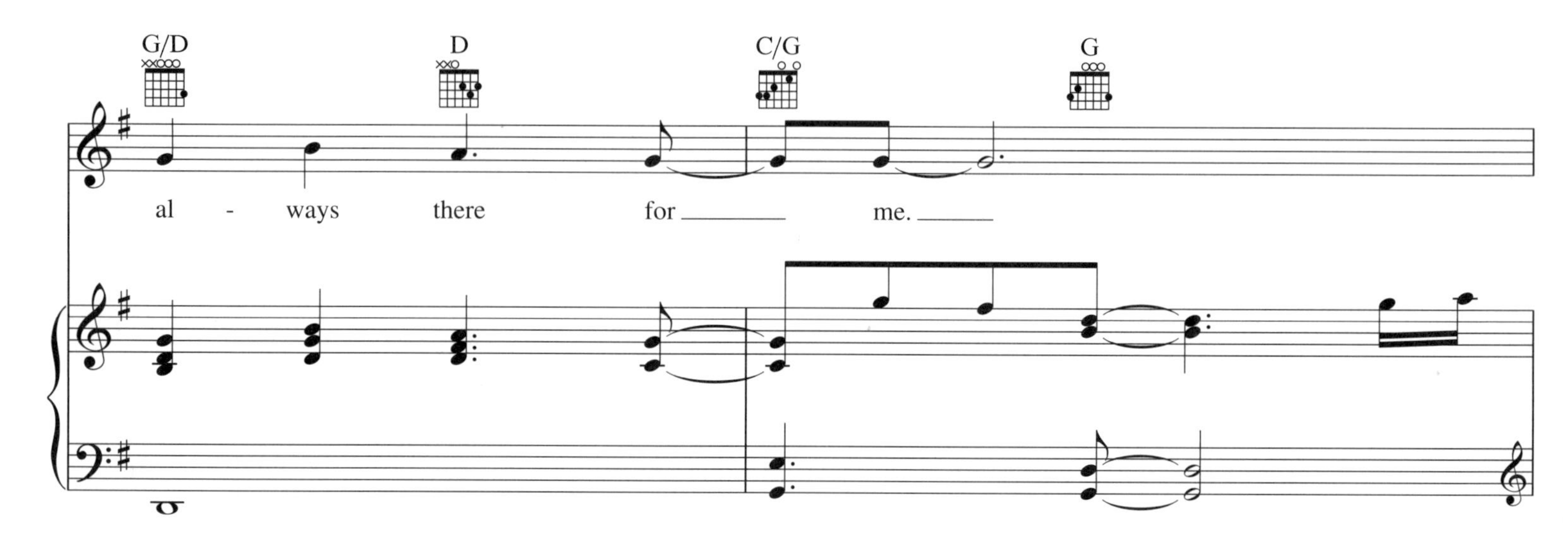
G/D
D
C/G
G
al - ways there for me.

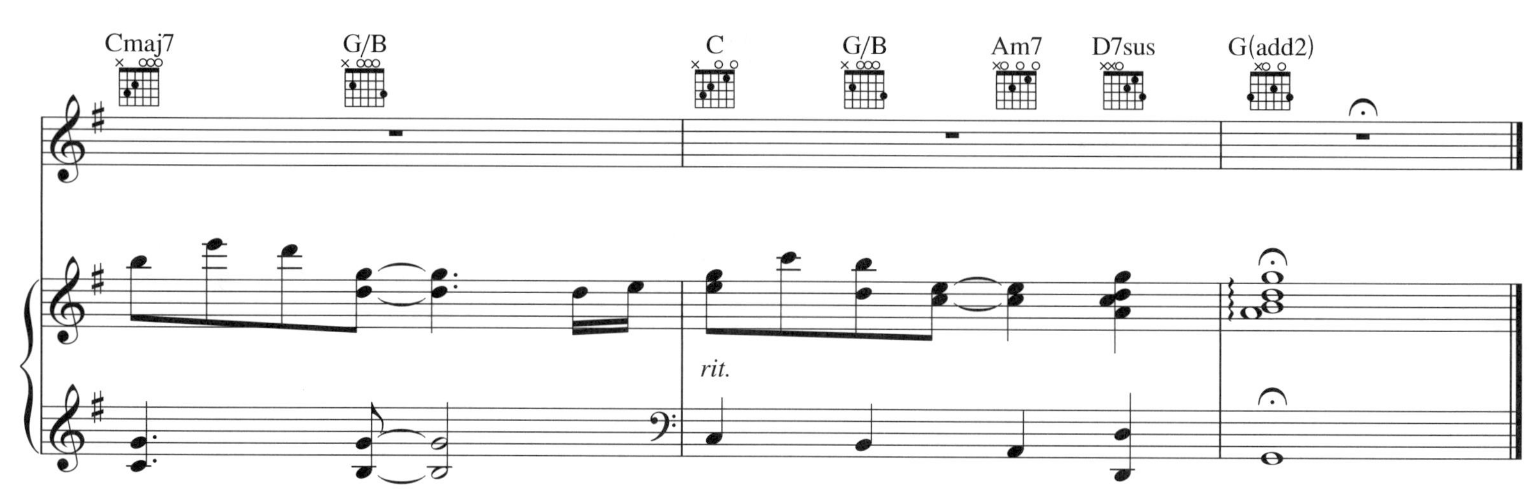
Cmaj7
G/B
C
G/B
Am7
D7sus
G(add2)
rit.

BLESS THE BROKEN ROAD

Words and Music by MARCUS HUMMON,
BOBBY BOYD and JEFF HANNA

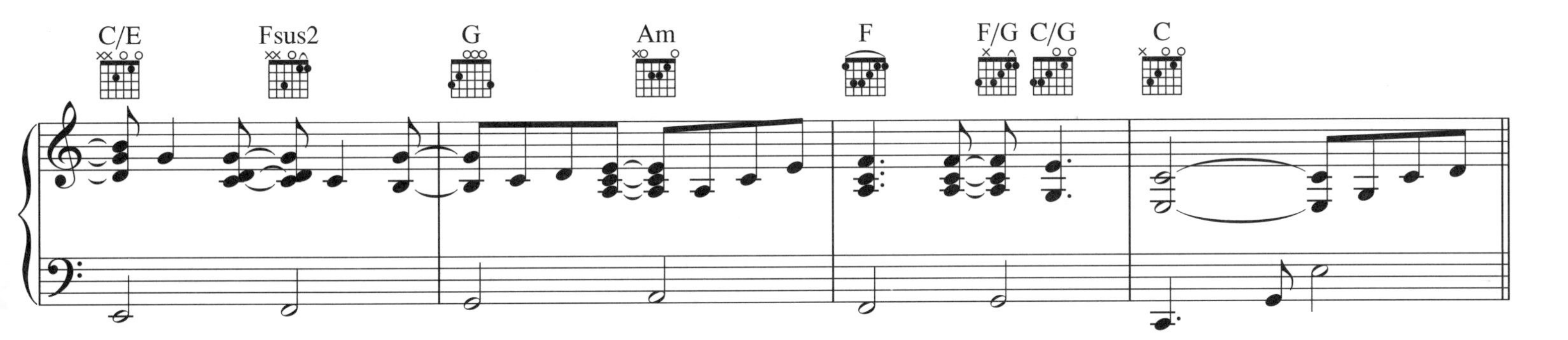

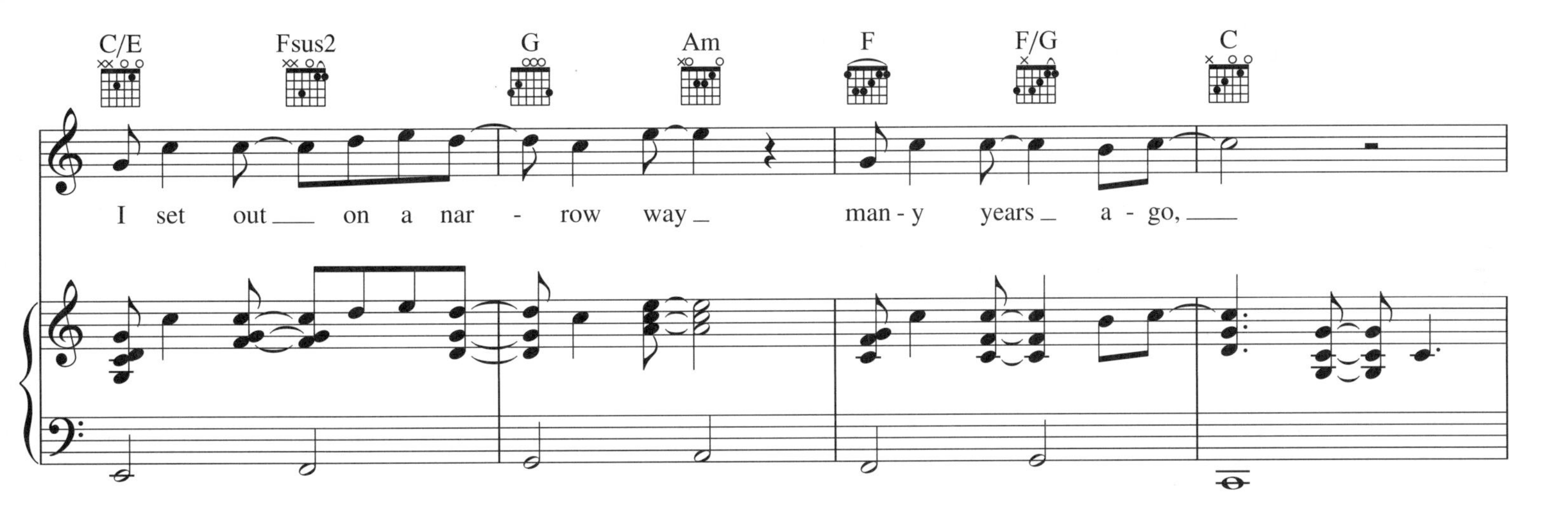

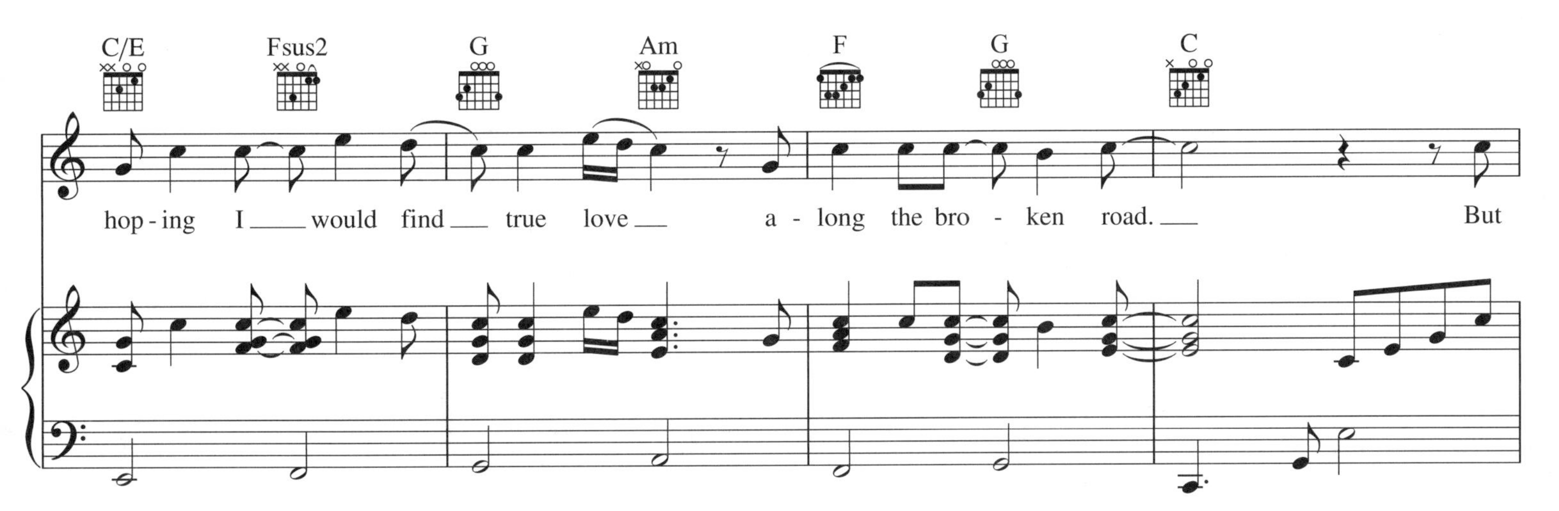

Am7 G F C/E Dm7 G7sus
I got lost a time or two, wiped my brow and kept push-in' through.

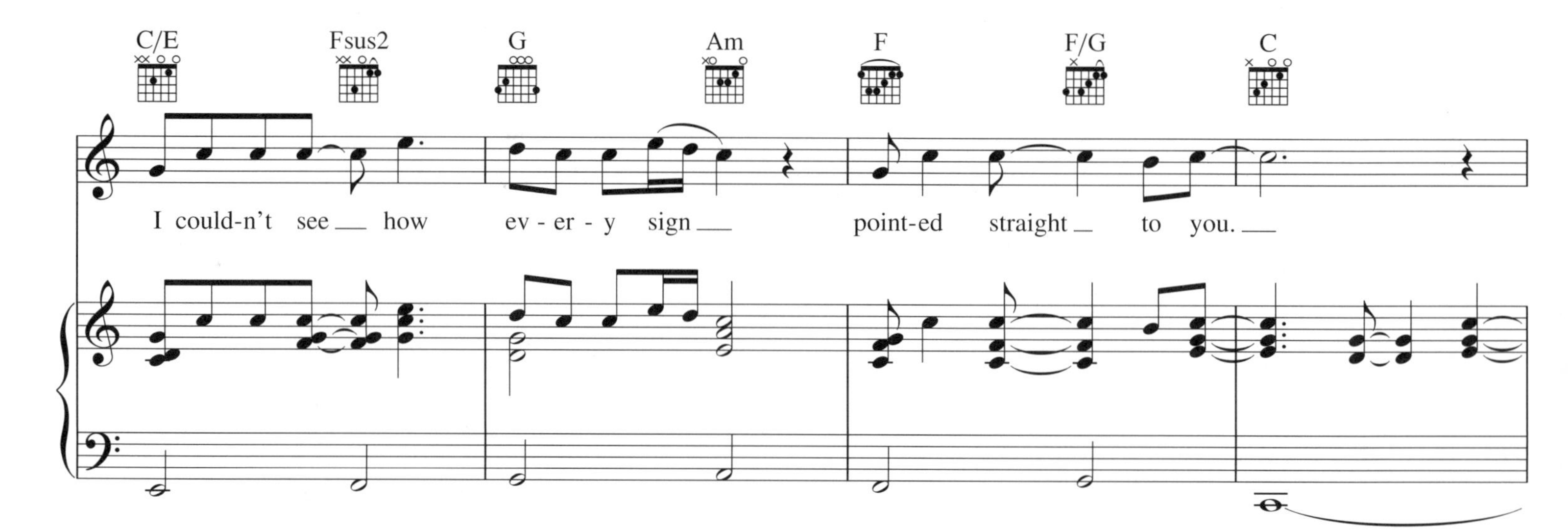
C/E Fsus2 G Am F F/G C
I could-n't see how ev-er-y sign point-ed straight to you.

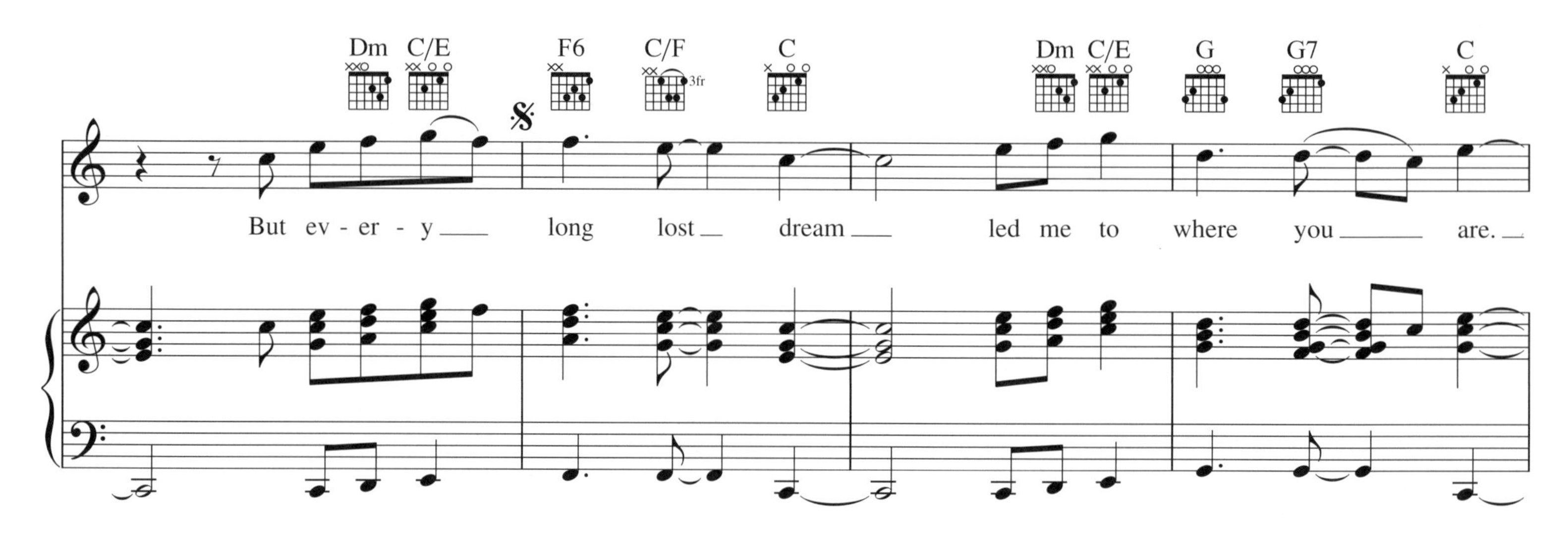
Dm C/E F6 C/F C Dm C/E G G7 C
3fr
But ev-er-y long lost dream led me to where you are.

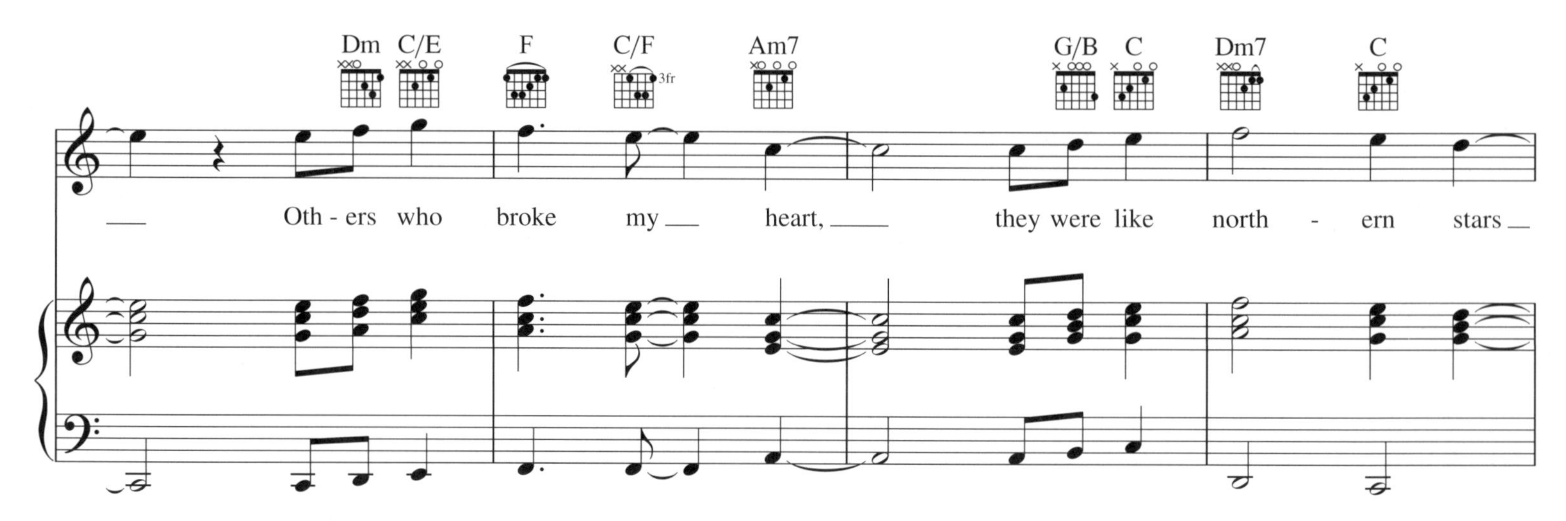
Dm C/E F C/F Am7 G/B C Dm7 C
3fr
Oth-ers who broke my heart, they were like north-ern stars

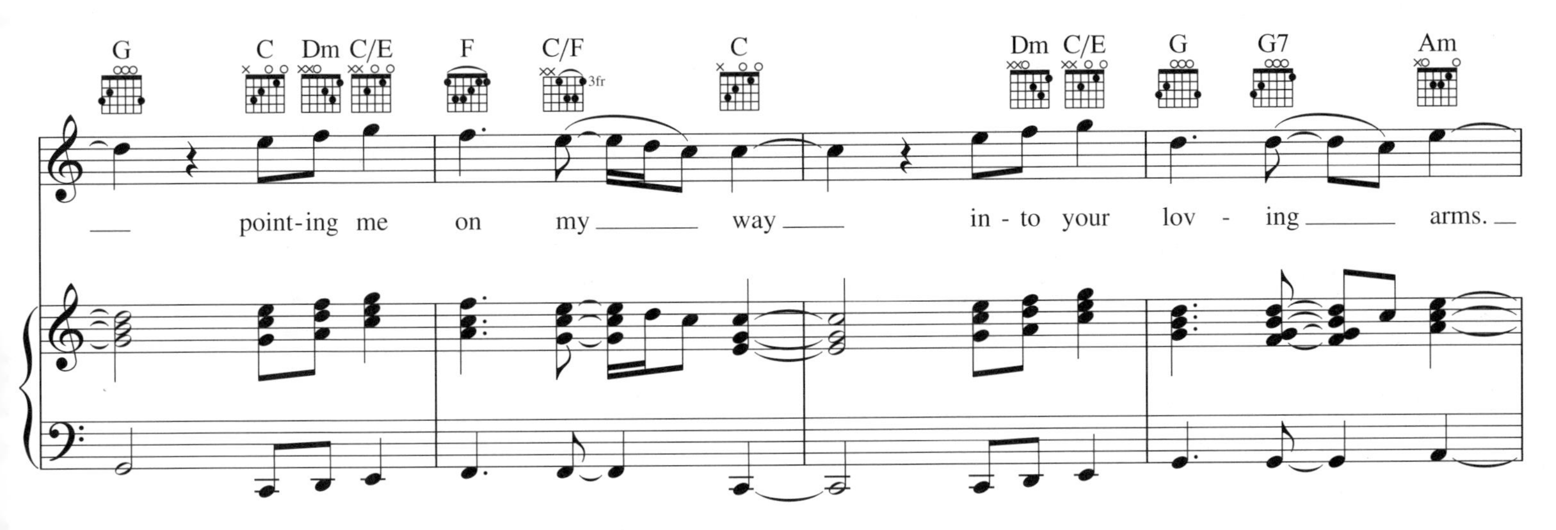
G C Dm C/E F C/F C Dm C/E G G7 Am
3fr
pointing me on my way into your lov - ing arms.

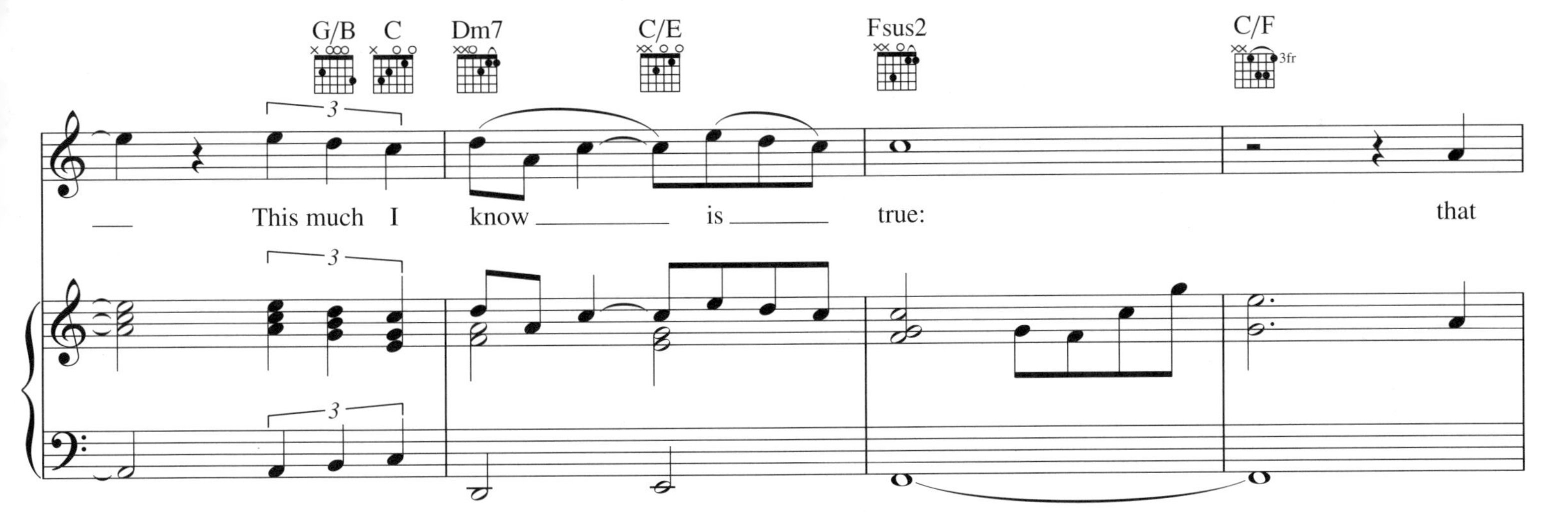
G/B C Dm7 C/E Fsus2 C/F
3fr
3
This much I know is true: that

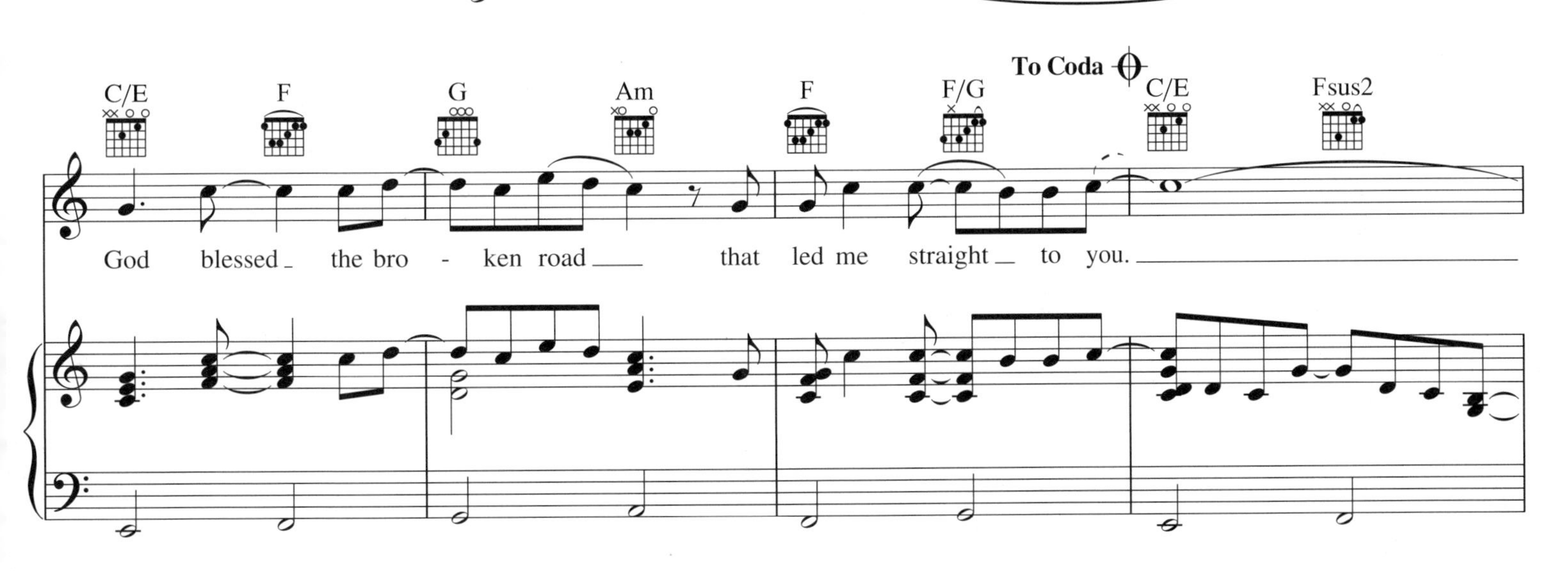
To Coda
C/E F G Am F F/G C/E Fsus2
God blessed the bro - ken road that led me straight to you.

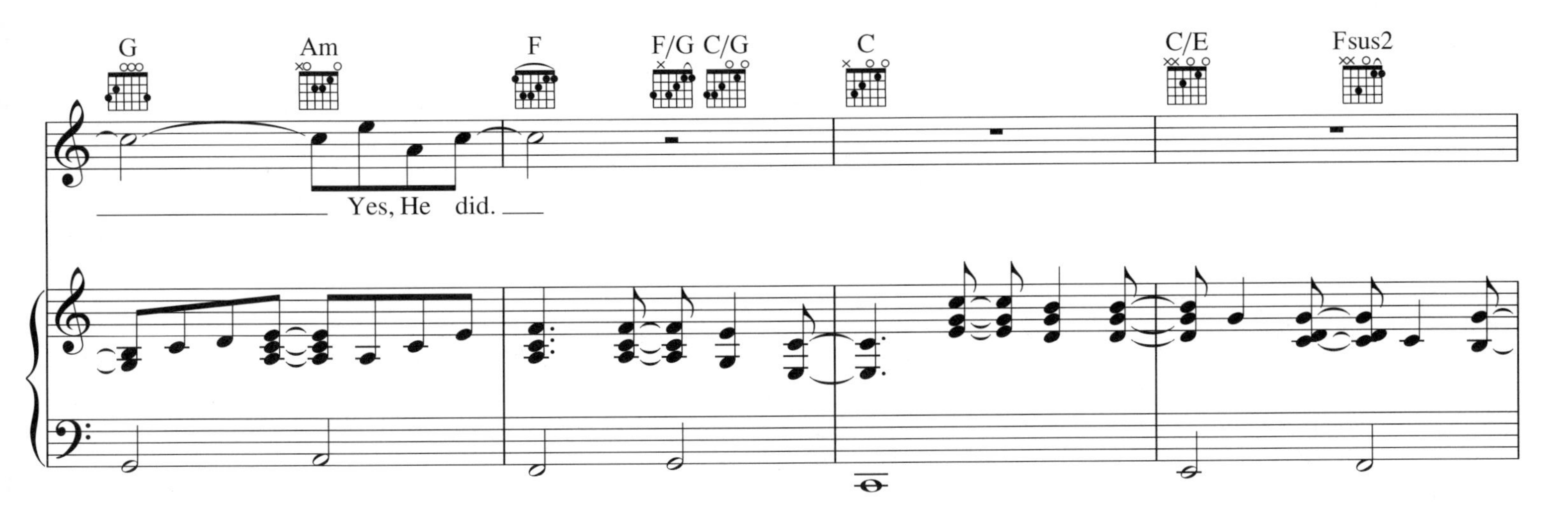
G Am F F/G C/G C C/E Fsus2
Yes, He did.

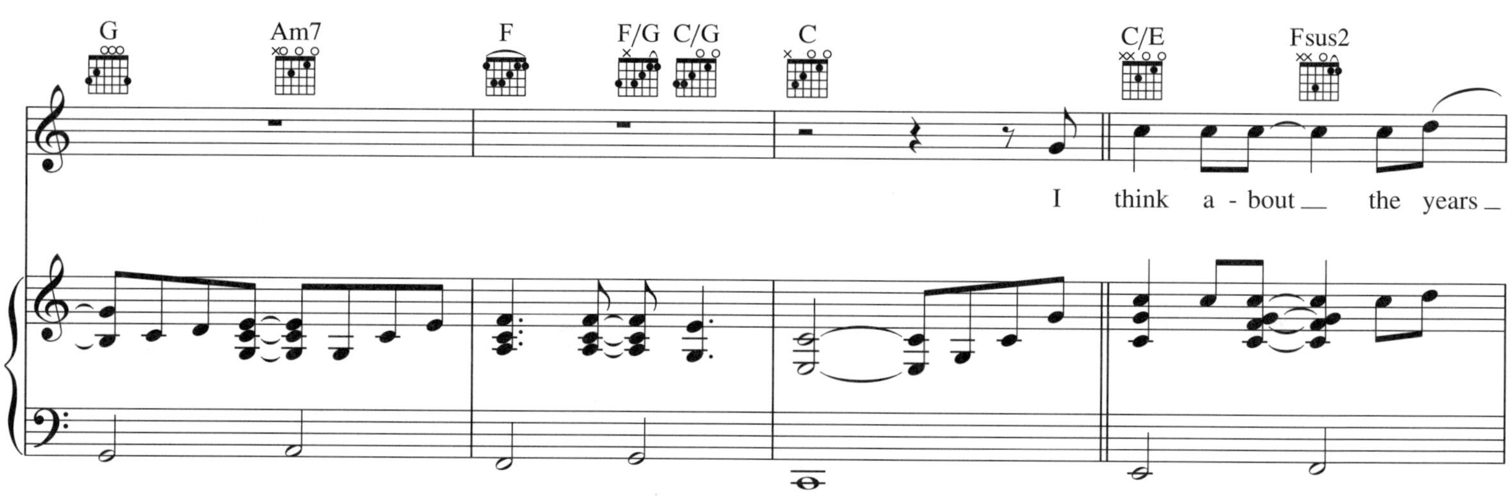
G Am7 F F/G C/G C C/E Fsus2
I think a - bout the years

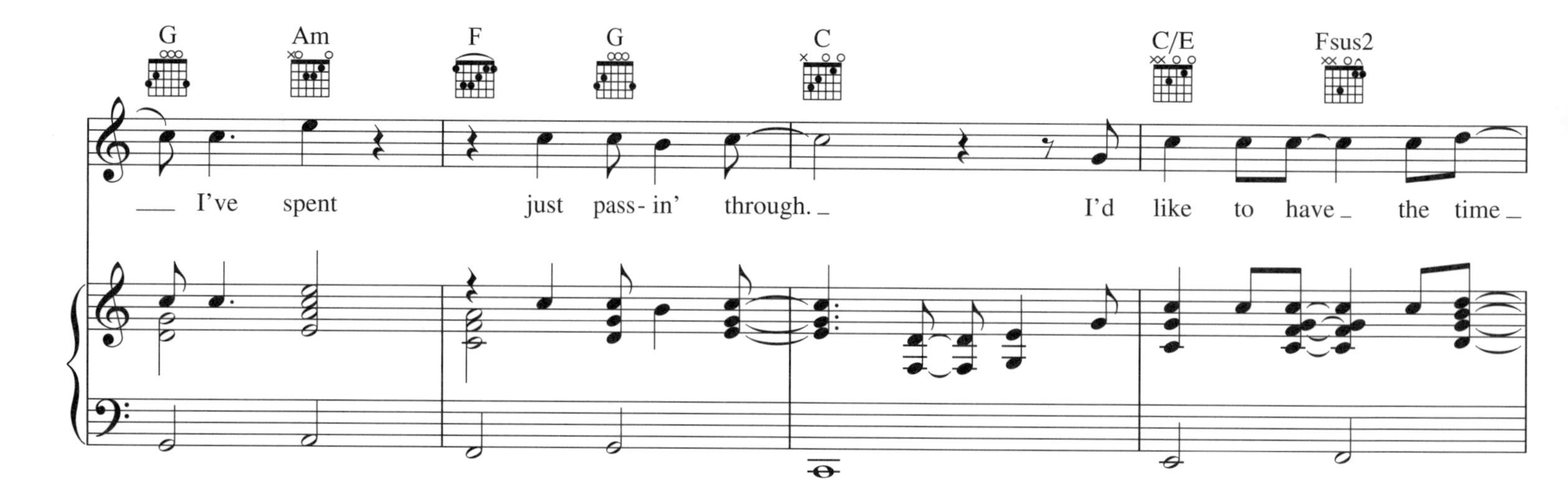
G Am F G C C/E Fsus2
I've spent just pass - in' through. I'd like to have the time

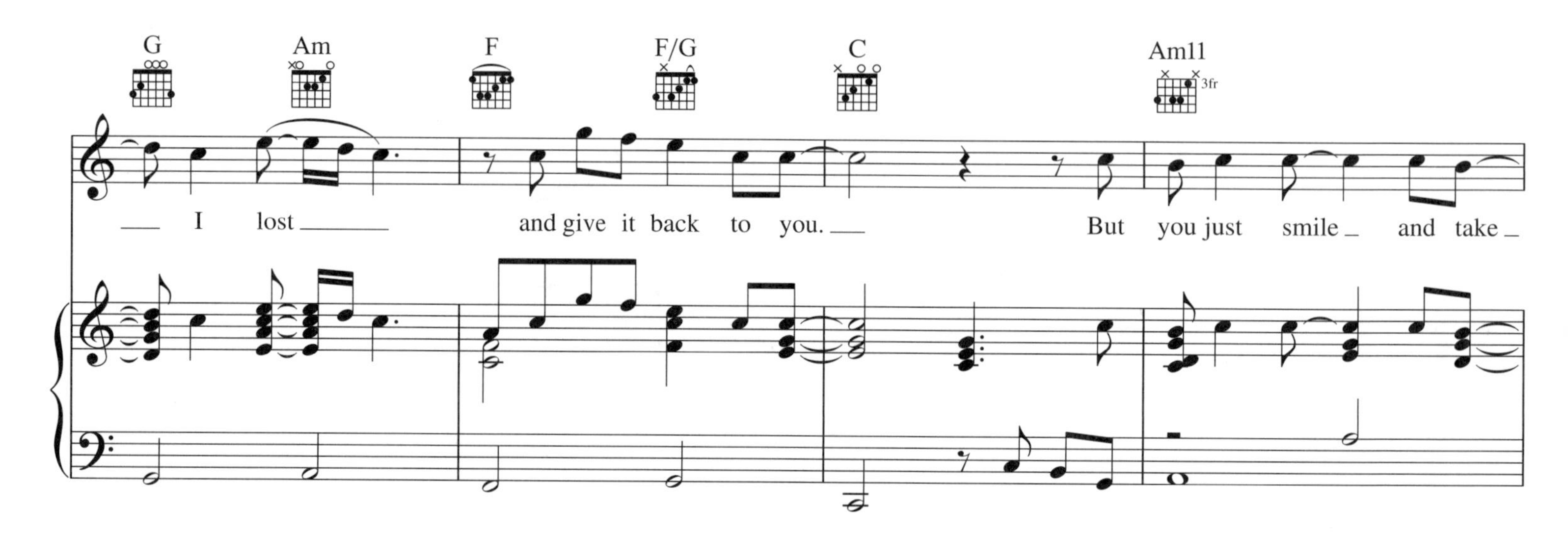
G Am F F/G C Am11
3fr
I lost and give it back to you. But you just smile and take

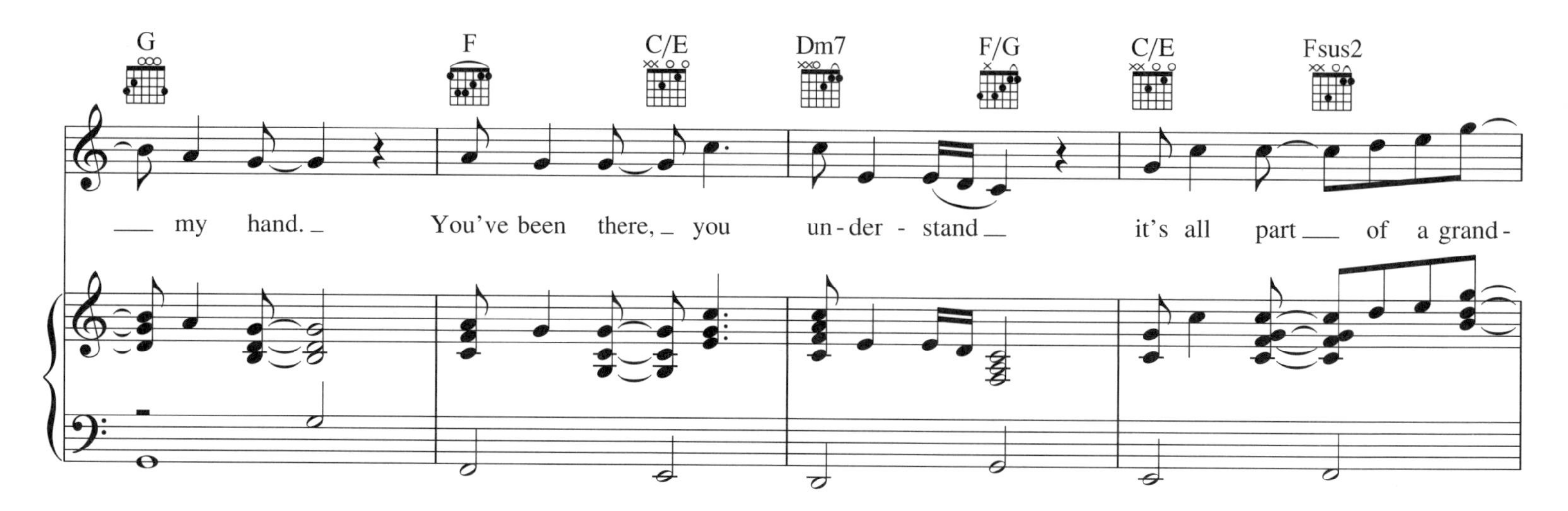
G F C/E Dm7 F/G C/E Fsus2
my hand. You've been there, you un - der - stand it's all part of a grand -

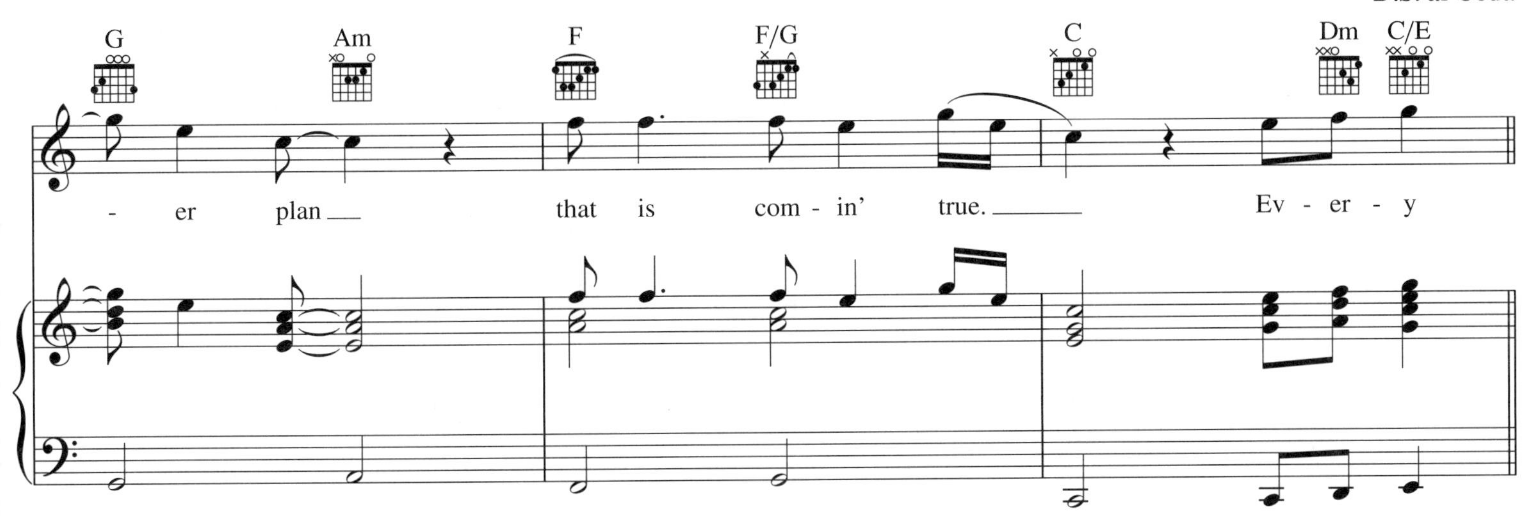
D.S. al Coda
G Am F F/G C Dm C/E
- er plan that is com - in' true. Ev - er - y

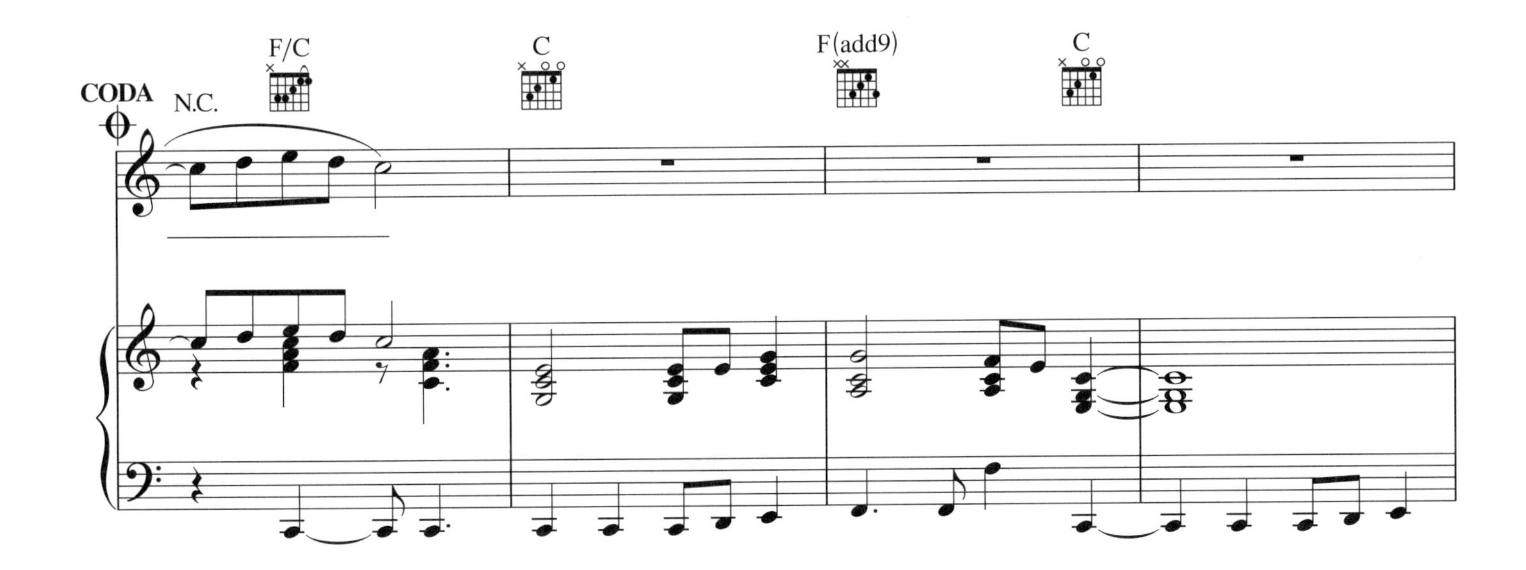
CODA
N.C.
F/C C F(add9) C

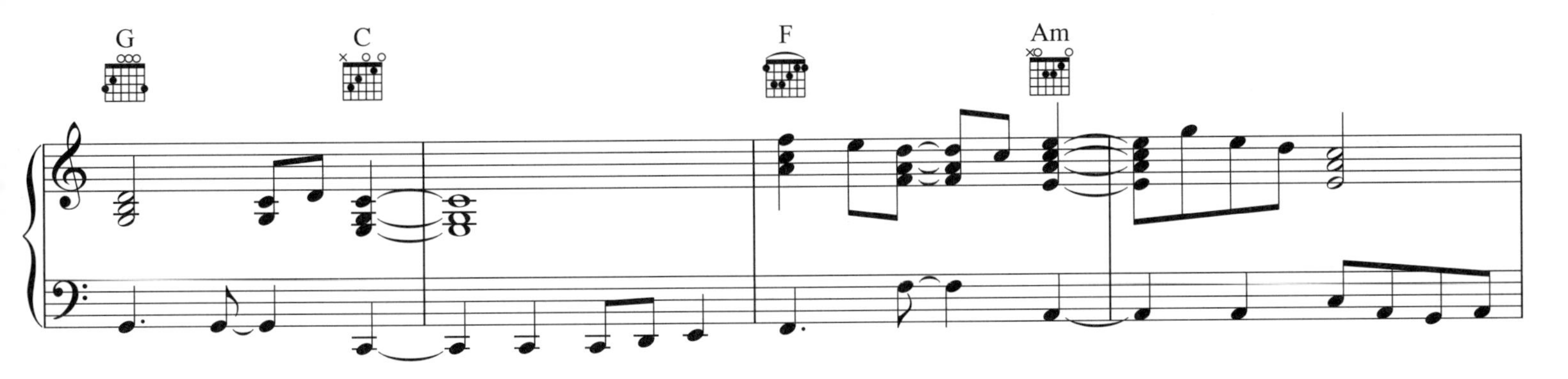
G C F Am

Dm C G/B C F F(add9) C
Now I'm just a - roll - in' home

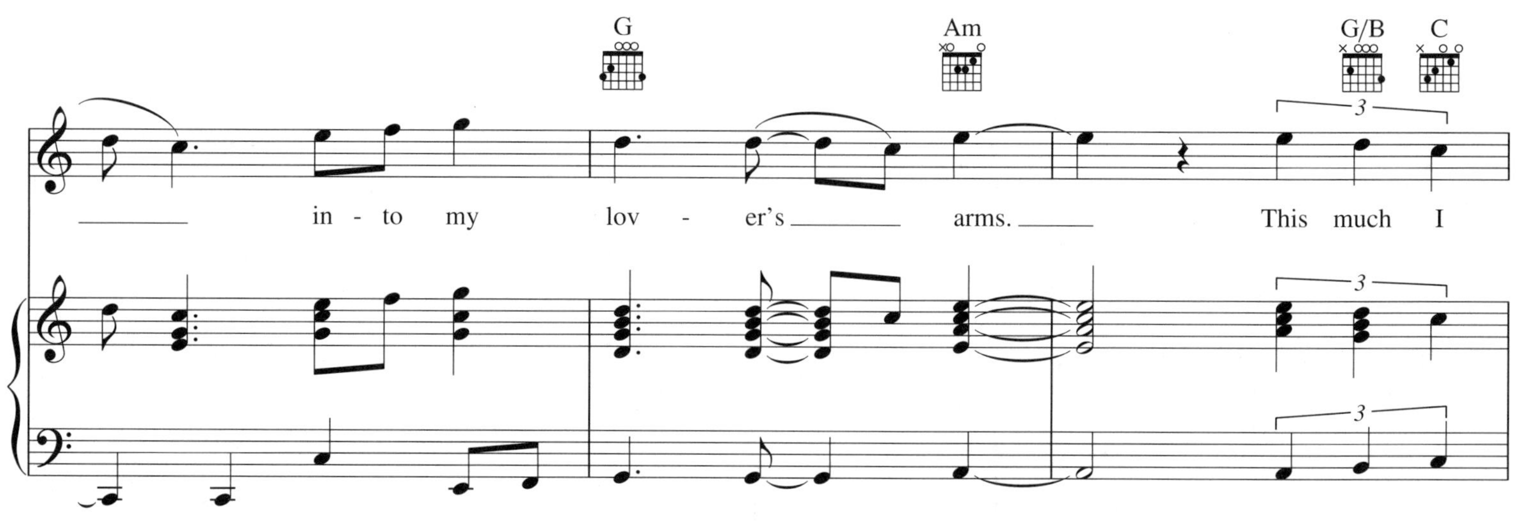
G
Am
G/B
C
3
into my lover's arms.
This much I

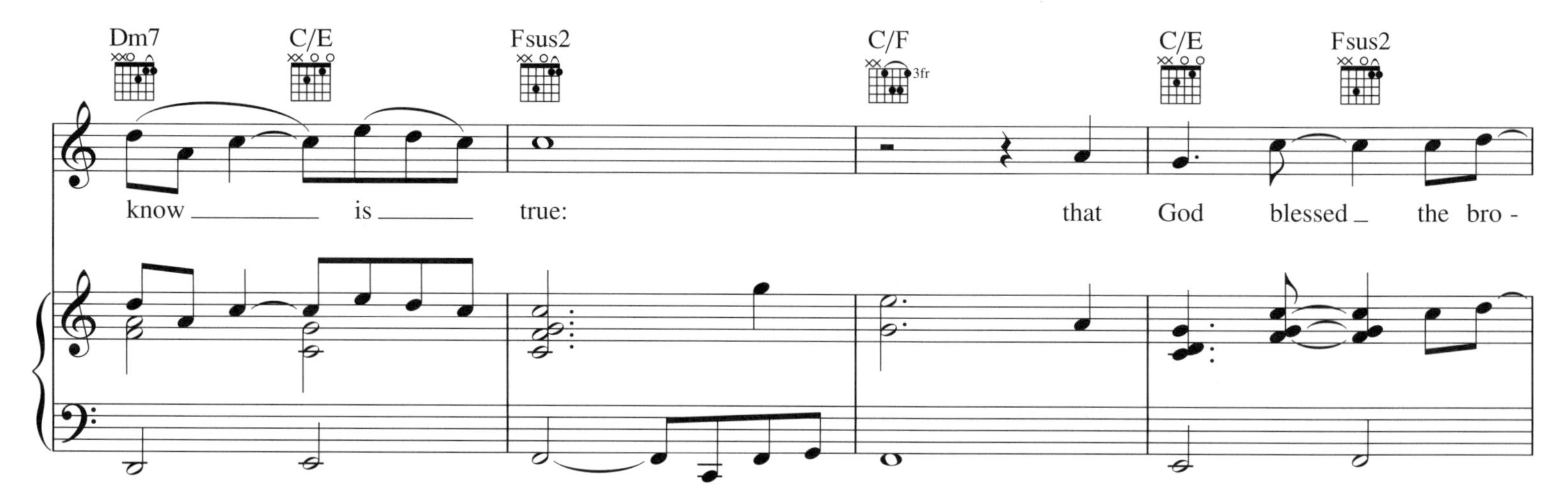
Dm7
C/E
Fsus2
C/F
3fr
C/E
Fsus2
know is true:
that God blessed the bro-

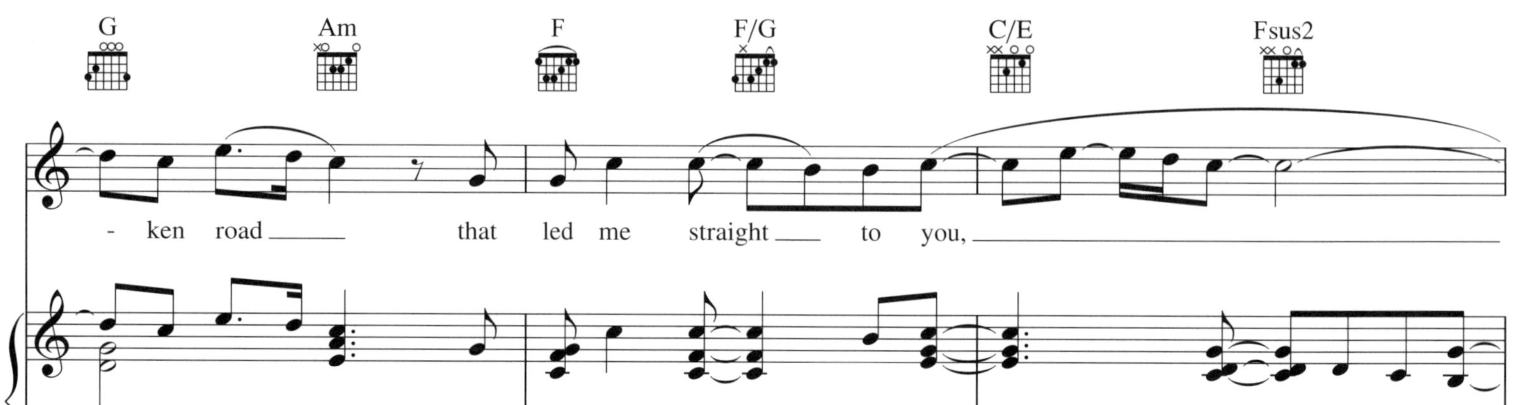
G
Am
F
F/G
C/E
Fsus2
-ken road that led me straight to you,

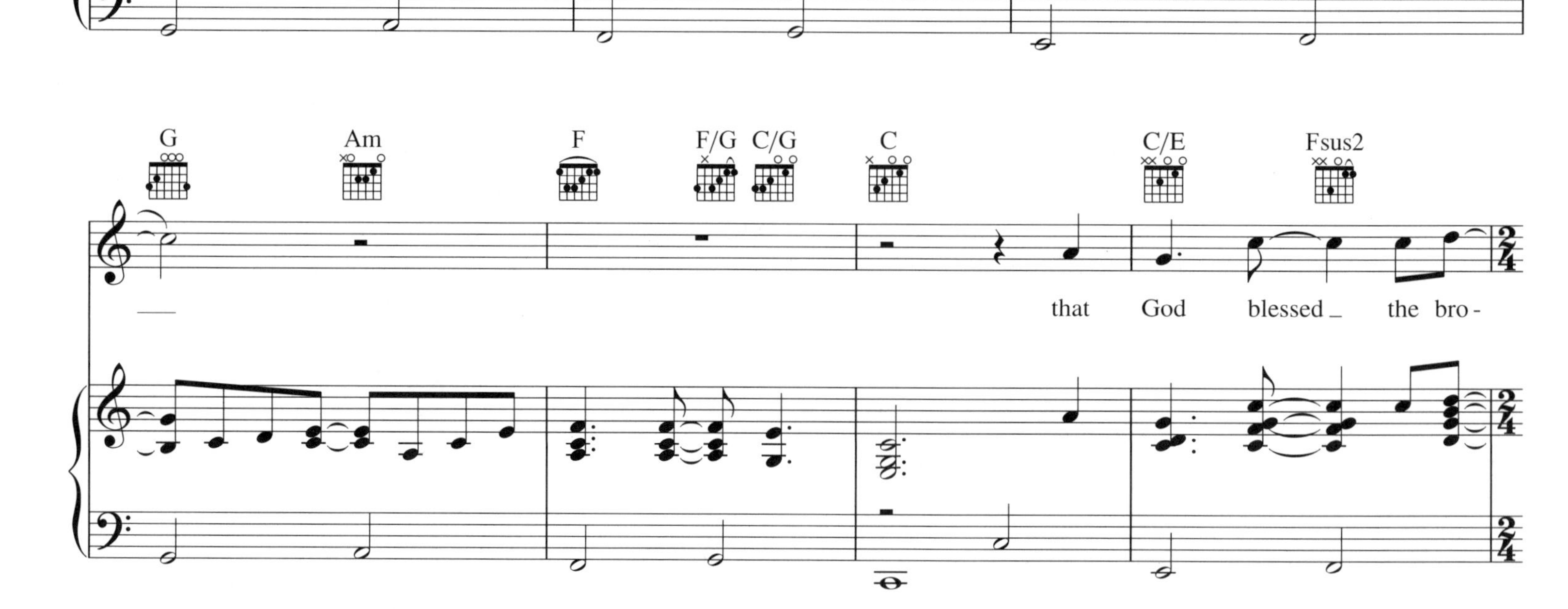
G
Am
F
F/G
C/G
C
C/E
Fsus2
that God blessed the bro-

G
Am
F
G
- ken road
that led me straight

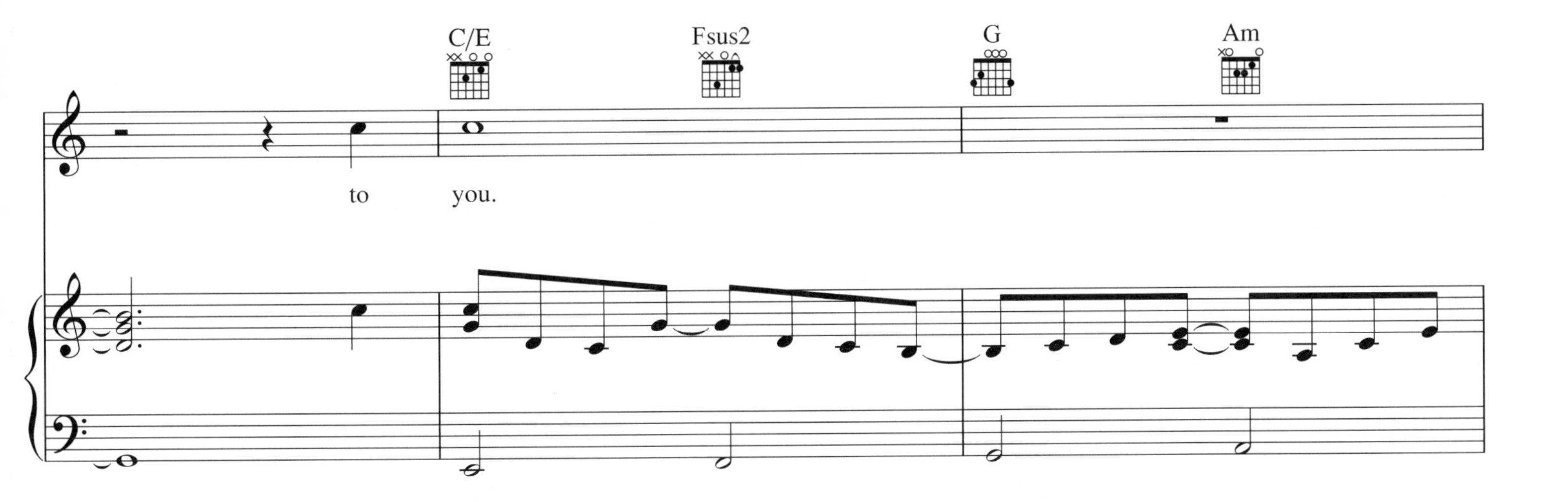
C/E
Fsus2
G
Am
to you.

F
F/G
C/G
C
C/E
Fsus2

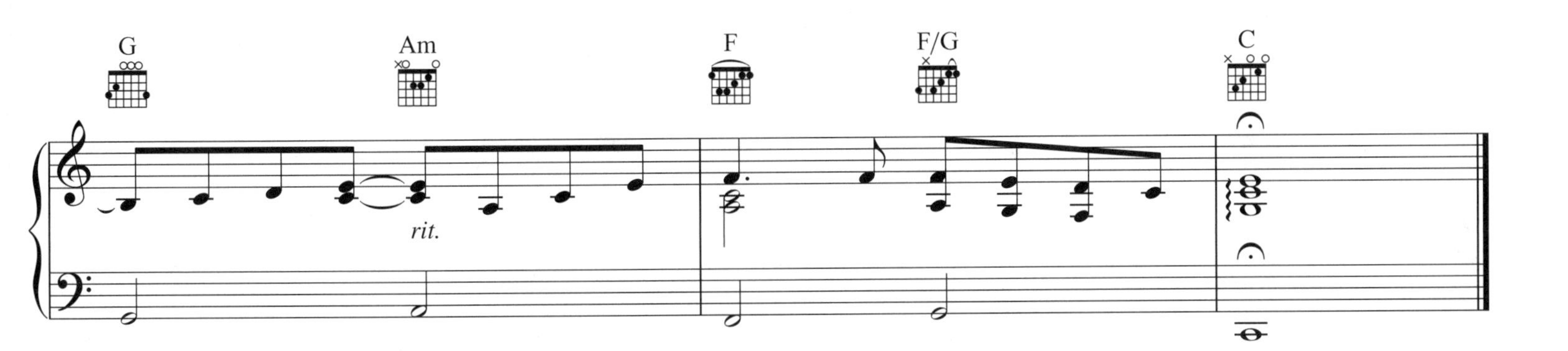
G
Am
F
F/G
C
rit.

BRAID MY HAIR

Words and Music by BRENT WILSON
and MARK GRAY

G♯m
4fr
E
But right now, treat - ments keep her sick in bed.

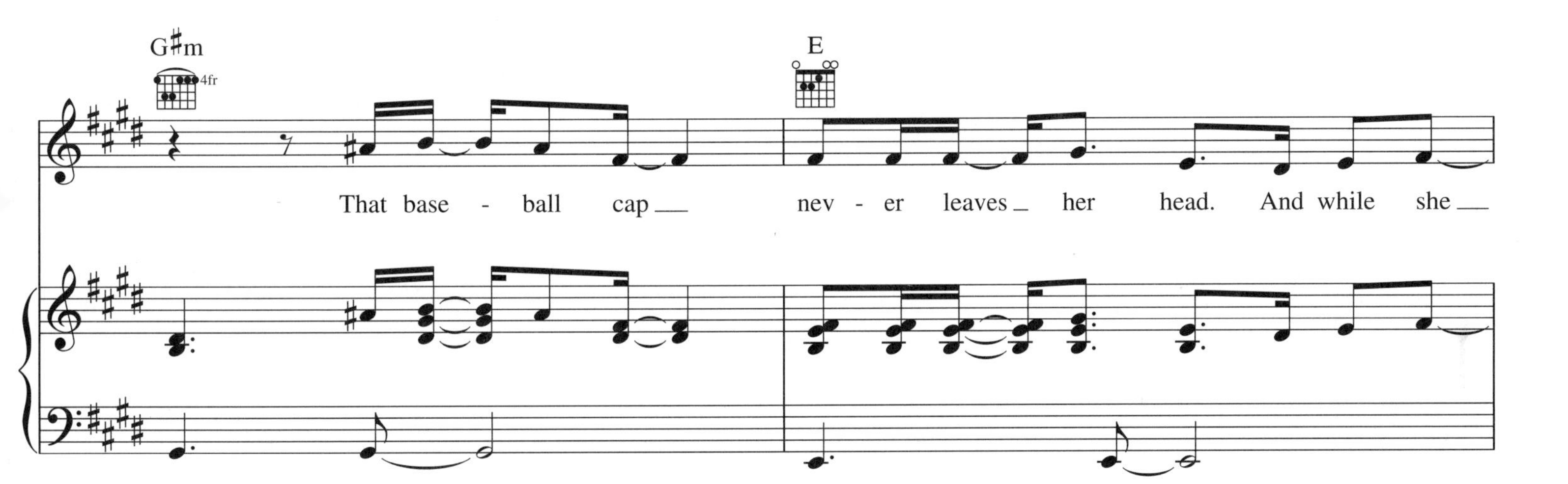
G♯m
4fr
E
That base - ball cap nev - er leaves her head. And while she

A
F♯
F♯m
E
sleeps, I sit and dream. One day I asked her, "What
mf

B
E
E/G♯
do you wan - na do when you grow up?"

F#m
A
I soon found out
I was - n't dream - ing big e -

B
E
nough.
She said, "I'm gon - na
ride my bike,
I'm gon - na
ride my bike,
for me to

B
E
climb a tree,
climb a tree.
I'm gon - na
fly a kite,
score a

A
B
G#m
4fr
E
run in Lit - tle League.
I'm gon - na
go to school,
make a friend,
be

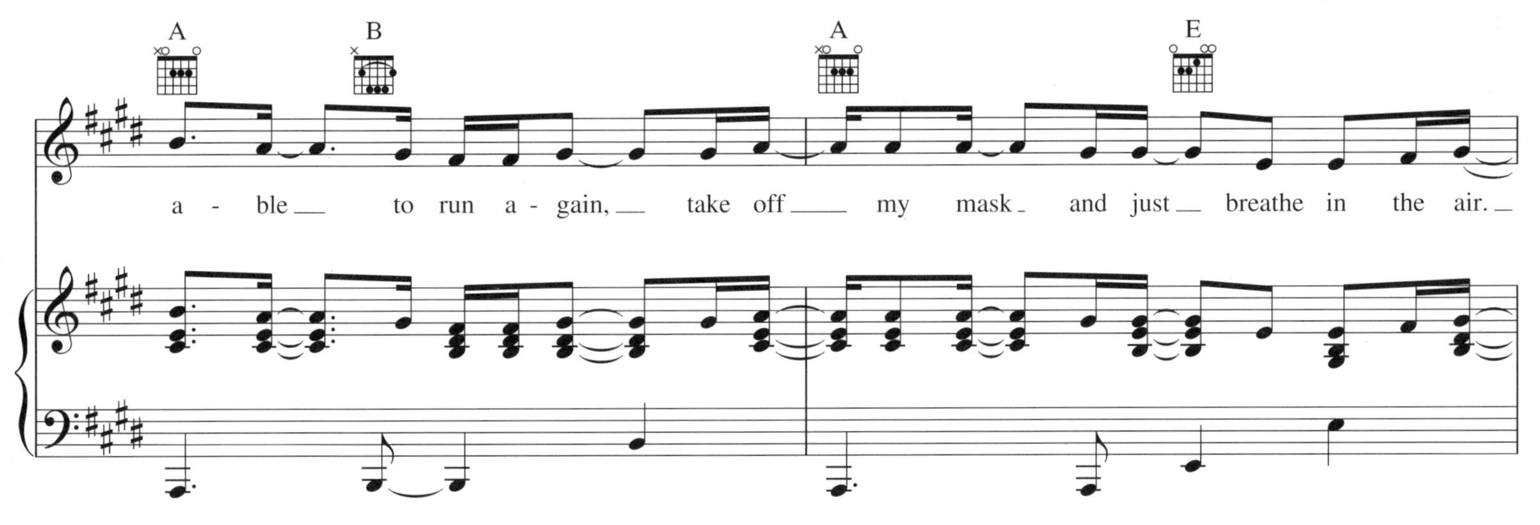
A
B
A
E
a - ble to run a - gain, take off my mask and just breathe in the air.

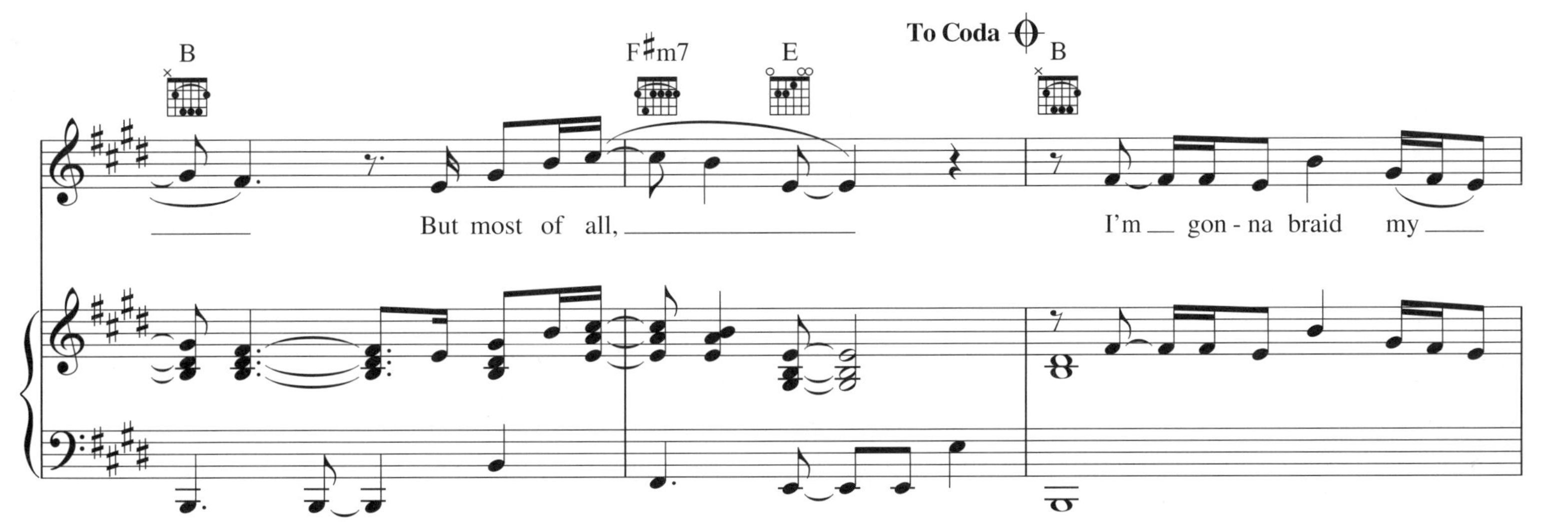
To Coda
B
F♯m7
E
B
But most of all, I'm gon - na braid my

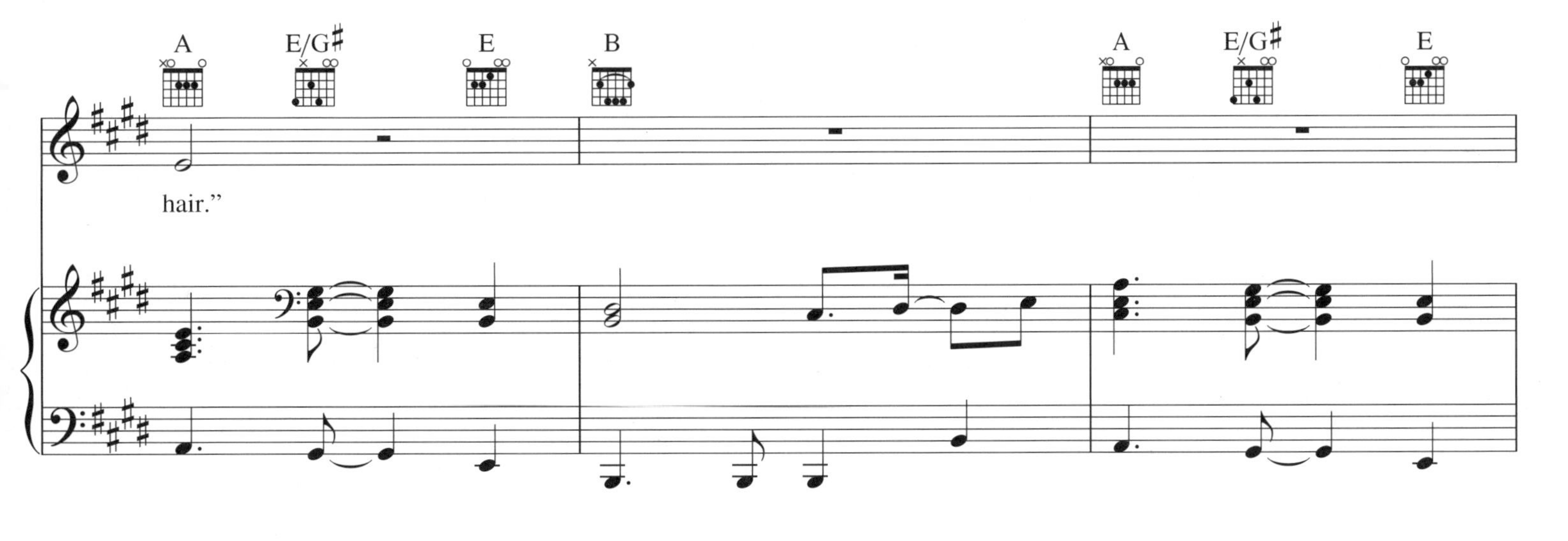
A
E/G♯
E
B
A
E/G♯
E
hair."

B
G♯m
4fr
E
She could ques - tion God; Lord knows, I would.

G♯m
4fr
E
She could just give up.
I don't think I could be that

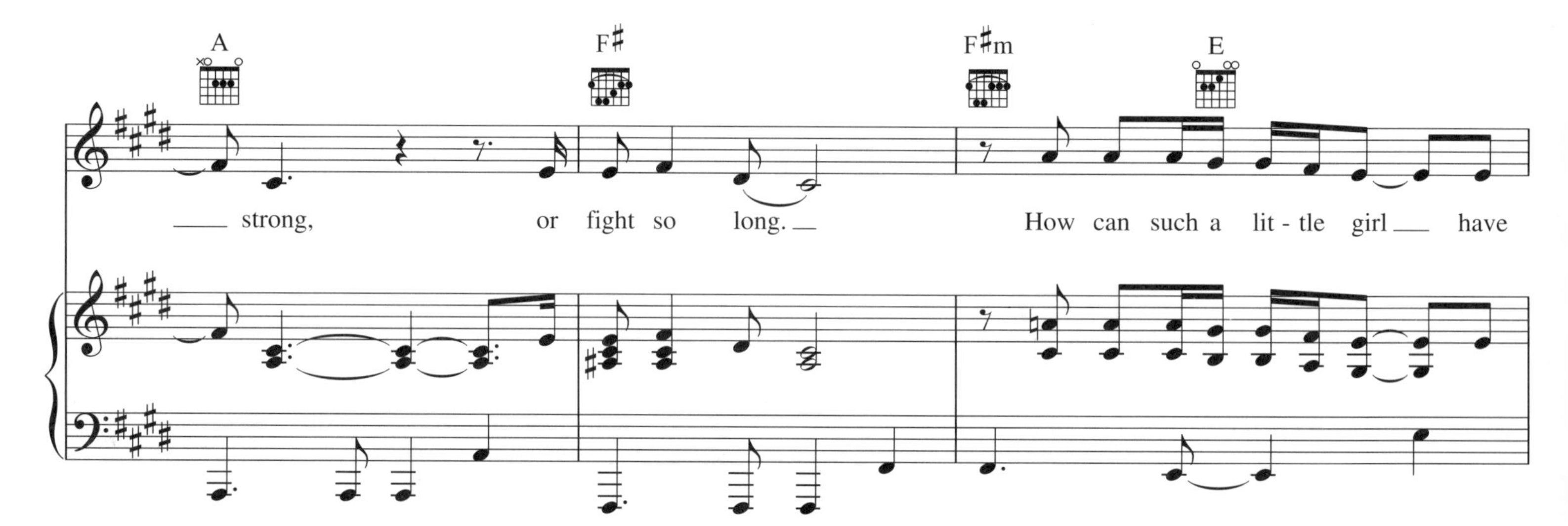
A
F♯
F♯m
E
strong,
or fight so long.
How can such a lit - tle girl have

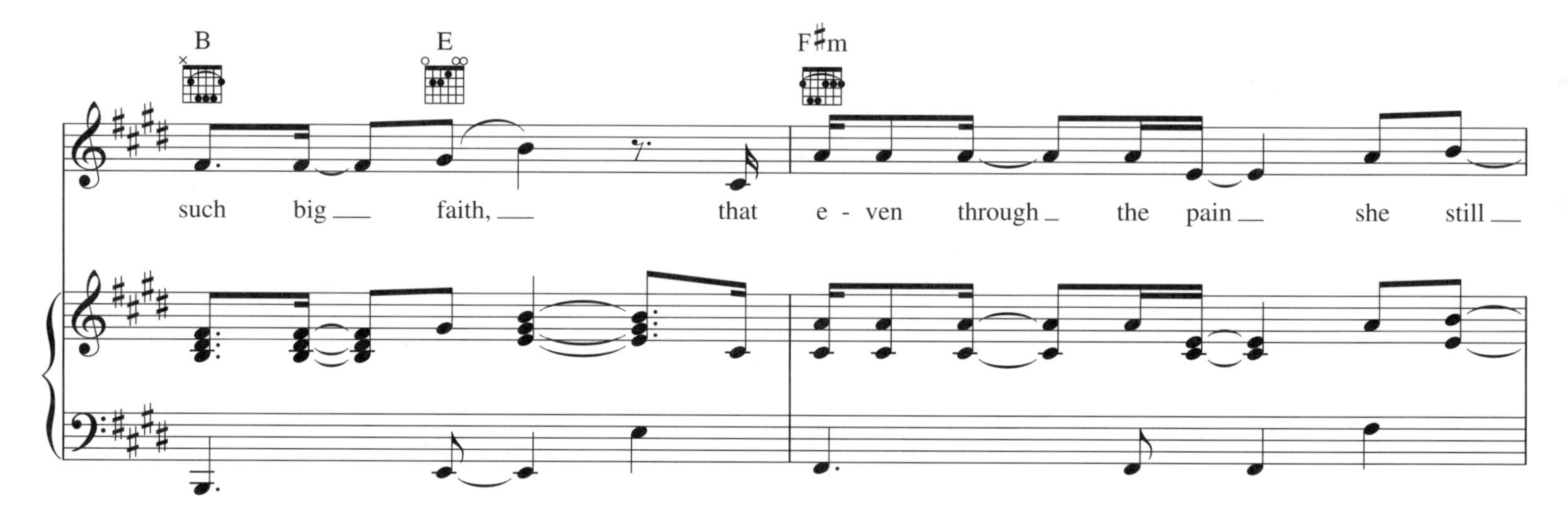
B
E
F♯m
such big faith,
that e - ven through the pain she still

B
D.S. al Coda
prays,
say - ing, "God will make a way for me to

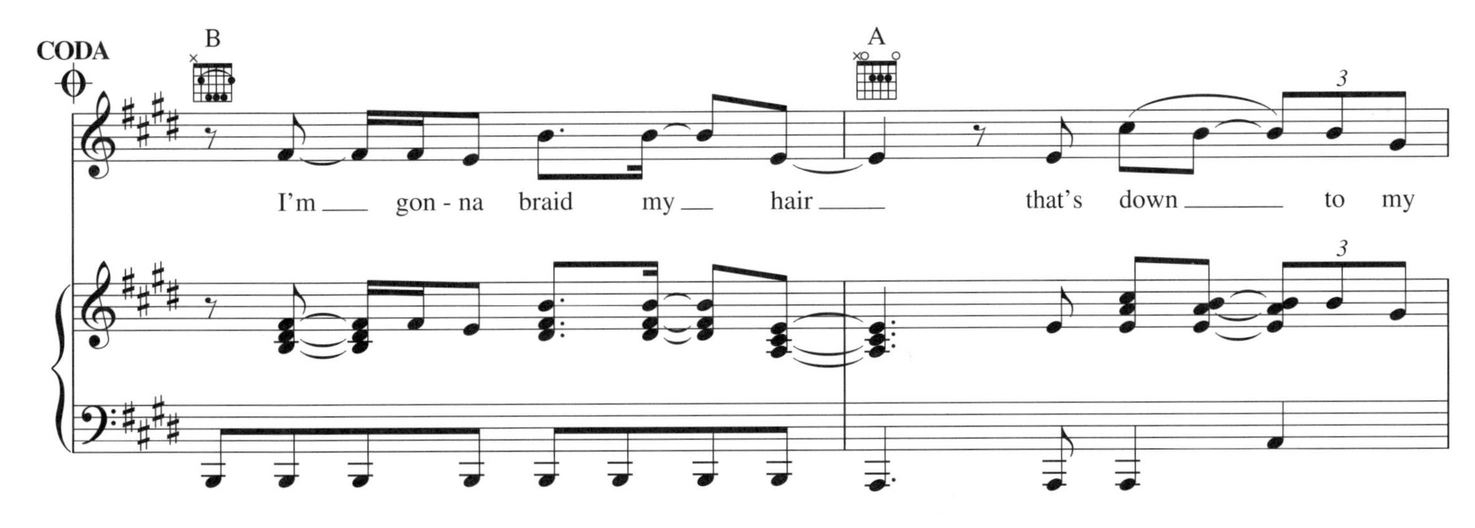
CODA
B
A
I'm gon-na braid my hair that's down to my
3

E/G♯
F♯m
E
B
waist. Then I'll get it cut so they can make locks of
dim.

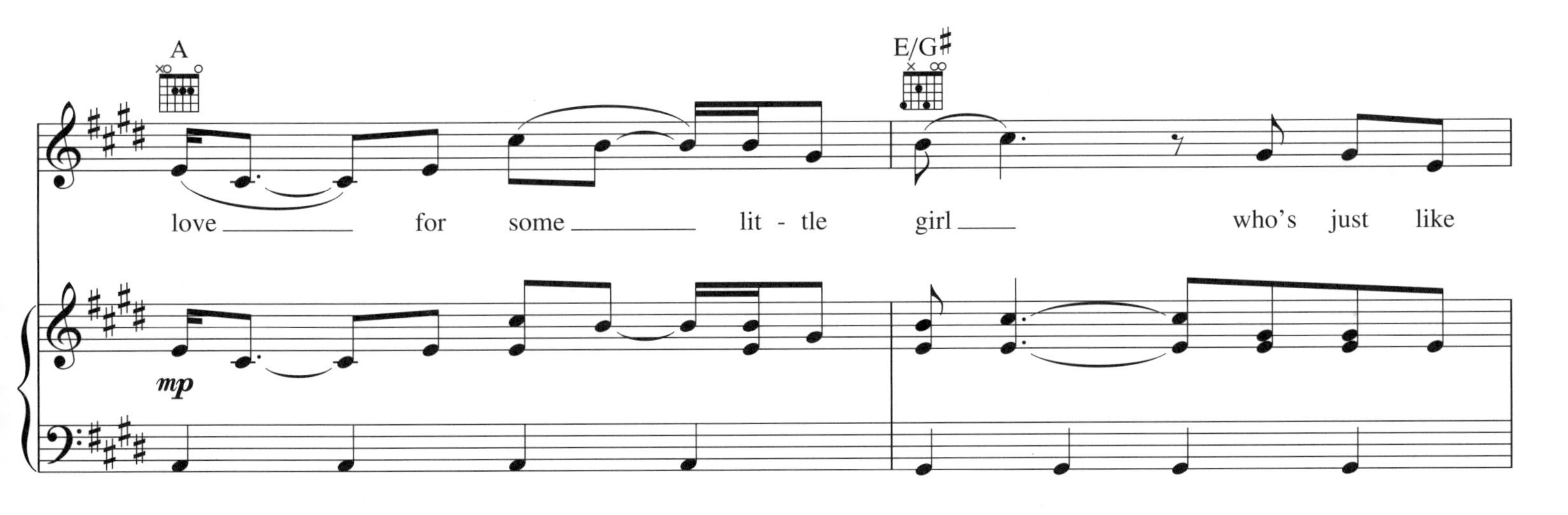
A
E/G♯
love for some lit-tle girl who's just like
mp

F♯m
E
B
me, and won-ders if she'll ev-er be a-ble to

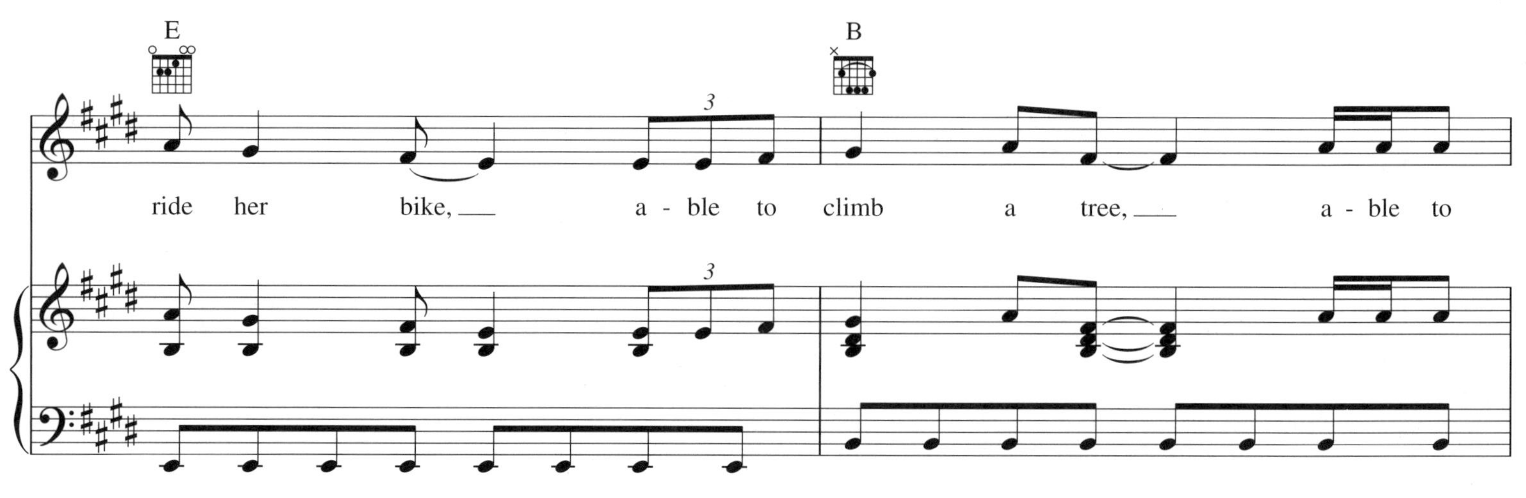
E
B
ride her bike, a - ble to climb a tree, a - ble to

E
A
B
fly her kite, and score a run in Lit - tle League, a - ble to go
cresc.
f

G♯m
4fr
E
A
B
to school, make new friends, be a - ble to run a - gain, take off

A
E
B
her mask and just breathe in the air. And most of all,

F♯m7
E
B
F♯m7
E
yeah, most of all,

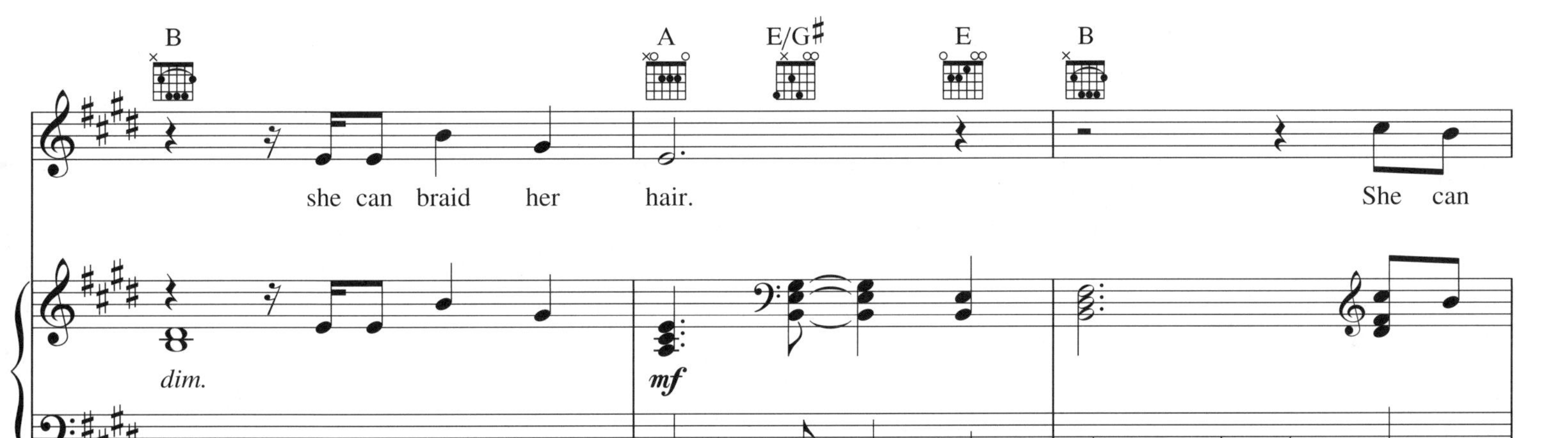
B
A
E/G♯
E
B
she can braid her hair.
She can
dim.
mf

A
E/G♯
E
B
A
E/G♯
E
braid her hair.

dim.

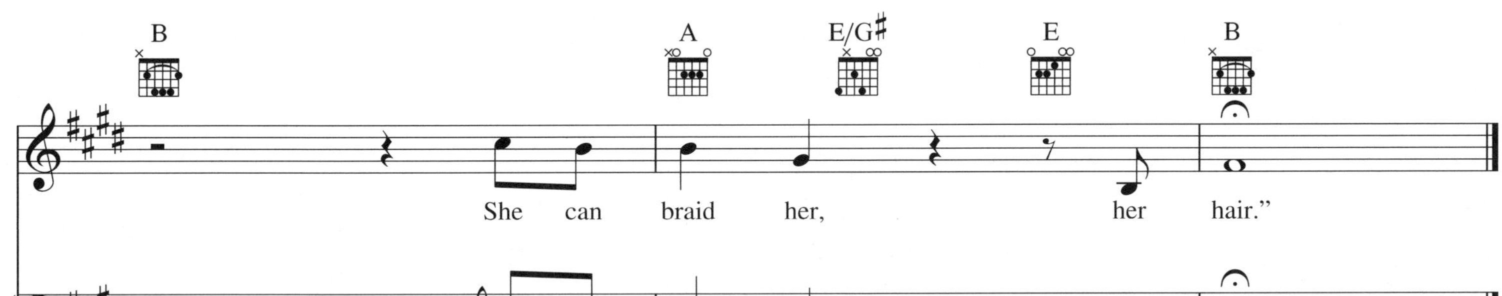
B
A
E/G♯
E
B
She can braid her, her hair.”

mp
rit.

FRIENDS

Words and Music by MICHAEL W. SMITH
and DEBORAH D. SMITH

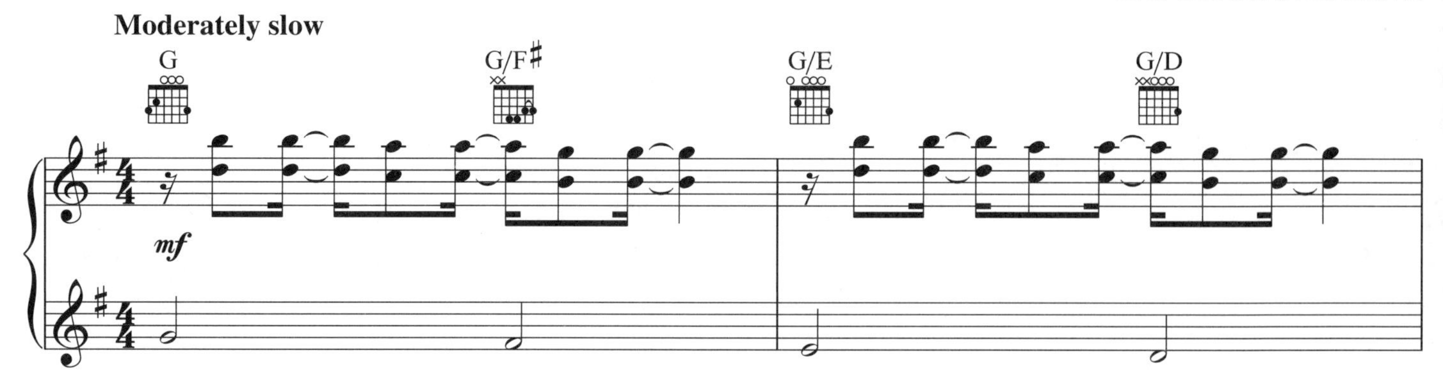

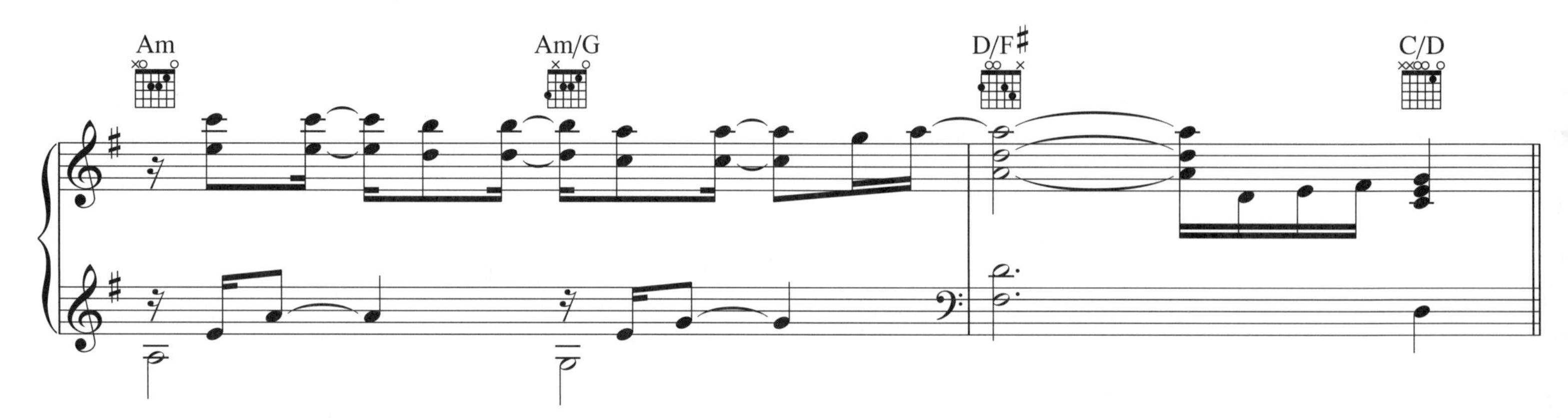

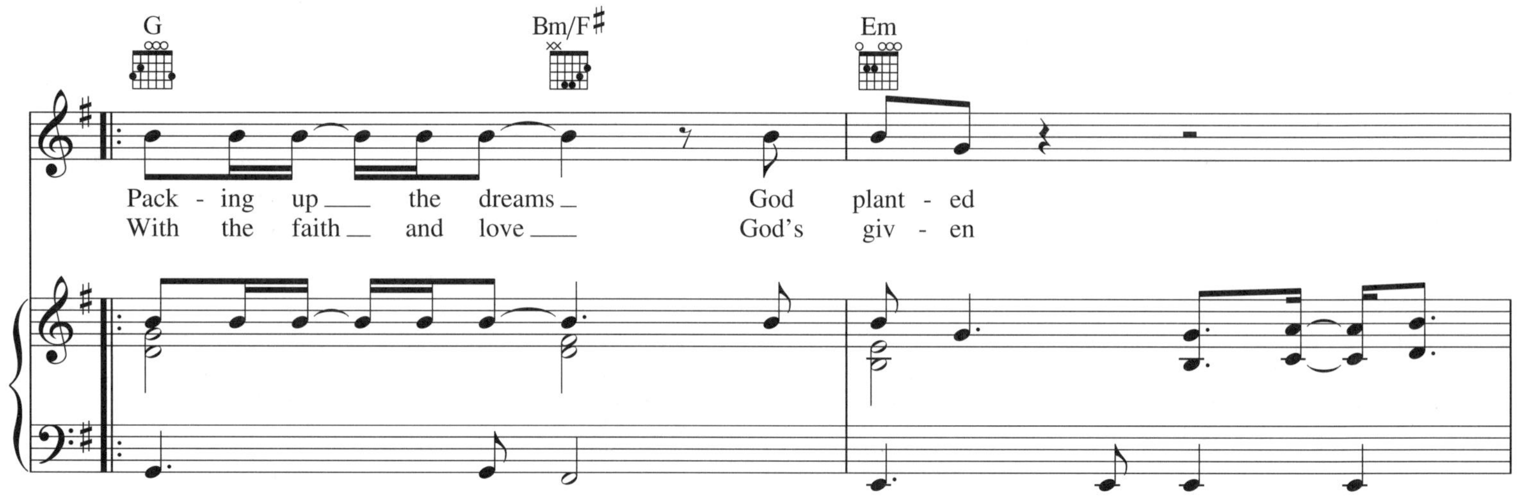

G
Bm/F♯
Em
can't be - lieve the hopes He's grant - ed means a
we will pray the joy you'll live in

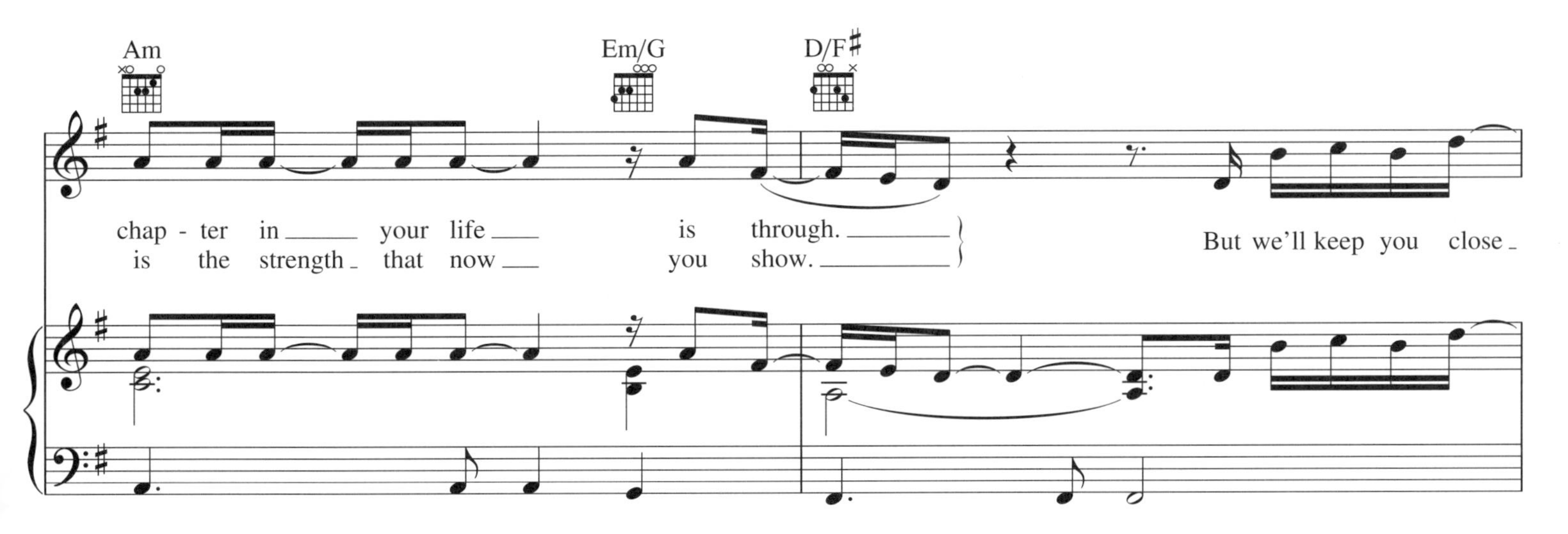
Am
Em/G
D/F♯
chap - ter in your life is through.
is the strength that now you show.
But we'll keep you close

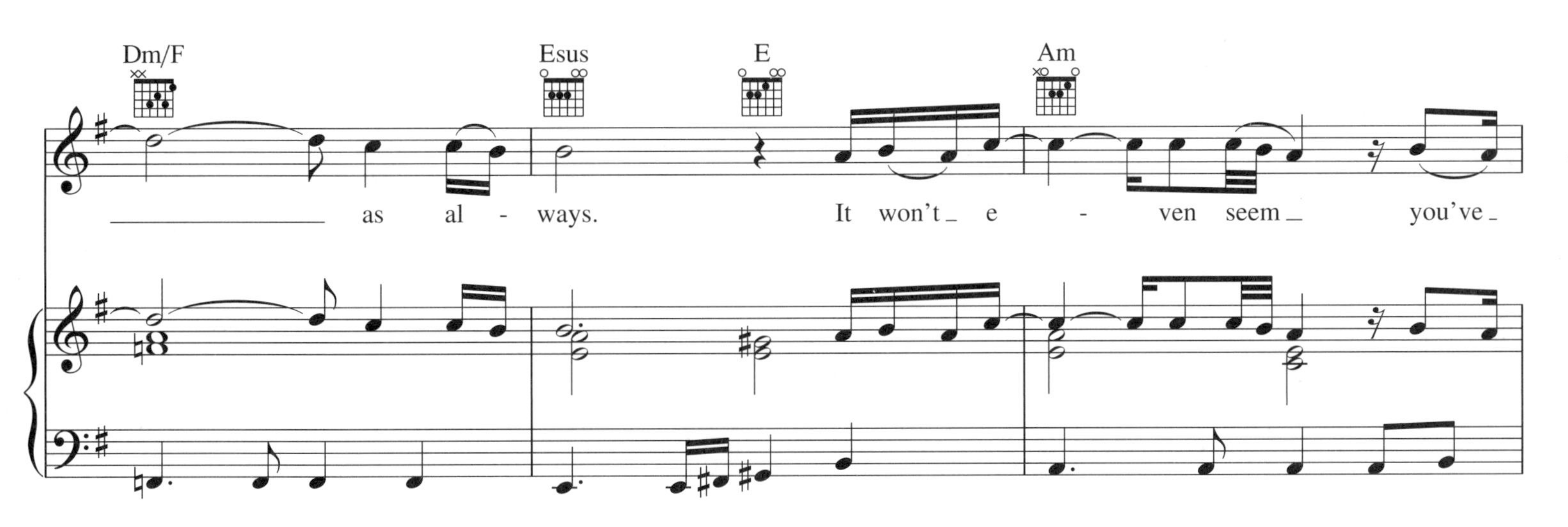
Dm/F
Esus
E
Am
as al - ways. It won't e - ven seem you've

Cm
3fr
G
Bm/F♯
Em
gone. 'Cause our hearts in big and small ways will

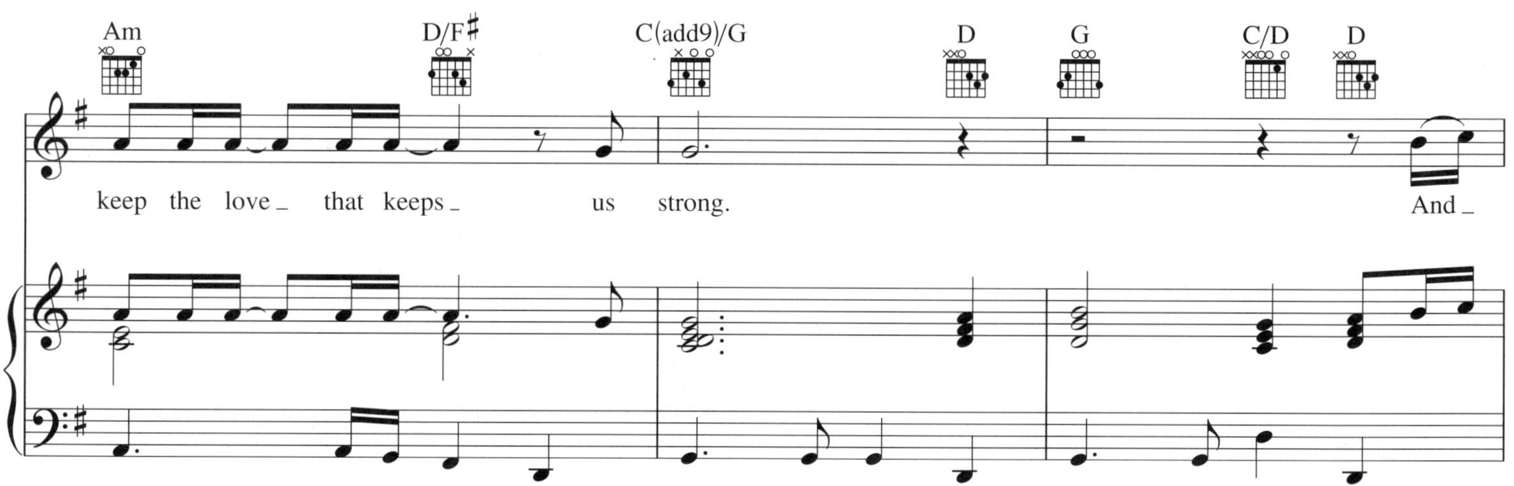
Am D/F♯ C(add9)/G D G C/D D
keep the love _ that keeps _ us strong. And _

G D/F♯ C/E Dsus D
friends are friends _ for - ev - er if the Lord's the Lord _ of them, _ and a

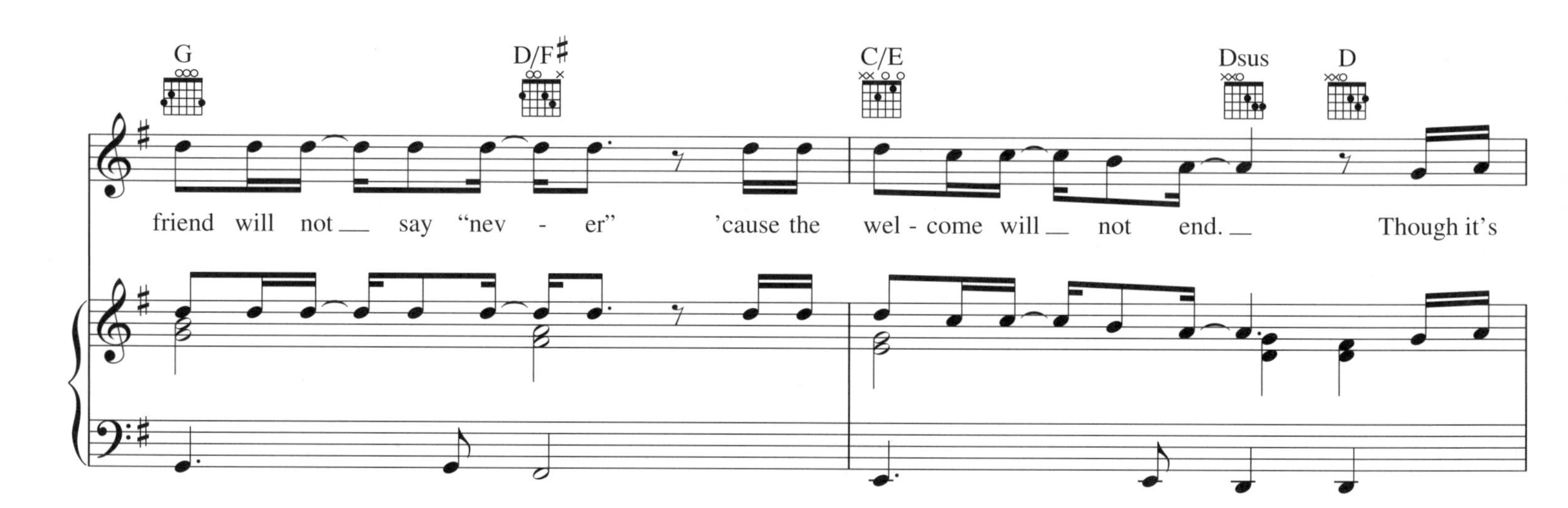
G D/F♯ C/E Dsus D
friend will not _ say "nev - er" 'cause the wel - come will _ not end. _ Though it's

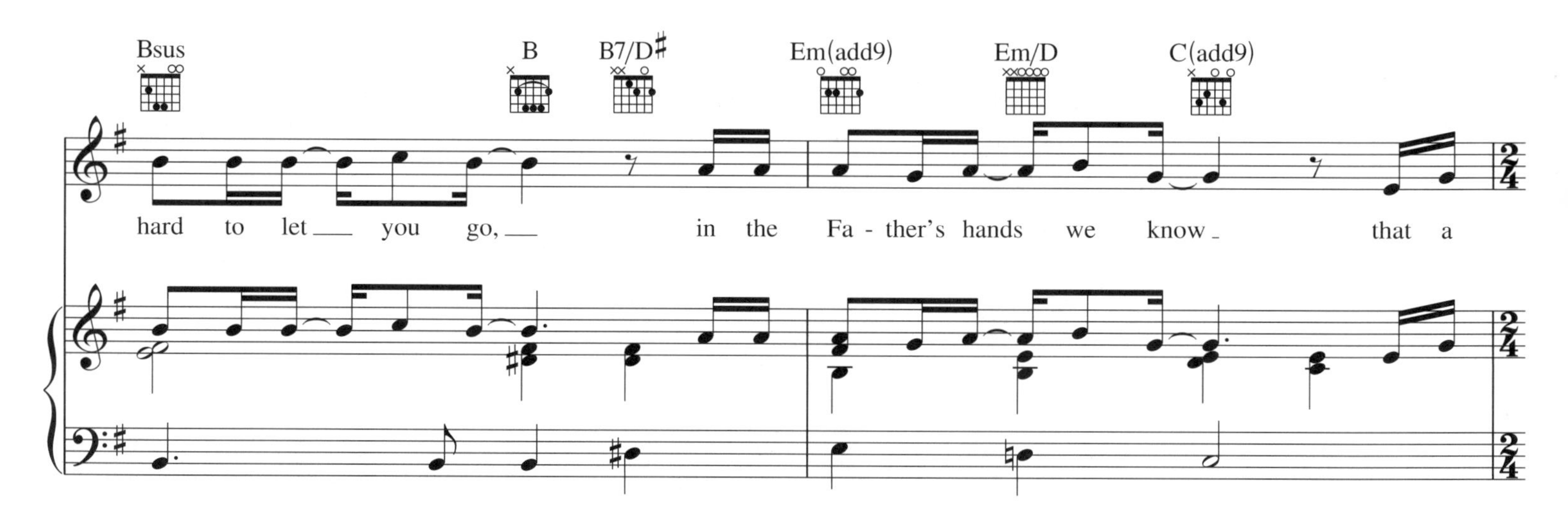
Bsus B B7/D♯ Em(add9) Em/D C(add9)
hard to let _ you go, _ in the Fa - ther's hands we know _ that a

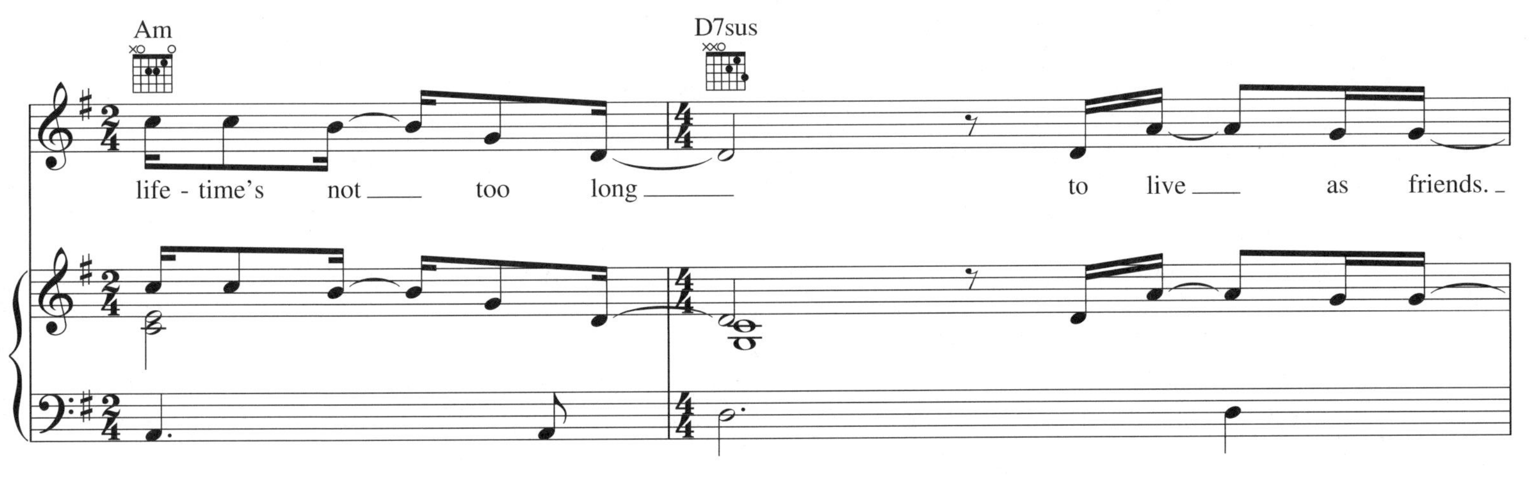
Am
D7sus
life - time's not too long to live as friends.

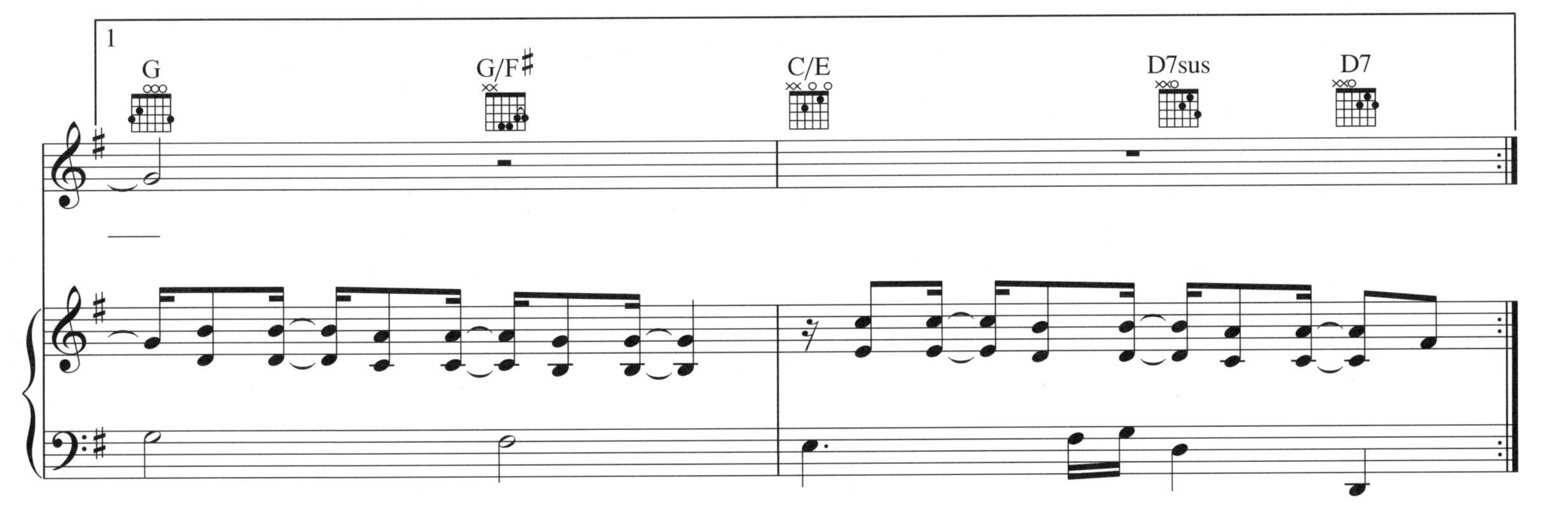
1
G
G/F♯
C/E
D7sus
D7

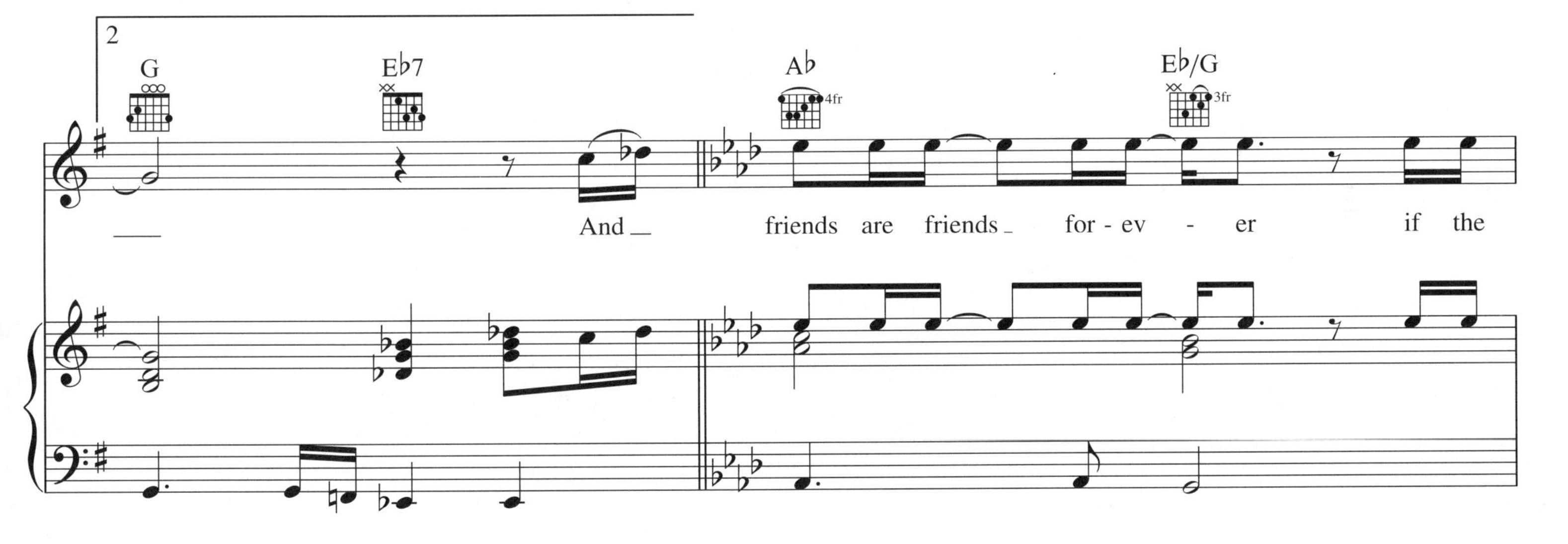
2
G
E♭7
A♭
E♭/G
And friends are friends for - ev - er if the

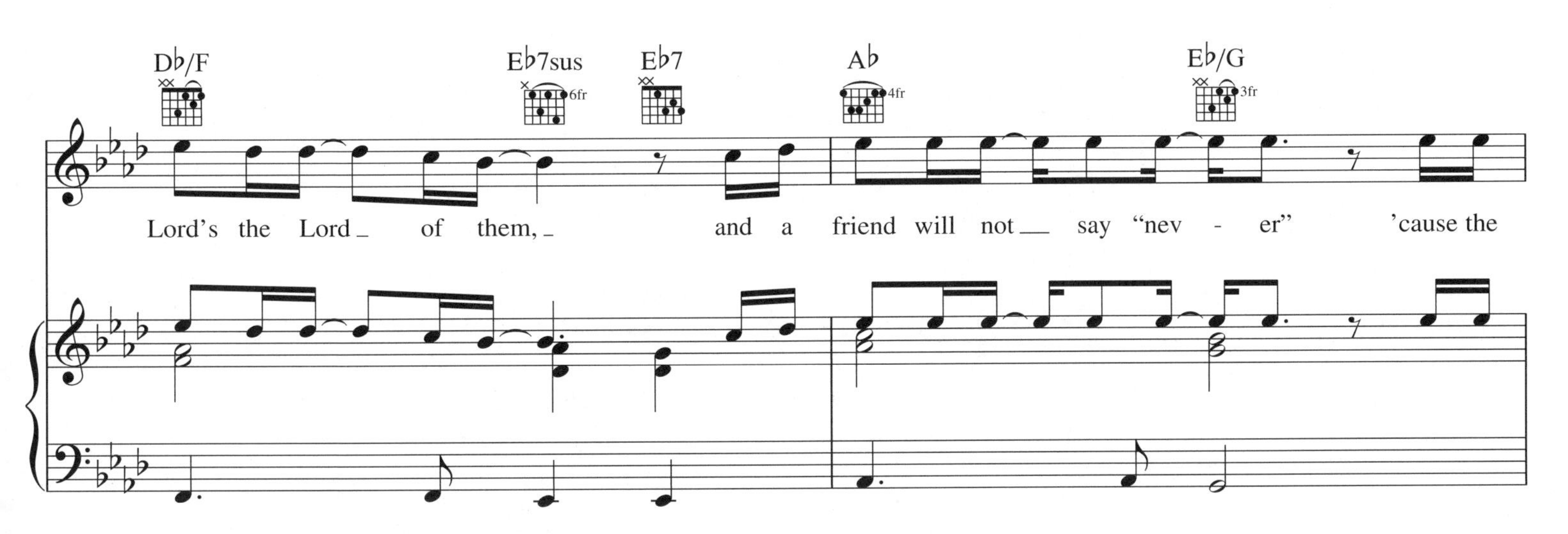
D♭/F
E♭7sus
E♭7
A♭
E♭/G
Lord's the Lord of them, and a friend will not say "nev - er" 'cause the

D♭/F
E♭7sus
E♭7
C7sus
C7
C7/E
wel - come will not end. Though it's hard to let you go, in the
Fm(add9)
Fm/E♭
D♭(add9)
B♭m7
E♭7sus
E♭7
Fa - ther's hands we know that a life-time's not too long to live as friends.
A♭
E♭/G
D♭/F
E♭sus
E♭
A♭
E♭/G
To live as friends.
D♭/F
E♭sus
E♭
C7sus
C7
C7/E
Though it's hard to let you go, in the

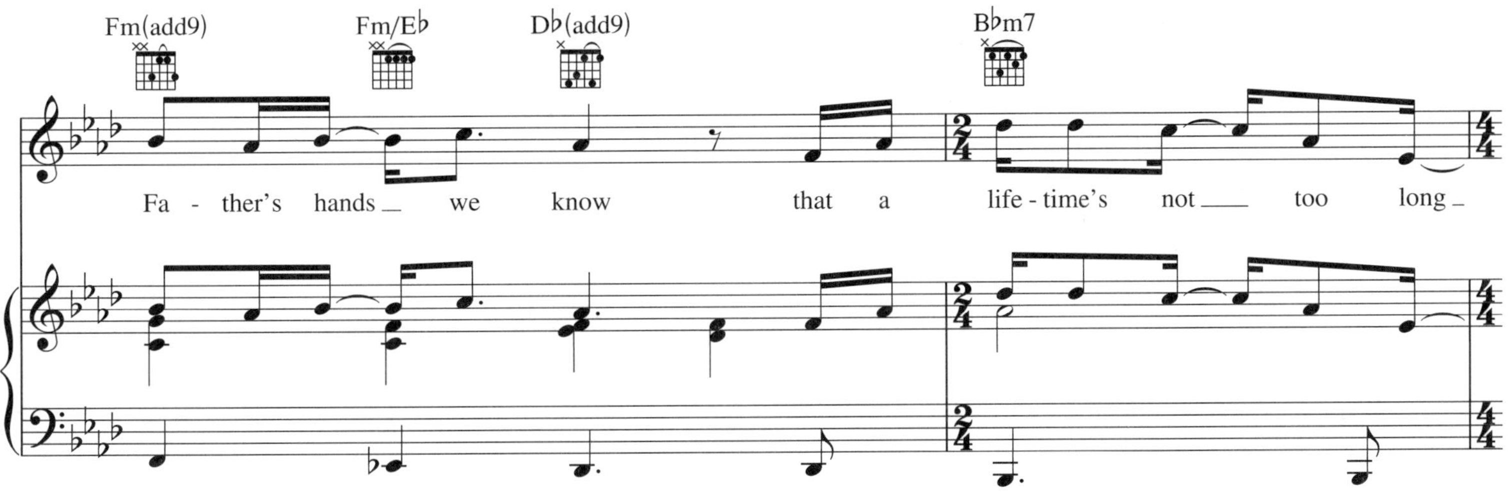
Fm(add9)
Fm/E♭
D♭(add9)
B♭m7
Fa - ther's hands we know that a life - time's not too long

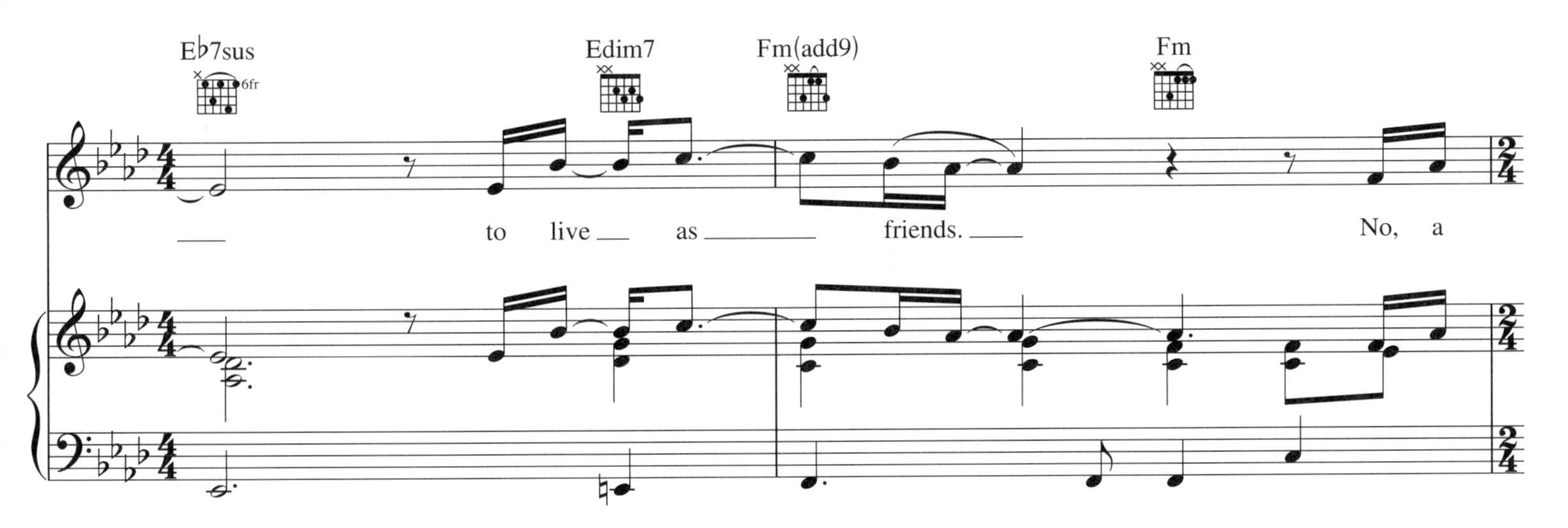
E♭7sus
6fr
Edim7
Fm(add9)
Fm
to live as friends. No, a

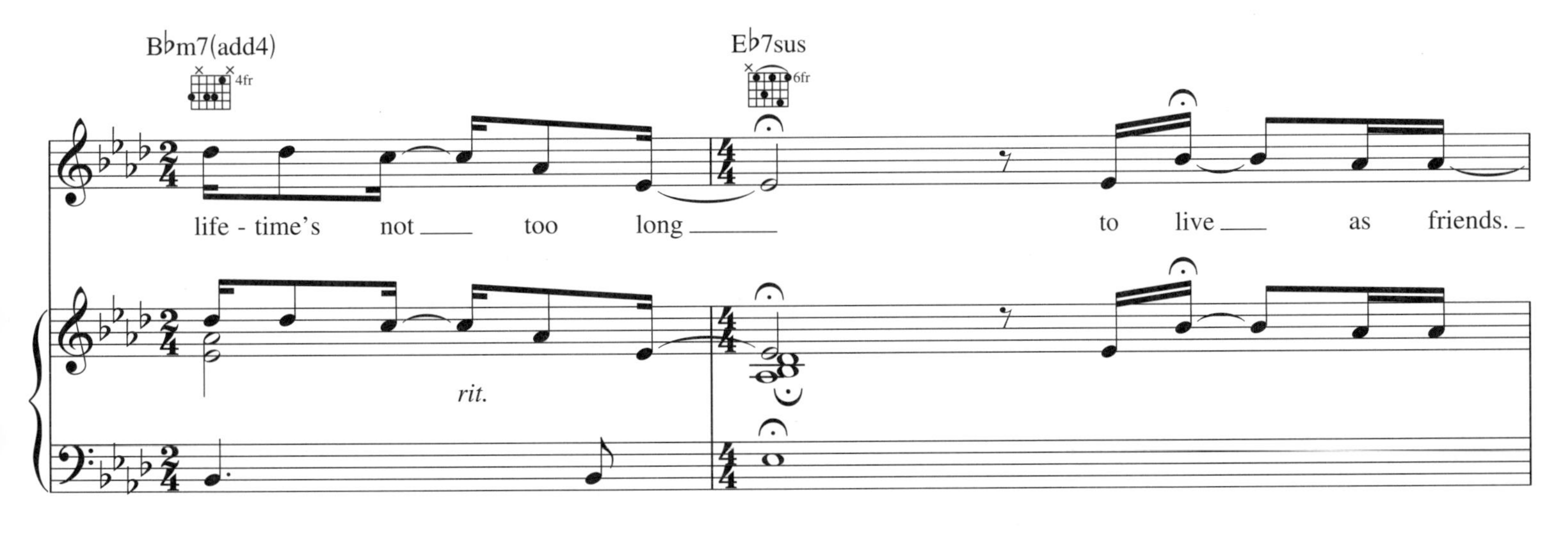
B♭m7(add4)
4fr
E♭7sus
6fr
life - time's not too long to live as friends.
rit.

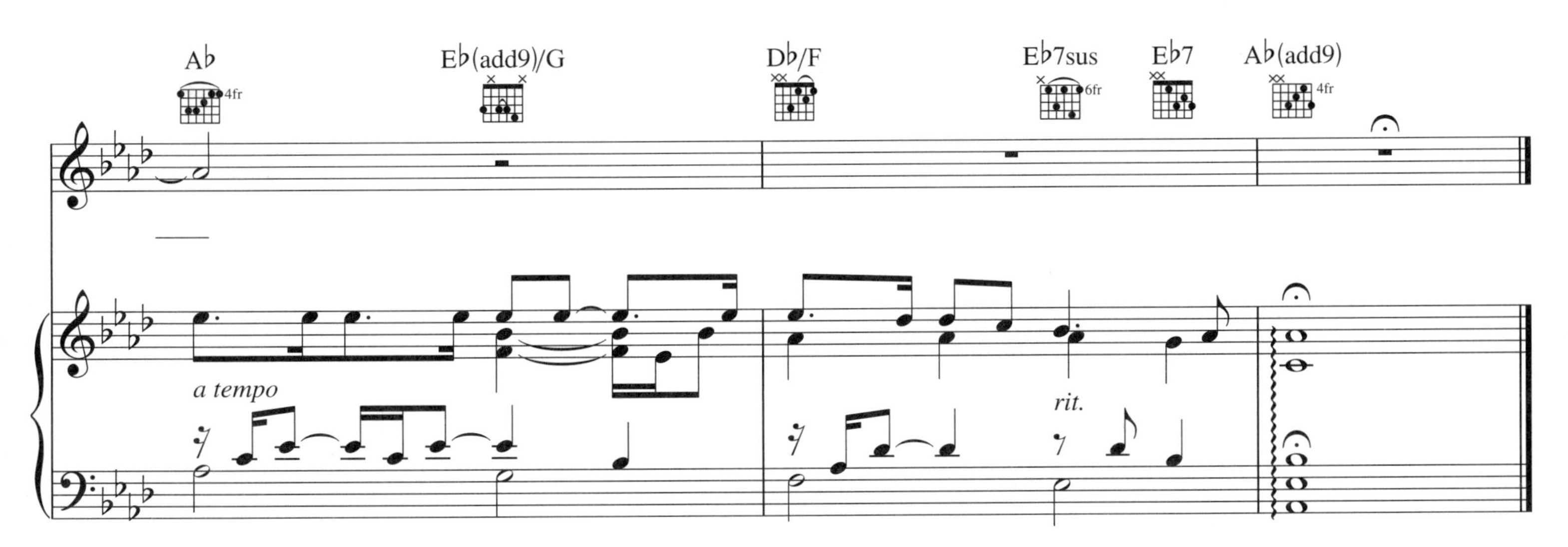
A♭
4fr
E♭(add9)/G
D♭/F
E♭7sus
6fr
E♭7
A♭(add9)
4fr
a tempo
rit.

FROM A DISTANCE

Words and Music by
JULIE GOLD

Moderately slow

G(add2) D/G C/G G C(add2) G/B D

mp

Em7 G/B C G/B Am Em/G D/F♯ D

From a

G(add2) C(add2)/G D/G G(add2)

dis - tance, the world looks blue and green, and the
dis - tance, we all have e - nough, and
dis - tance, you look like my friend e - ven

C D G D/G C(add2)/G G(add2) C(add2) C/E

snow - capped moun - tains white. From a dis - tance, the o - cean meets
no one is in need. There are no guns, no bombs and
though we are at war. From a dis - tance, I just can - not

D/F♯ G G/B C D
the stream, and the ea - gle takes to
no dis - eas - es, no hun - gry mouths to
com - pre - hend what all this fight - ing is
3
G D/G G Cmaj7 D
flight. From a dis - tance there is har -
feed. From a dis - tance, we are
for. From a dis - tance, there is har -
cresc.
mf
Em C G/B G/D D
- mo - ny, and it ech - oes through the land. It's the
in - stru - ments march - ing in a com - mon band, play - ing
- mo - ny, and it ech - oes through the land. It's the
C G/B C G/B To Coda C D
voice of hope, it's the voice of peace. It's the voice of ev - 'ry
songs of hope, play - ing songs of peace. They're the songs of ev - 'ry
hope of hopes, it's the love of loves. It's the

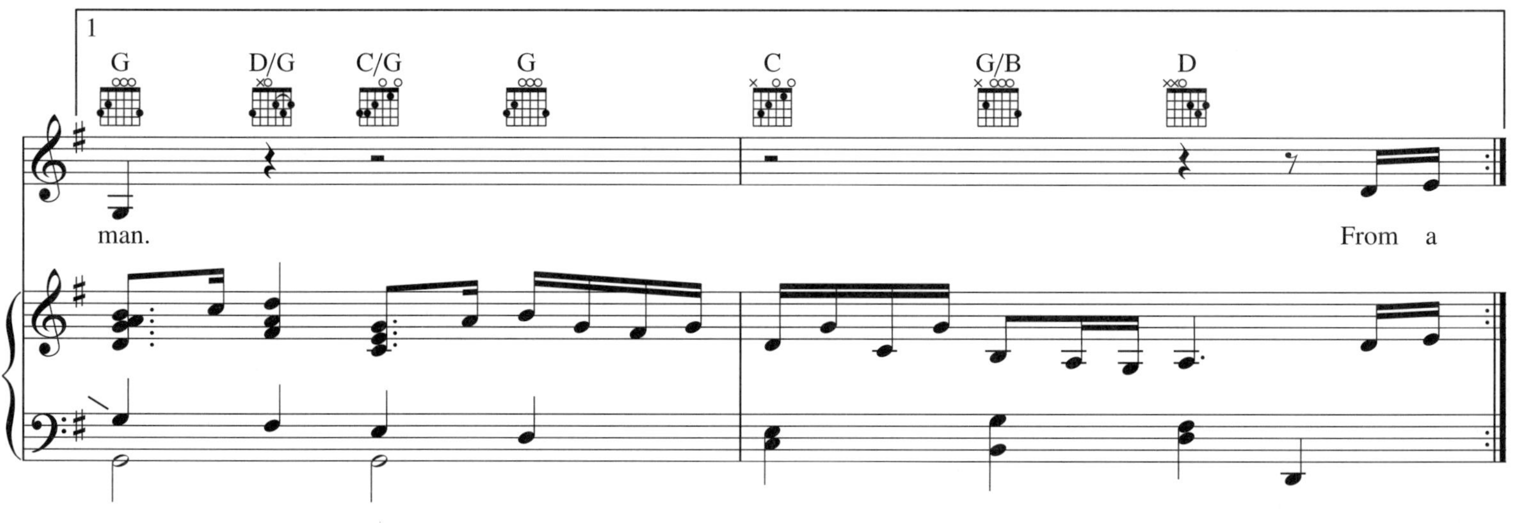
1
G D/G C/G G C G/B D
man. From a

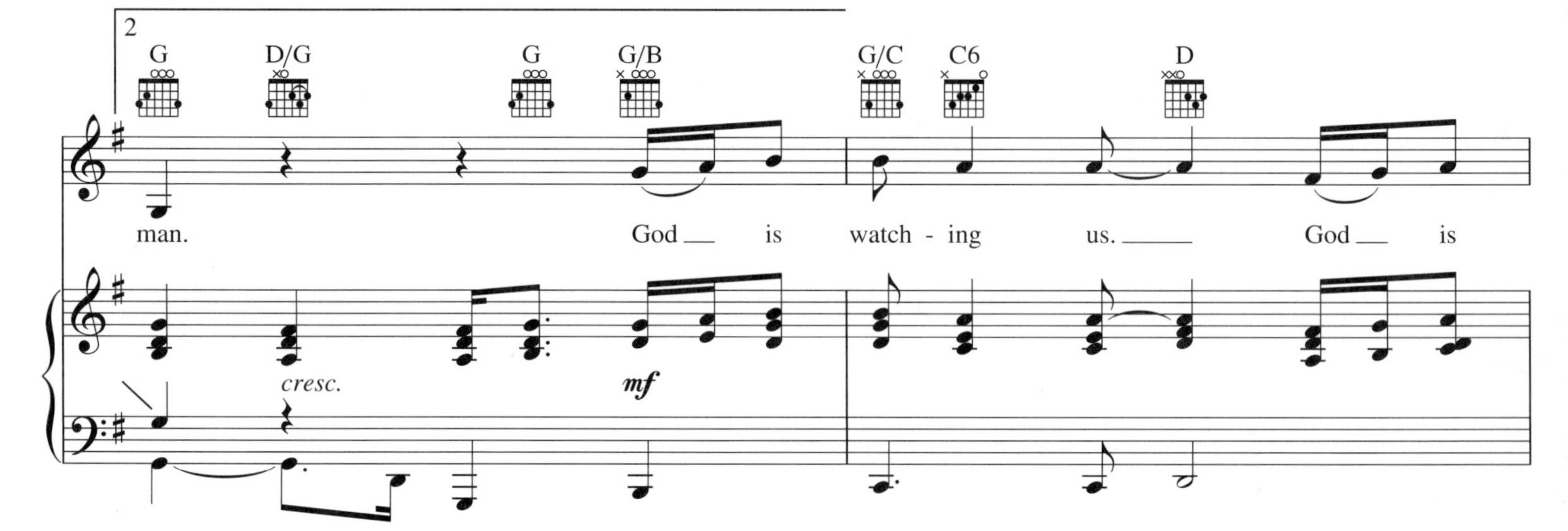
2
G D/G G G/B G/C C6 D
man. God is watch - ing us. God is
cresc.
mf

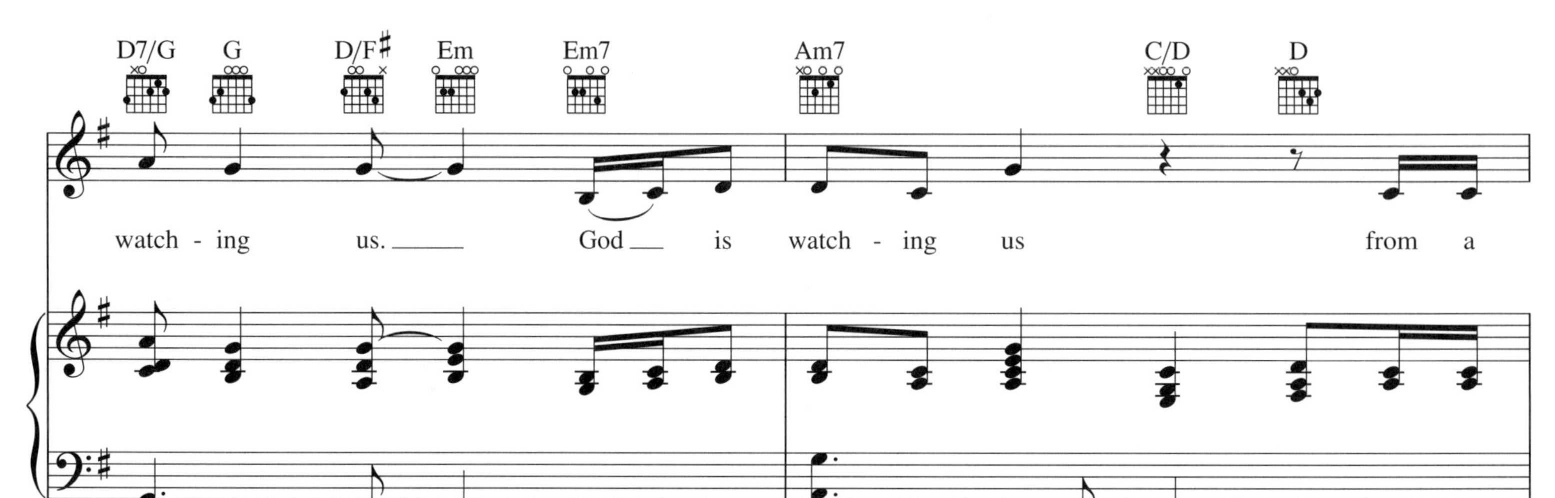
D7/G G D/F♯ Em Em7 Am7 C/D D
watch - ing us. God is watch - ing us from a

G G/B
dis - tance.
dim.
mp

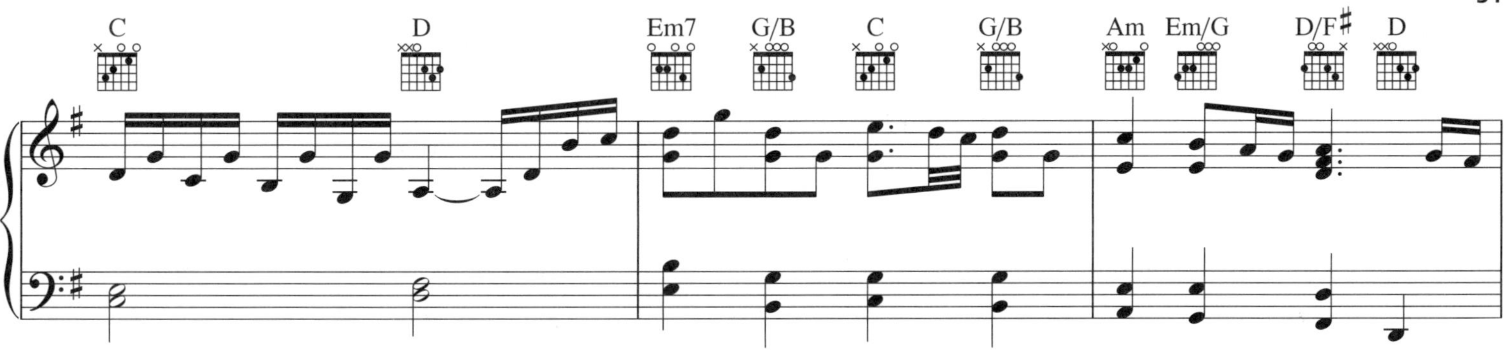
C D Em7 G/B C G/B Am Em/G D/F♯ D

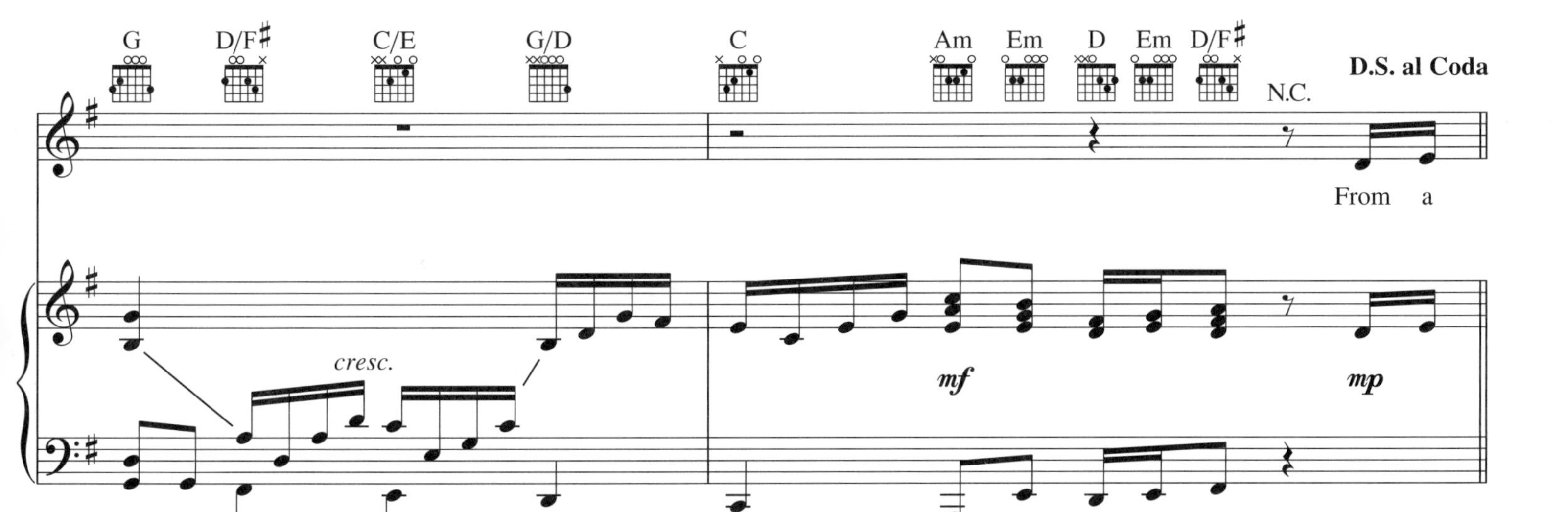
G D/F♯ C/E G/D C Am Em D Em D/F♯
N.C.
D.S. al Coda
From a
cresc.
mf
mp

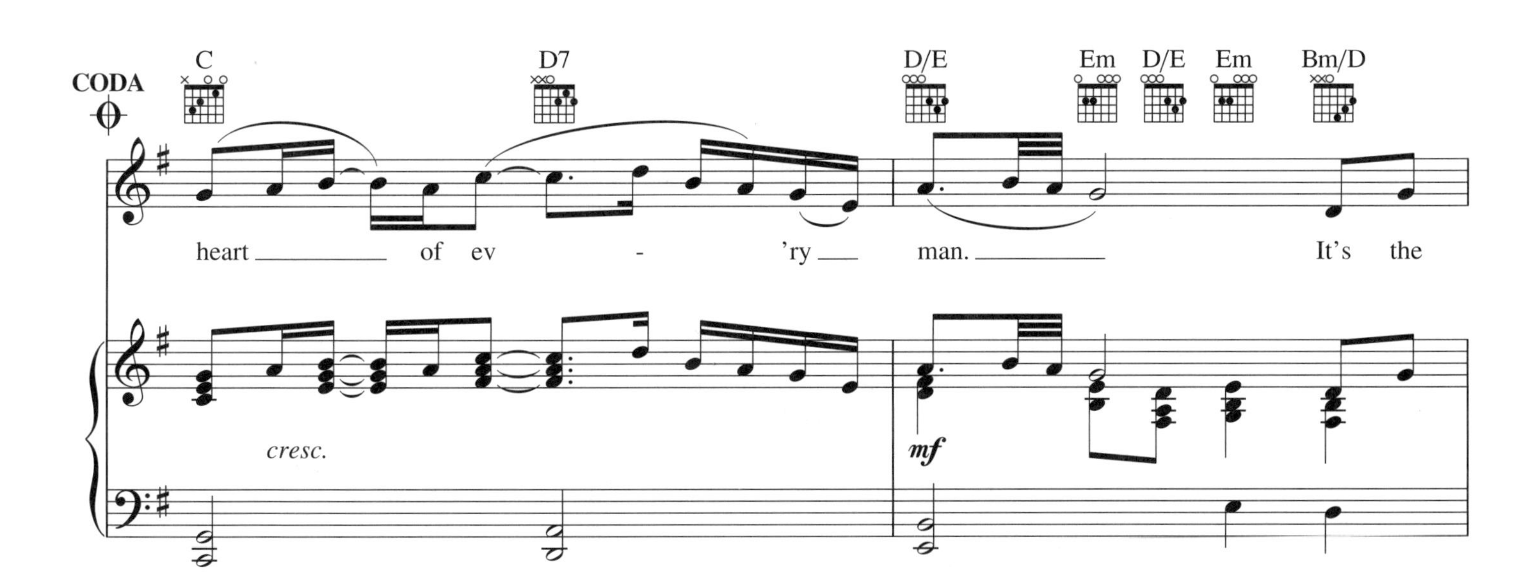
CODA
C D7 D/E Em D/E Em Bm/D
heart of ev - 'ry man. It's the
cresc.
mf

C G/B C G/B C D7
hope of hopes, it's the love of loves. This is the song of ev - 'ry
3

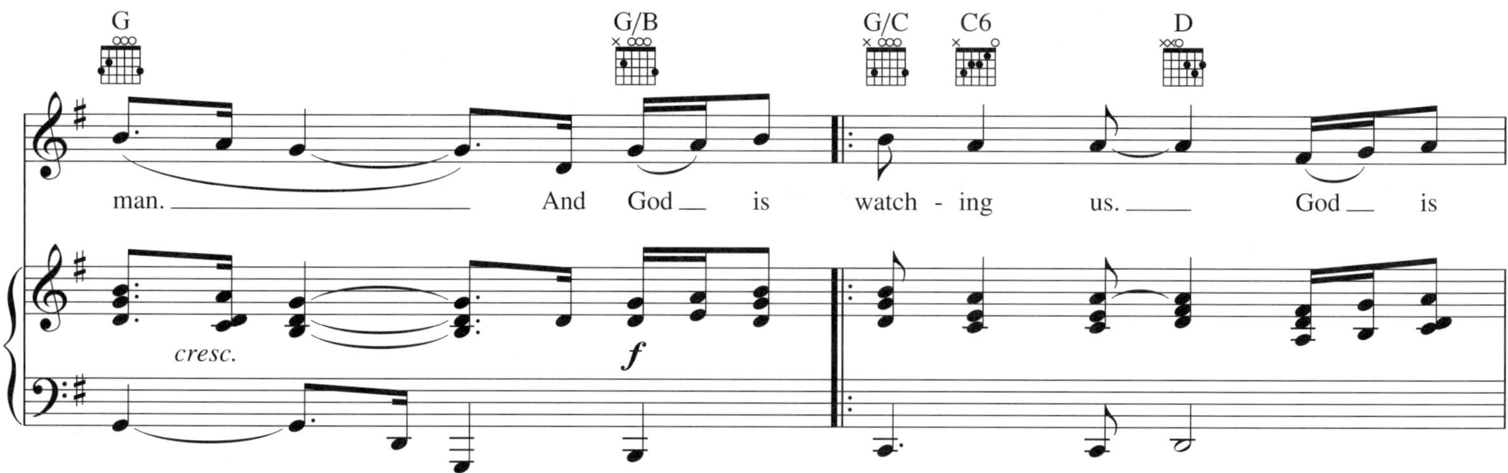
G
G/B
G/C
C6
D
man. And God is watch - ing us. God is
cresc.
f

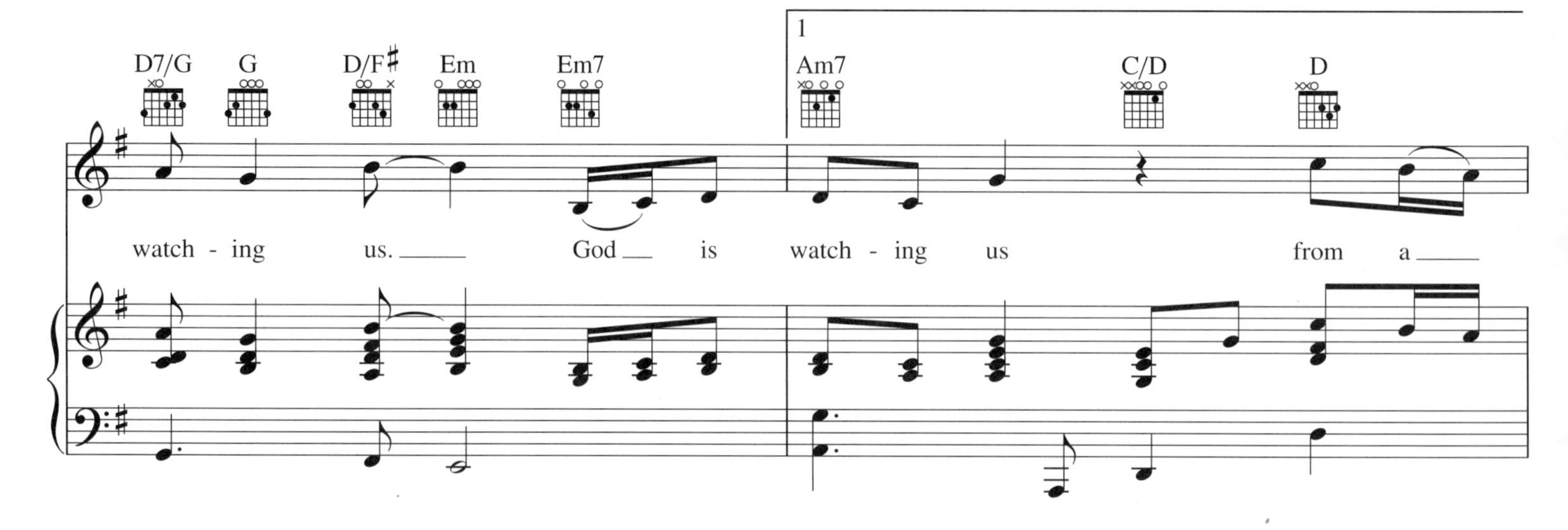
D7/G
G
D/F♯
Em
Em7
1
Am7
C/D
D
watch - ing us. God is watch - ing us from a

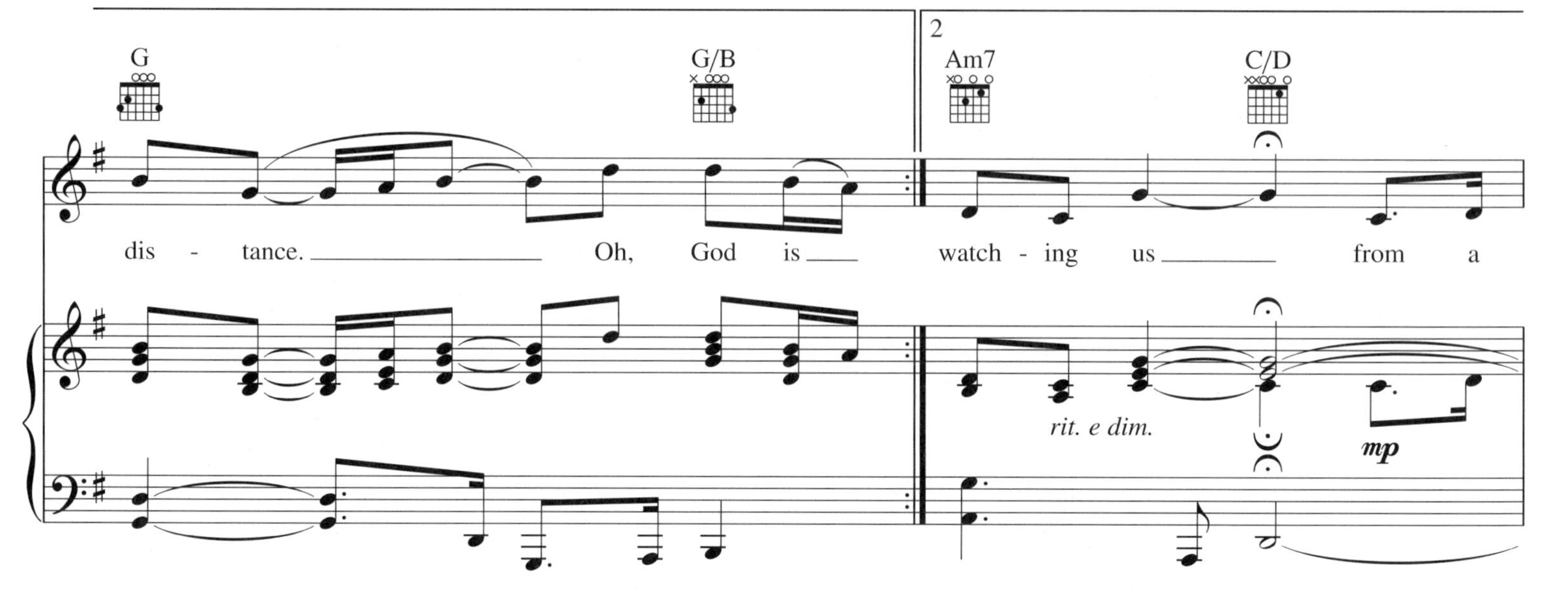
G
G/B
2
Am7
C/D
dis - tance. Oh, God is watch - ing us from a
rit. e dim.
mp

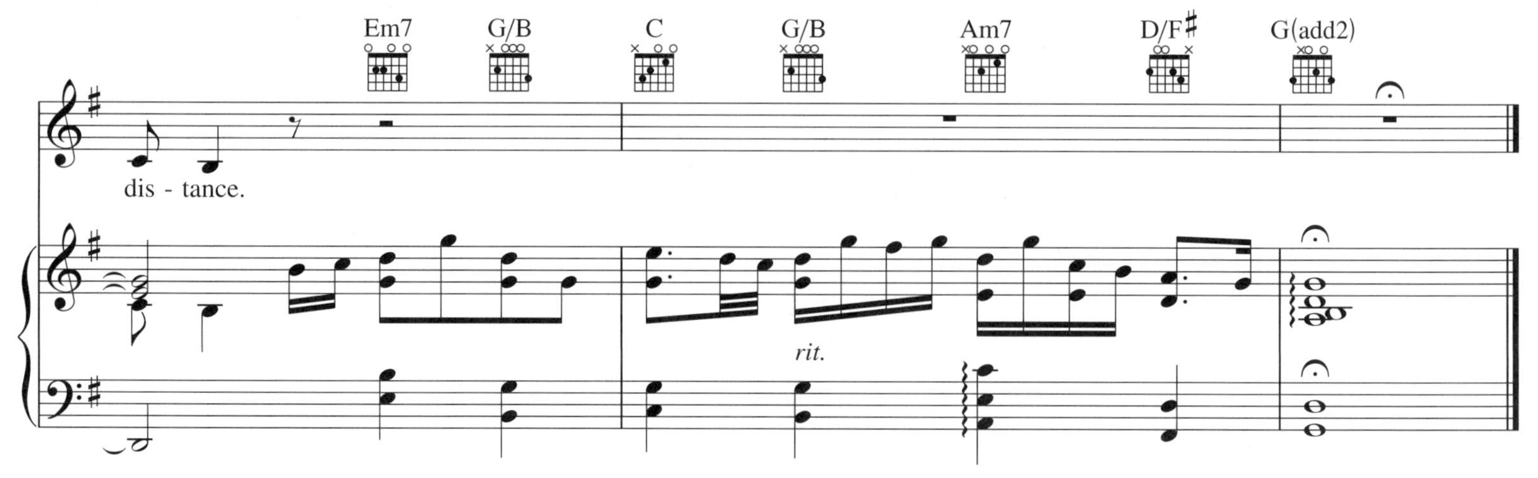
Em7
G/B
C
G/B
Am7
D/F♯
G(add2)
dis - tance.
rit.

GOD BLESS THE U.S.A.

Words and Music by
LEE GREENWOOD

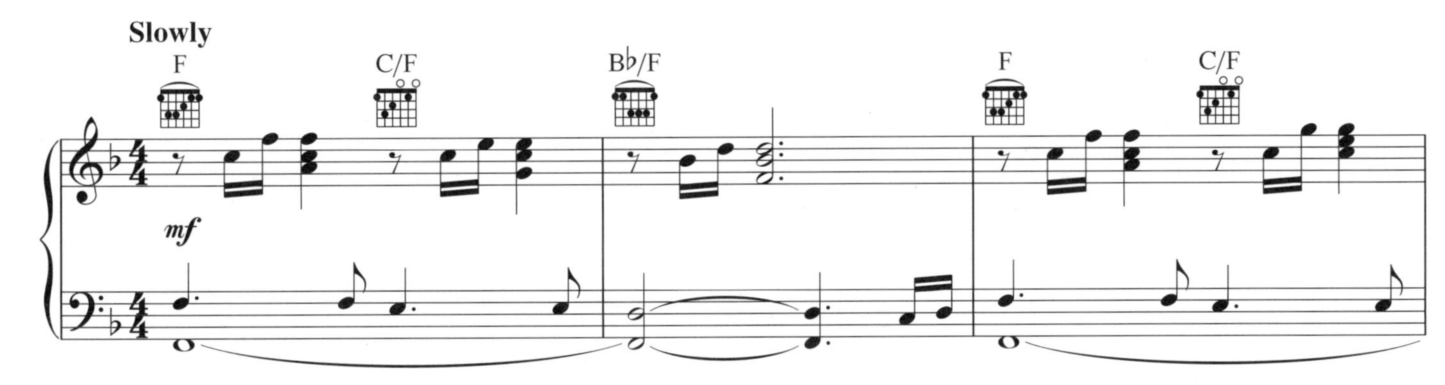

Am7
Gm7
liv - in' here to - day, 'cause the flag still stands for free - dom and they
Dm
B♭
can't take that a - way. And I'm
C/E
B♭/D
F
3
proud to be an A - mer - i - can where at least I know I'm free. And I
C/E
B♭/D
F
won't for - get the men who died, who gave that right to me. And I'd glad - ly

Dm
F/A
B♭
F/A
stand up next to you and de - fend her still to - day.
'Cause there

Gm7
F/A
To Coda
B♭
Gm7/C
F
Fmaj9
ain't no doubt I love this land,
God bless the U. S. A.

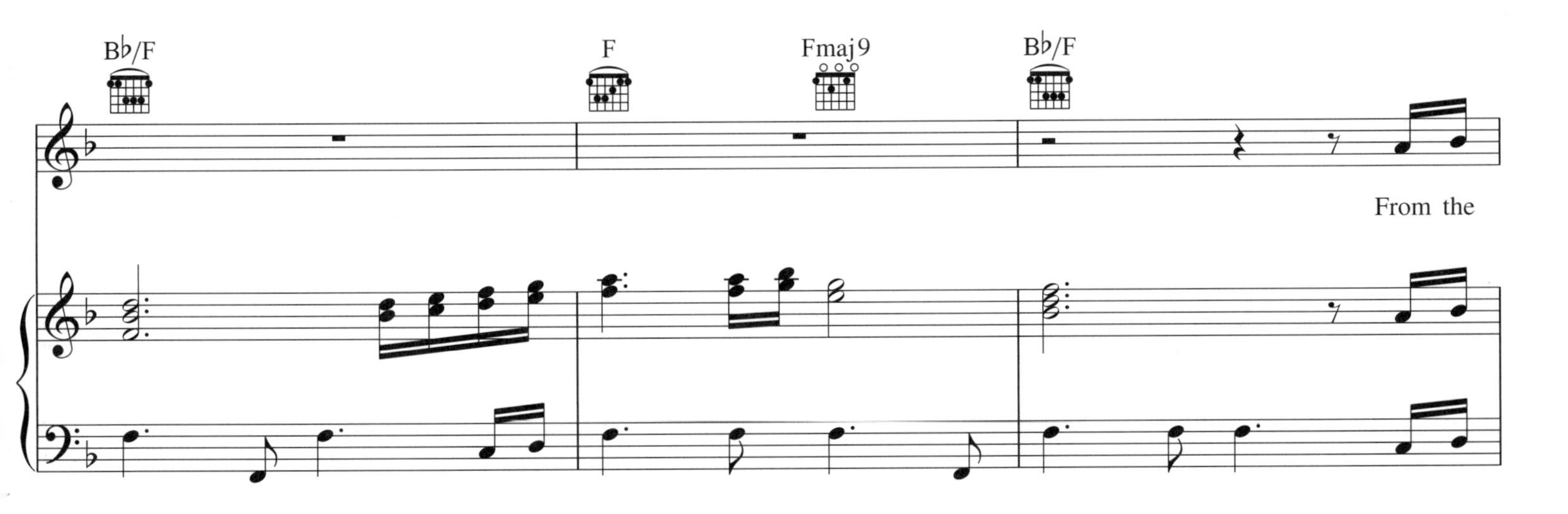
B♭/F
F
Fmaj9
B♭/F
From the

F
B♭/F
Gm7
lakes of Min - ne - so - ta, to the hills of Ten - nes - see,
a - cross the plains of Tex - as, from

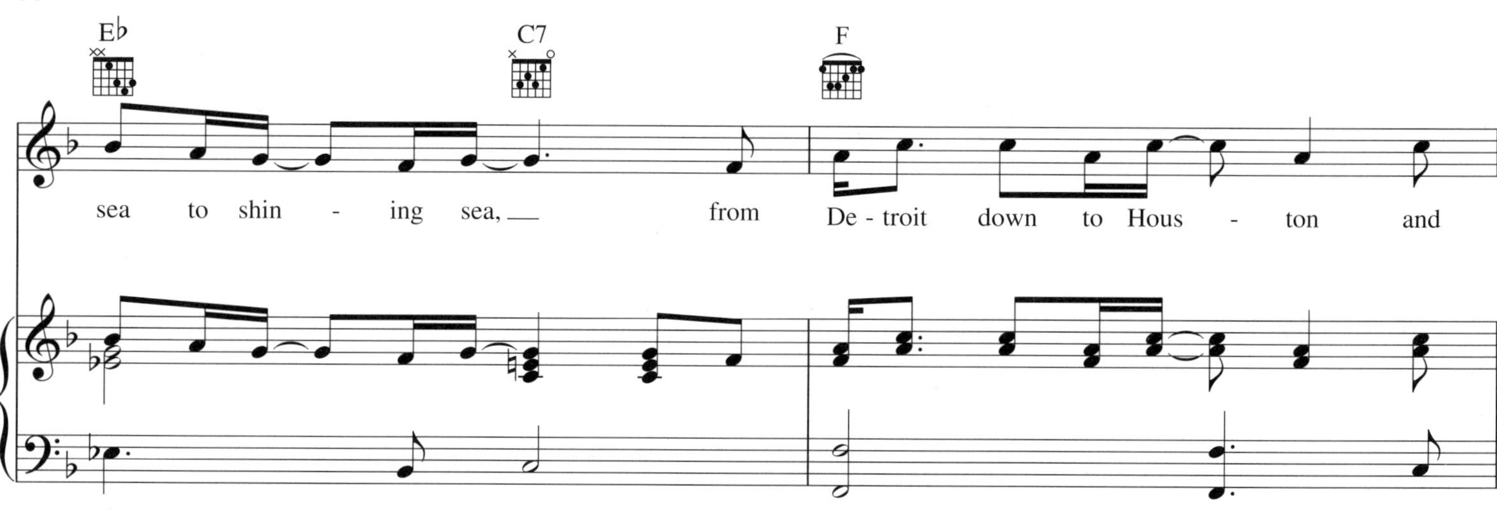
E♭
C7
F
sea to shin - ing sea, from De - troit down to Hous - ton and

Am7
Gm7
New York to L. A., well, there's pride in ev - 'ry A - mer - i - can heart, and it's

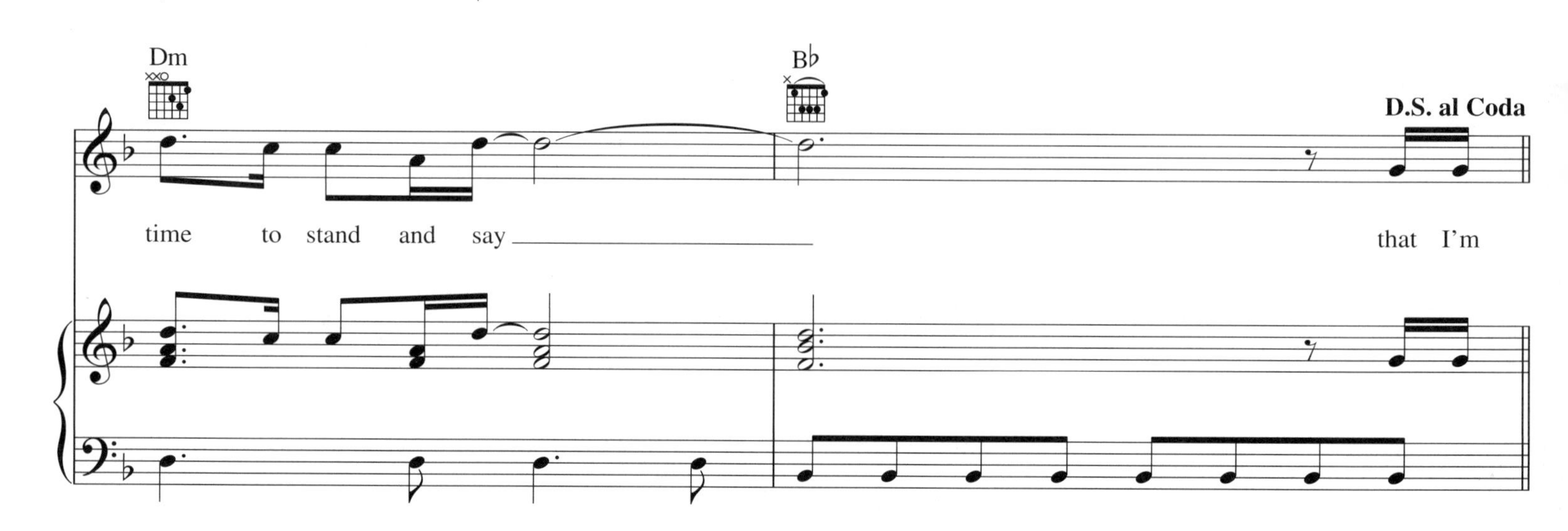
Dm
B♭
D.S. al Coda
time to stand and say that I'm

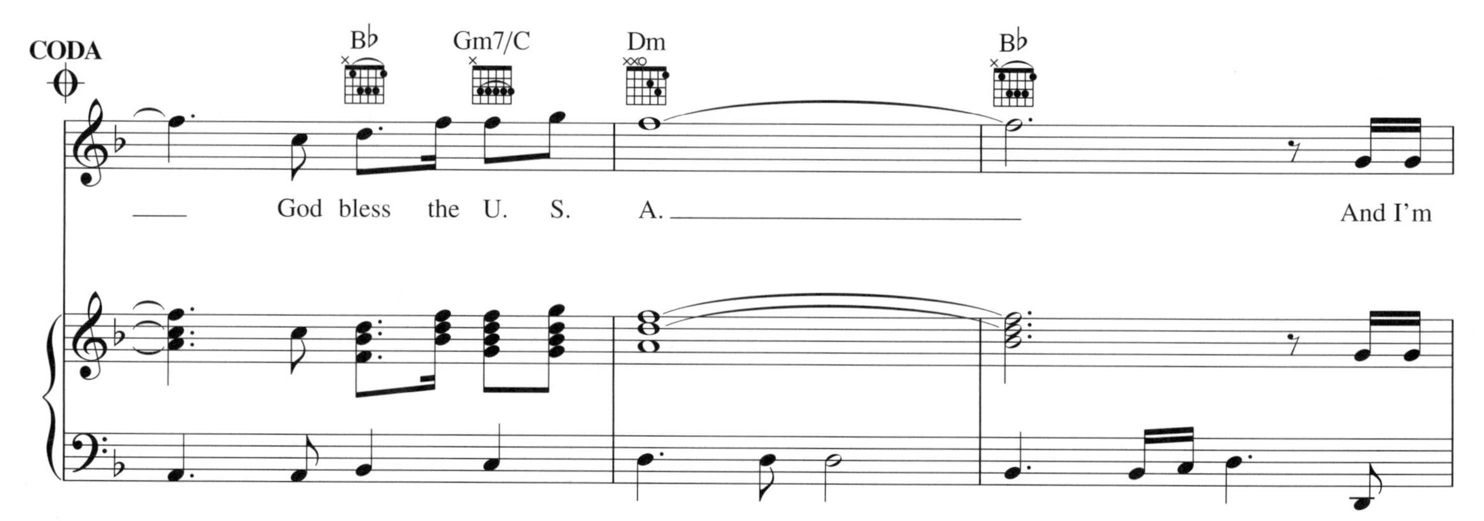
CODA
B♭
Gm7/C
Dm
B♭
God bless the U. S. A. And I'm

C/E
B♭/D
F
proud to be an A - mer - i - can where at least I know I'm free, and I
3
C/E
B♭/D
F
won't for - get the men who died, who gave that right to me. And I'd glad - ly
Dm
F/A
B♭
Am7
stand up next to you, and de - fend her still to - day. 'Cause there
Gm7
F/A
Gm7
Am7
B♭
C7
F
ain't no doubt I love this land, God bless the U. S. A.

HERO

Words and Music by MARIAH CAREY
and WALTER AFANASIEFF

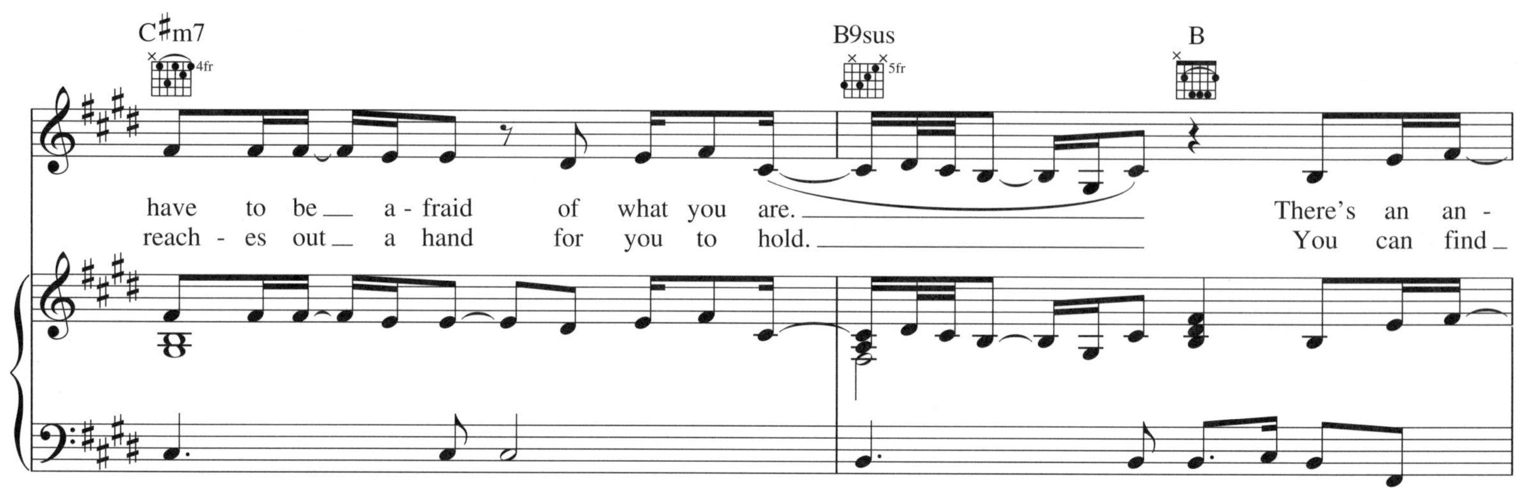

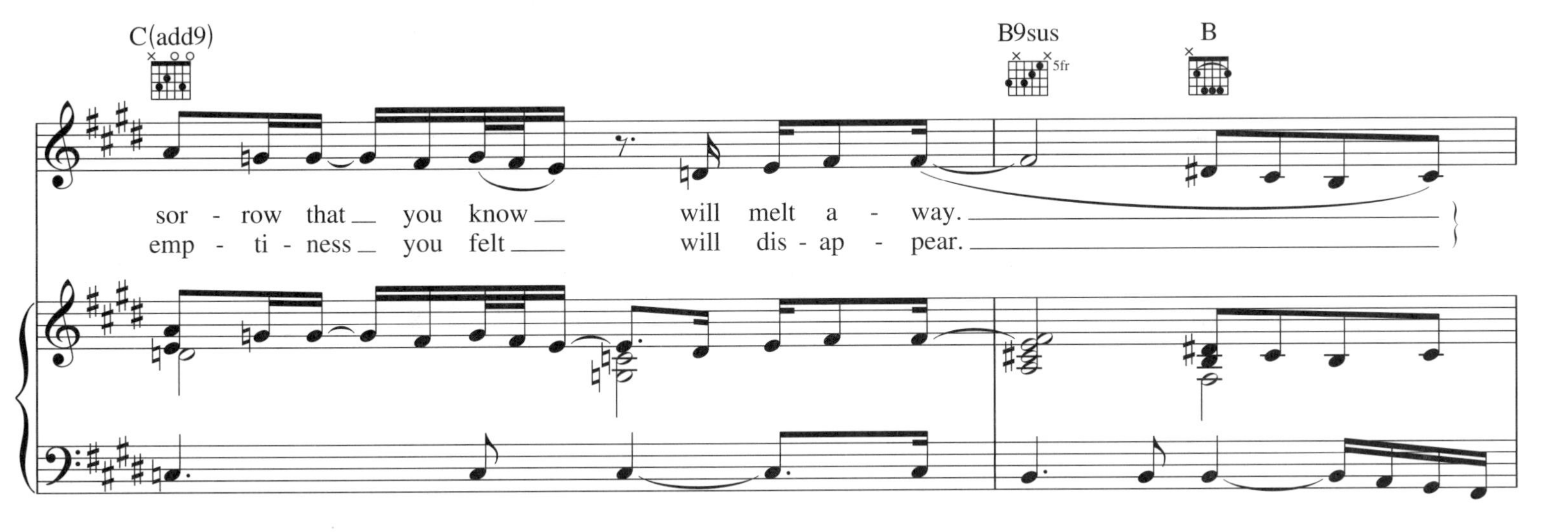
C(add9)
B9sus
5fr
B
sor - row that you know will melt a - way.
emp - ti - ness you felt will dis - ap - pear.

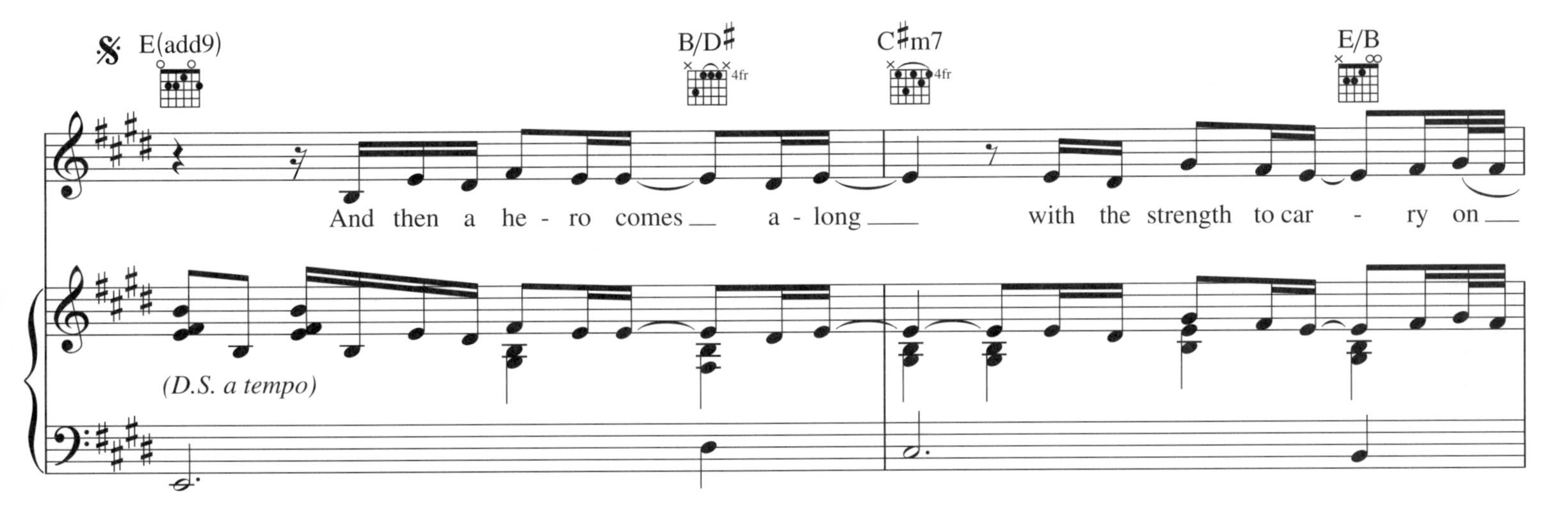
E(add9)
B/D♯
4fr
C♯m7
4fr
E/B
And then a he - ro comes a - long with the strength to car - ry on
(D.S. a tempo)

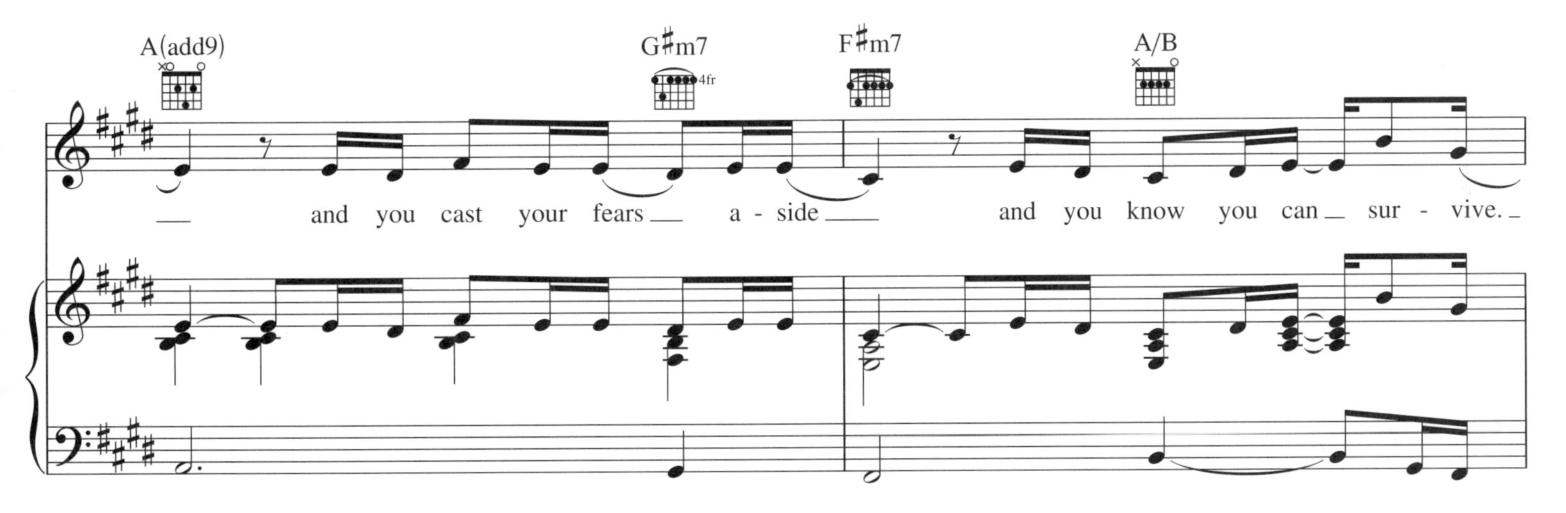
A(add9)
G♯m7
4fr
F♯m7
A/B
and you cast your fears a - side and you know you can sur - vive.

E
B/D♯
4fr
C♯m7
4fr
C♯m/B
So, when you feel like hope is gone, look in - side you and be strong

A(add9)
G#m7
F#m7
B9sus
To Coda
and you'll fi - n'ly see the truth
that a he - ro lies in you.

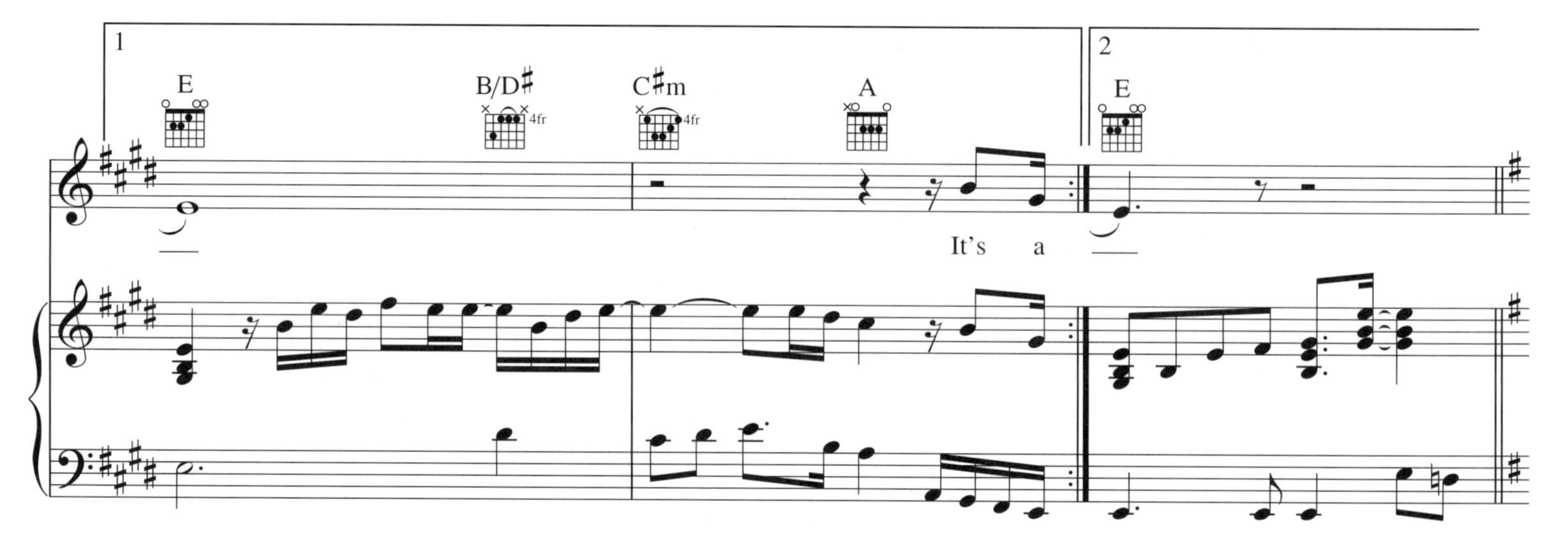
1
2
E
B/D#
C#m
A
E
It's a

C
G/B
G
D
Lord knows
dreams are hard to fol - low,

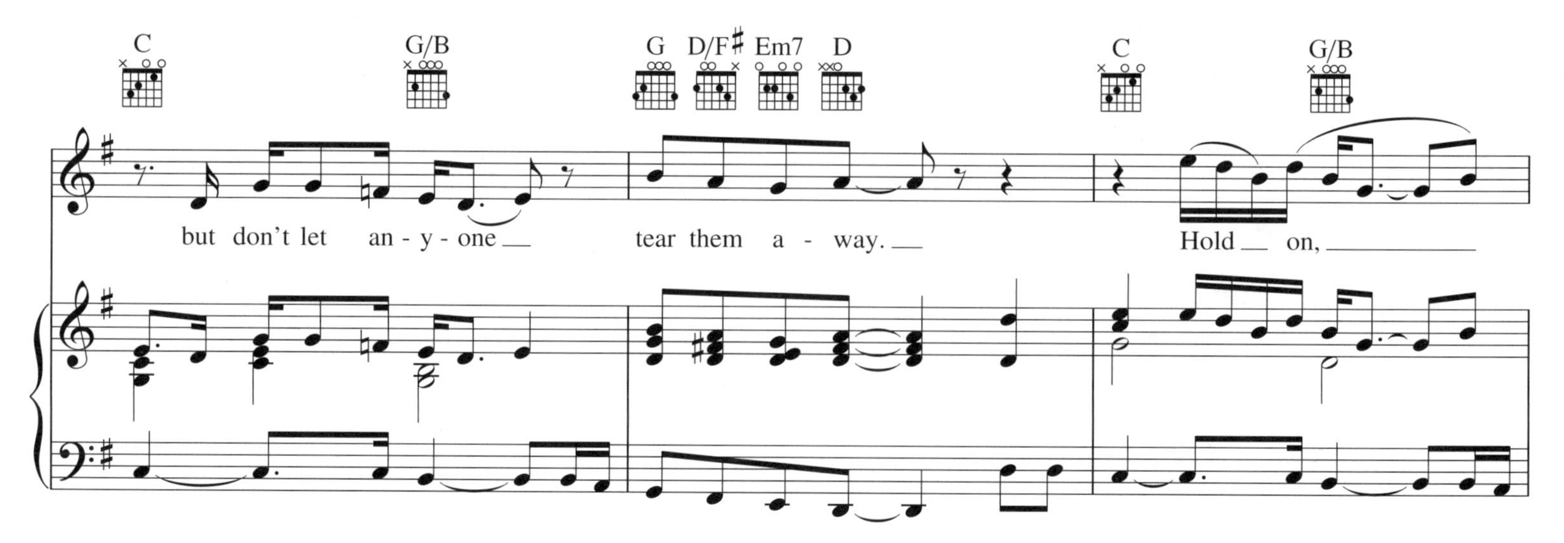
C
G/B
G
D/F#
Em7
D
C
G/B
but don't let an - y - one tear them a - way.
Hold on,

D.S. al Coda
G
D
C
G/B
A/B
B
there will be to - mor - row. In time you'll find the way.
rall.

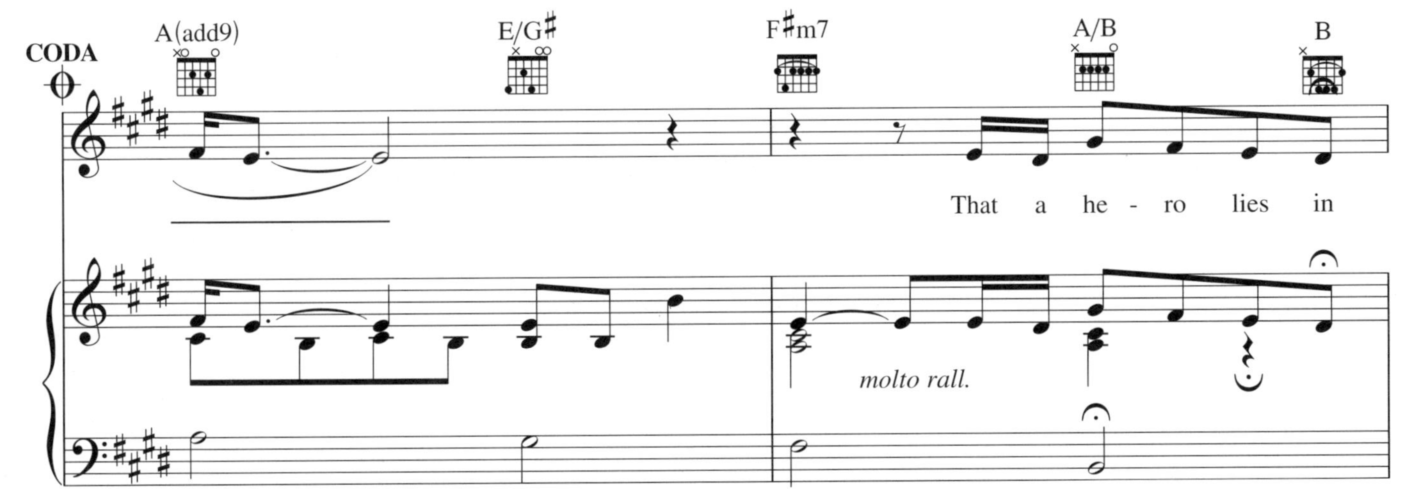
CODA
A(add9)
E/G#
F#m7
A/B
B
That a he - ro lies in
molto rall.

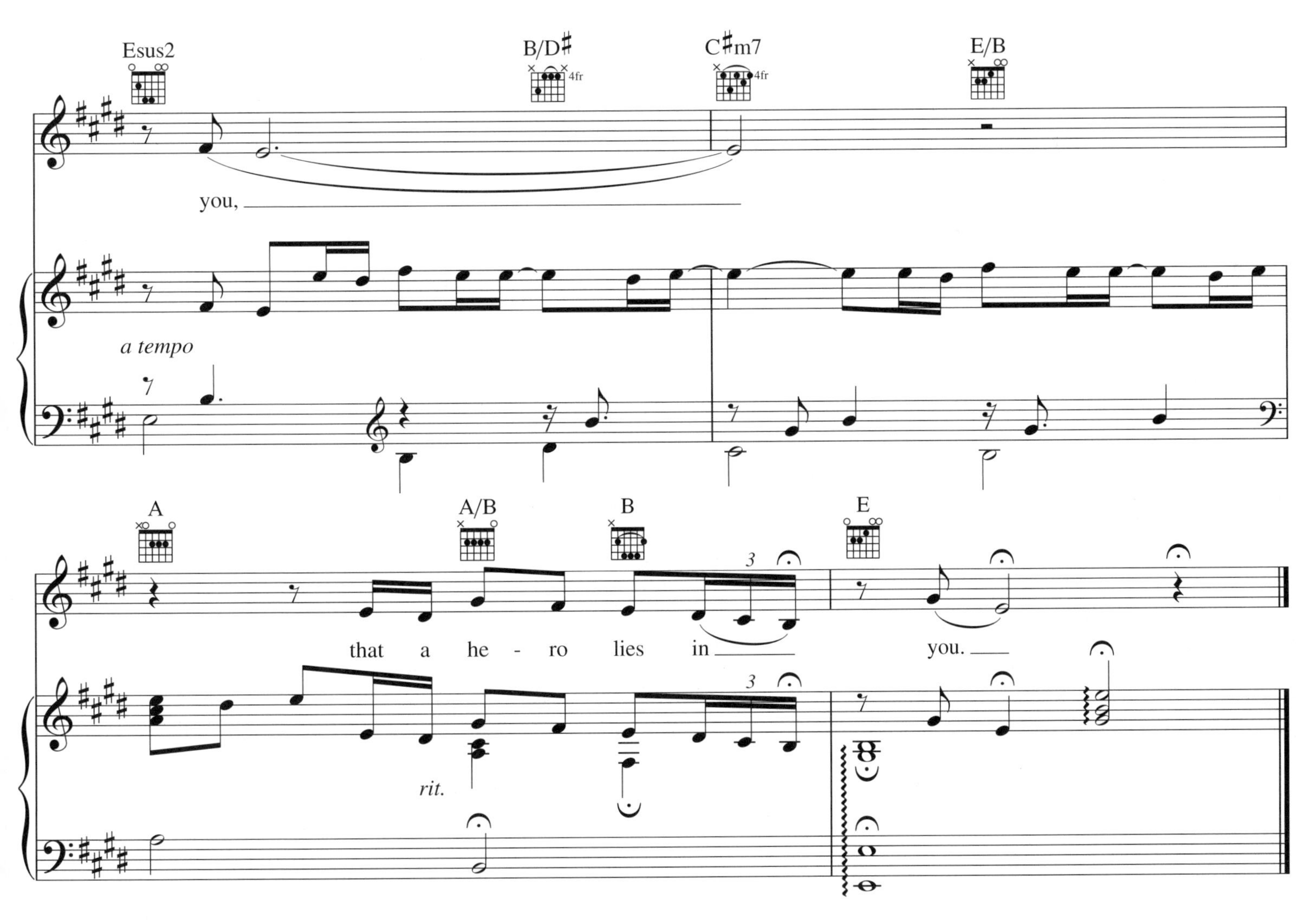
Esus2
B/D#
C#m7
E/B
you,
a tempo
A
A/B
B
E
that a he - ro lies in you.
rit.

I BELIEVE I CAN FLY

from SPACE JAM

Words and Music by
ROBERT KELLY

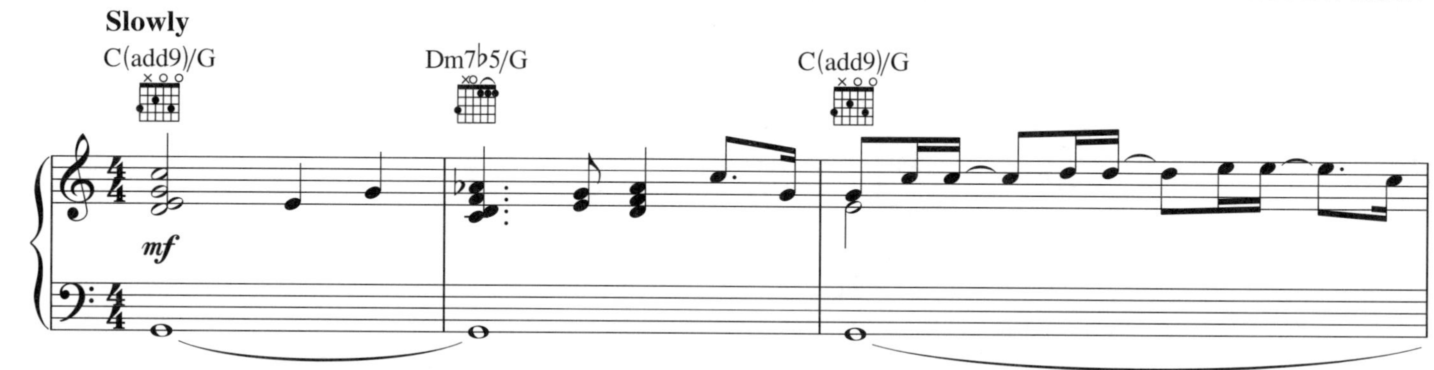

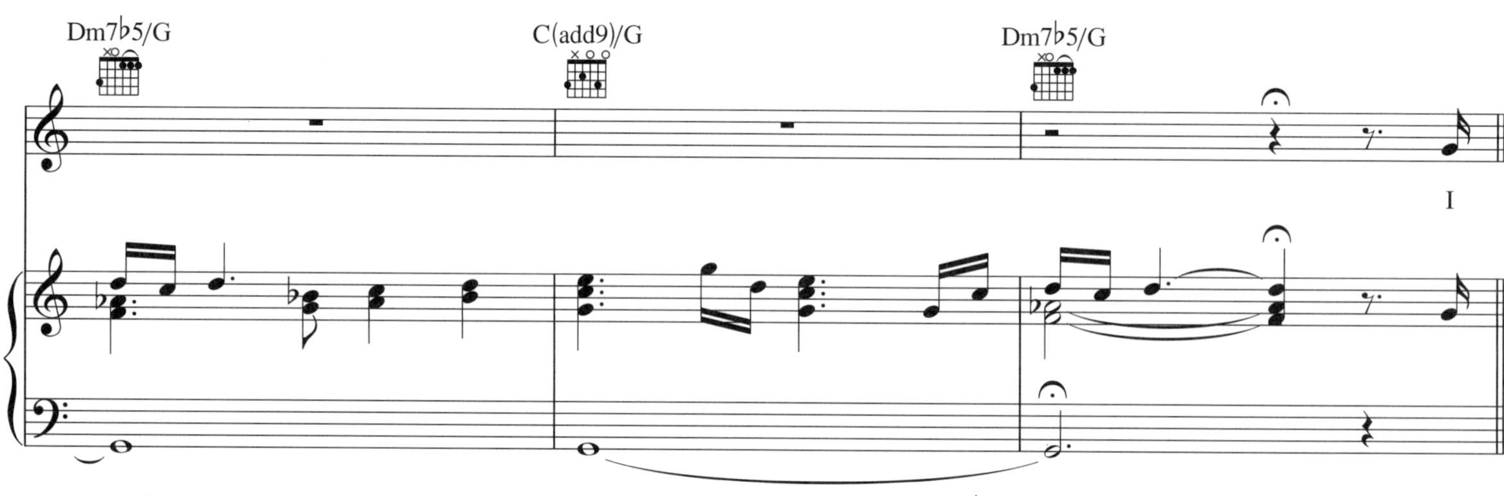

C
Dm7♭5/C
now I know the mean - ing of true love.
mir - a - cles in life I must a - chieve,
I'm
but
C
Dm7♭5/C
E7♯5
lean - ing on the ev - er - last - ing arm.
first I know it starts in - side of me.
If I can
Am7
Dm7♭5/A♭
C/G
see it, then I can do it; if I just be - lieve it, there's noth - ing
be
Dm7/G
C
to it. I be - lieve I can fly, I be - lieve I can

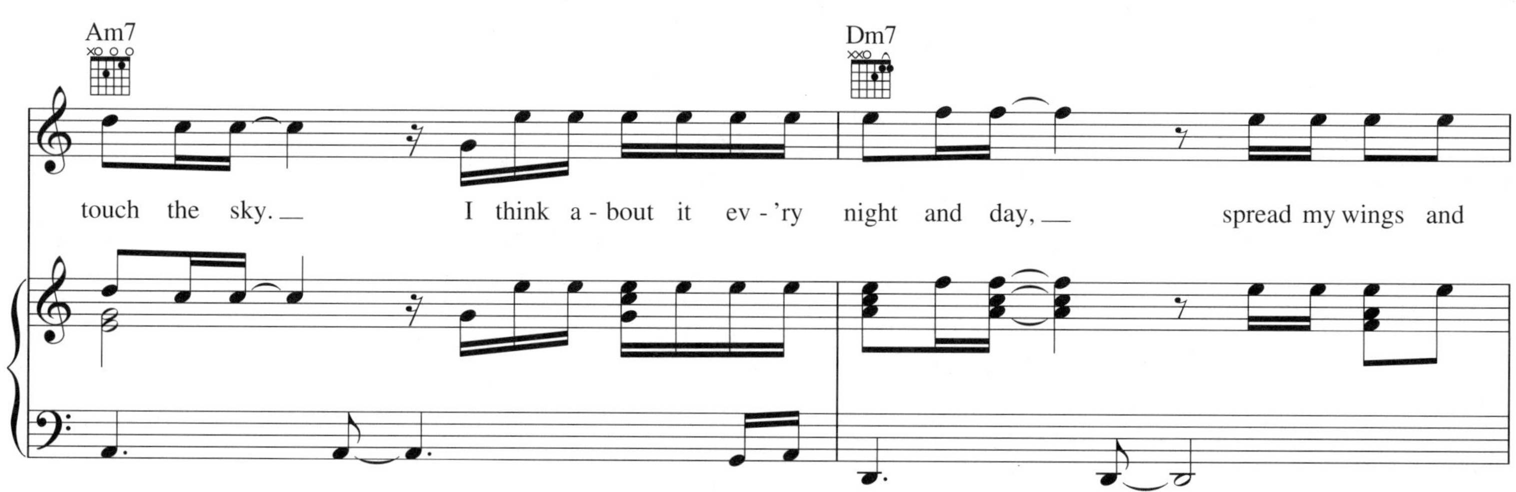
Am7
Dm7
touch the sky. I think a - bout it ev - 'ry night and day, spread my wings and

Dm7/G
G♯dim7
Am7
fly a - way. I be - lieve I can soar, I see me run - ning through that

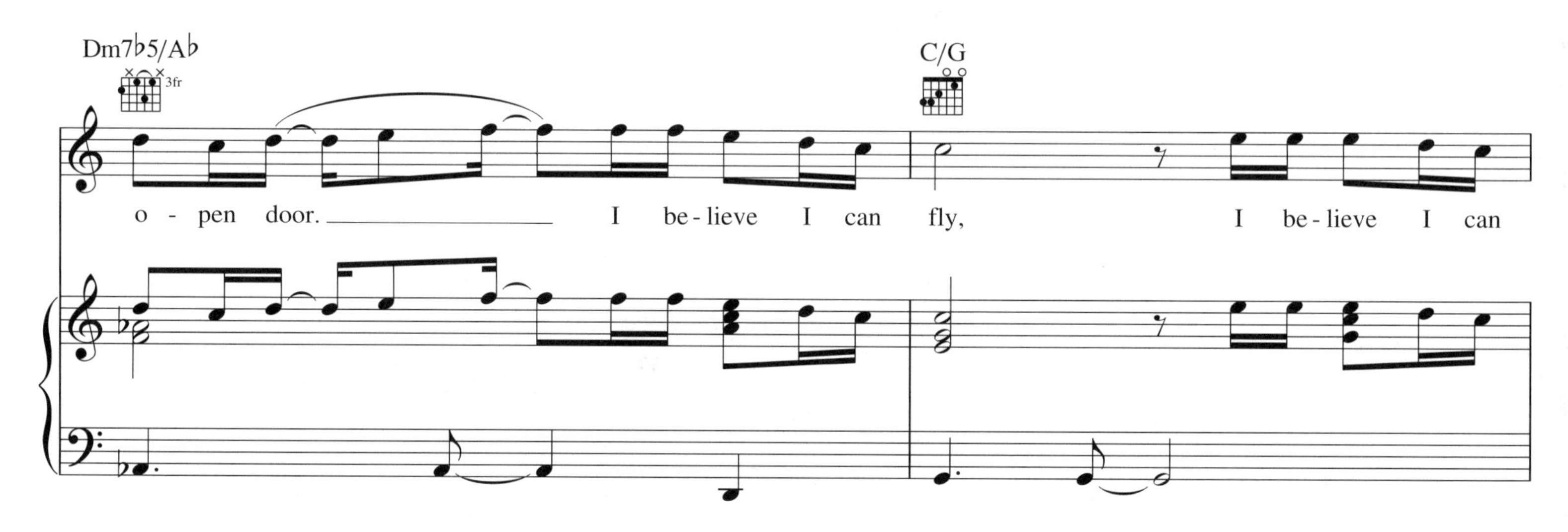
Dm7♭5/A♭
3fr
C/G
o - pen door. I be - lieve I can fly, I be - lieve I can

1
Dm7♭5/A♭
3fr
Am7
Fmaj7/G
fly, I be - lieve I can fly. See,

2
Dm7♭5/A♭
3fr
Am7
fly, oh, I be - lieve I can fly.

Dm7
C/E
Fmaj7/G
Hey, 'cause I be - lieve in me, oh. If I can

B♭m7
E♭m7♭5/A
D♭/A♭
4fr
see it, then I can do it; if I just be - lieve it, there's noth - ing

E♭m7/A♭
6fr
D♭
to it. I be - lieve I can fly, I be - lieve I can

B♭m7
E♭m7
6fr
touch the sky. I think a-bout it ev-ery night and day, spread my wings and

E♭m7/A♭
6fr
Adim7
B♭m7
fly a-way. I be-lieve I can soar, I see me run-ning through that

E♭m7♭5/A
D♭/A♭
4fr
o-pen door. I be-lieve I can fly, I be-lieve I can

E♭m7♭5/A
D♭/A♭
4fr
fly, I be-lieve I can fly, hey, if I just
3

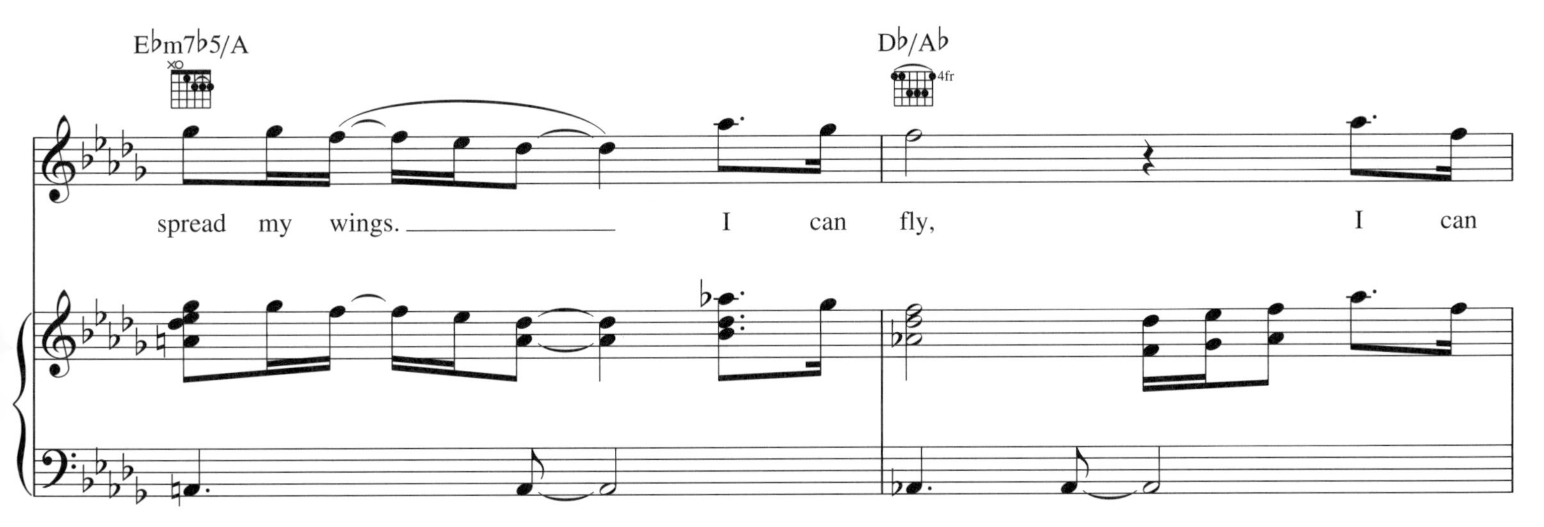
E♭m7♭5/A
D♭/A♭
4fr
spread my wings. I can fly, I can

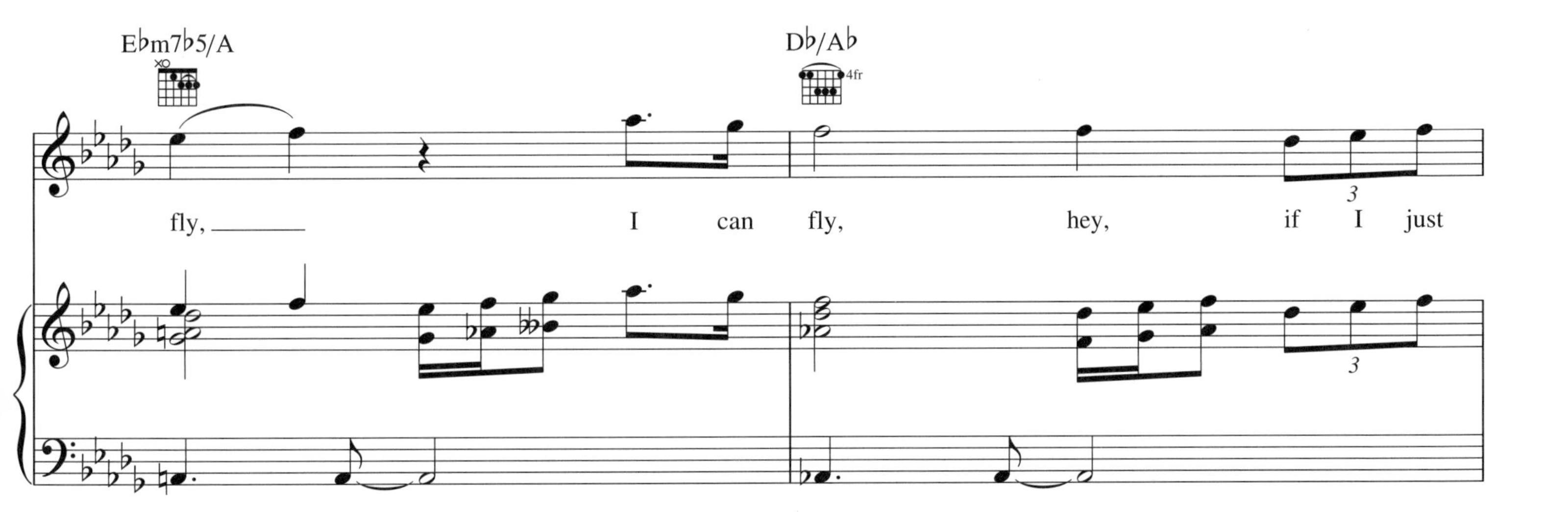
E♭m7♭5/A
D♭/A♭
4fr
fly, I can fly, hey, if I just
3
3

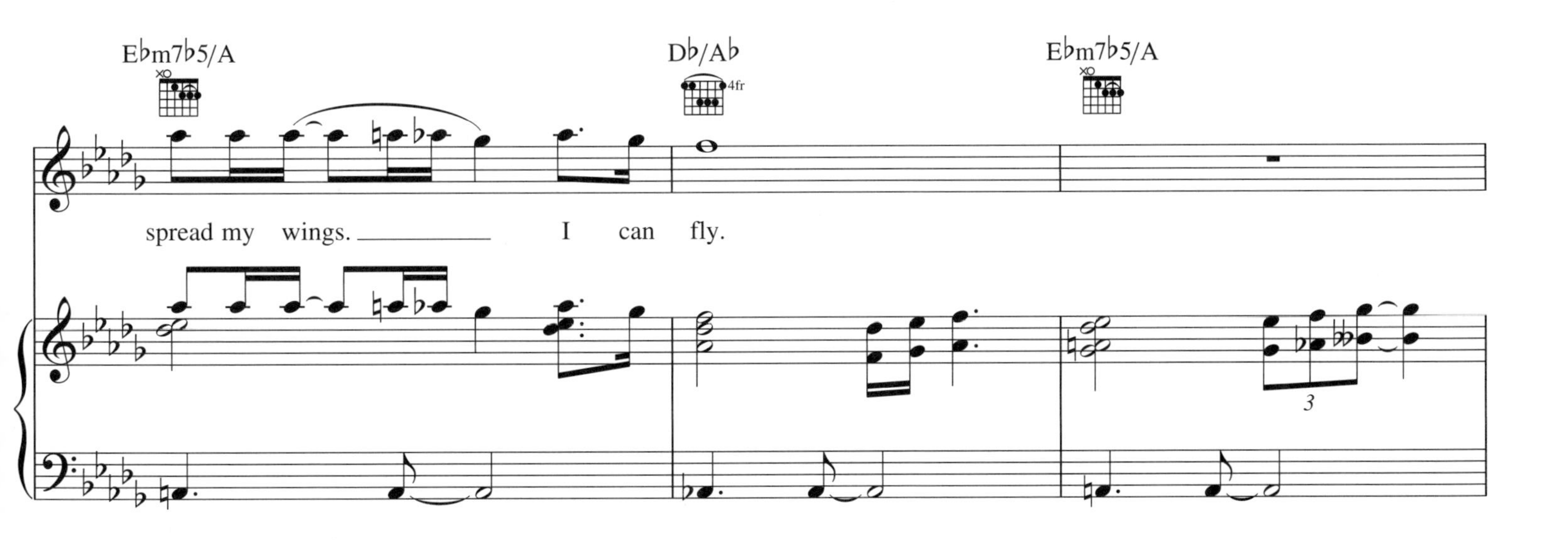
E♭m7♭5/A
D♭/A♭
4fr
E♭m7♭5/A
spread my wings. I can fly.
3

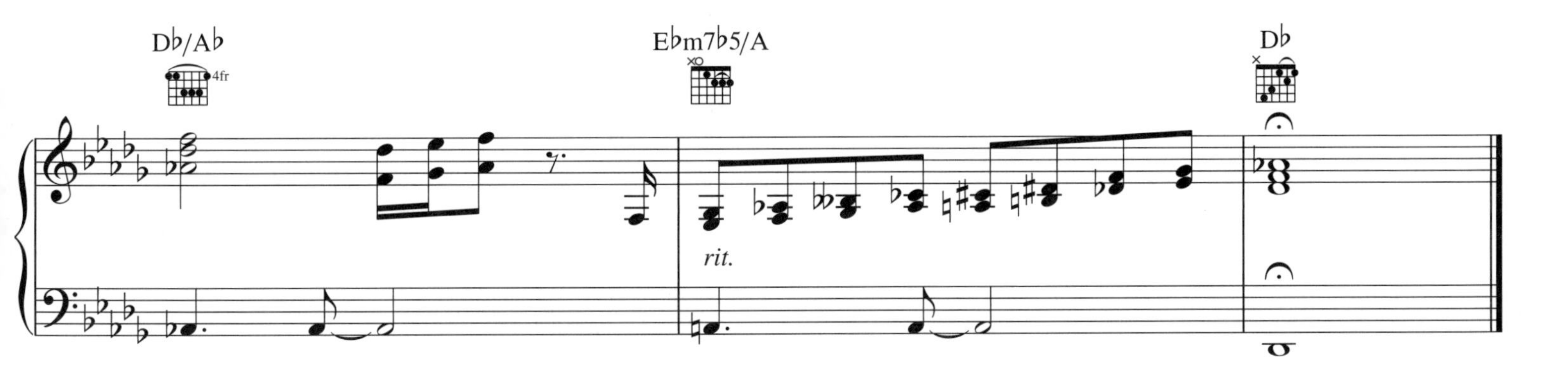
D♭/A♭
4fr
E♭m7♭5/A
D♭
rit.

I CAN ONLY IMAGINE

Words and Music by
BART MILLARD

Emaj9
Amaj9
mag - ine.

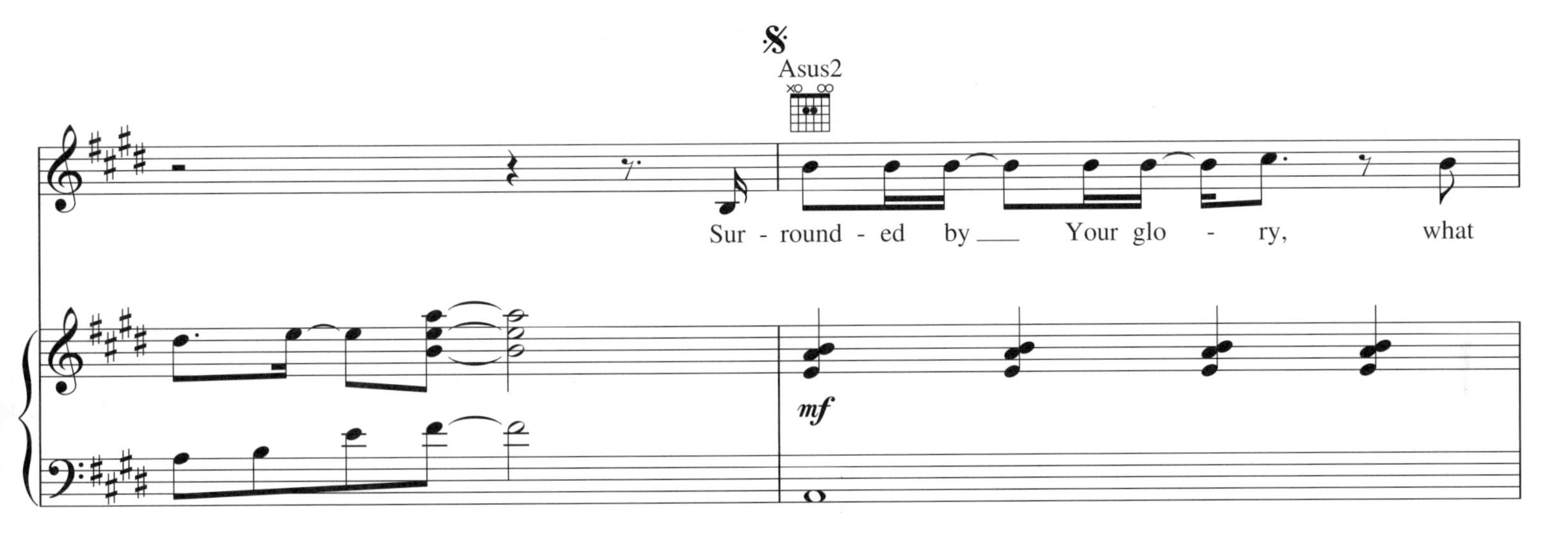
Asus2
Sur - round - ed by Your glo - ry, what
mf

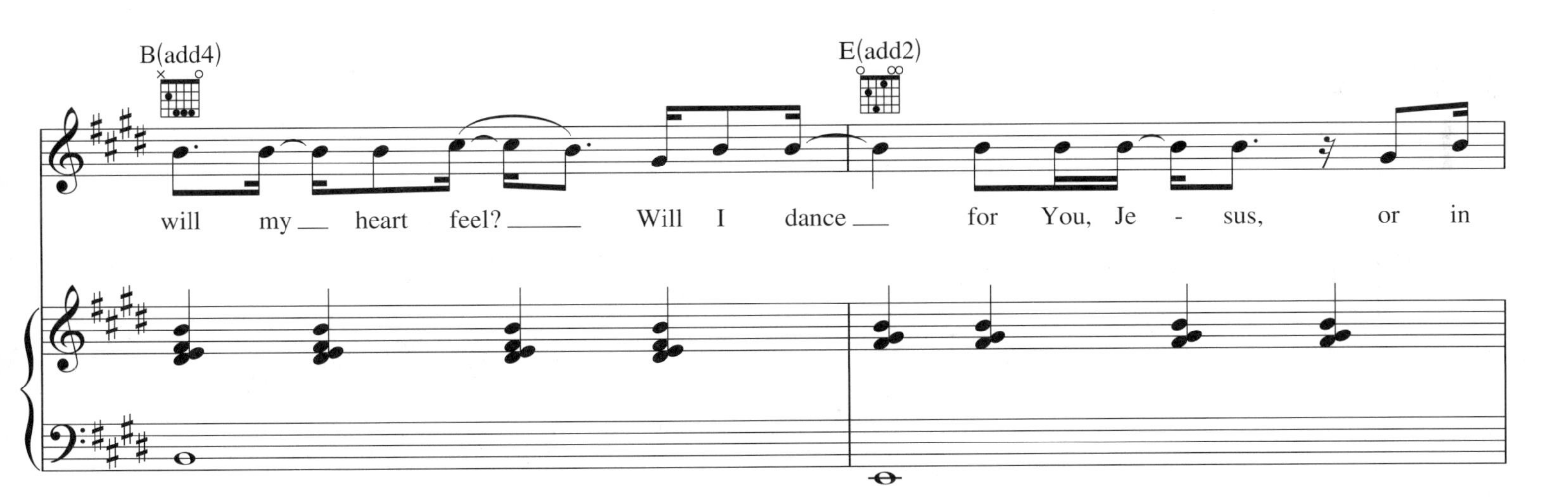
B(add4)
E(add2)
will my heart feel? Will I dance for You, Je - sus, or in

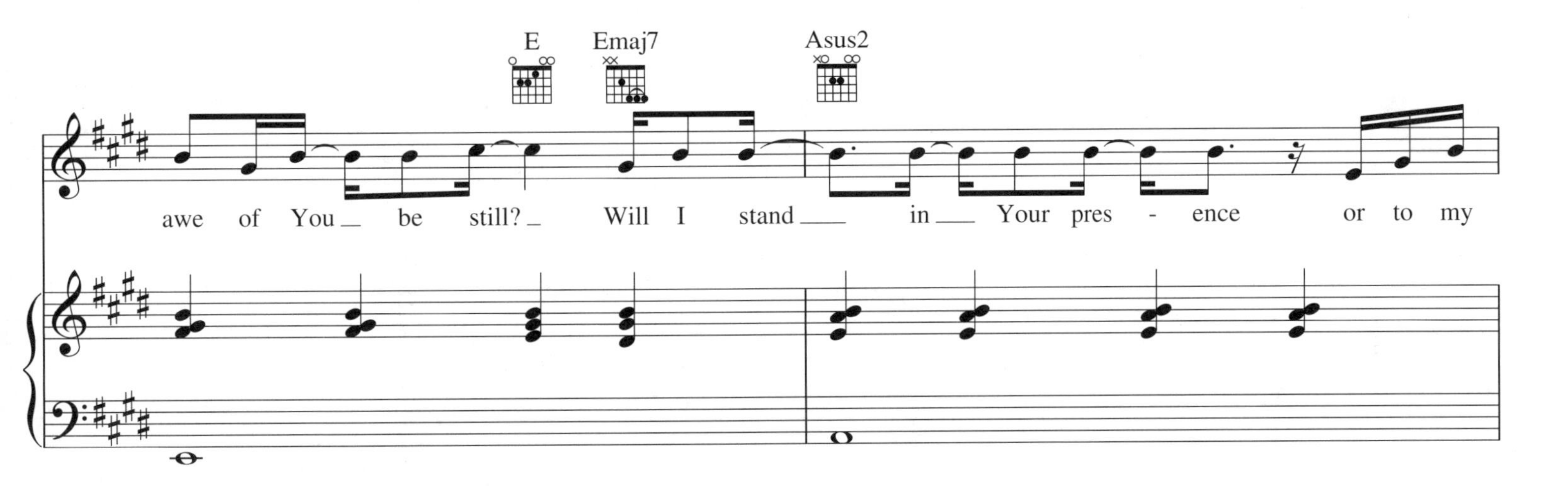
E
Emaj7
Asus2
awe of You be still? Will I stand in Your pres - ence or to my

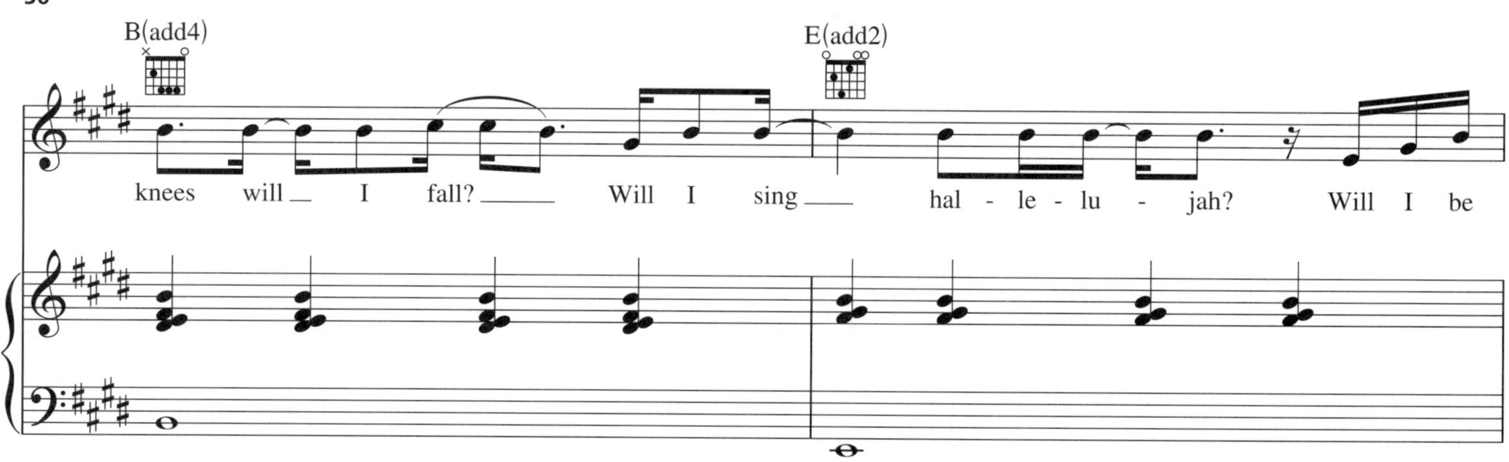
B(add4)
E(add2)
knees will I fall? Will I sing hal - le - lu - jah? Will I be

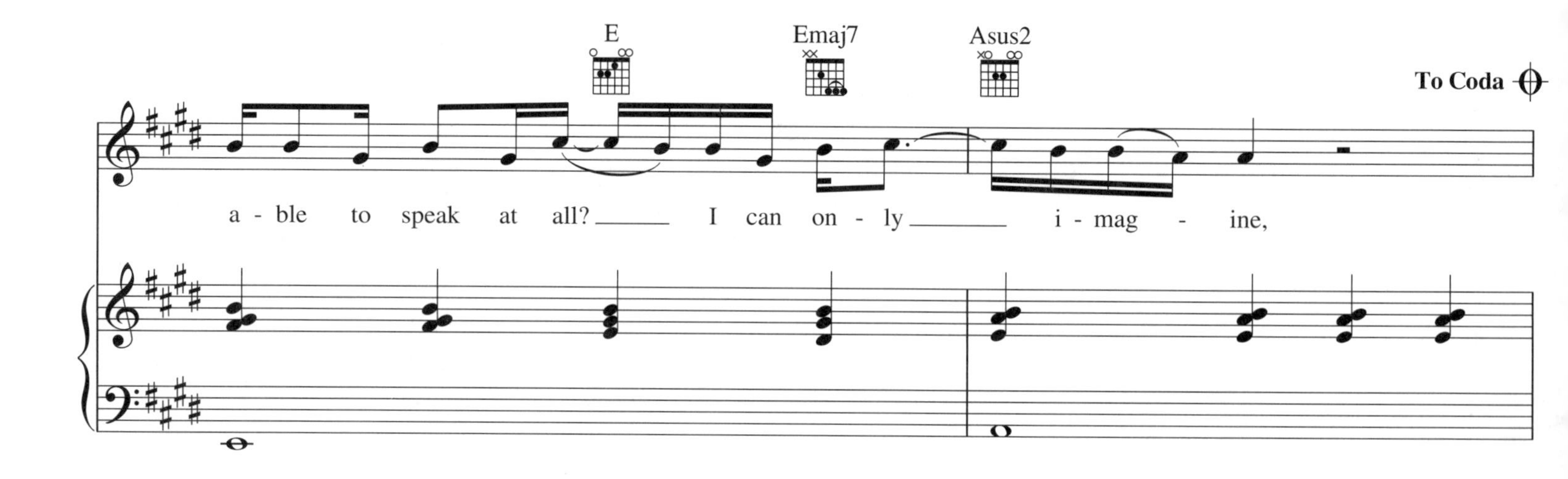
E
Emaj7
Asus2
To Coda
a - ble to speak at all? I can on - ly i - mag - ine,

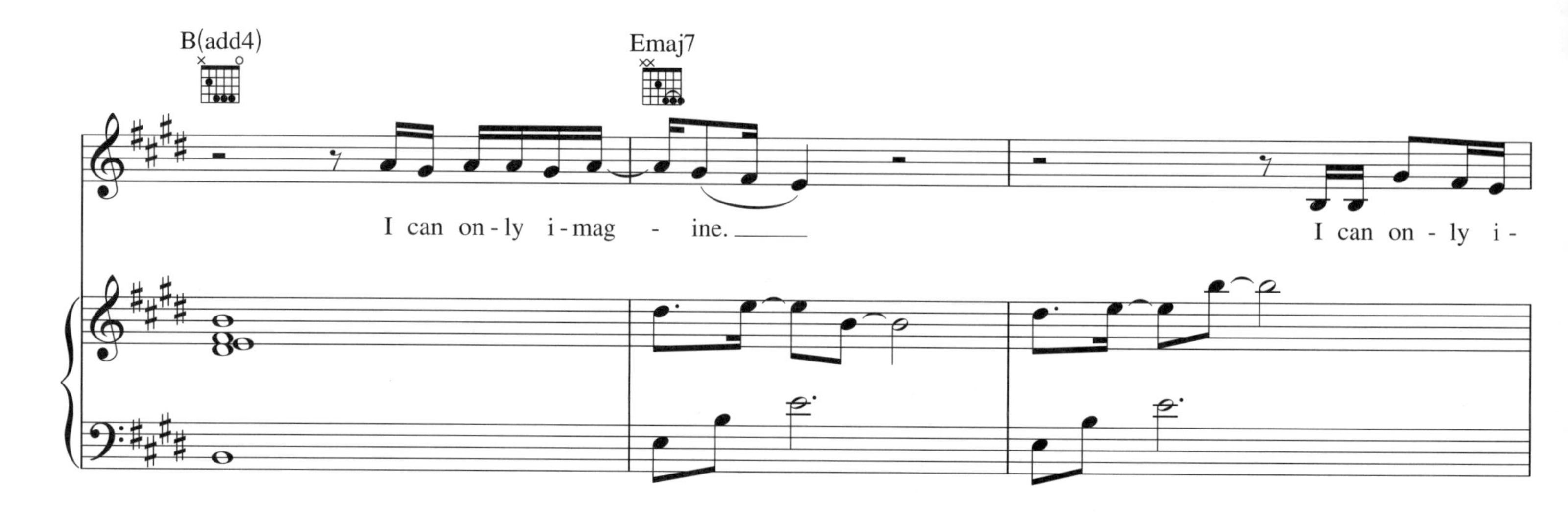
B(add4)
Emaj7
I can on - ly i - mag - ine. I can on - ly i -

Amaj9
mag - ine when that day comes and I find my - self stand - ing in

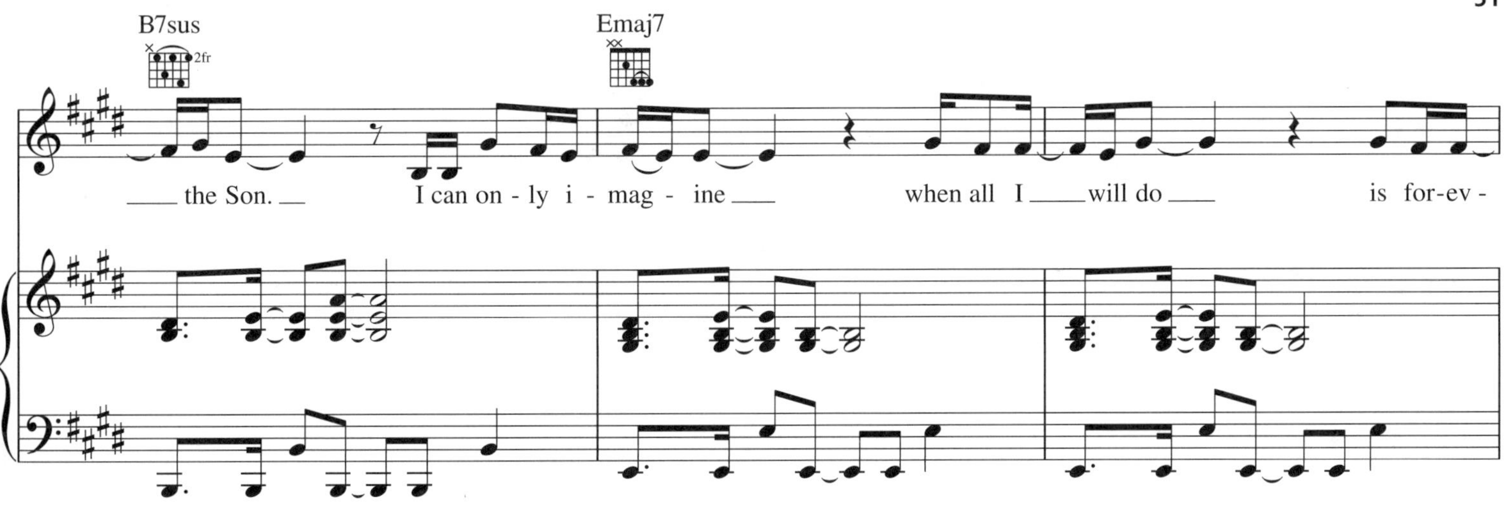
B7sus
Emaj7
the Son. I can on-ly i-mag-ine when all I will do is for-ev-

Amaj9
B7sus
Emaj7
-er, for-ev-er wor-ship You. I can on-ly i-mag-ine,

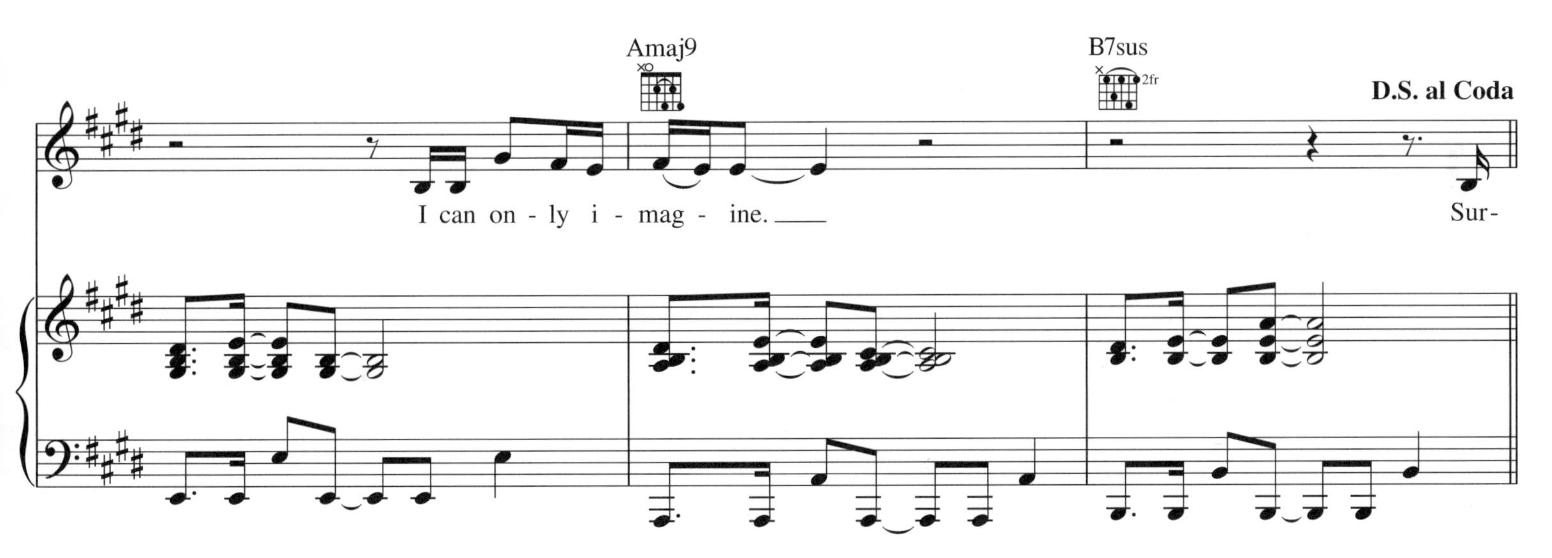
Amaj9
B7sus
D.S. al Coda
I can on-ly i-mag-ine. Sur-

CODA
B(add4)
E
I can on-ly i-mag-ine.

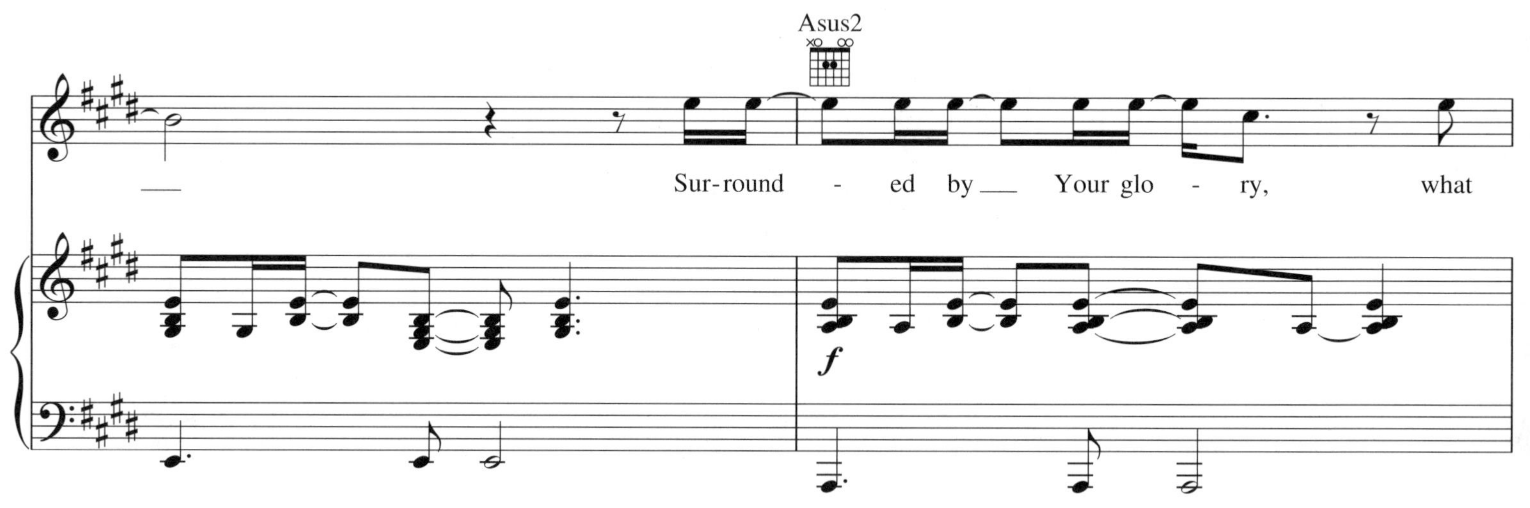
Asus2
Sur-round - ed by Your glo - ry, what
f

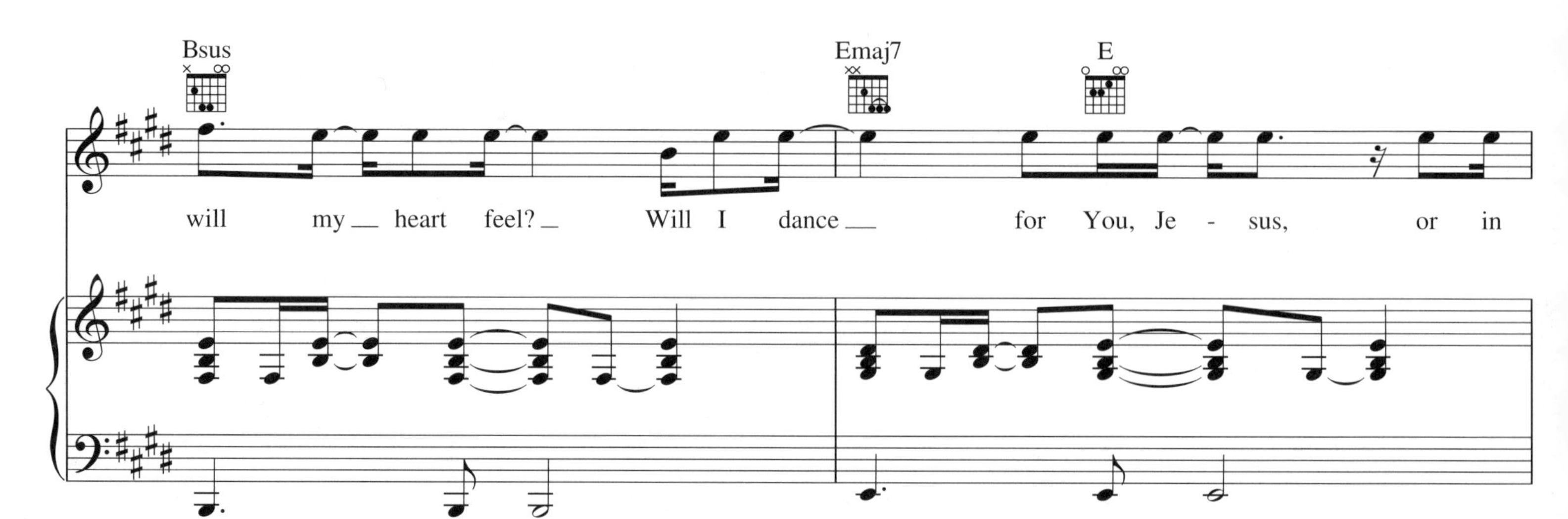
Bsus
Emaj7
E
will my heart feel? Will I dance for You, Je - sus, or in

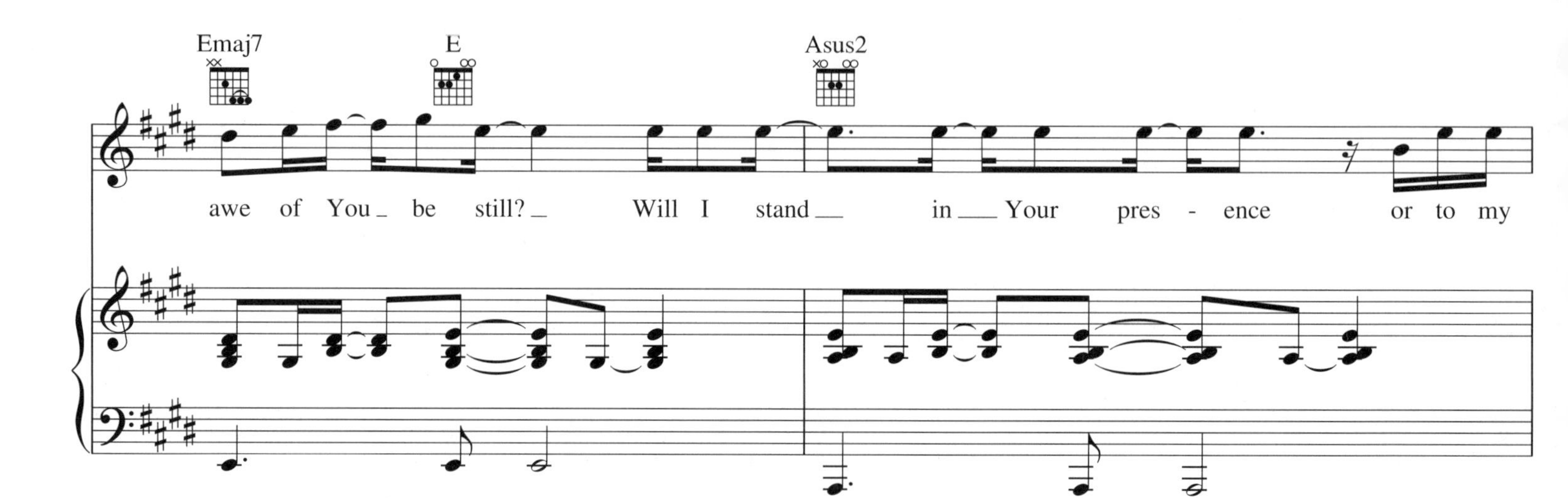
Emaj7
E
Asus2
awe of You be still? Will I stand in Your pres - ence or to my

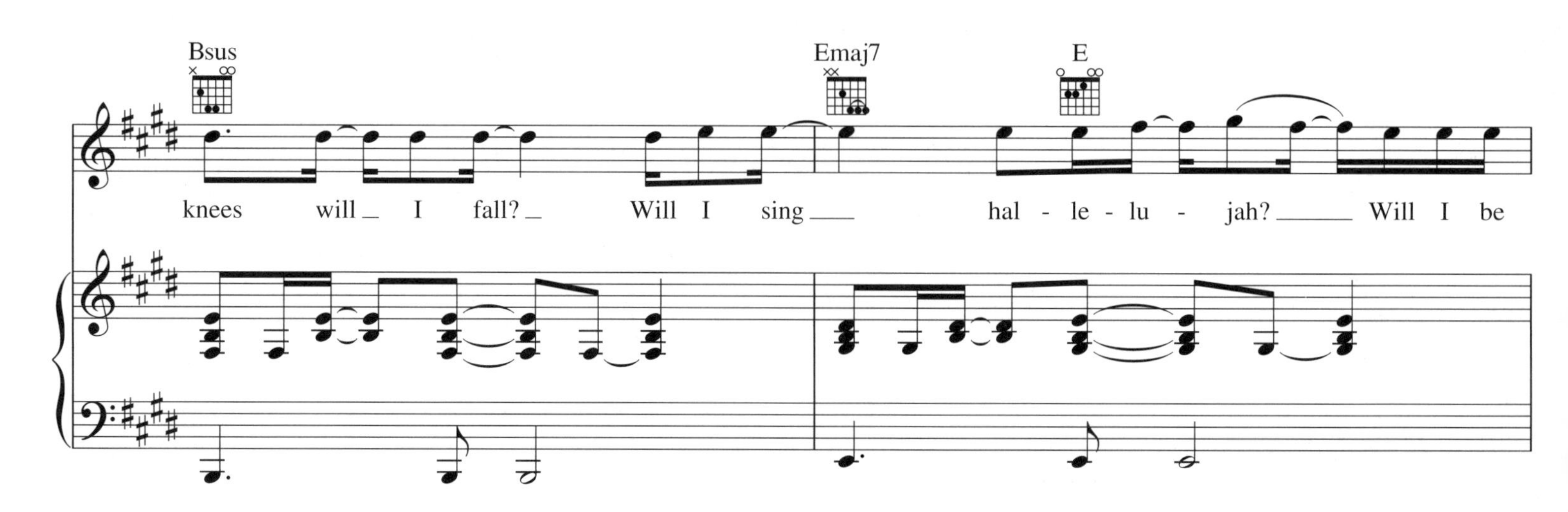
Bsus
Emaj7
E
knees will I fall? Will I sing hal - le - lu - jah? Will I be

Emaj7
E
Asus2
a - ble to speak at all? I can on - ly i - mag - ine, yeah,
Bsus
Emaj7
E
Emaj7
E
I can on-ly i-mag - ine. I can on-ly i-mag-
Asus2
Bsus
- ine, yeah, I can on - ly i - mag -
Emaj7
E
Emaj7
E
- ine. I can on - ly i - mag -

Asus2
Bsus
C♯m9
- ine,
I can on-ly i-mag - ine.
Amaj7
I can on - ly i - mag - ine
when all I
mp
B(add4)
G♯m/C♯
C♯m
E
will do
is for-ev - er,
for - ev - er wor - ship You.
4fr
Amaj9
B
E
I can on - ly i - mag - ine.

LIVE LIKE YOU WERE DYING

Words and Music by CRAIG WISEMAN
and TIM J. NICHOLS

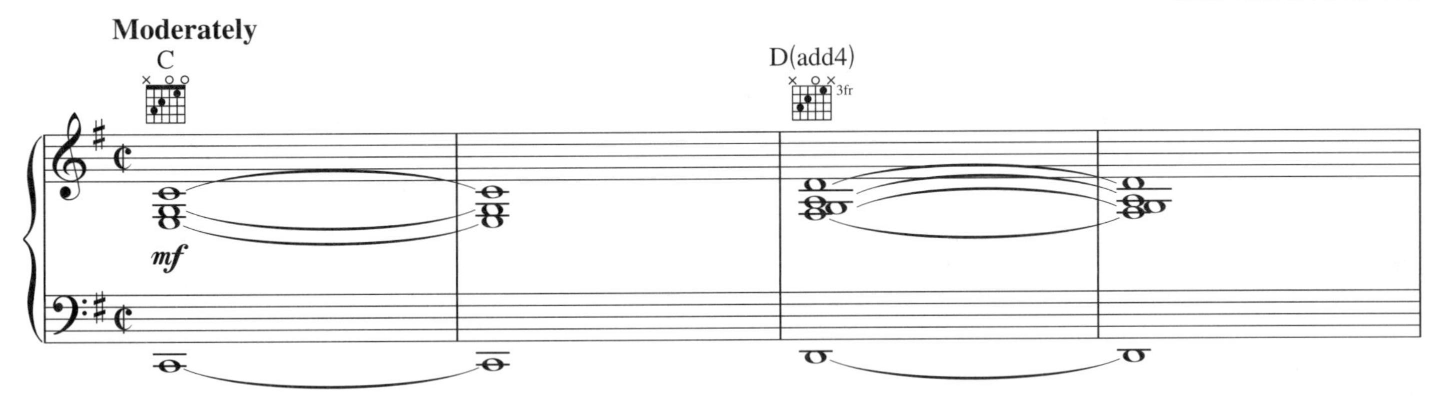

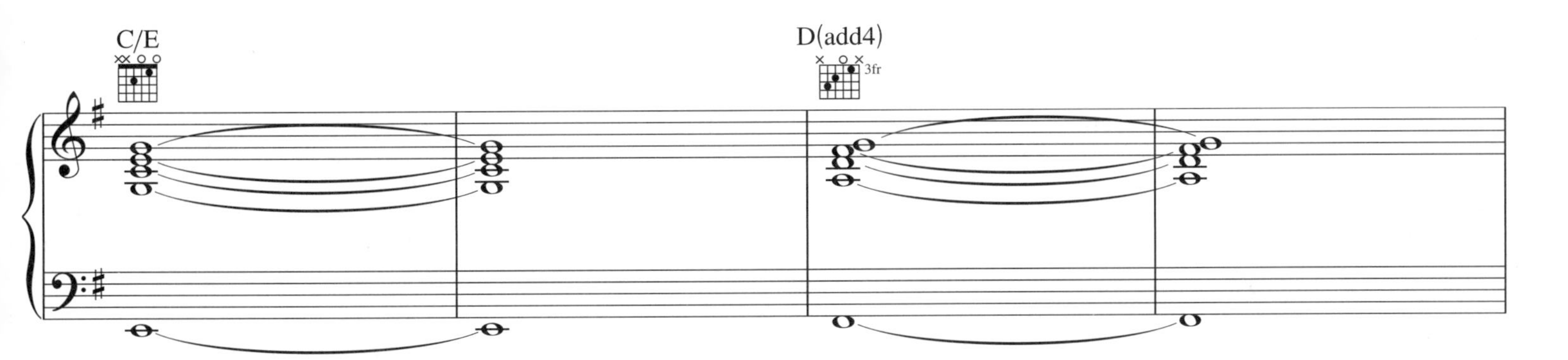

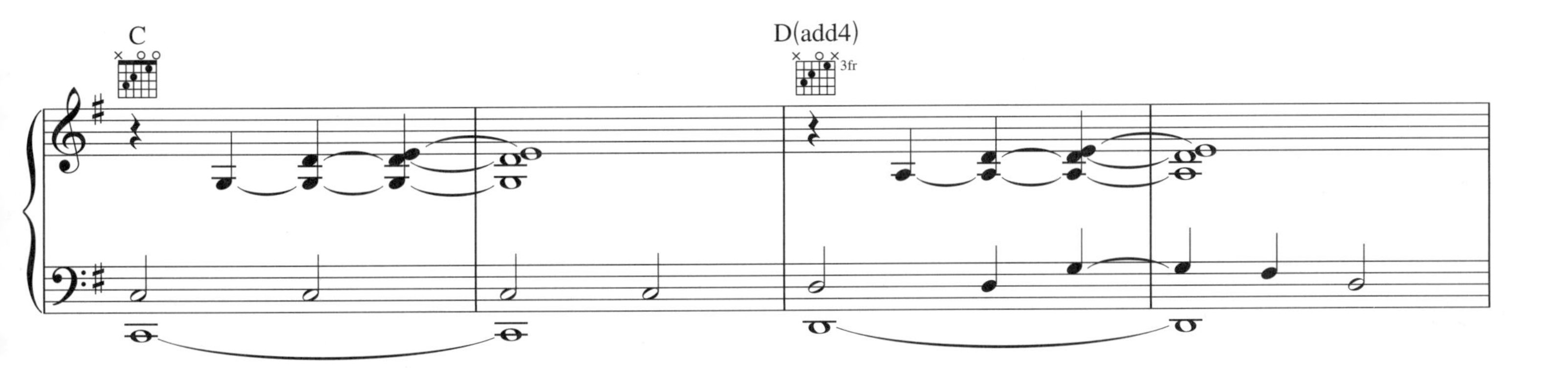

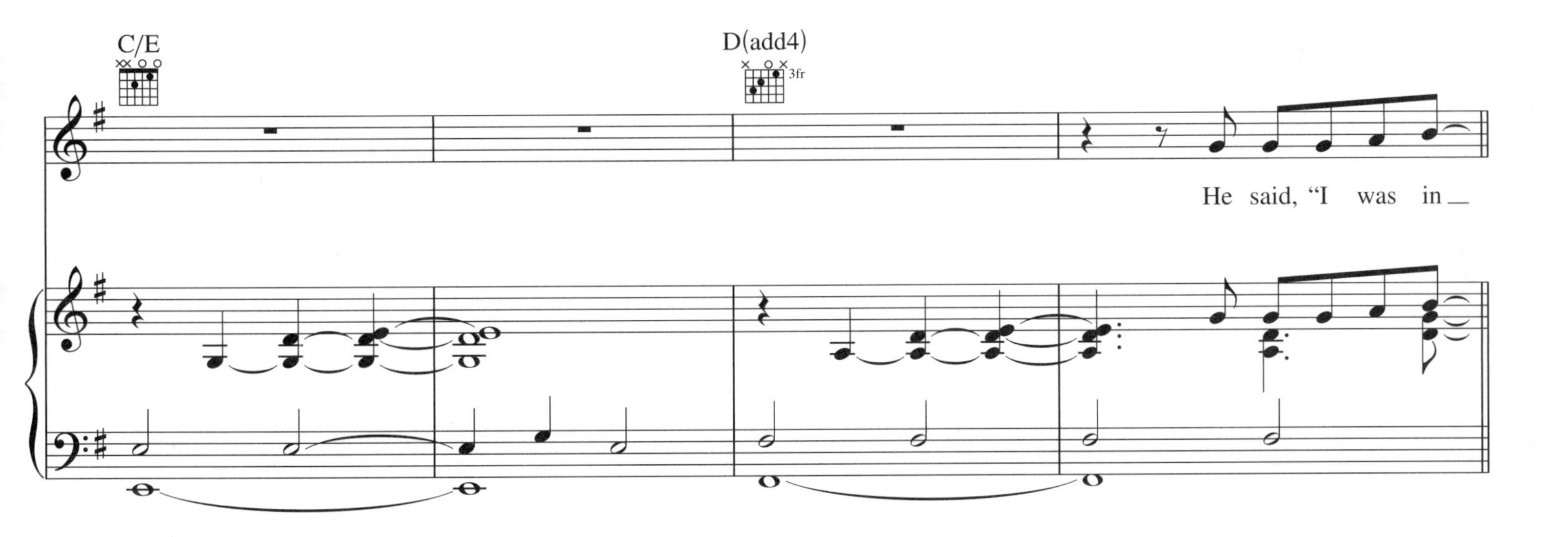

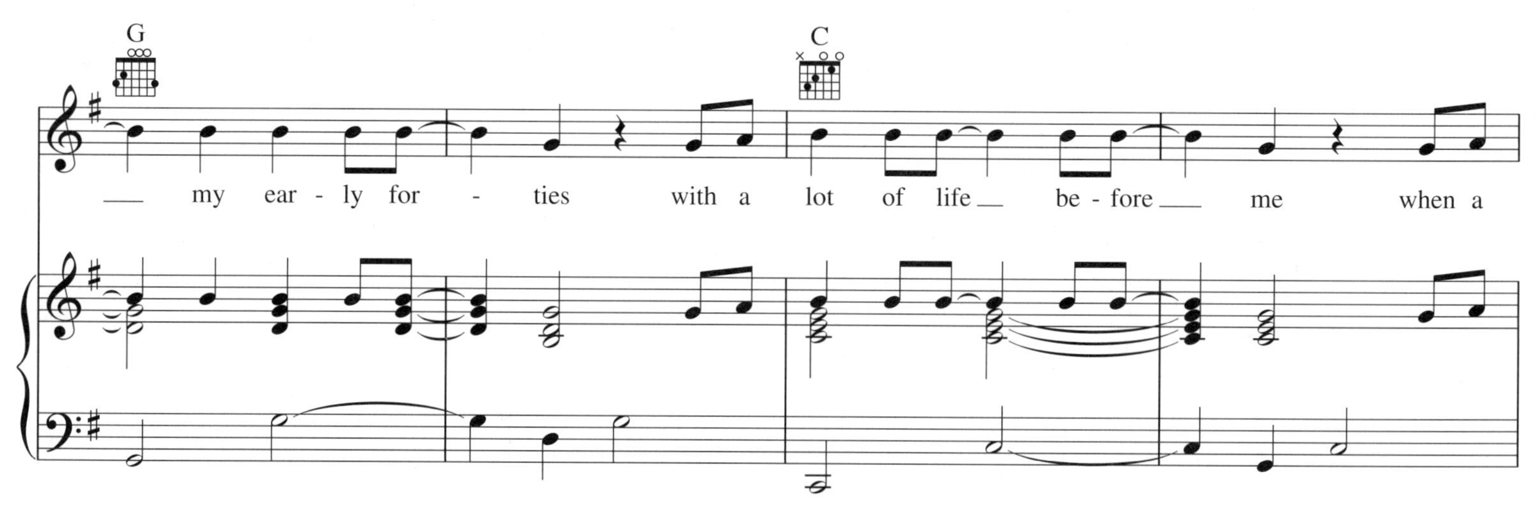
G
C
my ear - ly for - ties with a lot of life be - fore me when a

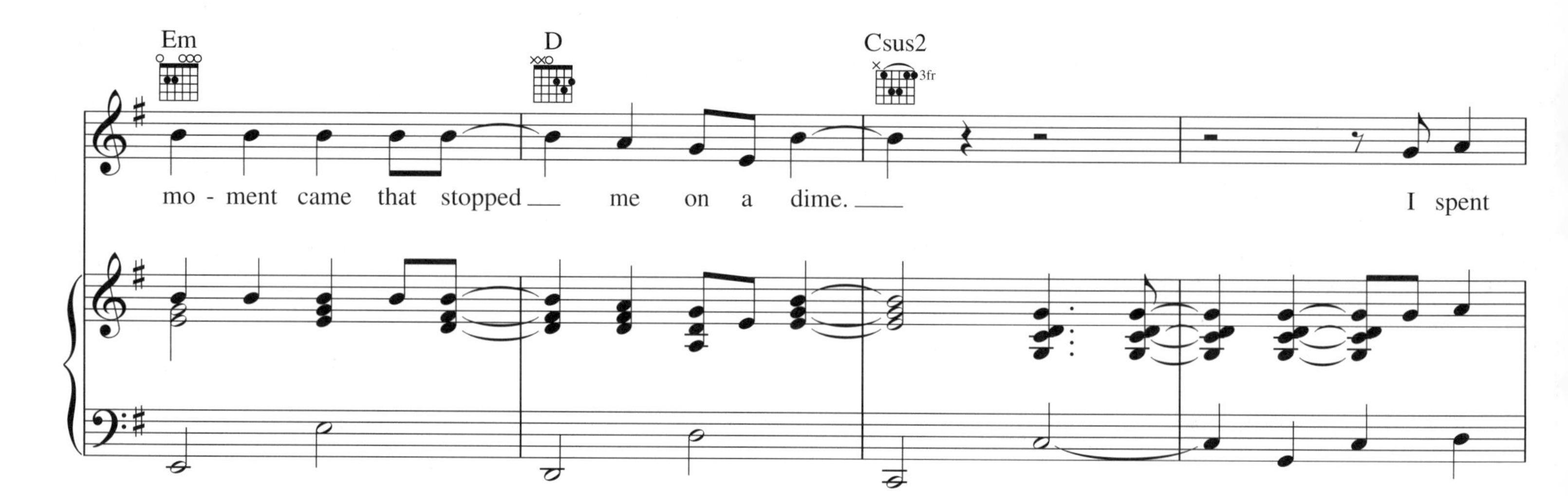
Em
D
Csus2
3fr
mo - ment came that stopped me on a dime.
I spent

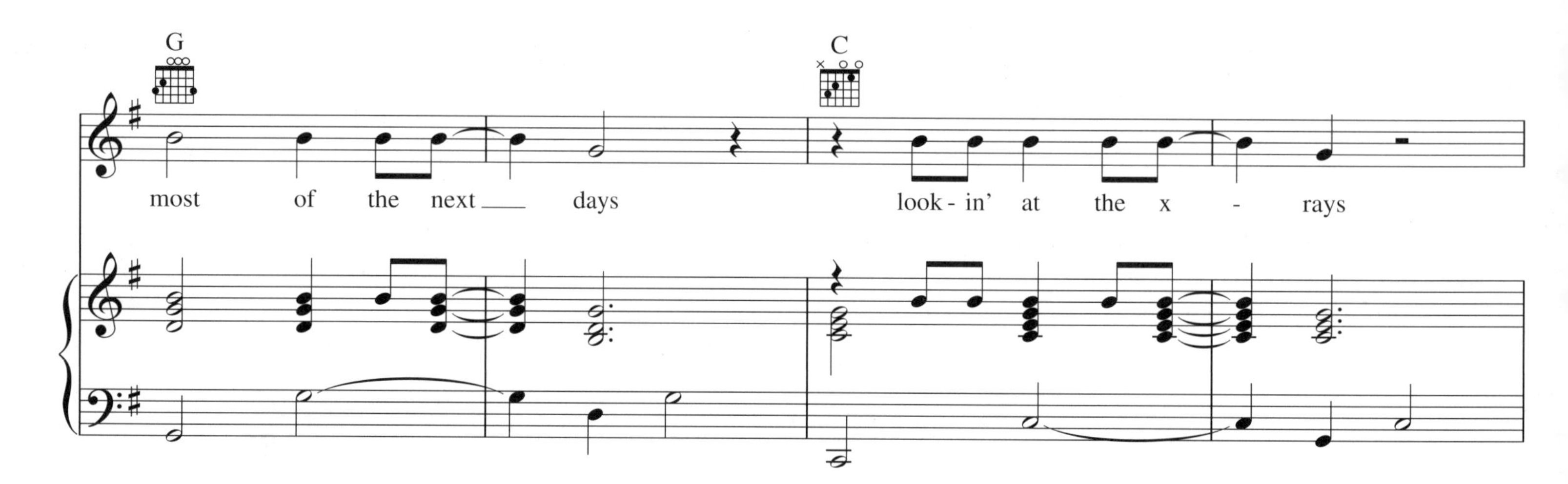
G
C
most of the next days look - in' at the x - rays

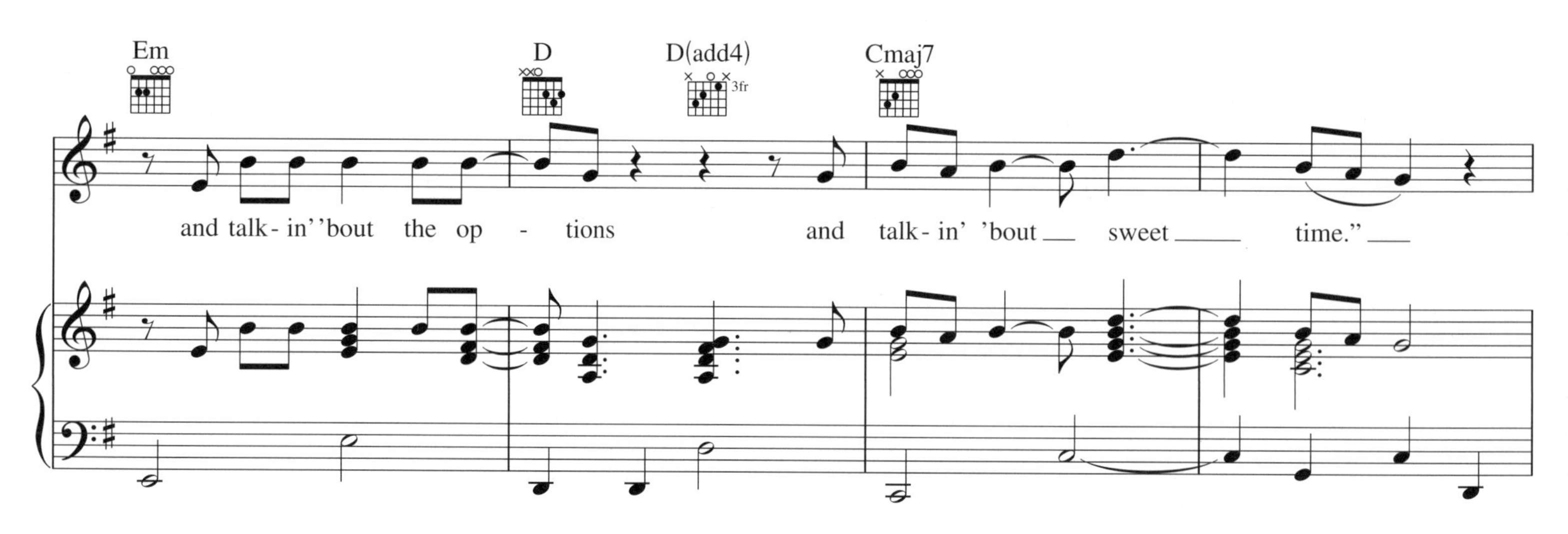
Em
D
D(add4)
3fr
Cmaj7
and talk - in' 'bout the op - tions and talk - in' 'bout sweet time."

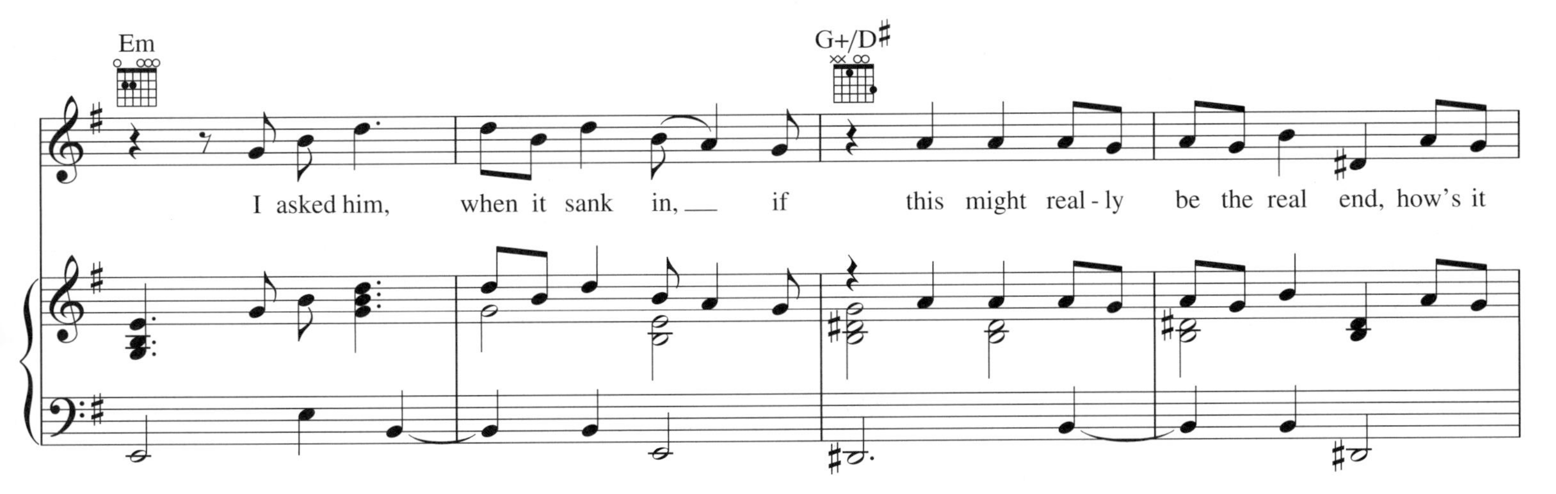
Em
G+/D♯
I asked him, when it sank in, if this might real-ly be the real end, how's it

G/D
Cmaj9
hit you when you get that kind of news?
Man, what'd you do?

N.C.
G
And he said, "I went sky - div - in', I went

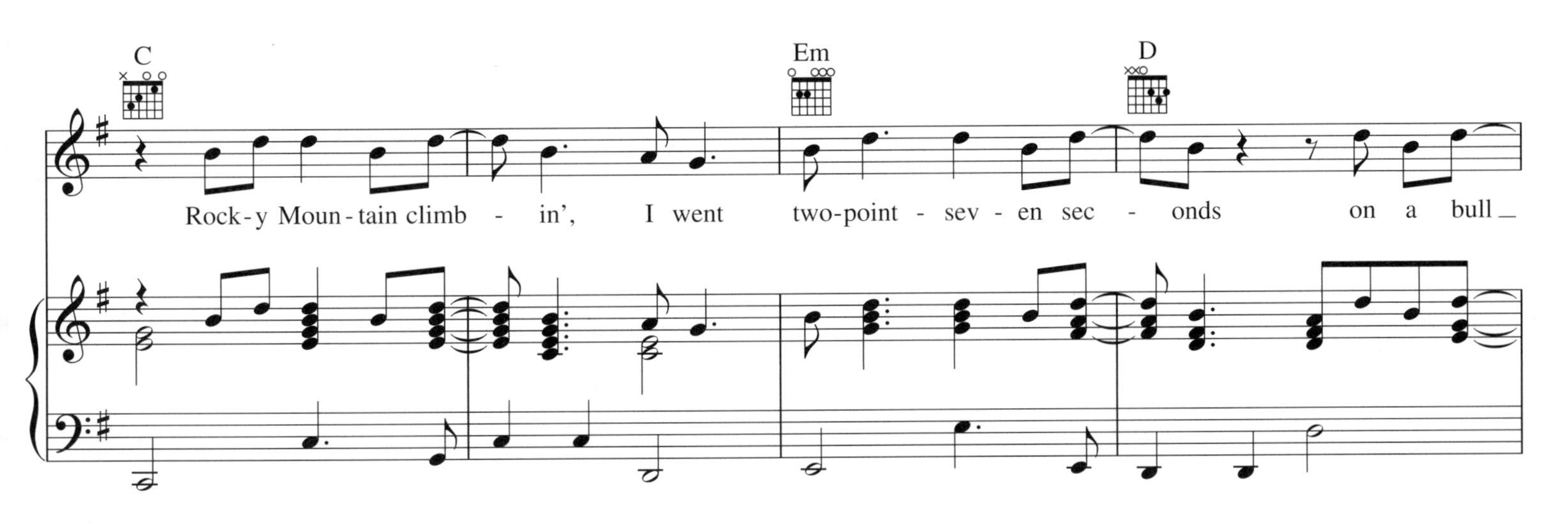
C
Em
D
Rock-y Moun-tain climb - in', I went two-point - sev - en sec - onds on a bull

C
G
named Fu Man - chu.
And I
loved deep - er and I

B7
Em
D
spoke sweet - er and I
gave for-give - ness I'd been de-ny -

C
To Coda
- in'."
And he said, "Some - day I hope you get the chance

D
G
to live like you were dy - in'."

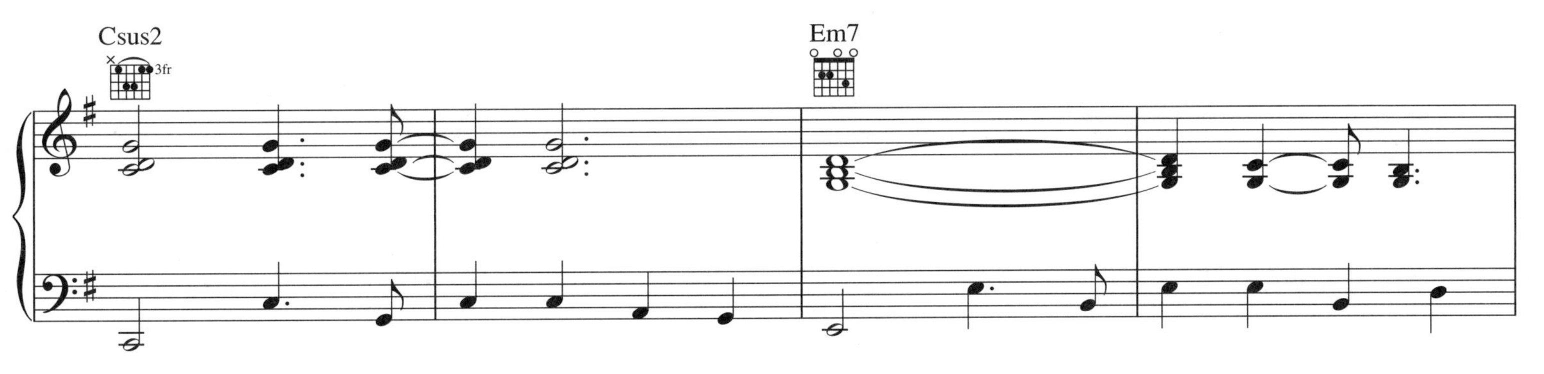
Csus2
3fr
Em7

Csus2
3fr
G
He said, "I was fi - nal - ly the hus - band

C
Em
D
that most the time I was - n't and I be - came a friend a friend would like to have.

C
G
And all the sud - den go - in' fish - in' was - n't

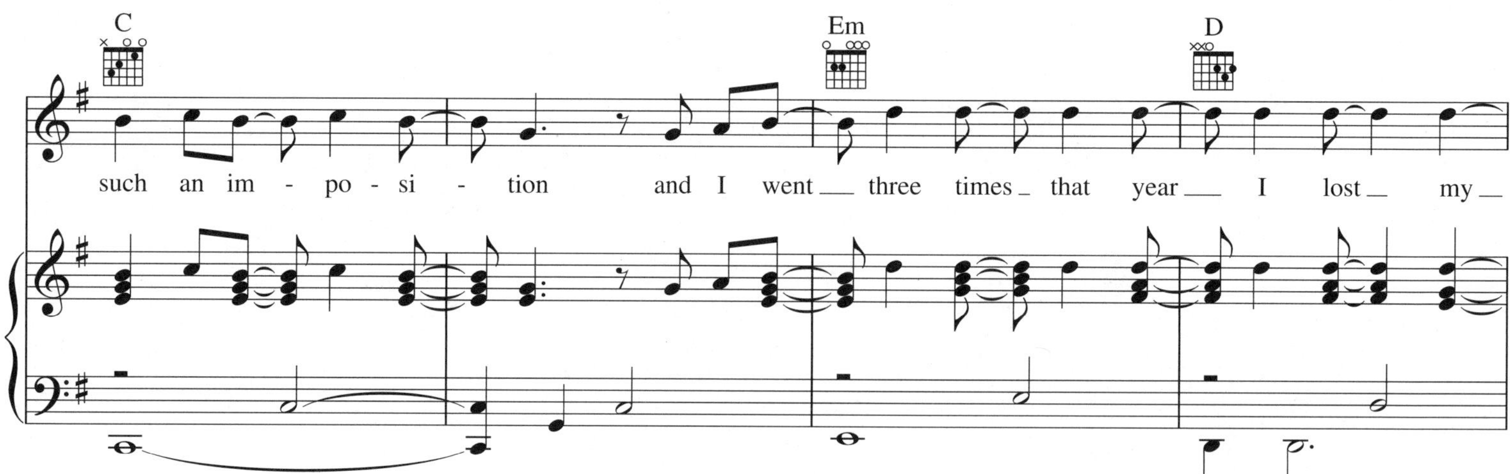
C
Em
D
such an im - po - si - tion and I went three times that year I lost my

C
Em
dad. Well, I, I fin-'lly read the Good Book and I

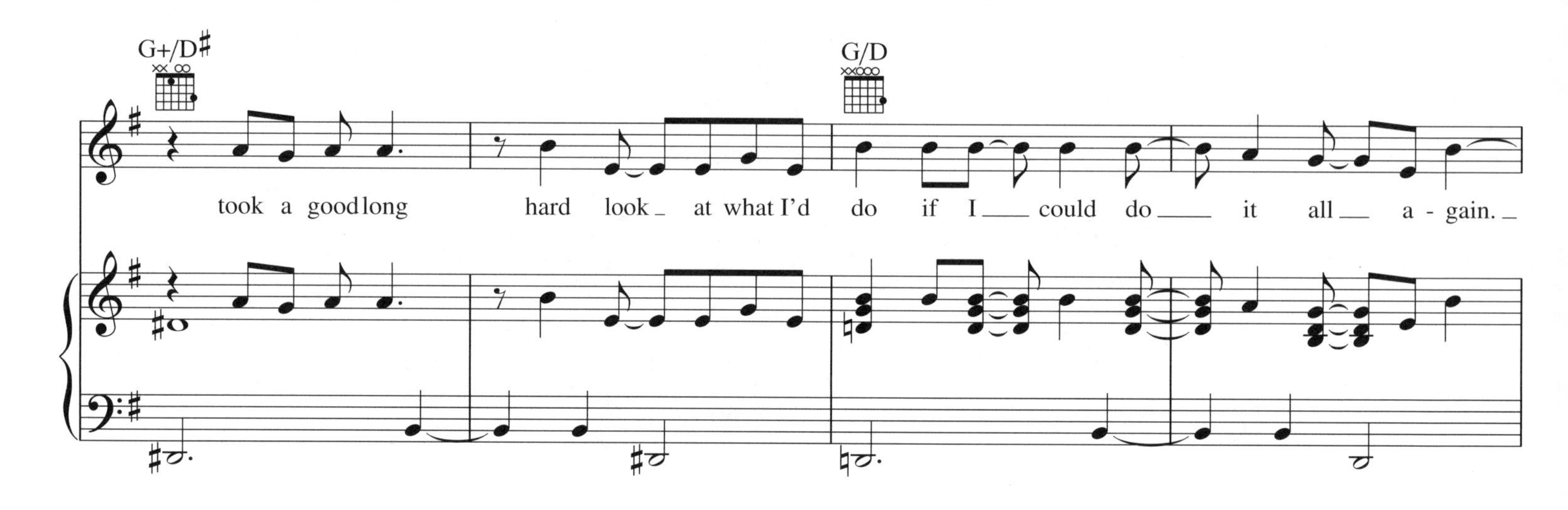
G+/D#
G/D
took a good long hard look at what I'd do if I could do it all a - gain.

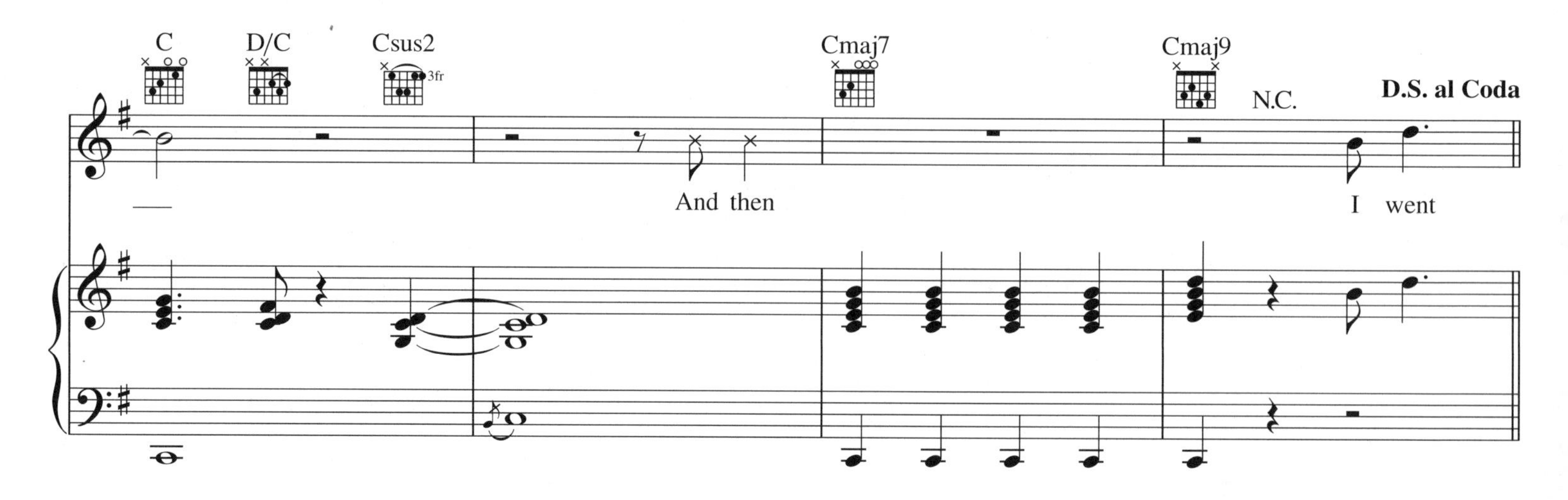
C
D/C
Csus2
3fr
Cmaj7
Cmaj9
N.C.
D.S. al Coda
And then I went

CODA
D
Em
to live like you were dy - in', like to-mor-

G+/D#
G/D
- row was a gift and you got e - ter - ni - ty to think

C
a - bout what you'd do with it, what could you do

D/C
C
with it, what did I do with it, what would I do

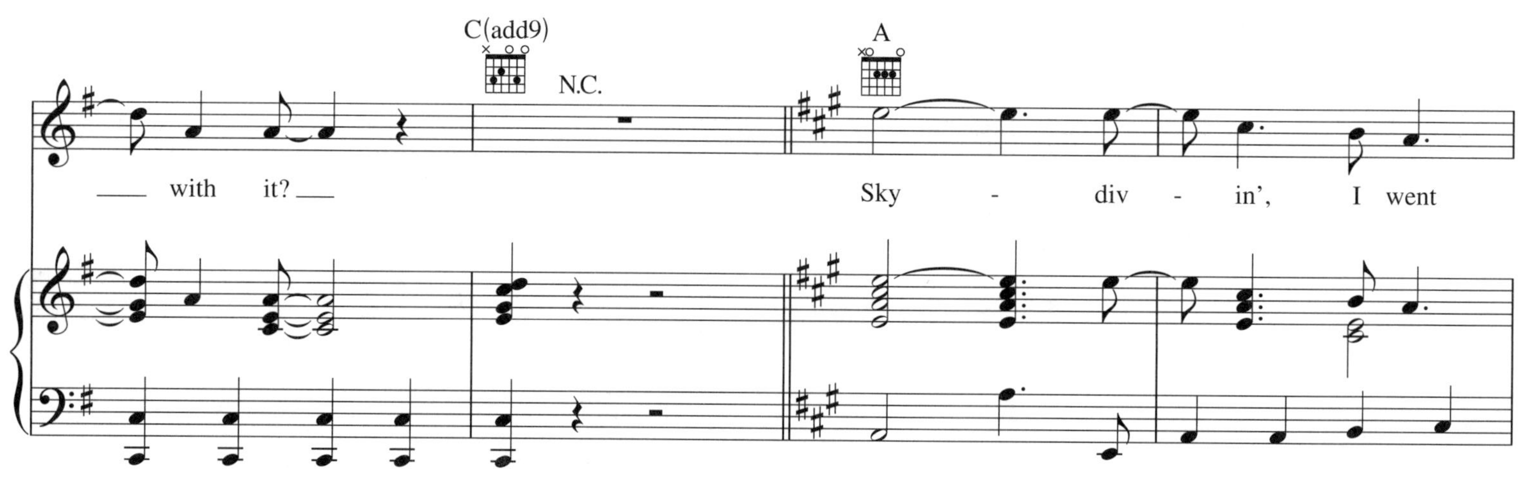
C(add9)
N.C.
A
with it?
Sky - div - in', I went

D
F♯m7
Rock - y Moun - tain climb - in', I went two-point - sev - en sec -

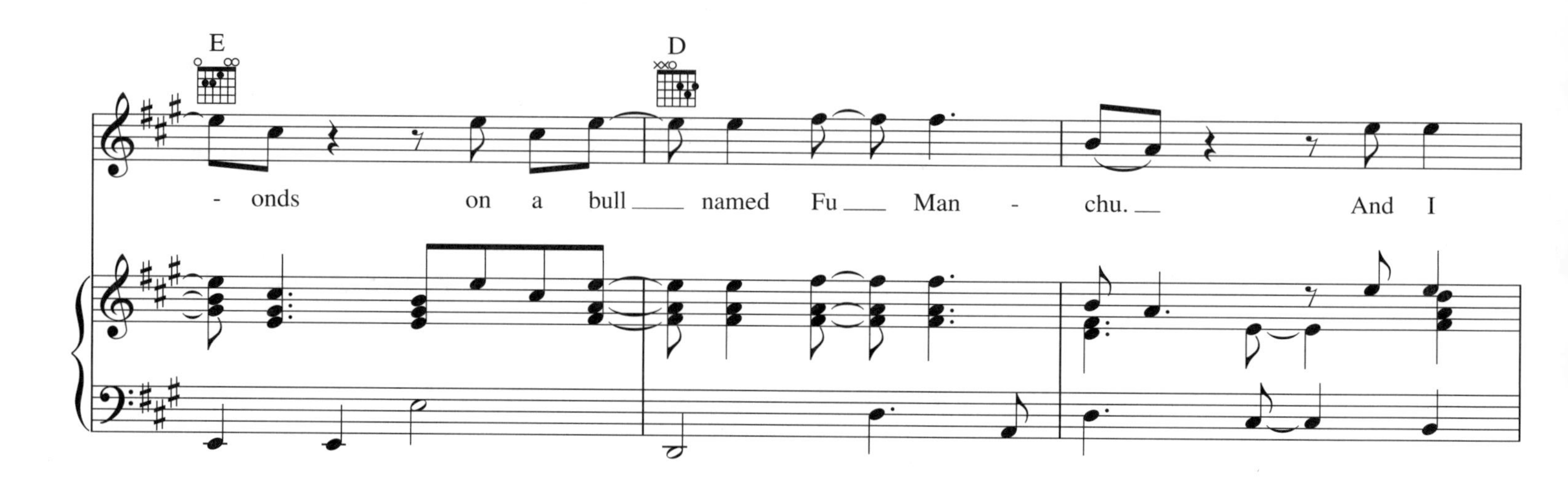
E
D
- onds on a bull named Fu Man - chu. And I

A
C♯7
loved deep - er and I spoke sweet -

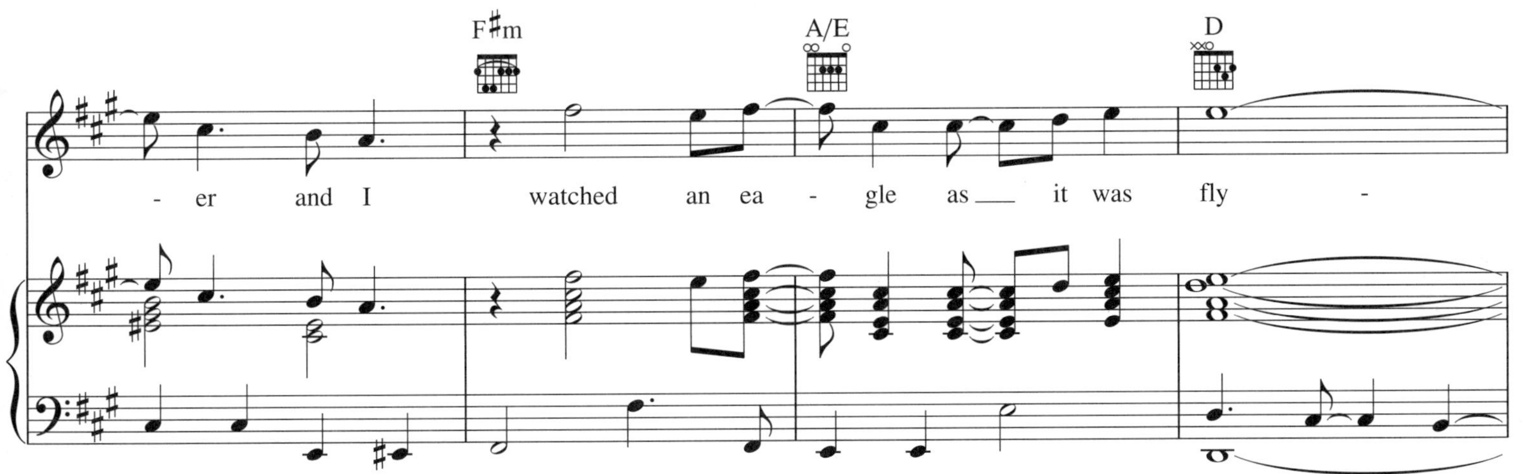
F♯m
A/E
D
-er and I watched an ea - gle as it was fly -

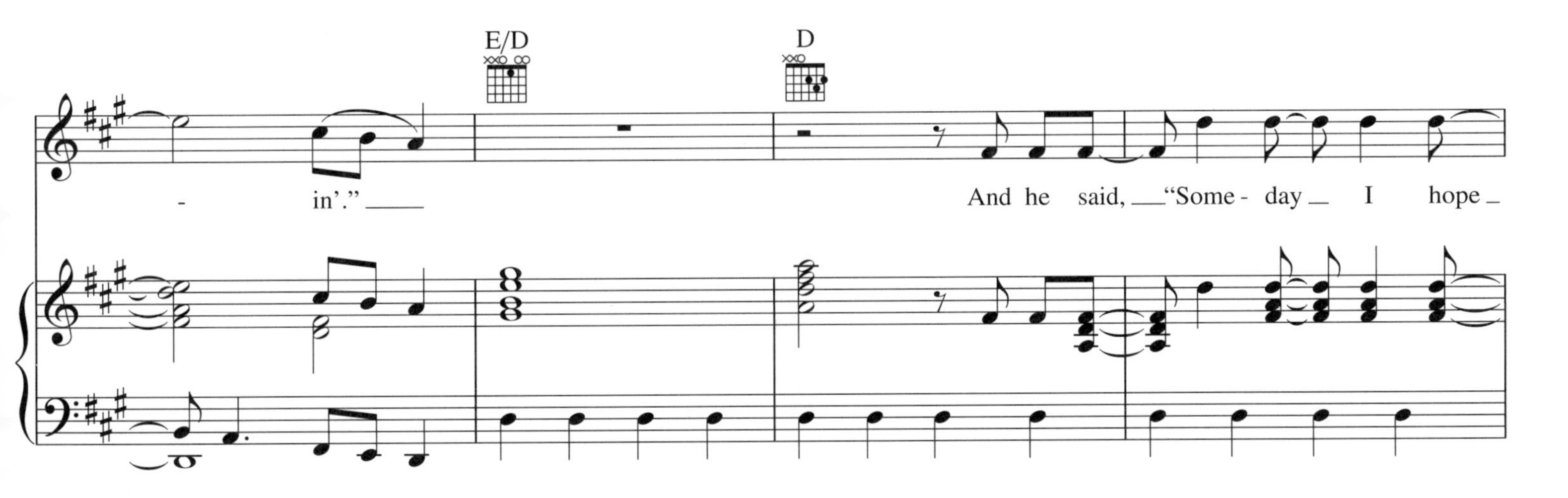
E/D
D
- in'."
And he said, "Some - day I hope

E
A
you get the chance
to live like you were dy - in',

D(add9)
A
to live like you were dy - in',

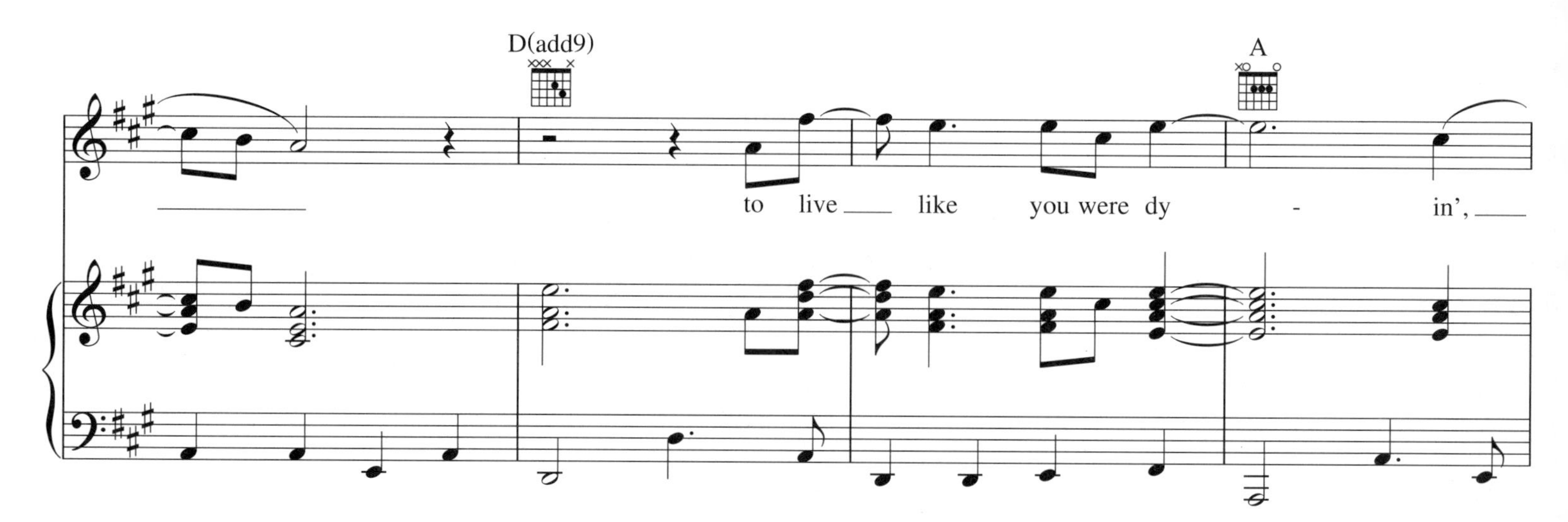
D(add9)
A
to live like you were dy - in',

D(add9)
A
to live like you were dy - in',

D(add9)
A
to live like you were dy -

D(add9)
A

D(add9)
A
in'."

D(add9)
A

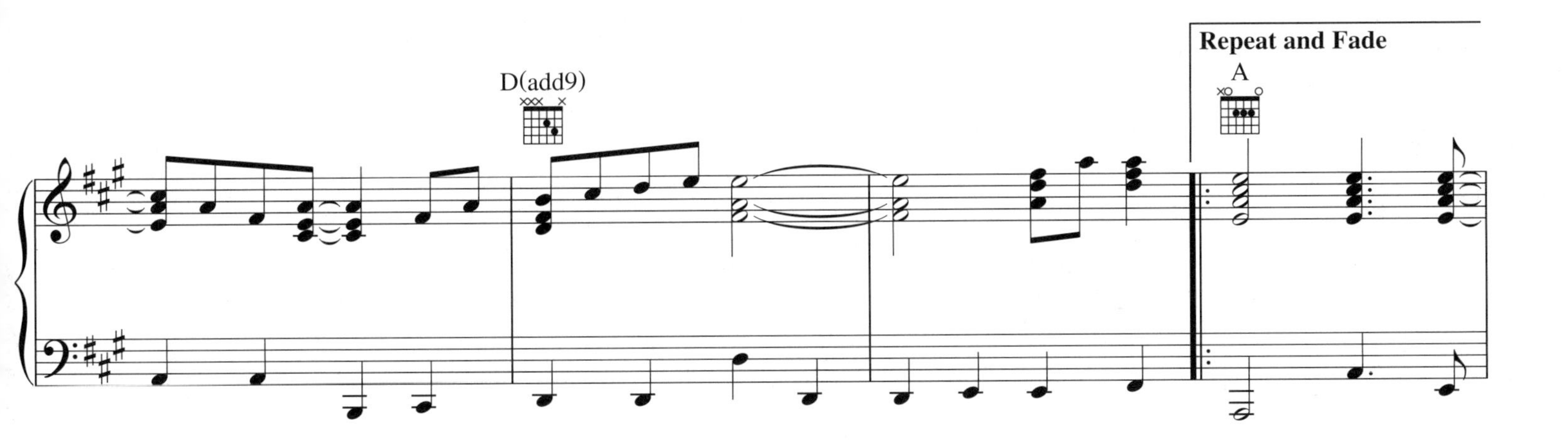
D(add9)
Repeat and Fade
A

D(add9)
Optional Ending
A

I HOPE YOU DANCE

Words and Music by TIA SILLERS
and MARK D. SANDERS

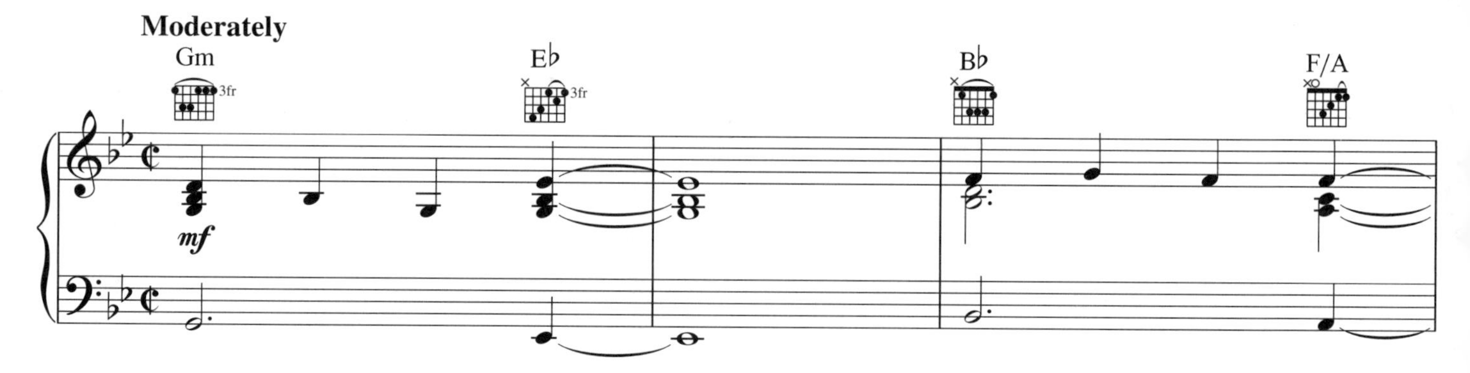

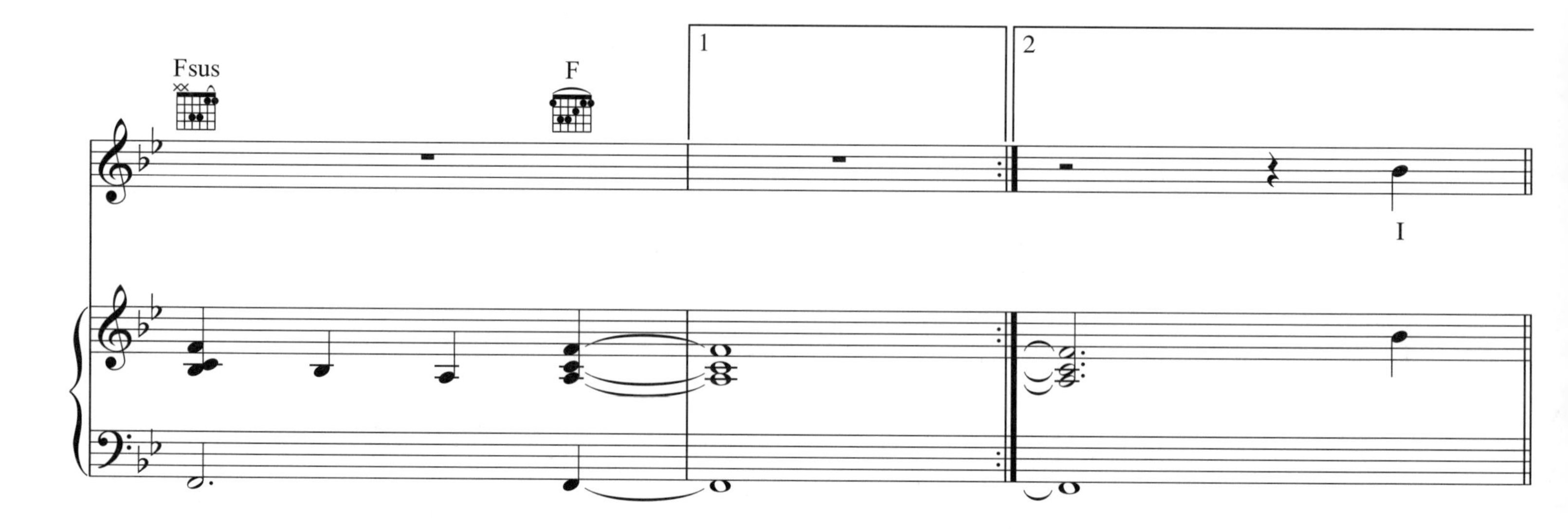

Gm7
You get your fill to eat, but al - ways keep that
Nev - er set - tle for the path of least re -
hun - ger.
sist - ance.
E♭
3fr
May you nev - er take one
Liv - in' might mean tak - in'
sin - gle breath for grant - ed.
chanc - es if they're worth tak - in'.
God for - bid
Lov - in' might

F
love ev - er leave you emp - ty - hand - ed.
be a mis - take, but it's worth mak - in'.

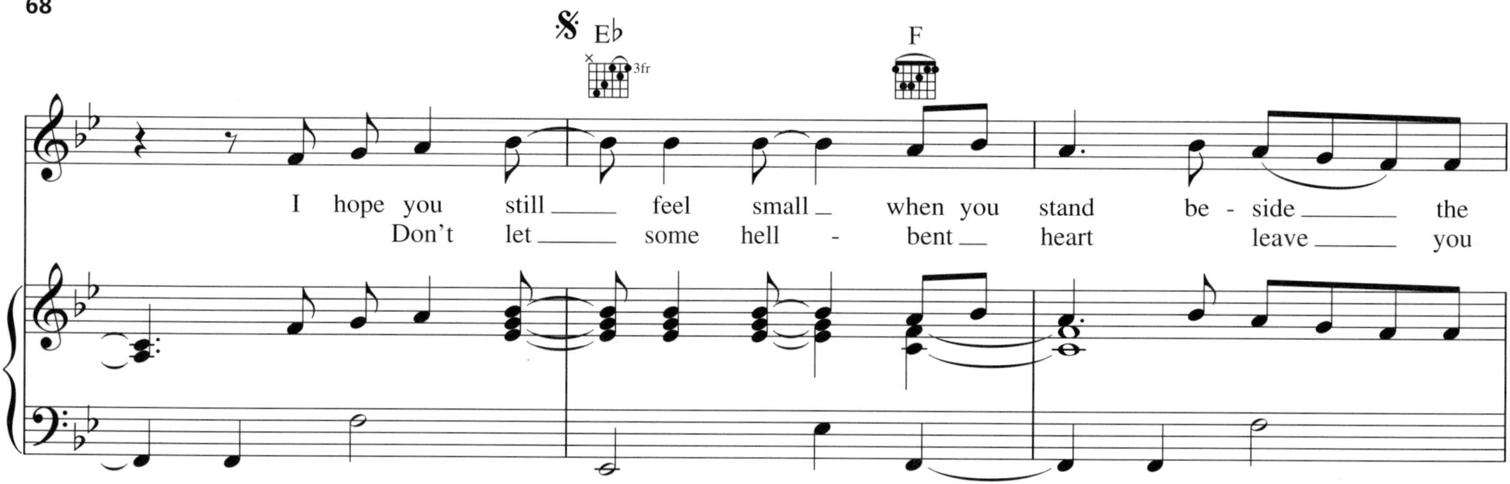
E♭
3fr
F
I hope you still feel small when you stand be - side the
Don't let some hell - bent heart leave you

B♭
E♭
3fr
F
o - cean. When - ev - er one door clos - es, I
bit - ter. When you come close to sell - in' out,

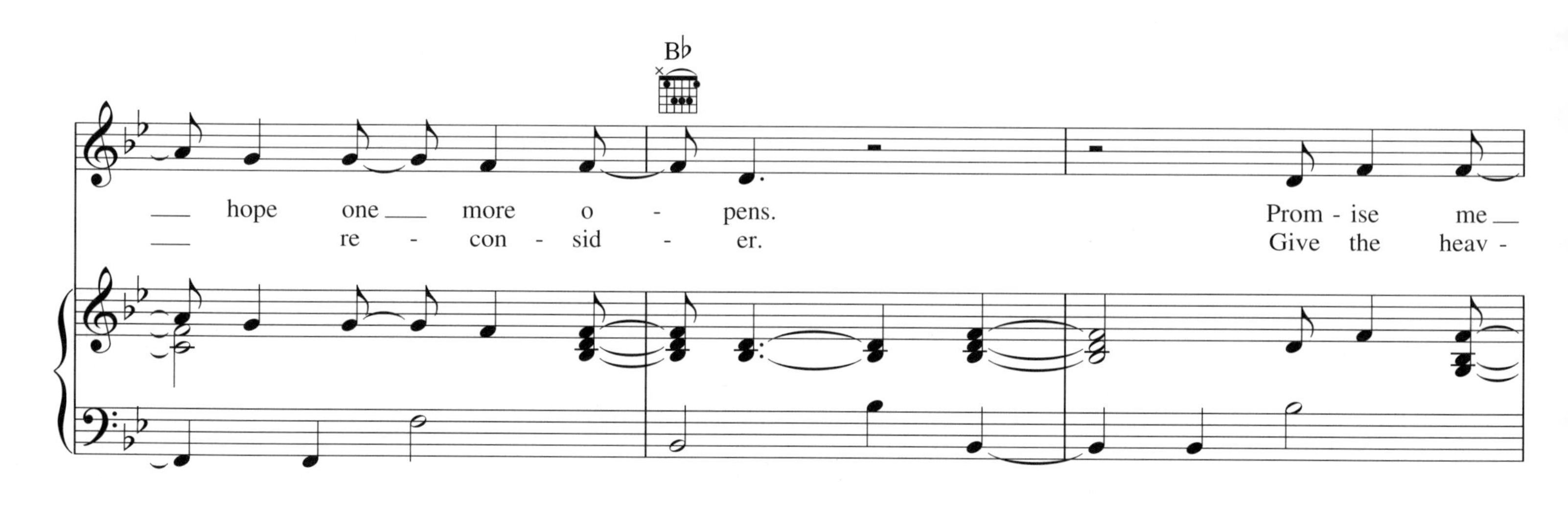
B♭
hope one more o - pens. Prom - ise me
re - con - sid - er. Give the heav -

Cm7
3fr
B♭/D
that you'll give faith a fight - ing
- ens a - bove more than just a pass - ing

E♭
3fr
chance.
glance.
And when you get the choice to

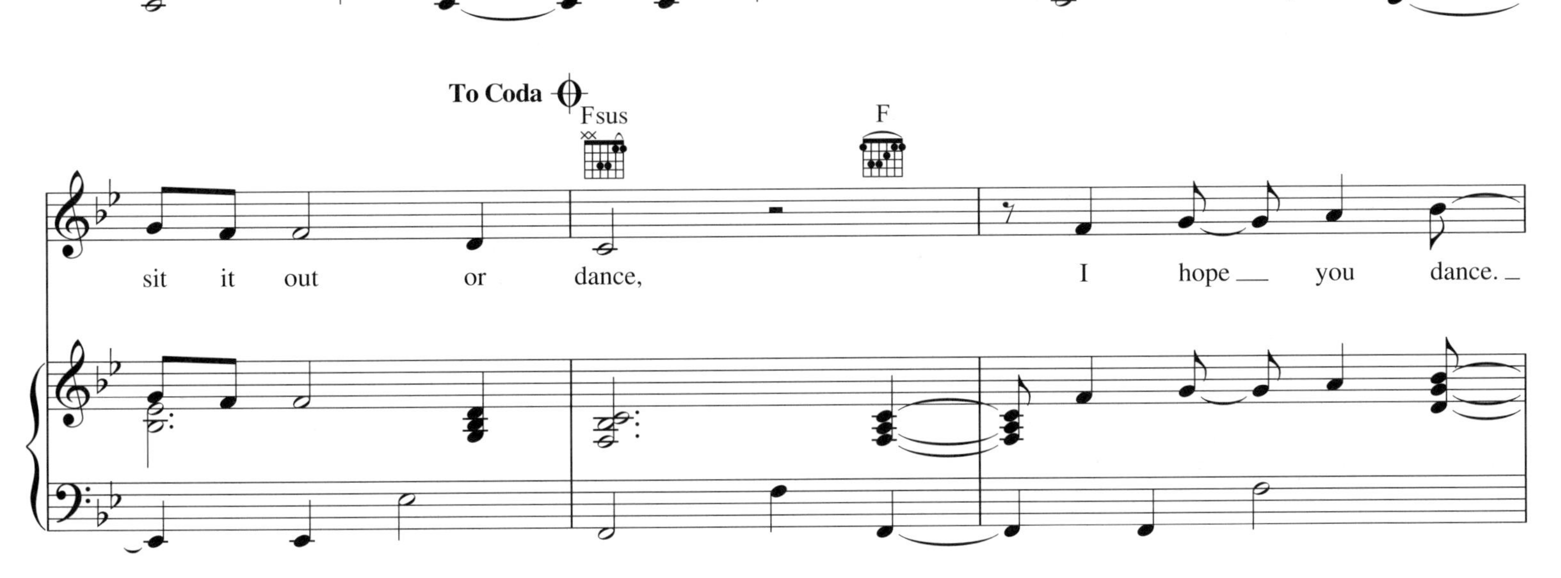
To Coda
Fsus
F
sit it out or dance,
I hope you dance.

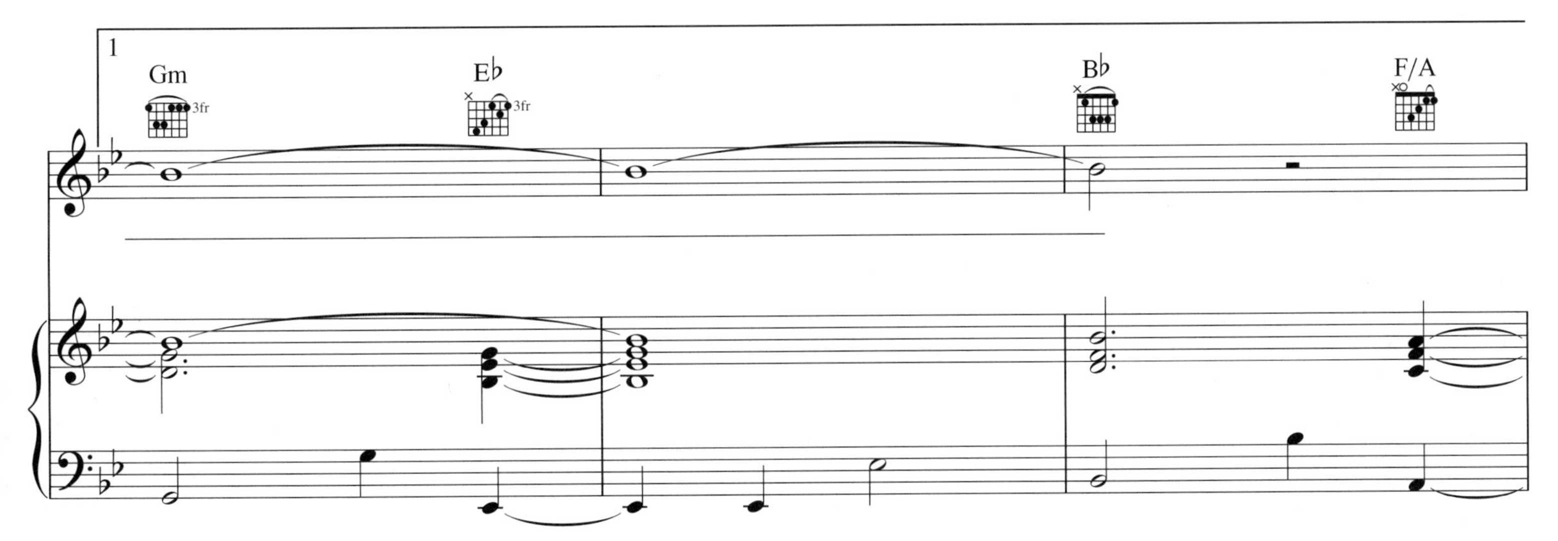
1
Gm
3fr
E♭
3fr
B♭
F/A

Gm
3fr
E♭
3fr
I hope you dance.

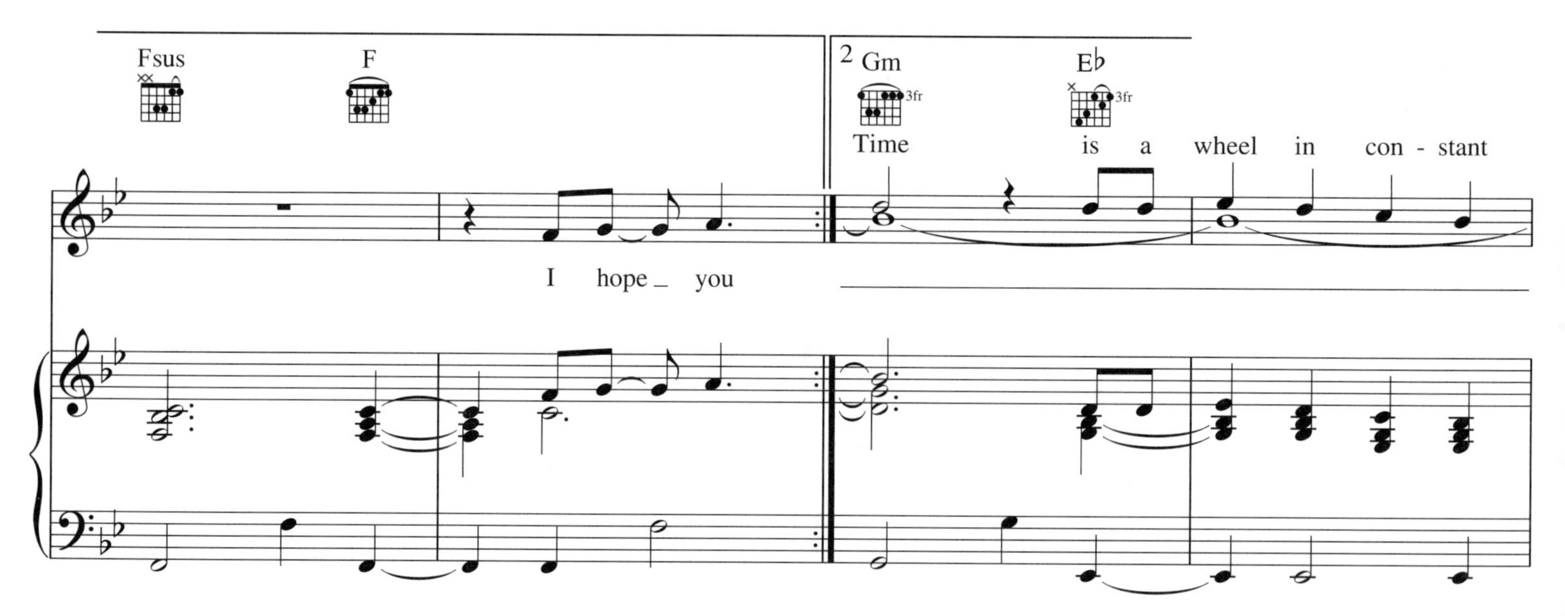
Fsus
F
2 Gm
E♭
3fr
Time is a wheel in con - stant
I hope _ you

B♭
F/A
Gm
E♭
3fr
mo - tion, al - ways roll - ing us _ a - long. _
I hope _ you dance. _

Fsus
F
Gm
E♭
3fr
Tell me, who wants to look back on their
I hope _ you dance. _

Bb
F/A
Gm
3fr
Eb
3fr
youth and won - der where those years have gone?
I hope you dance.

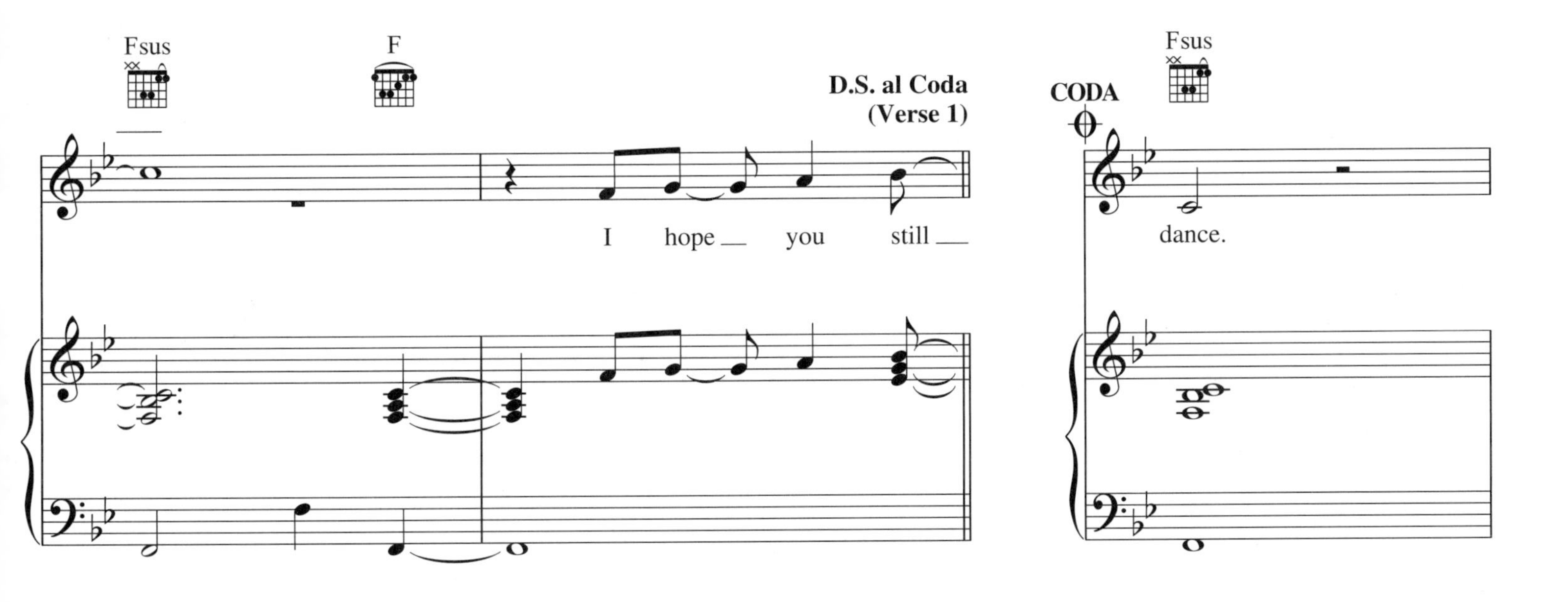
Fsus
F
D.S. al Coda
(Verse 1)
I hope you still
CODA
Fsus
dance.

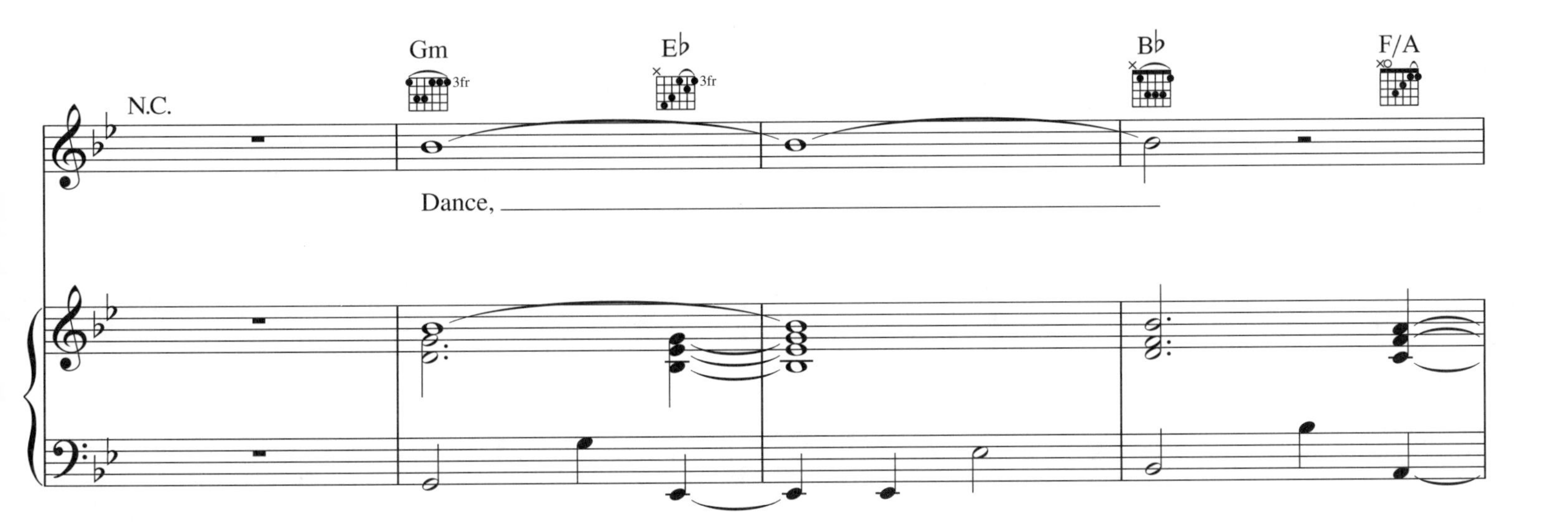
N.C.
Gm
3fr
Eb
3fr
Bb
F/A
Dance,

Gm
3fr
E♭
3fr
Fsus
F
I hope _ you dance.

Gm
3fr
E♭
3fr
B♭
F/A
Time is a wheel in con - stant mo - tion, al -
I hope _ you dance.

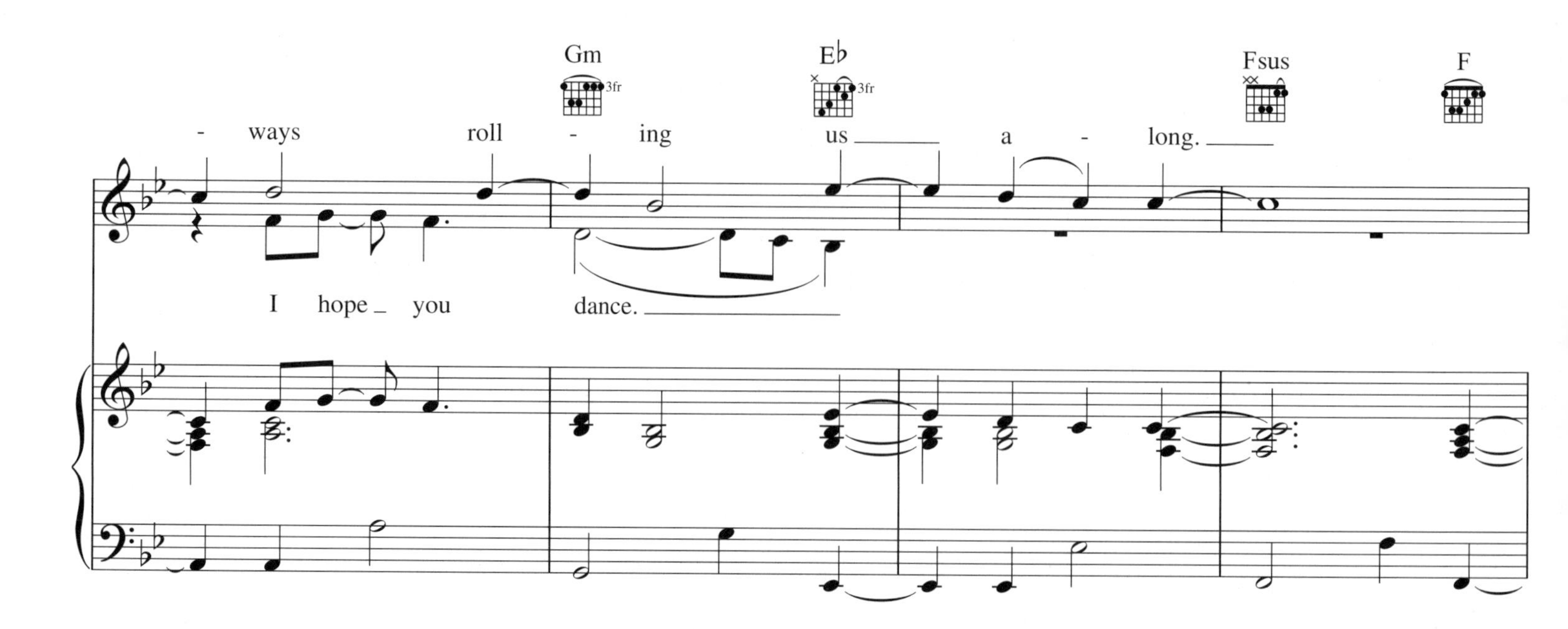
Gm
3fr
E♭
3fr
Fsus
F
- ways roll - ing us _ a - long. _
I hope _ you dance.

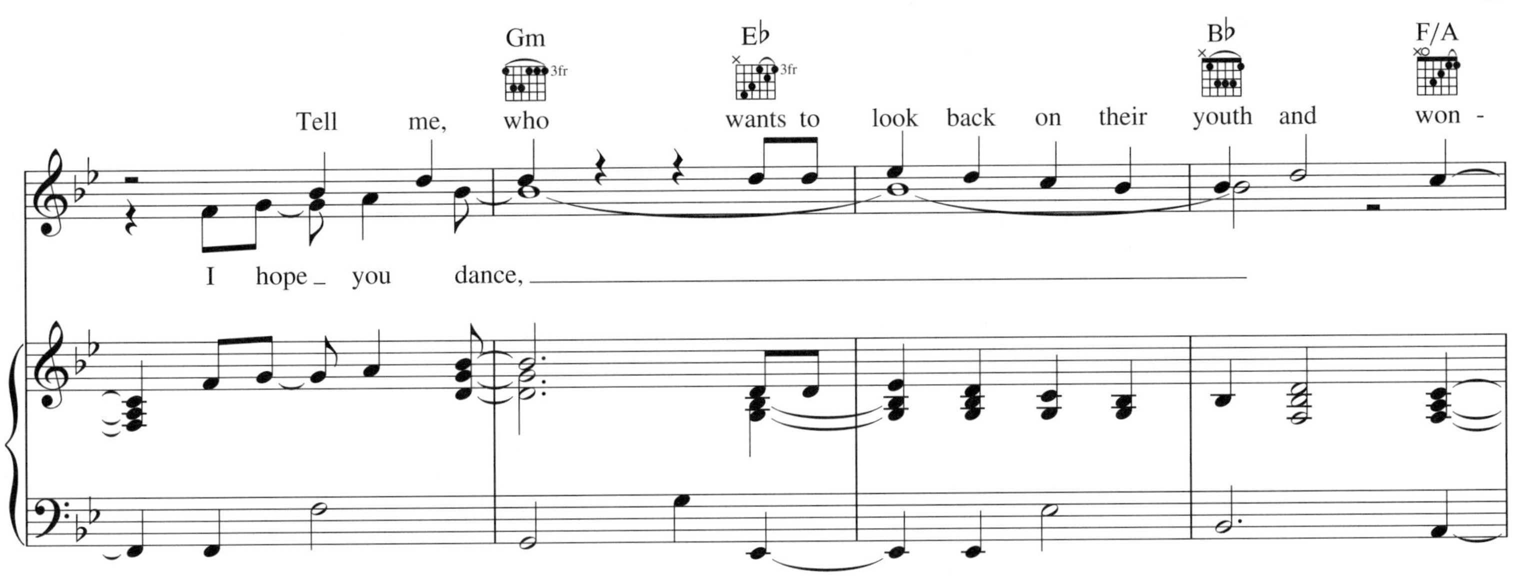
Gm
3fr
Eb
3fr
Bb
F/A
Tell me, who wants to look back on their youth and won -
I hope _ you dance, _

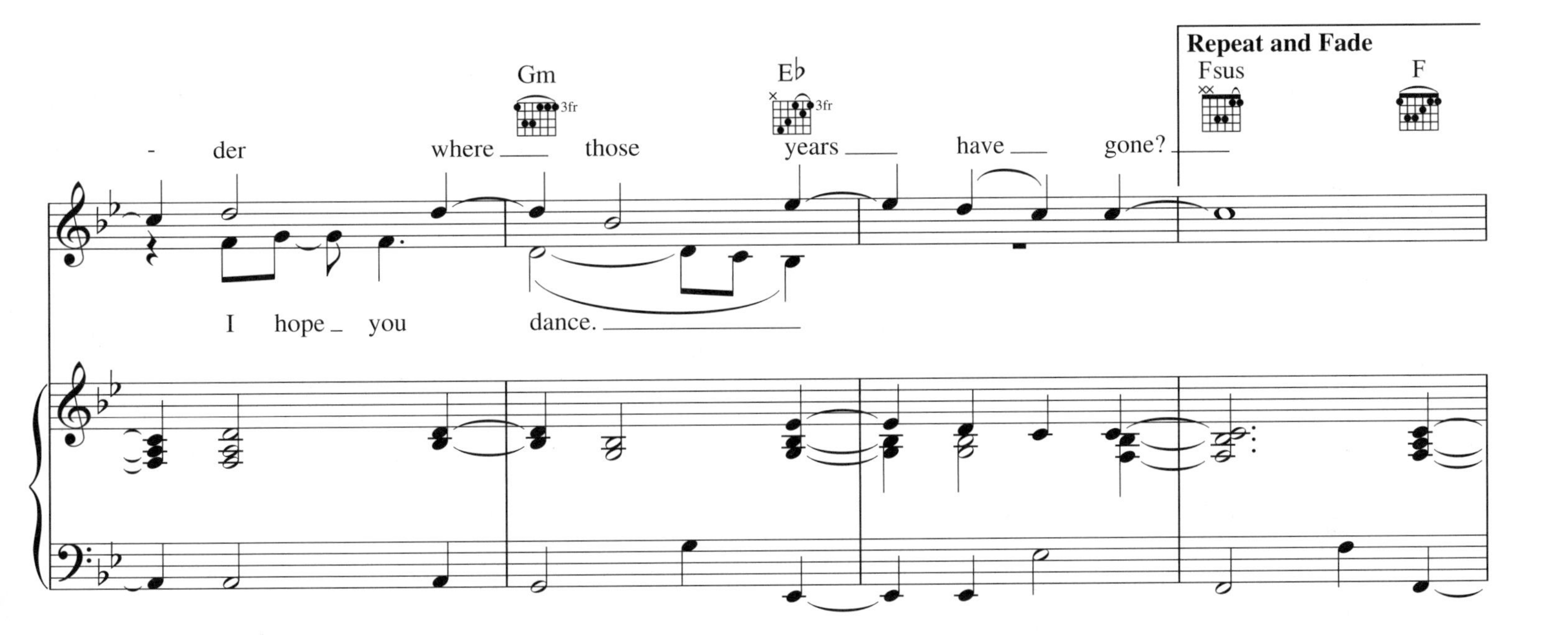
Repeat and Fade
Gm
3fr
Eb
3fr
Fsus
F
- der where _ those years _ have _ gone? _
I hope _ you dance. _

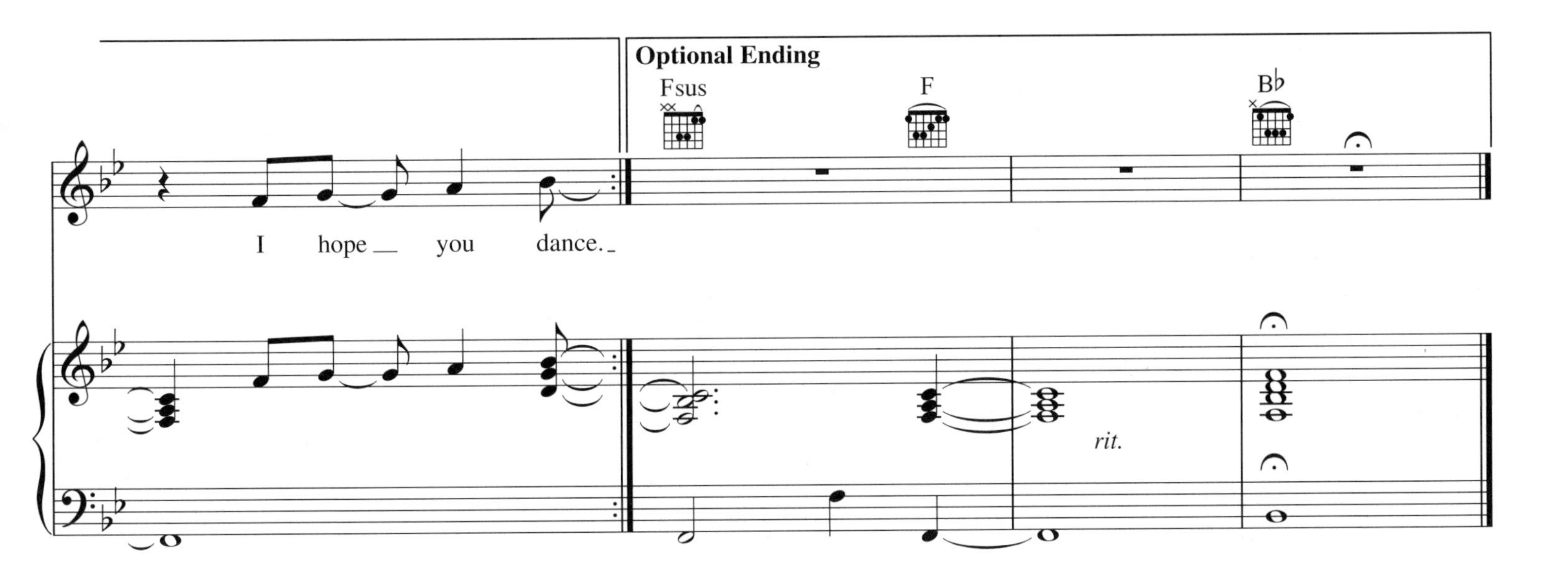
Optional Ending
Fsus
F
Bb
I hope _ you dance. _
rit.

I WILL BE HERE FOR YOU

Words and Music by MICHAEL W. SMITH
and DIANE WARREN

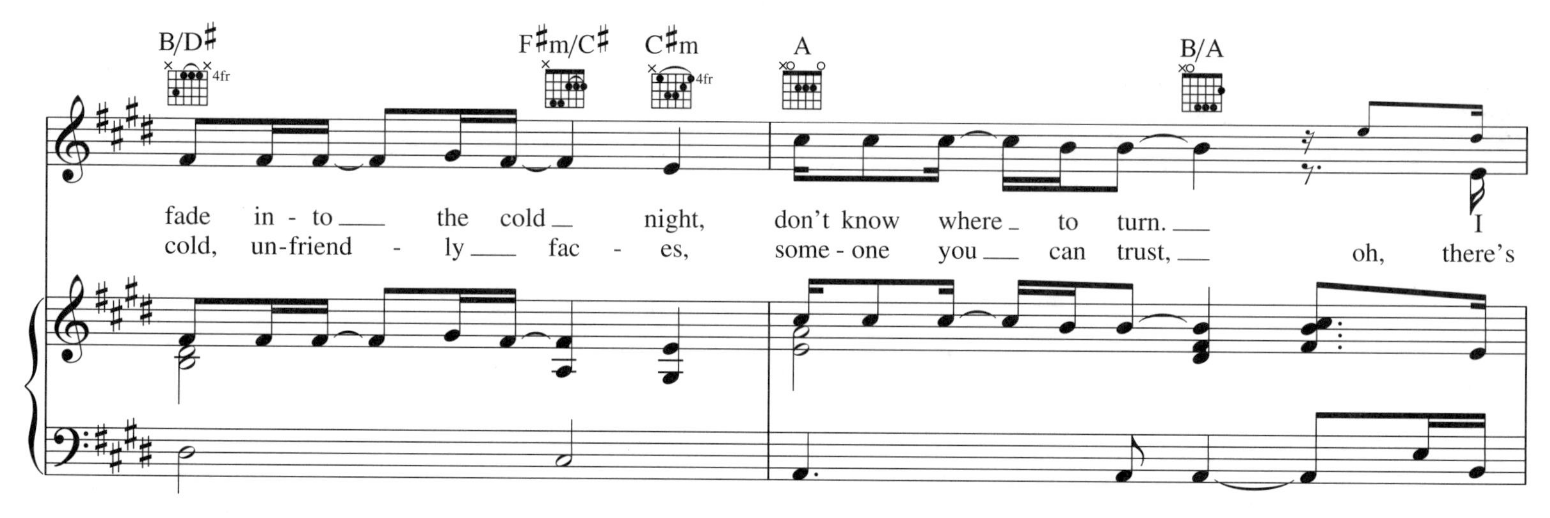

B/D♯
4fr
F♯m/C♯
C♯m
4fr
A
B/A
seem to lose their mean - ing. Let me in your world. Ba - by,
I'll give you my shoul - der. Just reach out for my love.

A
G♯m7
4fr
C♯/E♯
F♯m
let me in your world. All you need is
Reach out for my love. Call my name

E/G♯
A
D
C♯/E♯
F♯m
some - one you can hold. Don't be sad. You're not a -
and my heart will hear. I will be there; there's noth - ing to
3
3

Esus
E/G♯
A
C♯m7
4fr
- lone. I will be here for you
fear.

F#m
D6
Esus
E/D
some - where in the night,

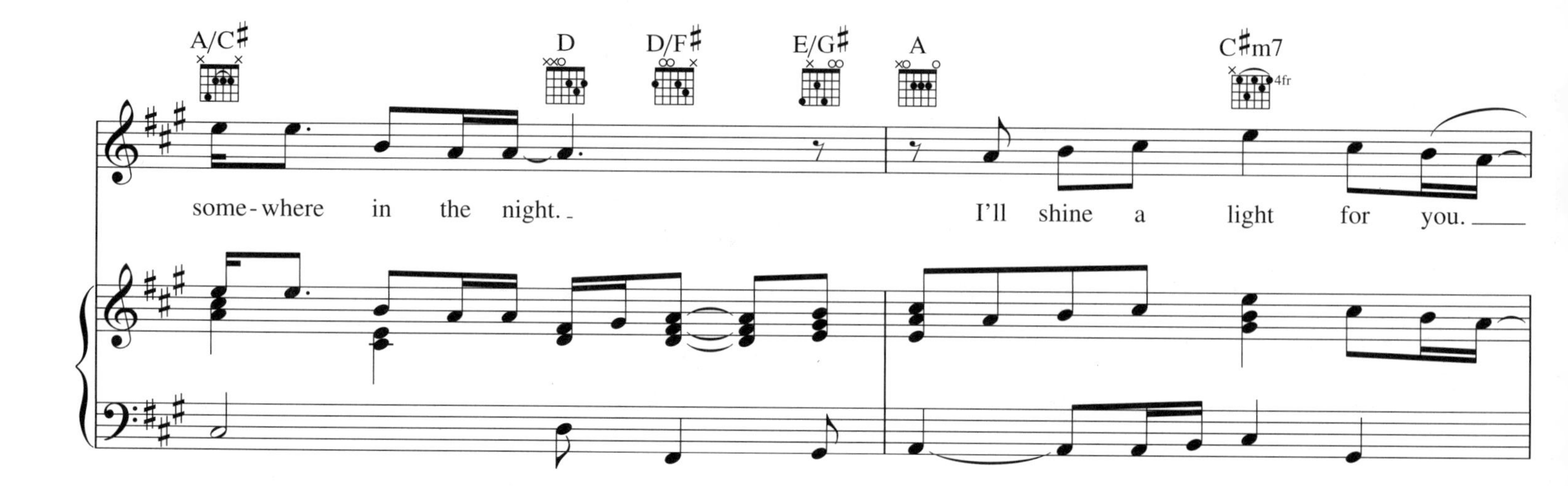
A/C#
D
D/F#
E/G#
A
C#m7
4fr
some - where in the night.
I'll shine a light for you.

F#m
B/D#
4fr
Ddim7
Some - where in the night

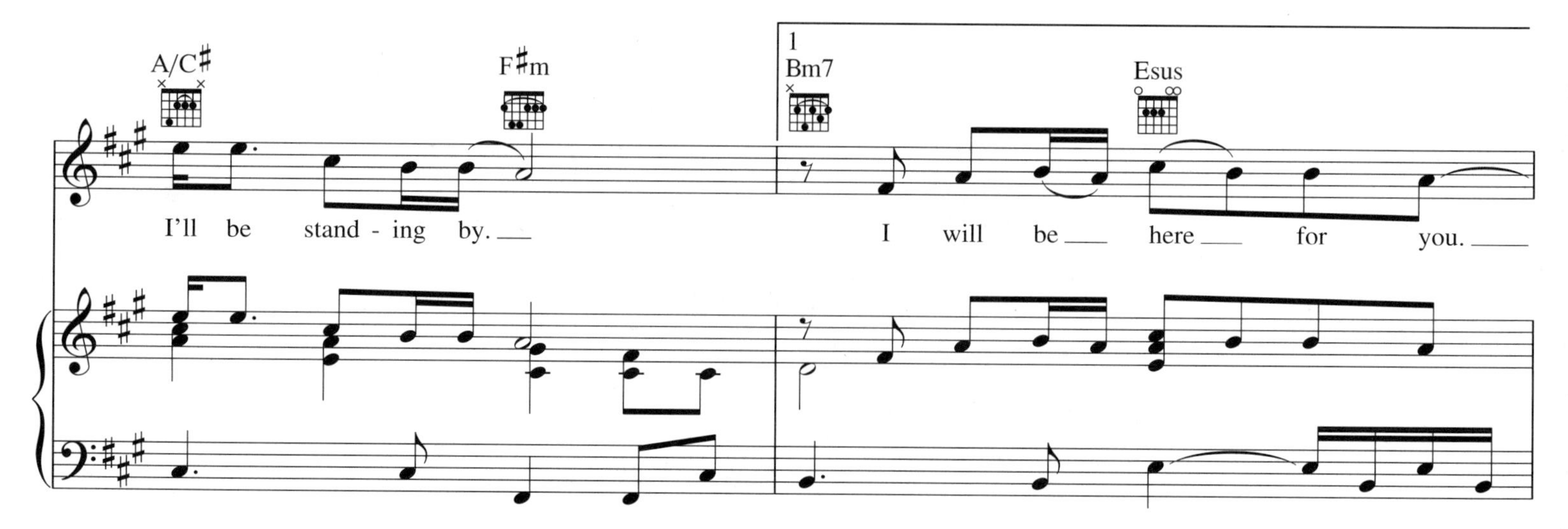
A/C#
F#m
1
Bm7
Esus
I'll be stand - ing by.
I will be here for you.

A
B/A
A
B/D♯
4fr
Well,

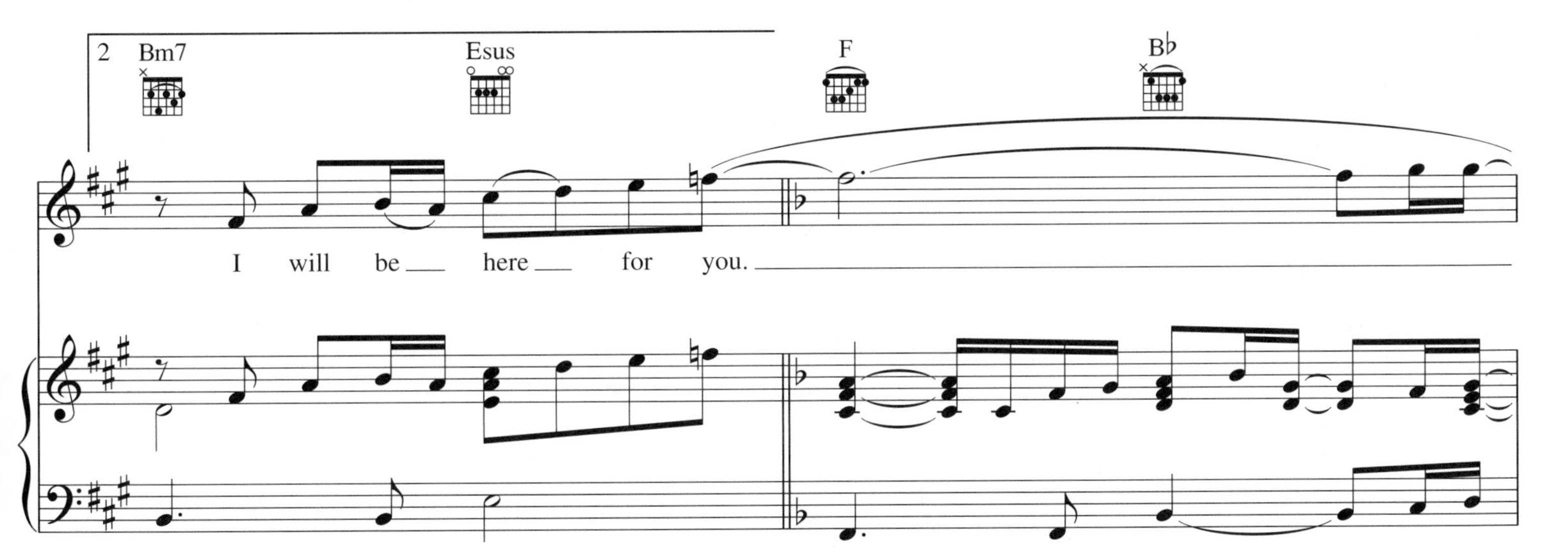
2
Bm7
Esus
F
B♭
I will be here for you.

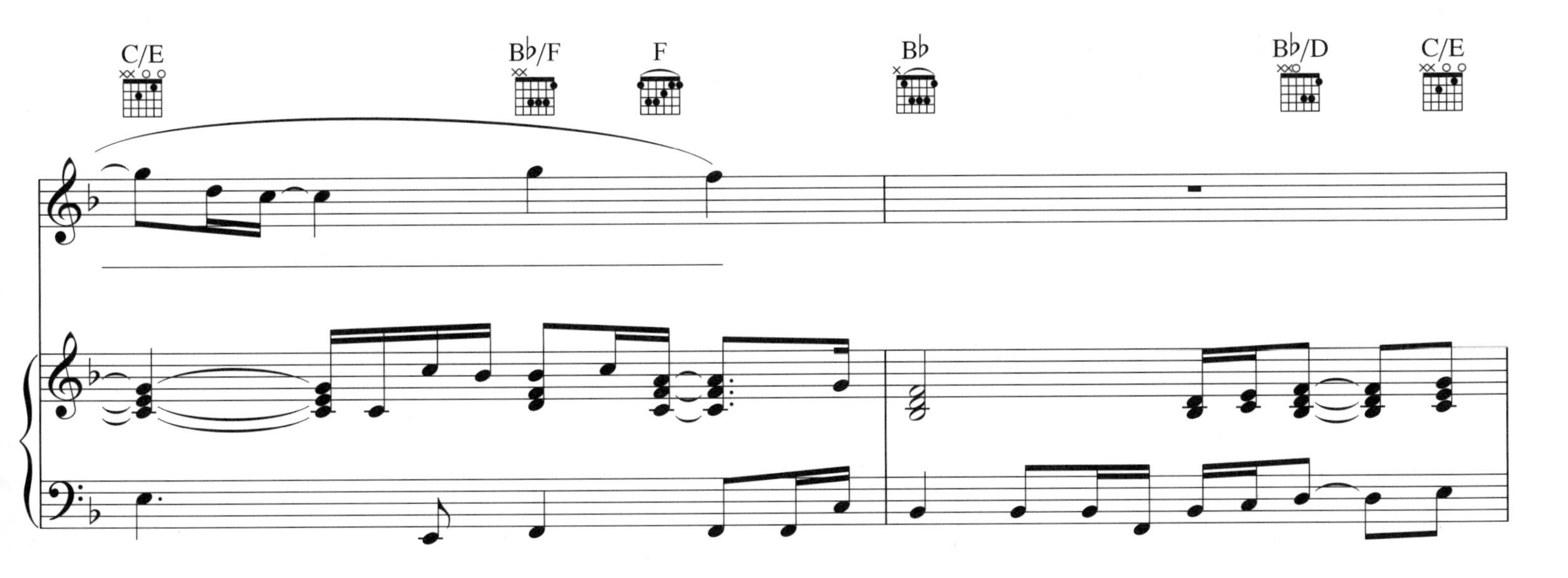
C/E
B♭/F
F
B♭
B♭/D
C/E

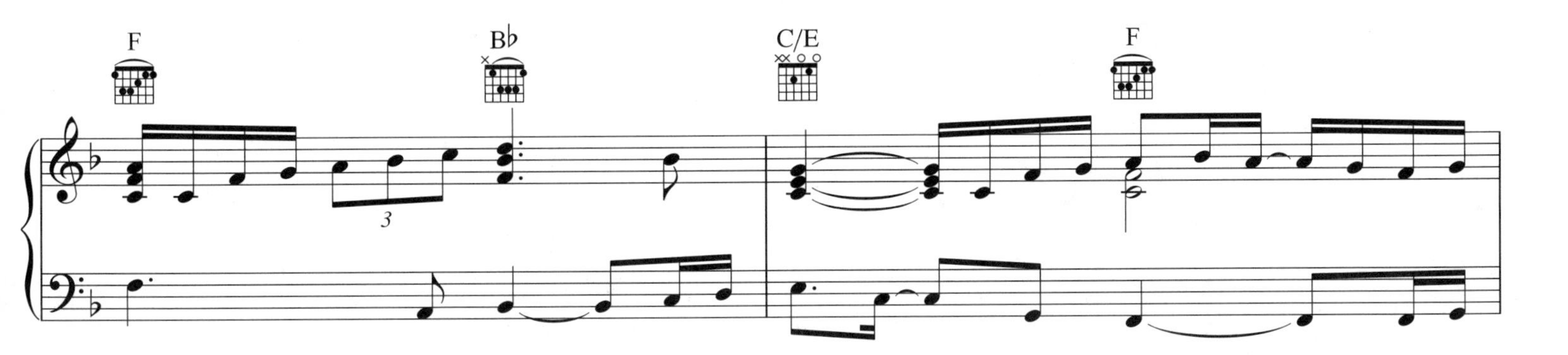
F
B♭
C/E
F
3

B♭/D
C/E
Gm7
F/A

F7
B♭
Dm7
Gm
3fr
I will be here for you

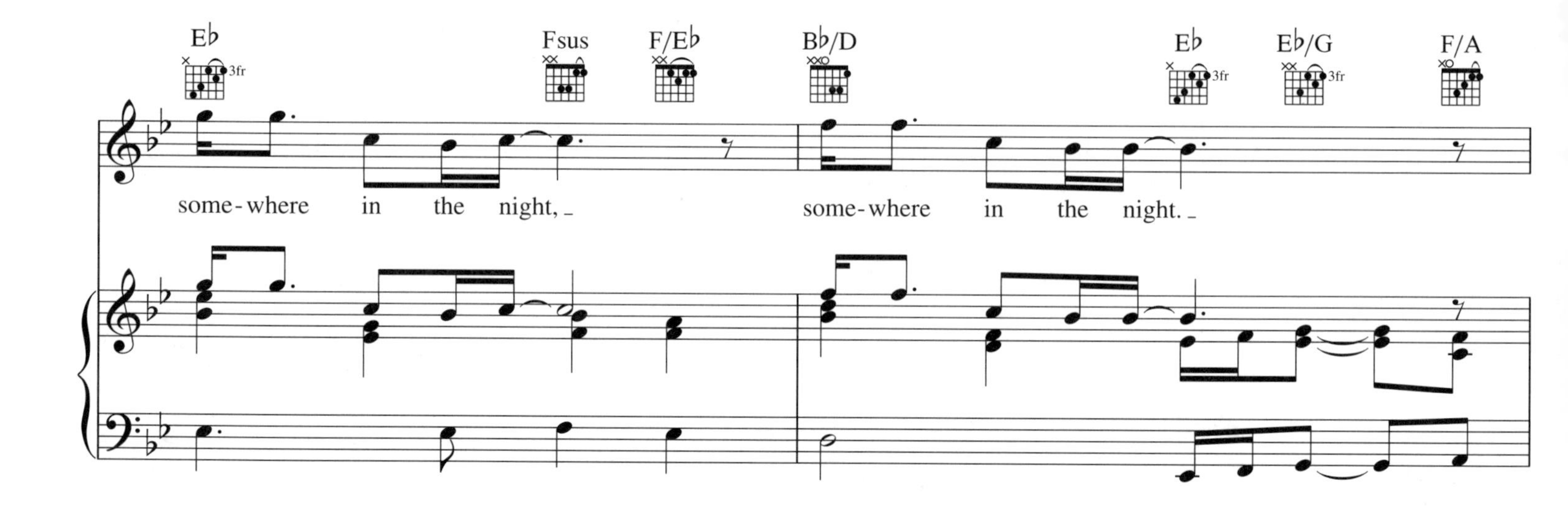
E♭
3fr
Fsus
F/E♭
B♭/D
E♭
3fr
E♭/G
3fr
F/A
some-where in the night,
some-where in the night.

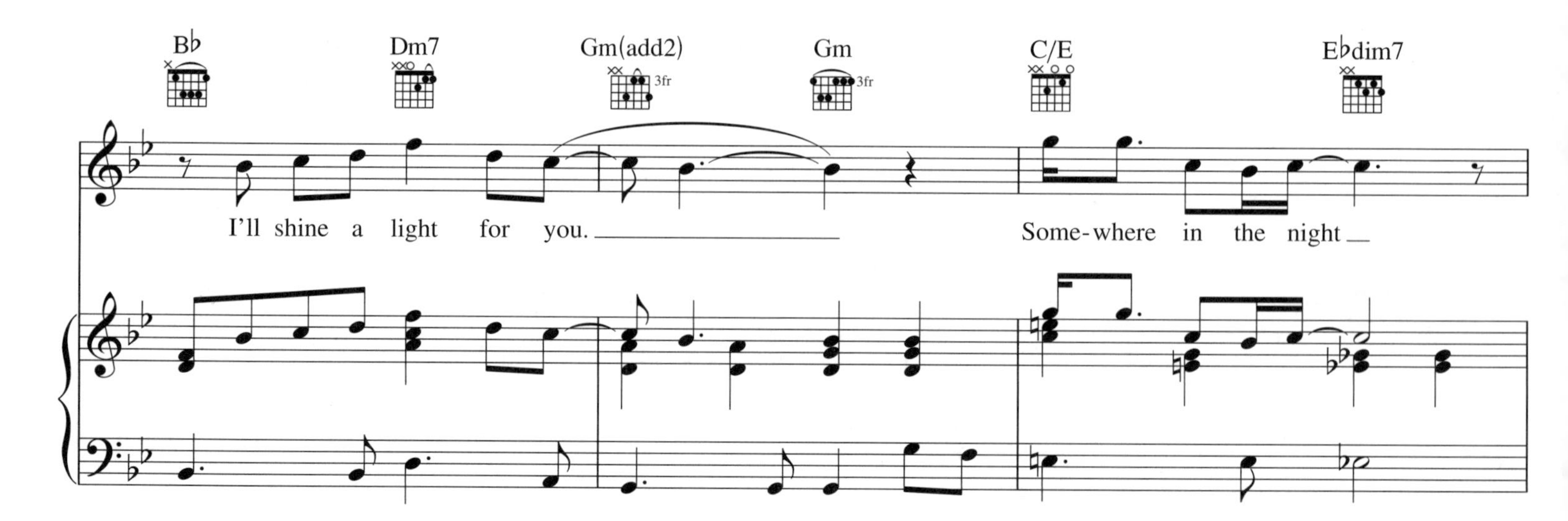
B♭
Dm7
Gm(add2)
3fr
Gm
3fr
C/E
E♭dim7
I'll shine a light for you.
Some-where in the night

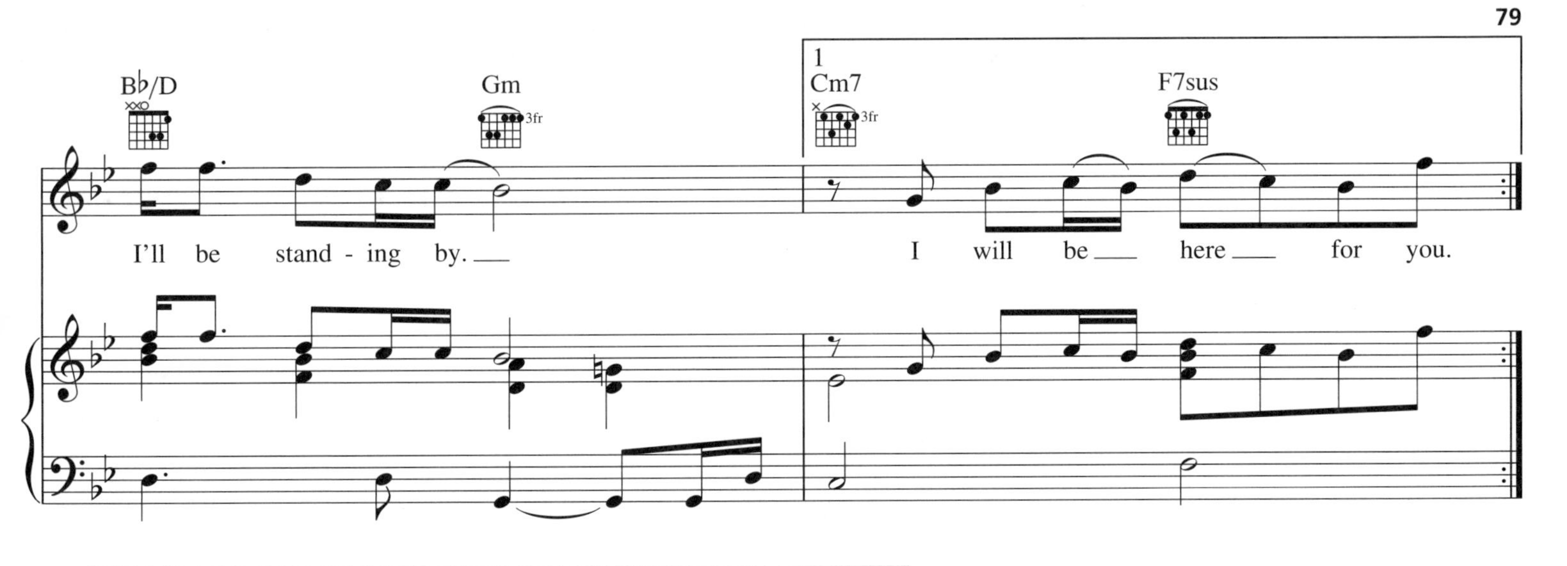
1
B♭/D
Gm
Cm7
F7sus
I'll be stand - ing by.
I will be here for you.

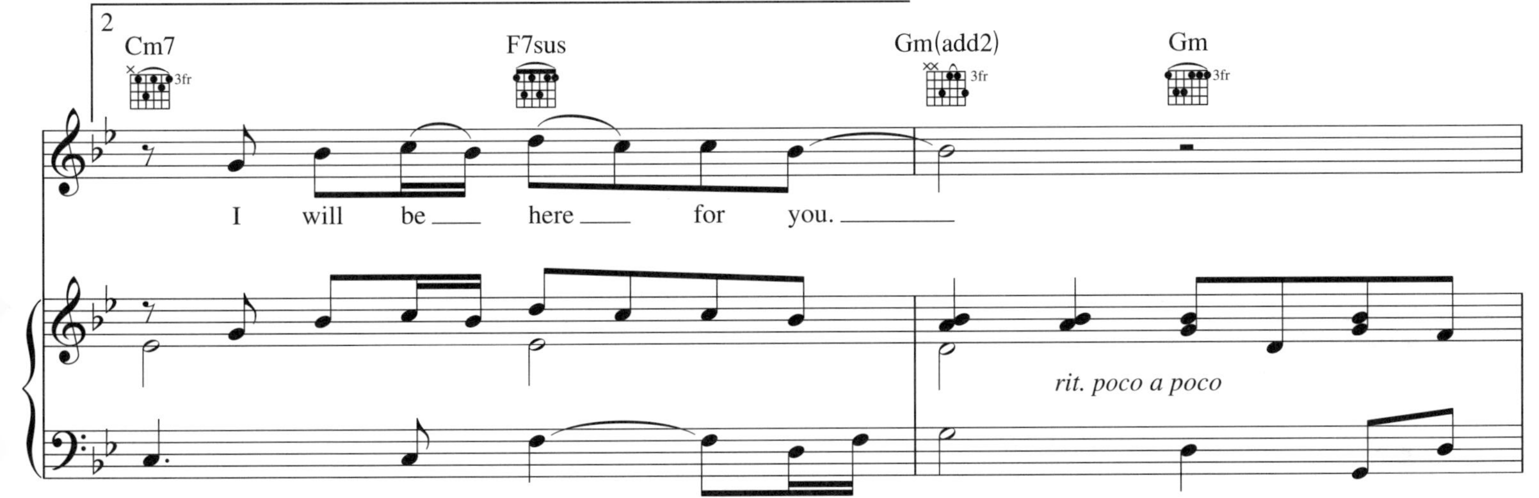
2
Cm7
F7sus
Gm(add2)
Gm
I will be here for you.
rit. poco a poco

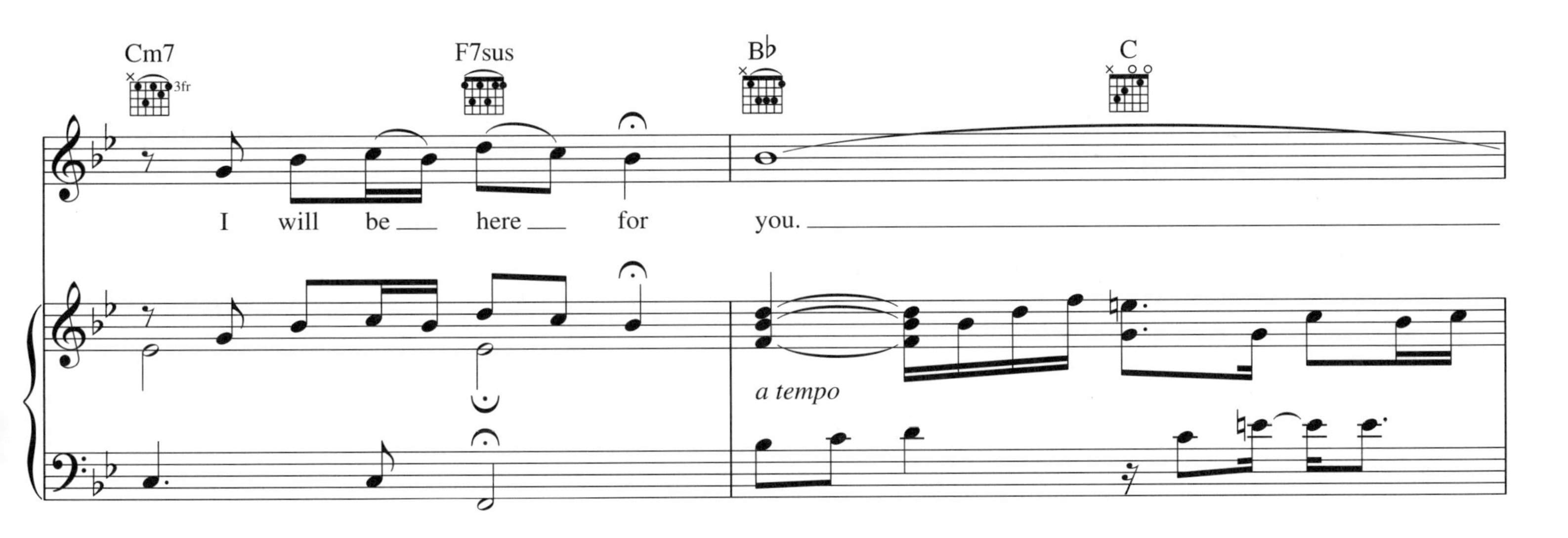
Cm7
F7sus
B♭
C
I will be here for you.
a tempo

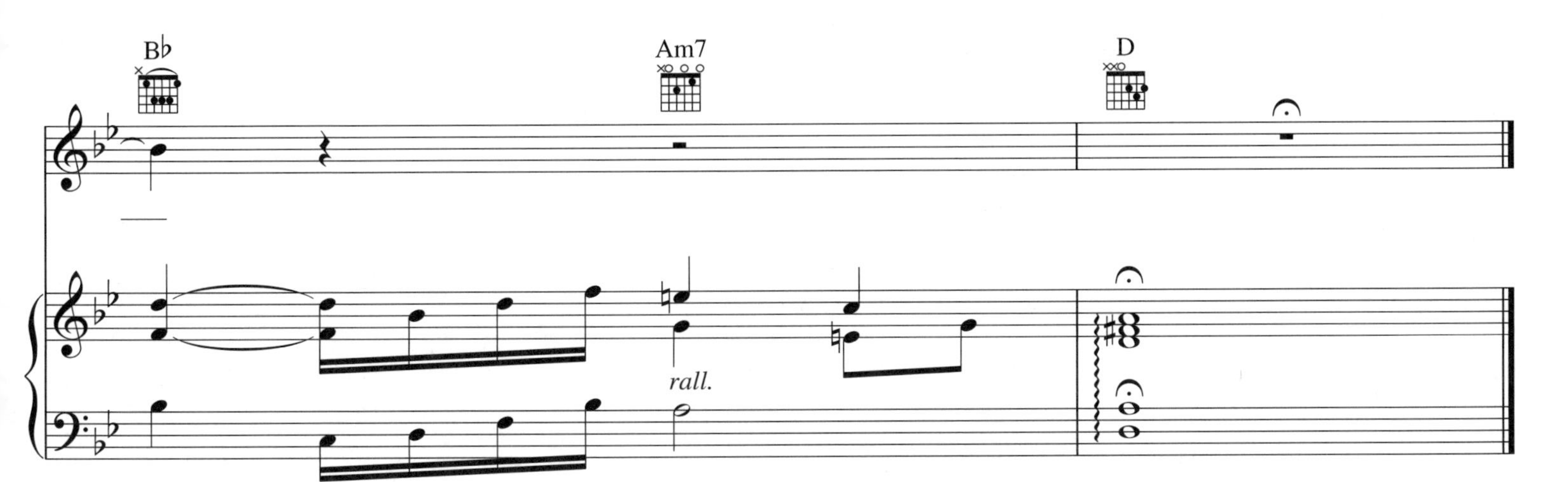
B♭
Am7
D
rall.

I'M ALREADY THERE

Words and Music by GARY BAKER, FRANK MYERS and RICHIE McDONALD

Gently

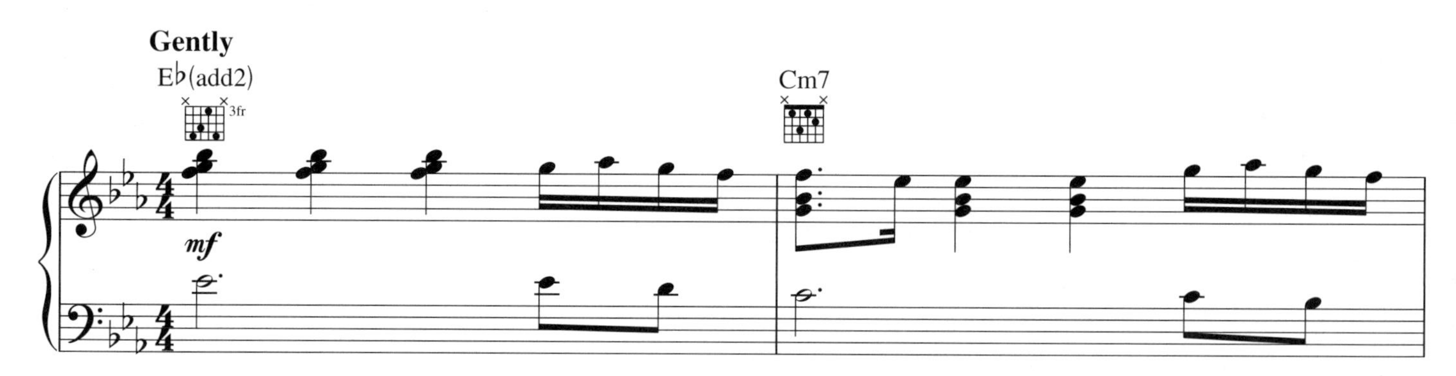

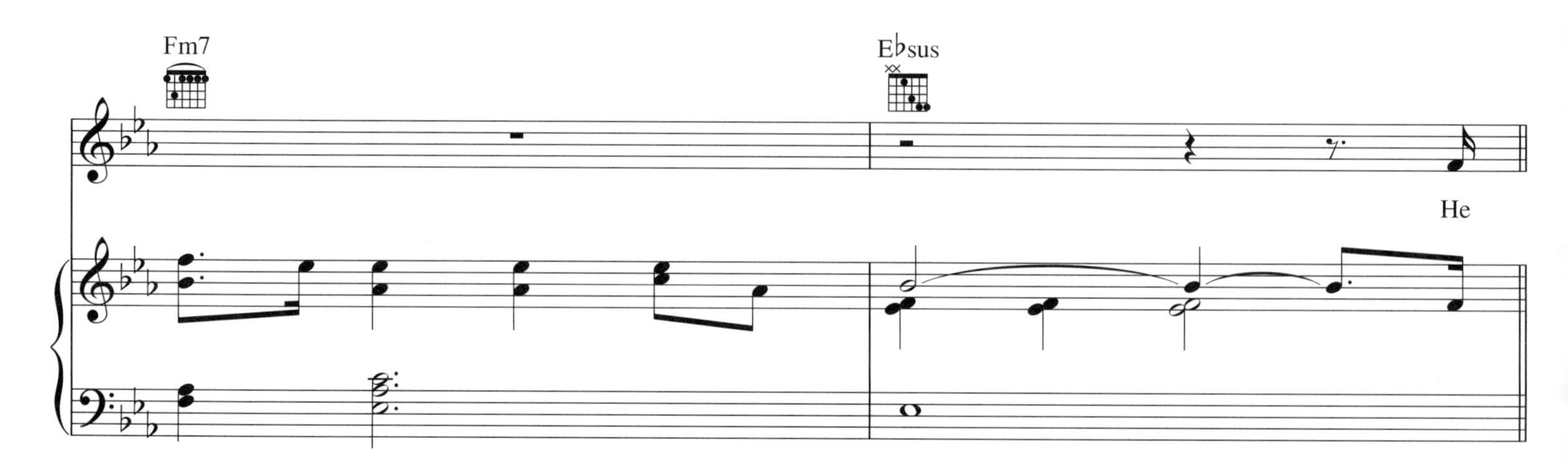

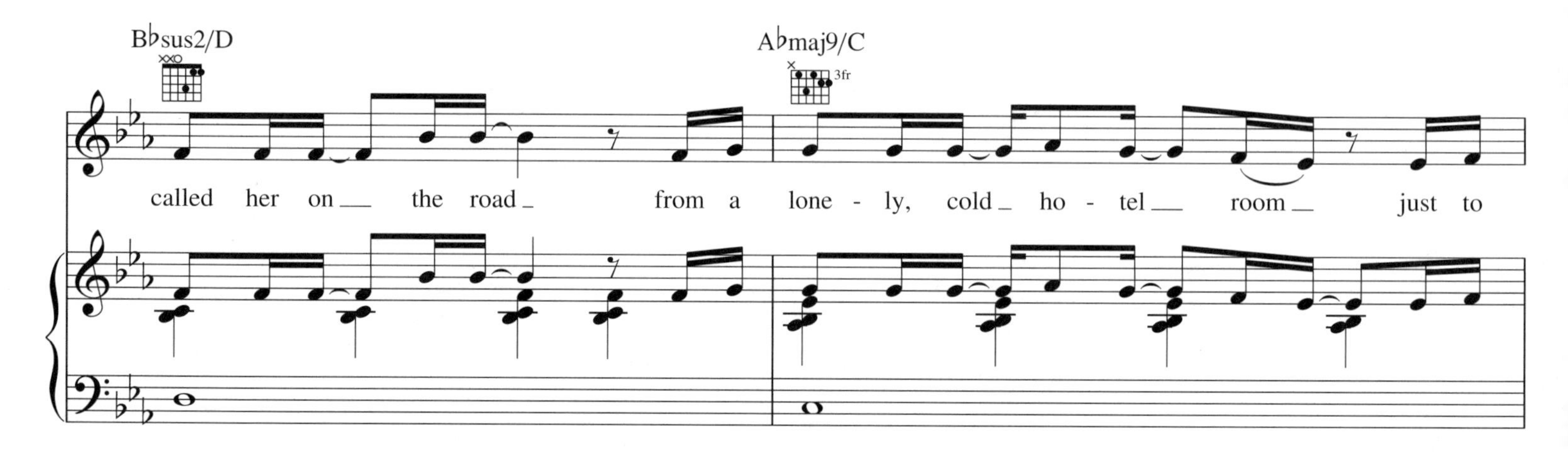

B♭/D
A♭maj9
4fr
when he heard the sound of the kids laugh - in' in the back - ground he had to

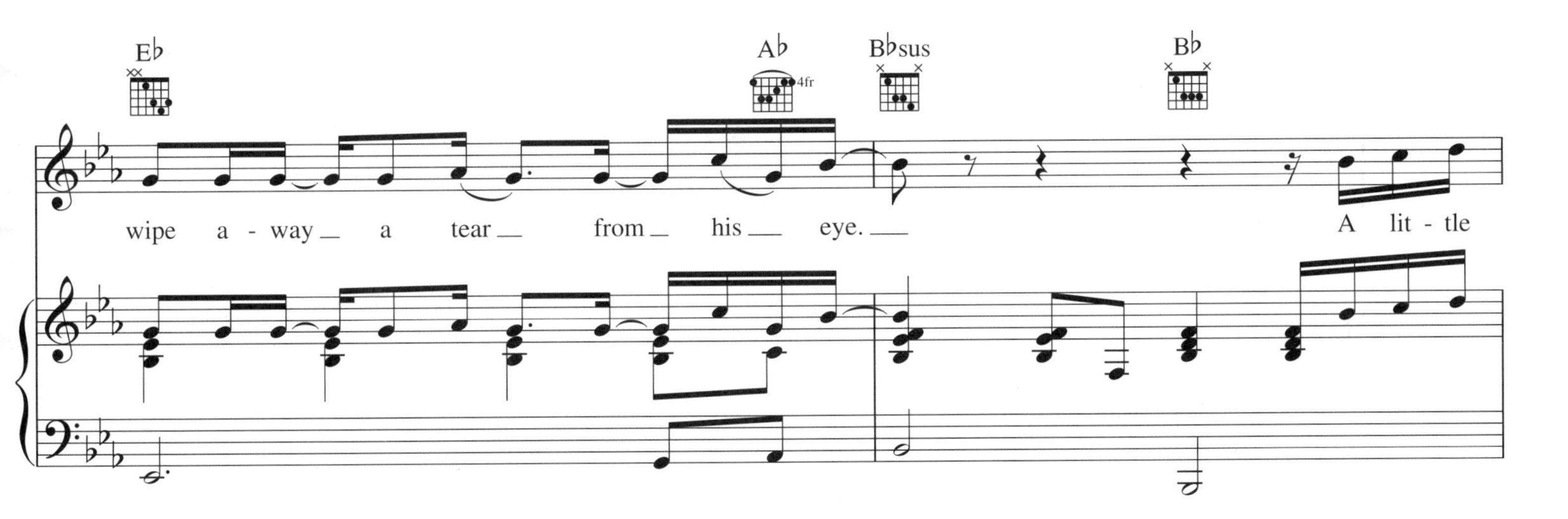
E♭
A♭
4fr
B♭sus
B♭
wipe a - way a tear from his eye. A lit - tle

Cm
B♭/D
voice came on the phone and said, "Dad - dy, when you com - in' home?" He said the

E♭
Fm
E♭/G
3fr
A♭
4fr
A♭/B♭
B♭
first thing that came to his mind: I'm al - read - y there.

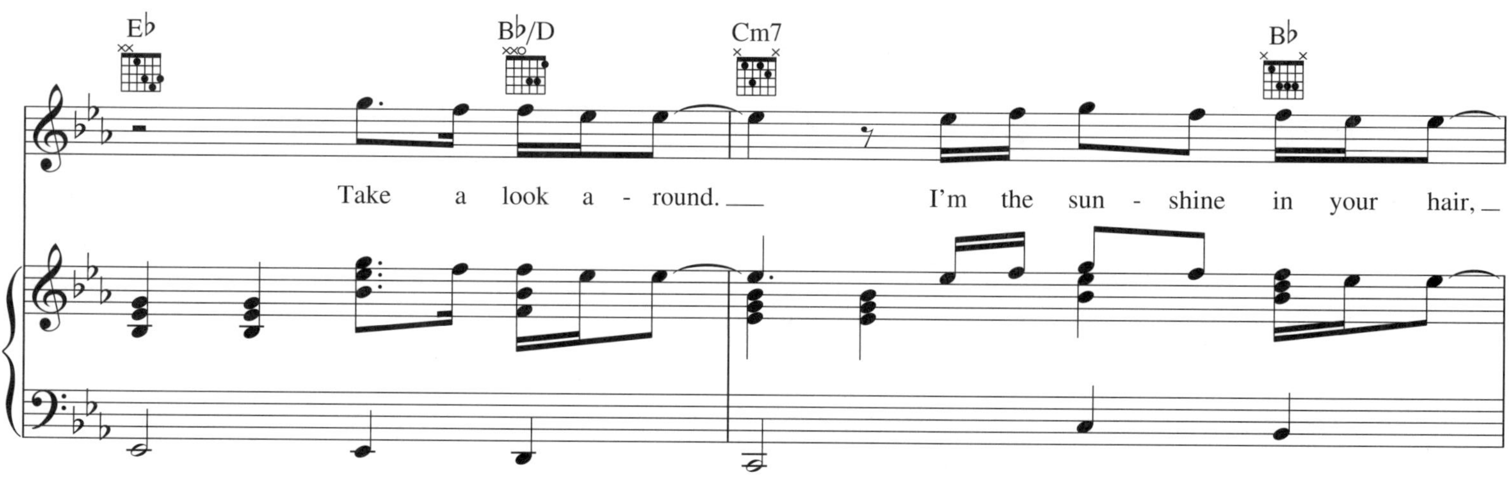
E♭
B♭/D
Cm7
B♭
Take a look a - round.
I'm the sun - shine in your hair,

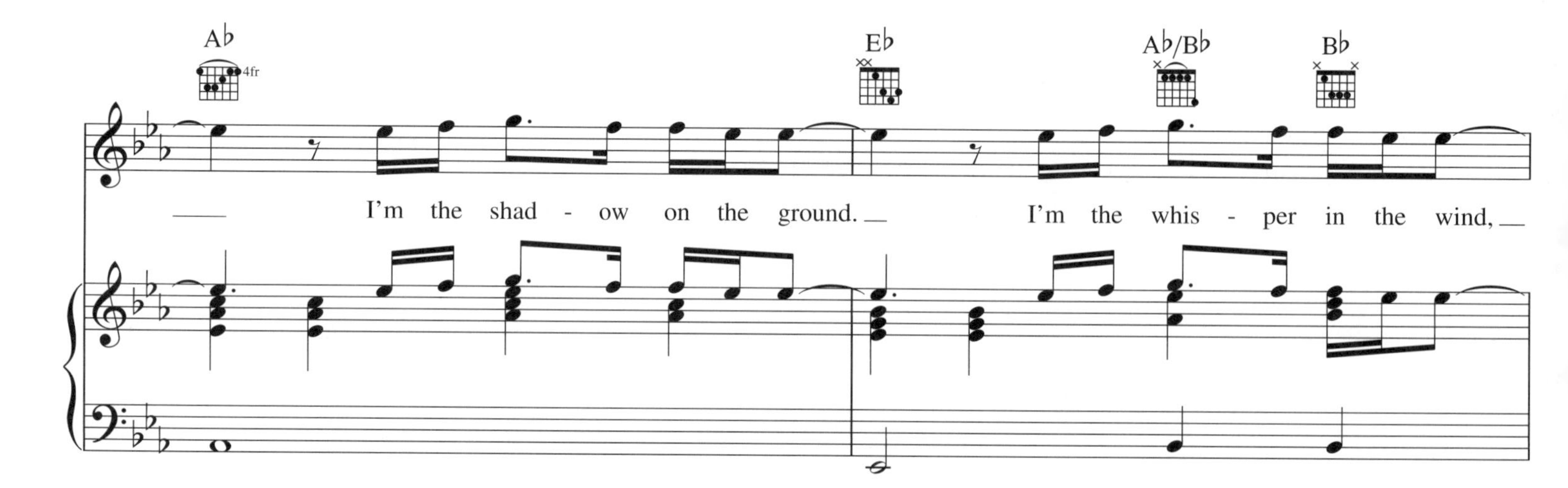
A♭
4fr
E♭
A♭/B♭
B♭
I'm the shad - ow on the ground.
I'm the whis - per in the wind,

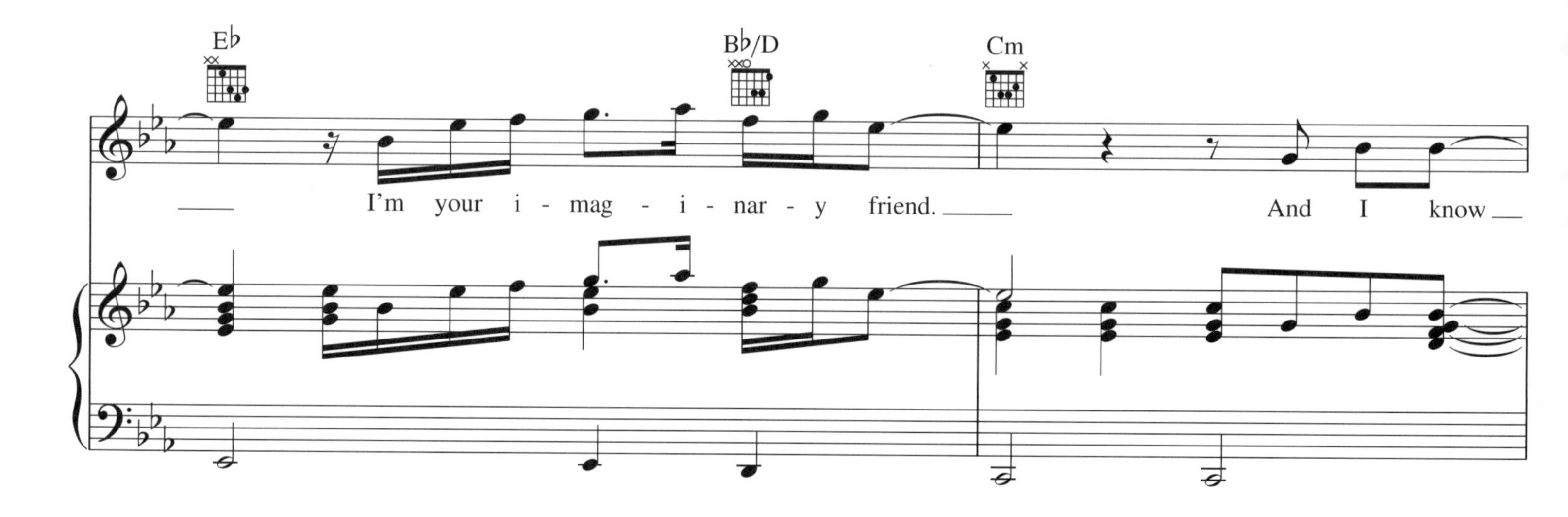
E♭
B♭/D
Cm
I'm your i - mag - i - nar - y friend.
And I know

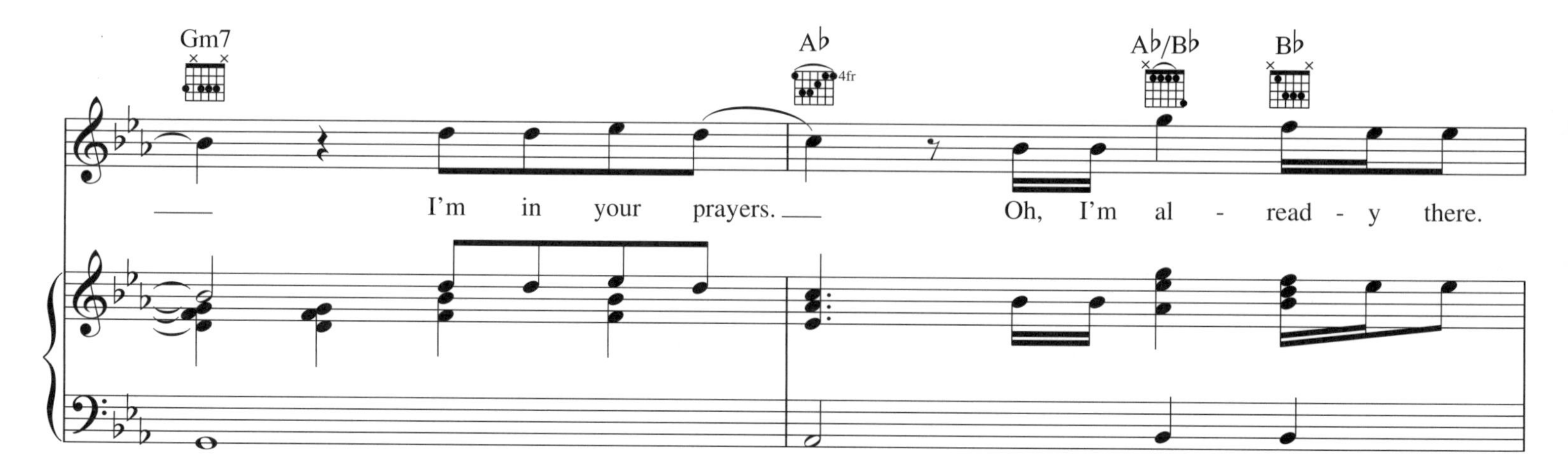
Gm7
A♭
4fr
A♭/B♭
B♭
I'm in your prayers.
Oh, I'm al - read - y there.

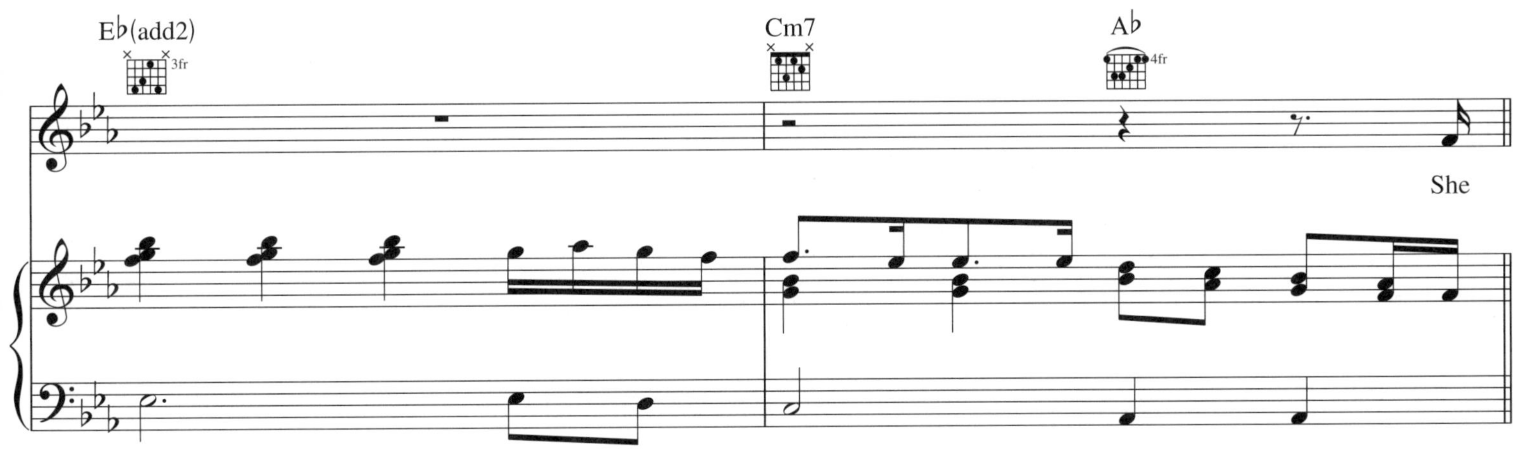

E♭(add2)
Cm7
A♭
She

B♭/D
A♭maj9
got back on the phone said, "I real-ly miss you, dar-lin'. Don't

E♭
B♭sus
B♭
A♭/C
wor-ry a-bout the kids; they'll be al-right. I wish

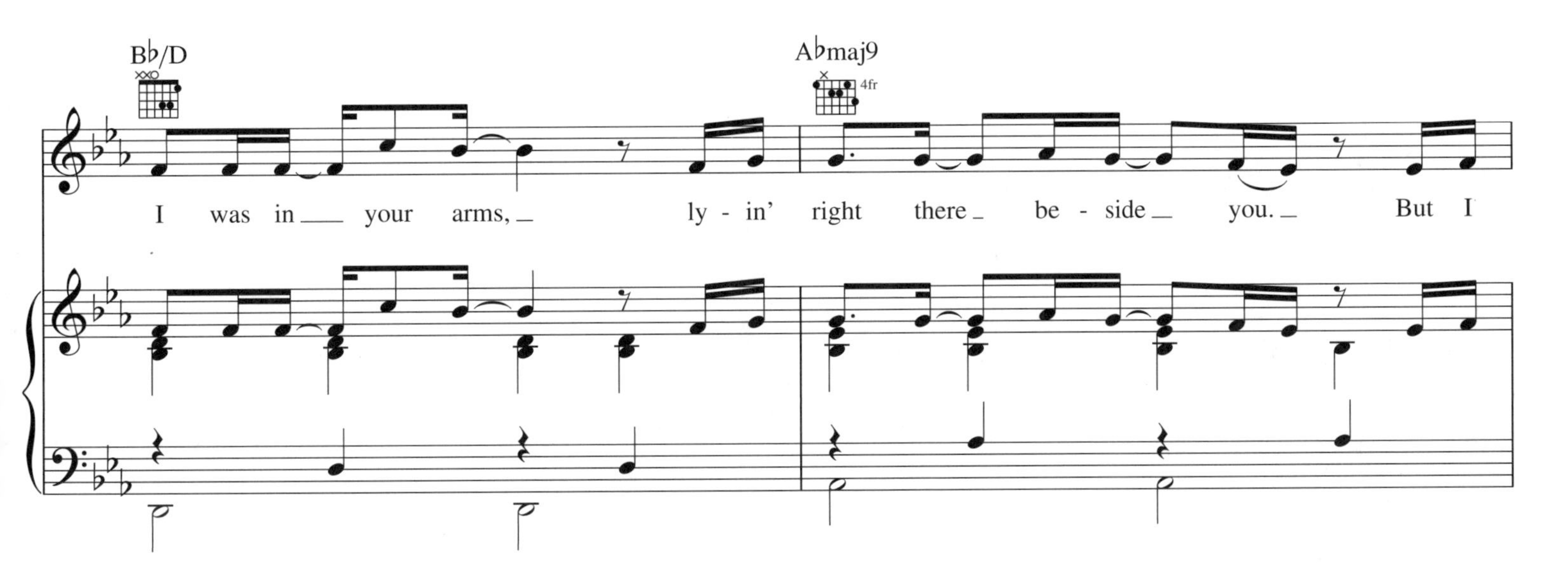

B♭/D
A♭maj9
I was in your arms, ly-in' right there be-side you. But I

E♭
B♭sus
B♭
know that I'll be in your dreams to - night. And I'll

Cm
B♭/D
gen - tly kiss your lips, touch you with my fin - ger - tips. So, turn

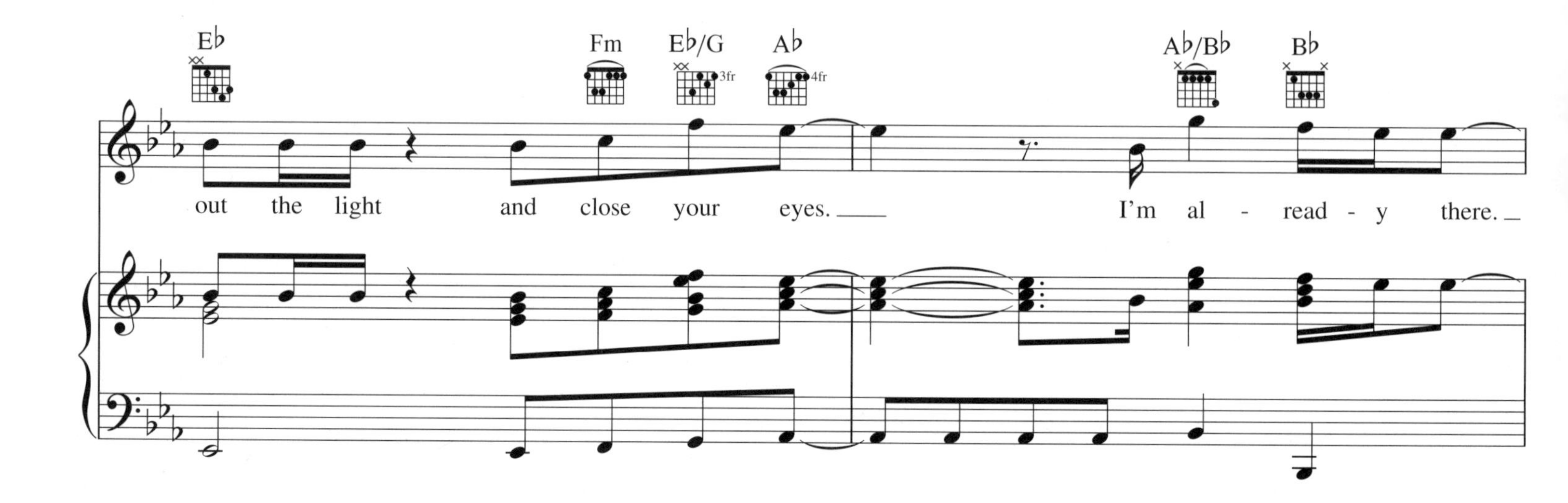
E♭
Fm
E♭/G
A♭
A♭/B♭
B♭
3fr
4fr
out the light and close your eyes. I'm al - read - y there.

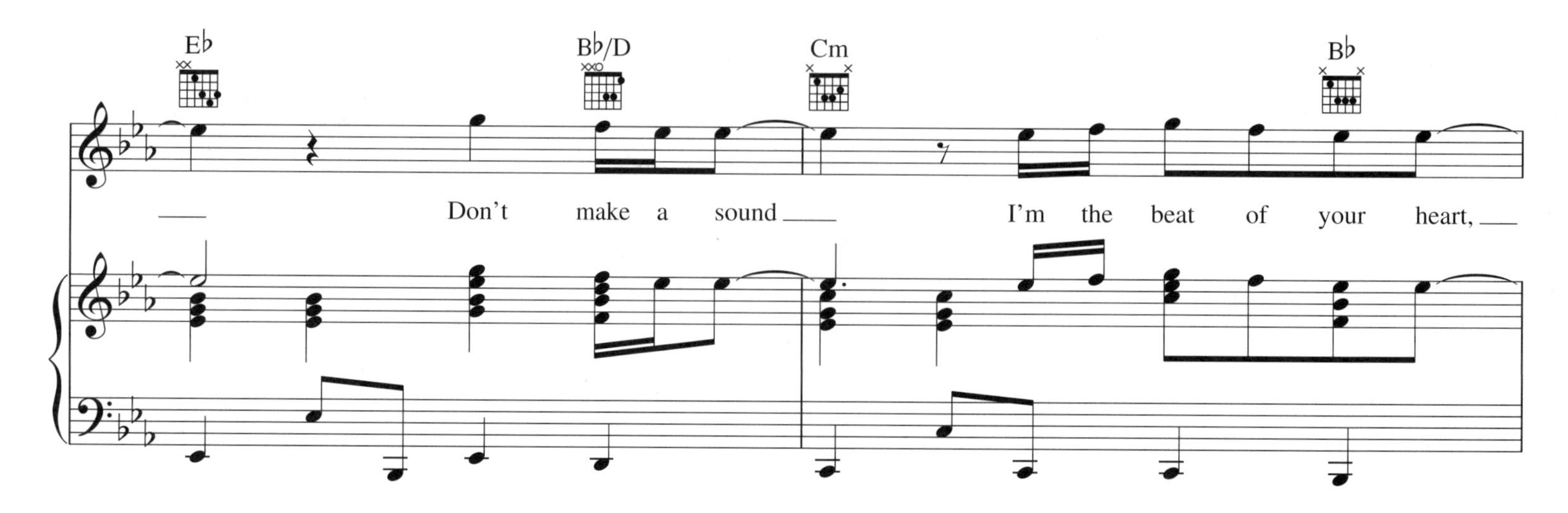
E♭
B♭/D
Cm
B♭
Don't make a sound I'm the beat of your heart,

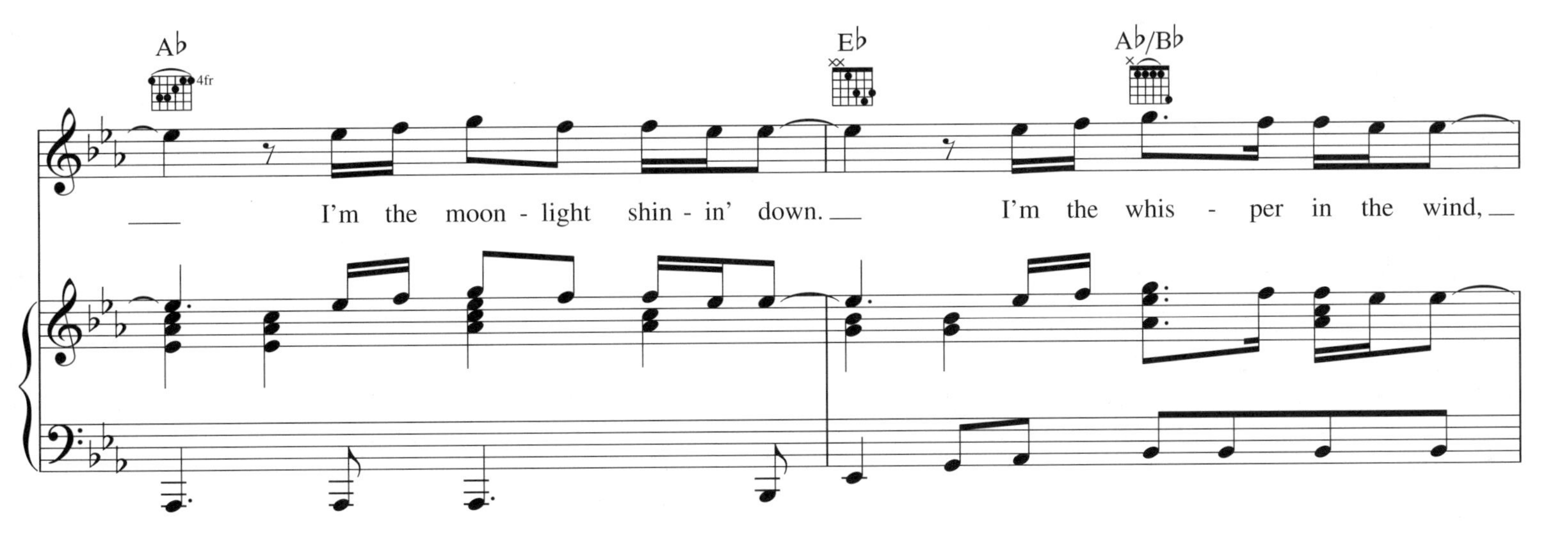
A♭
4fr
E♭
A♭/B♭
I'm the moon - light shin - in' down.
I'm the whis - per in the wind,

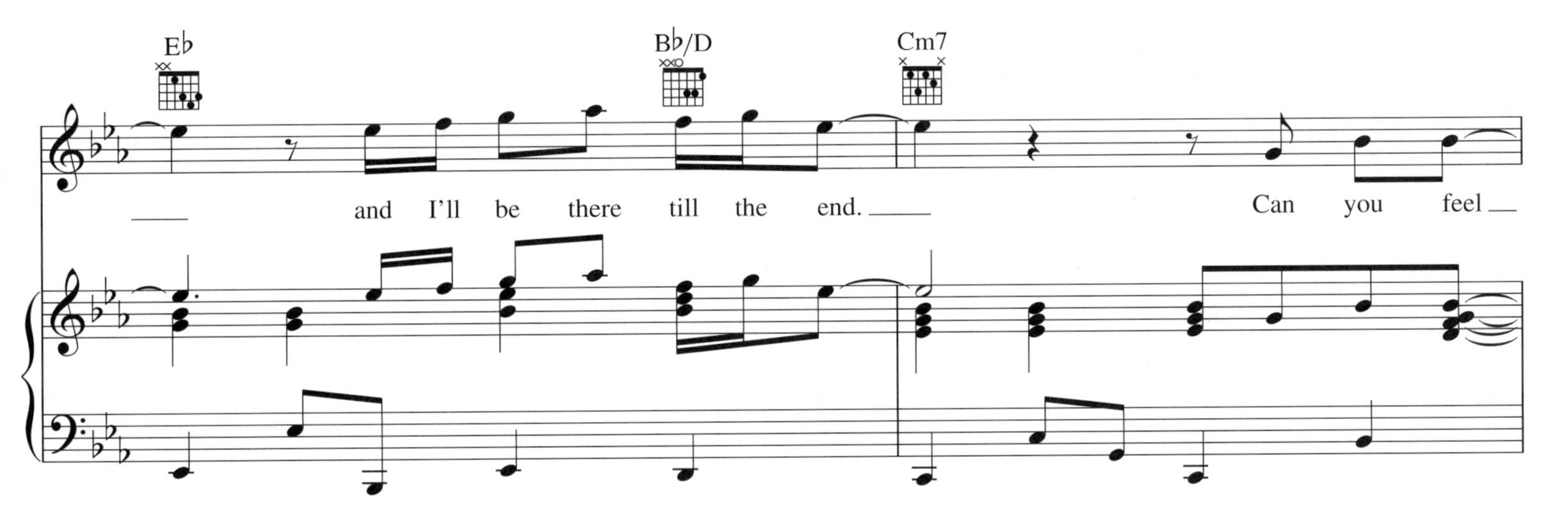
E♭
B♭/D
Cm7
and I'll be there till the end.
Can you feel

Gm7
A♭
4fr
B♭sus
B♭
the love that we've shared?
Oh, I'm al - read - y there."

E♭
Fm
E♭/G
3fr
We may be a thou -

A♭
4fr
G♭
D♭/F
- sand miles a - part,
but I'll be with you wher -

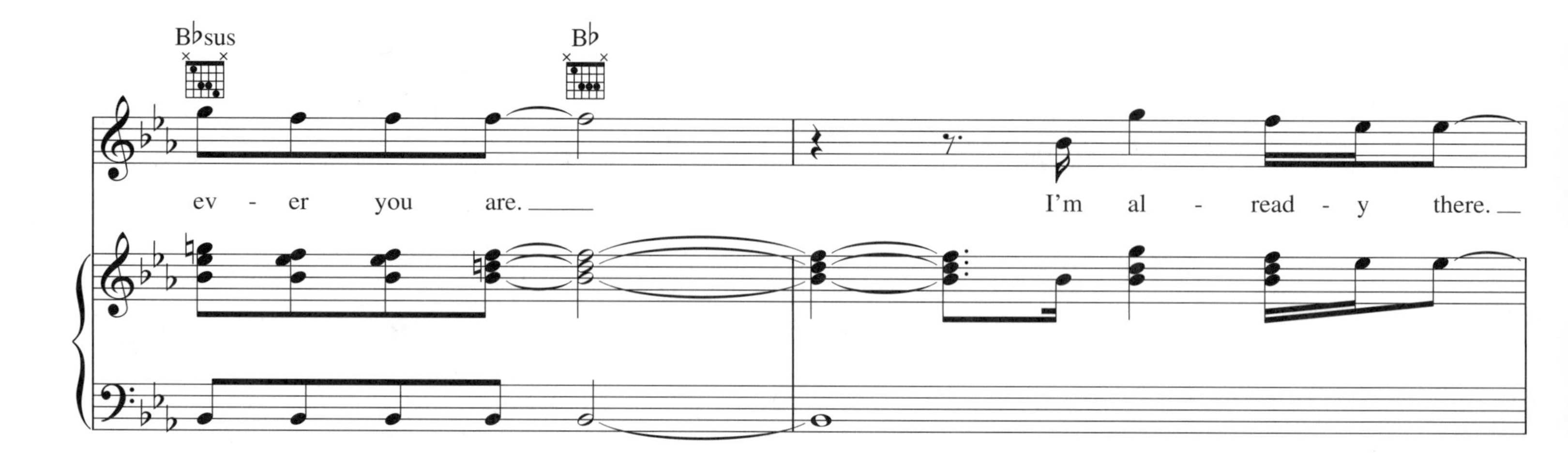
B♭sus
B♭
ev - er you are.
I'm al - read - y there.

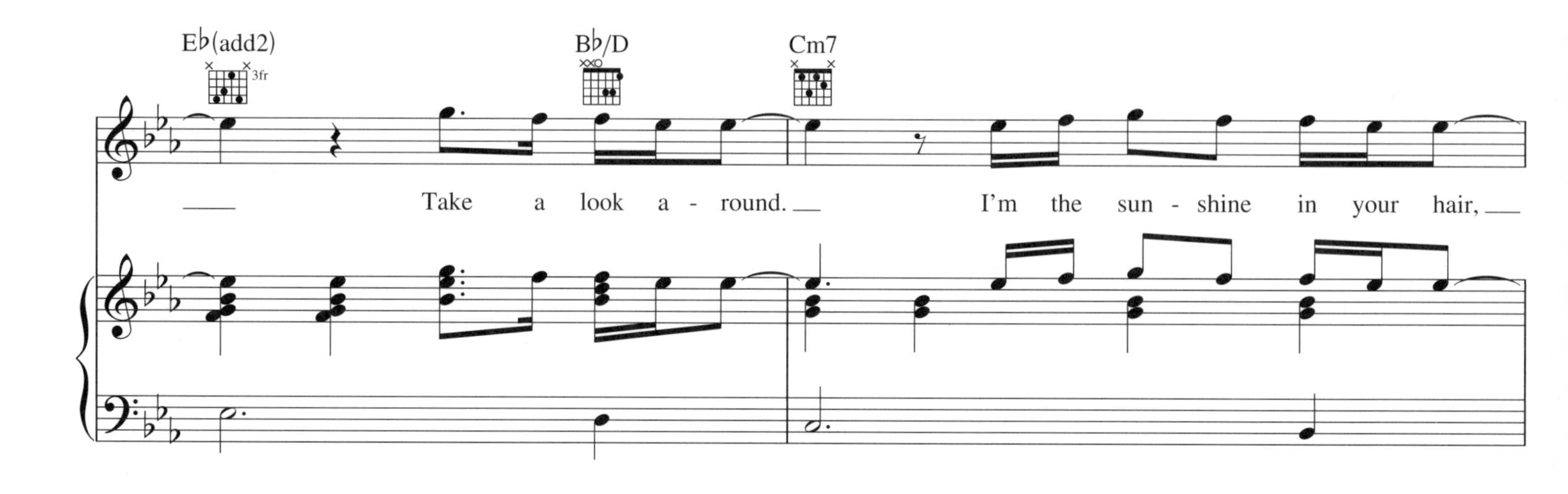
E♭(add2)
3fr
B♭/D
Cm7
Take a look a - round.
I'm the sun - shine in your hair,

A♭sus2
N.C.
B♭
I'm the shad - ow on the ground.
I'm the whis - per in the wind,

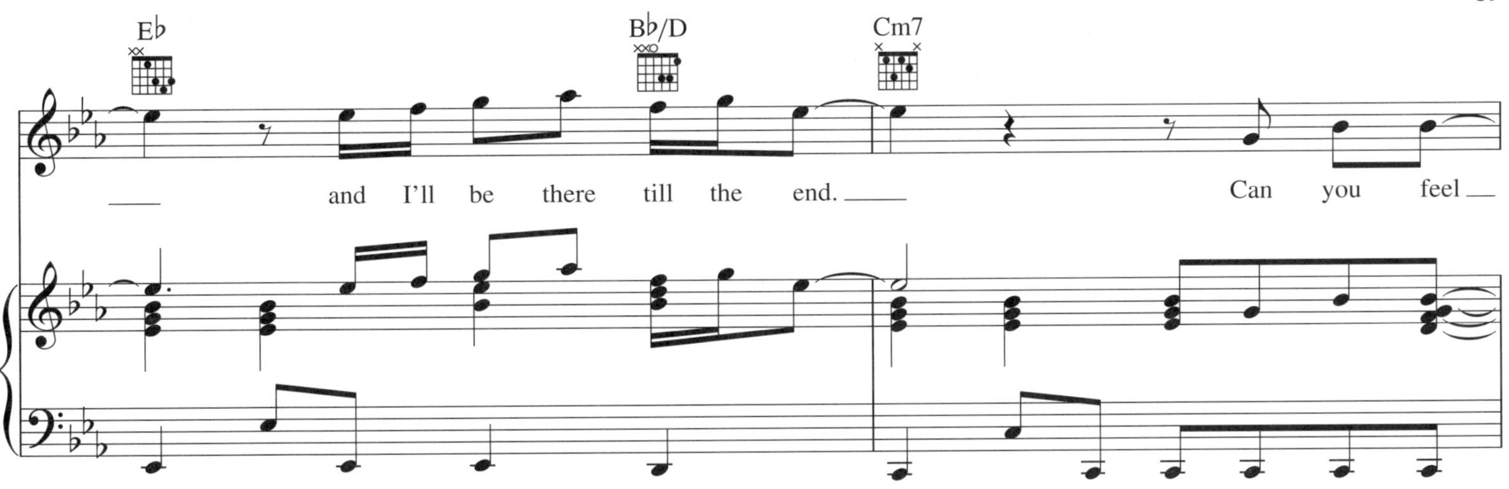
E♭
B♭/D
Cm7
and I'll be there till the end.
Can you feel

Gm7
A♭
4fr
B♭
the love that we've shared?
Oh, I'm al - read - y there.

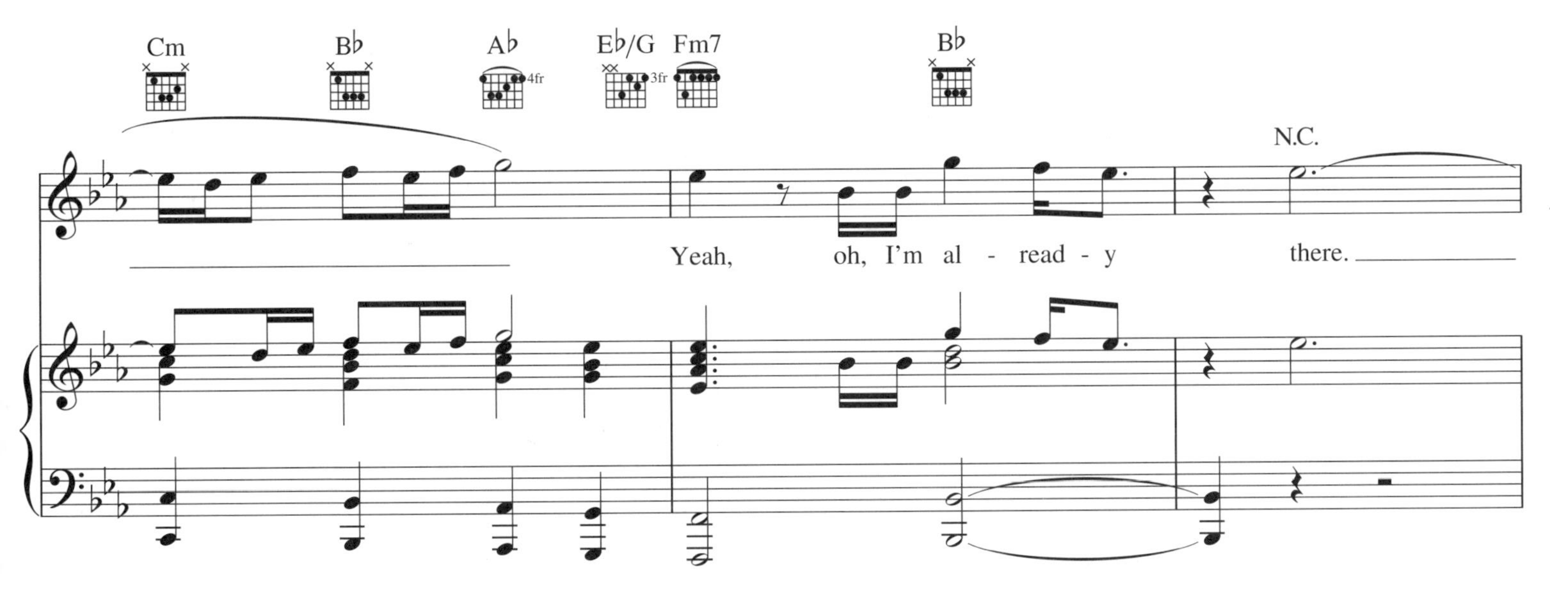
Cm
B♭
A♭
4fr
E♭/G
3fr
Fm7
B♭
N.C.
Yeah, oh, I'm al - read - y there.

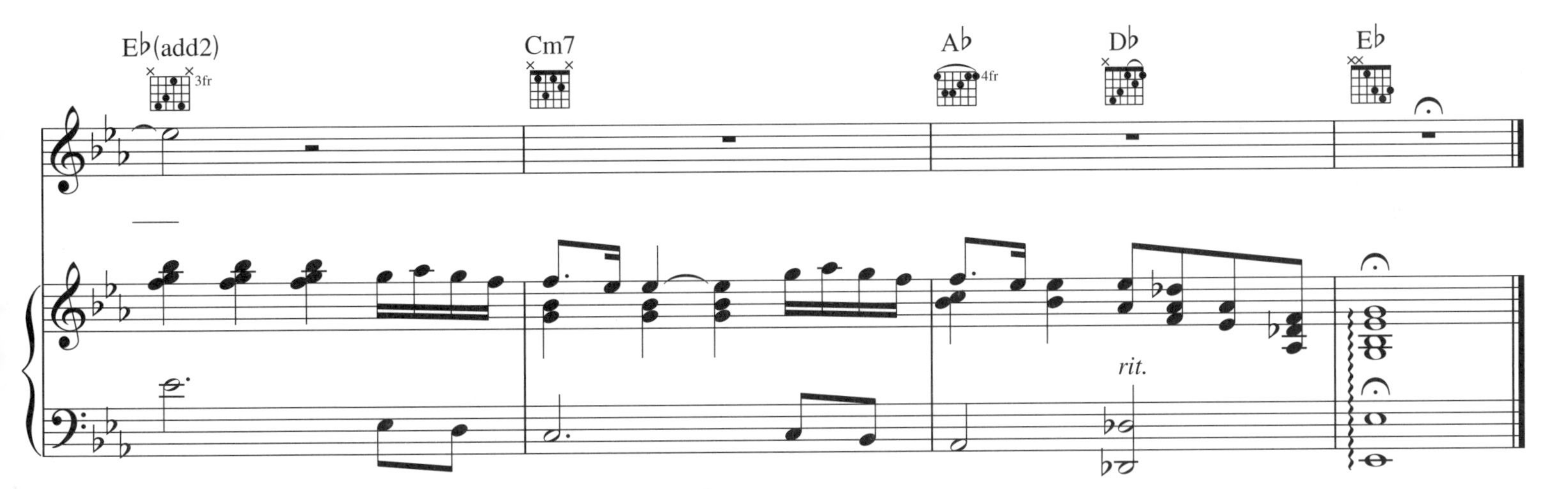
E♭(add2)
3fr
Cm7
A♭
4fr
D♭
E♭
rit.

JESUS TAKE THE WHEEL

Words and Music by BRETT JAMES,
GORDIE SAMPSON and HILLARY LINDSEY

1
Bm7
A
Gsus2
faith and gas - o - line.
It'd been a long hard year.
She had a

2
Bm7
A
Gsus2
she did - n't e - ven have time to cry.
She was so scared.
She threw her

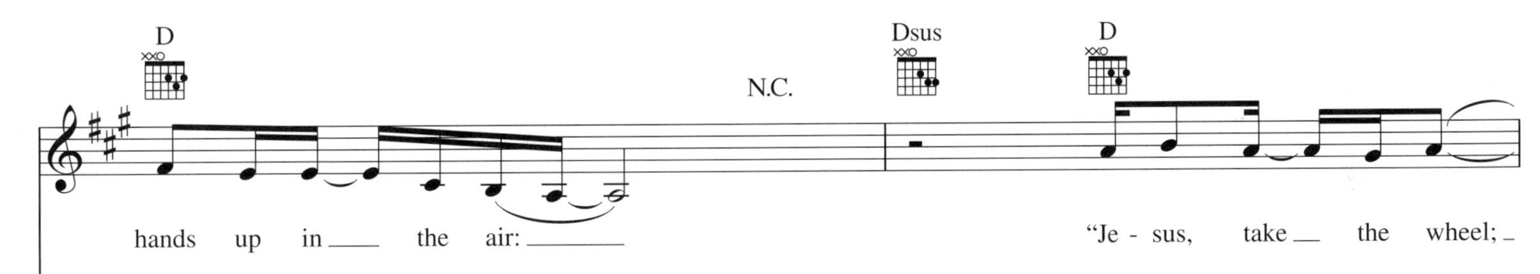
D
N.C.
Dsus
D
hands up in the air:
"Je - sus, take the wheel;

A
E
Bm
A/C♯
take it from my hands,
'cause I can't do this on my own.

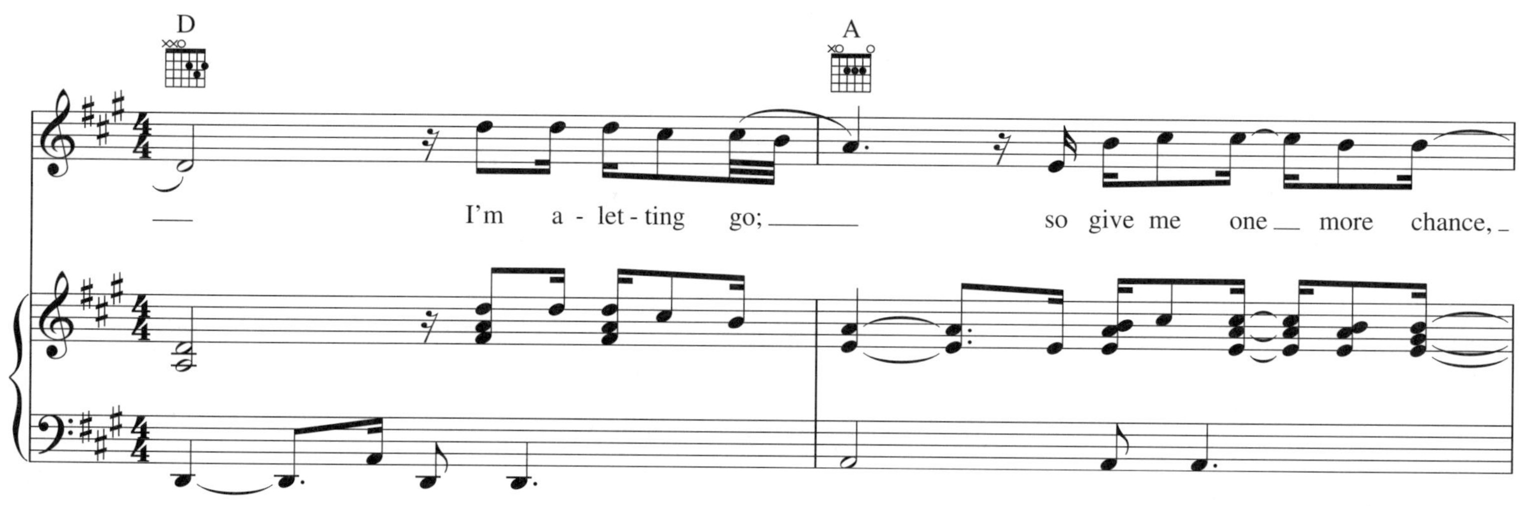
D
A
I'm a - let - ting go;
so give me one more chance,

To Coda
E
Bm
A/C♯
D
Dsus
save me from this road I'm on.

D
A/C♯
Bm7
A
Je - sus, take the wheel."

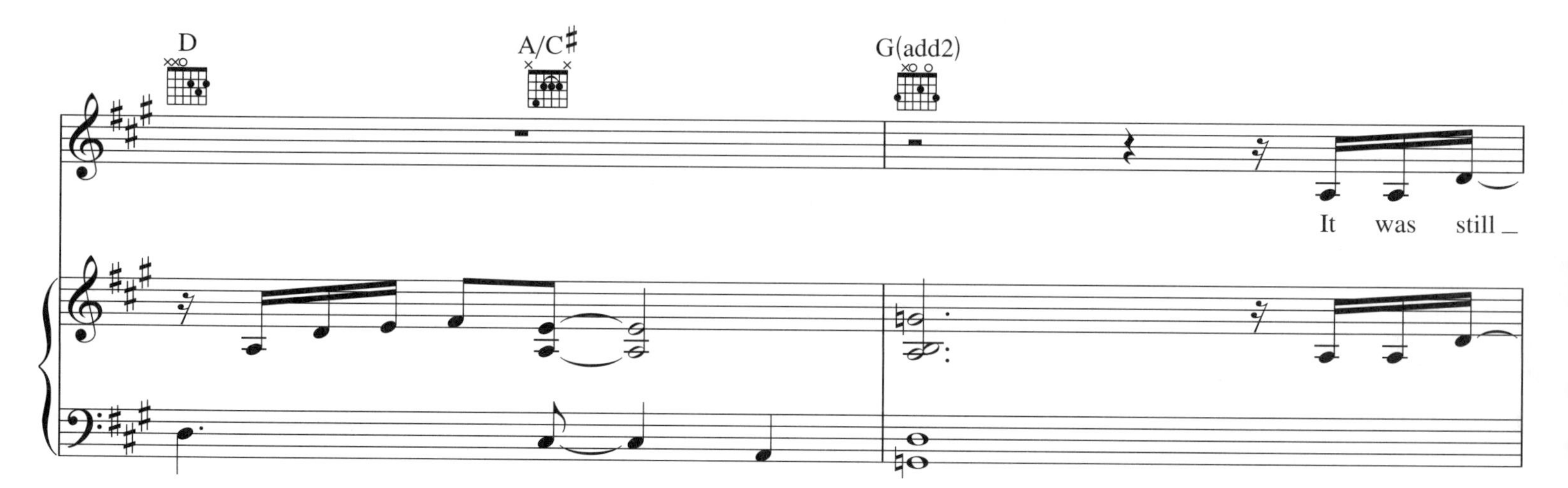
D
A/C♯
G(add2)
It was still

D
A/C♯
Bm7
A
get-ting cold-er when she made it to the shoul-der and the car came to a stop; and she cried

D
A/C♯
Bm7
A
when she saw that ba-by in the back seat, sleep-ing like a rock. And for the first

D
A/C♯
Bm7
A
time in a long time, she bowed her head to pray. She said, "I'm

Gsus2
D/F♯
Gsus2
3
sor-ry for the way I've been liv-ing my life. I know I've got to change; so from

D
Dsus
D
D.S. al Coda
now on, to - night,
Je - sus, take the wheel;

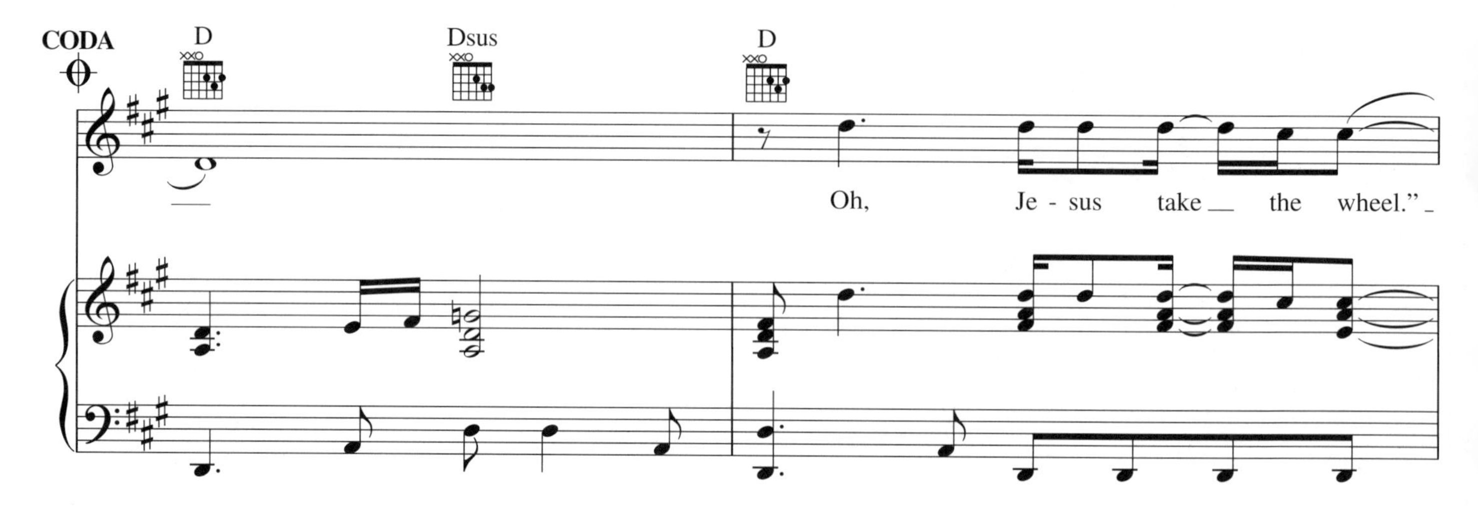
CODA
D
Dsus
D
Oh, Je - sus take the wheel.”

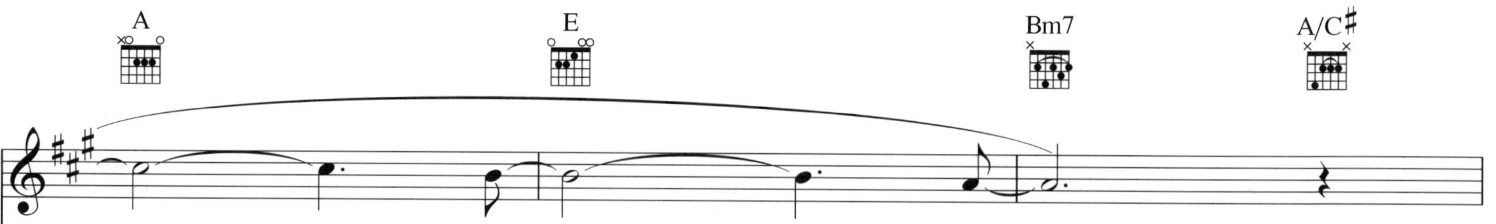
A
E
Bm7
A/C♯

D
A
“Oh, I'm a - let - ting go;
so give me one more

E
Bm
A/C♯
chance, save me from this road I'm on,
D
Bm
A/C♯
D
Dsus
from this road I'm on.
D
D
A/C♯
Bm7
A
Je - sus, take the wheel.
Oh, take it,
1
D
A/C♯
Bm7
A
take it from me."
Vocal continues ad lib.
2
D
A/C♯
G(add2)

LOVE OF MY LIFE

Words and Music by JIM BRICKMAN
and TOM DOUGLAS

Gsus
G/B
Csus
C
G/B
fall through the cracks and lose my track in this crazy, lonely world. Sometimes it's
think if I'd never met you, about all the things I'd missed. Sometimes it's
Am
C/G
so hard to believe, when my nights can be so long, and
so hard to believe when a love can be so strong, and
D/F♯
Gsus
G
C/E
faith gave me the strength and kept me holding on.
faith gave me the strength and kept me holding on.
You are the love
F
G
C
G/B
Am7
Gsus
of my life, and I'm so glad you found me. You are the love

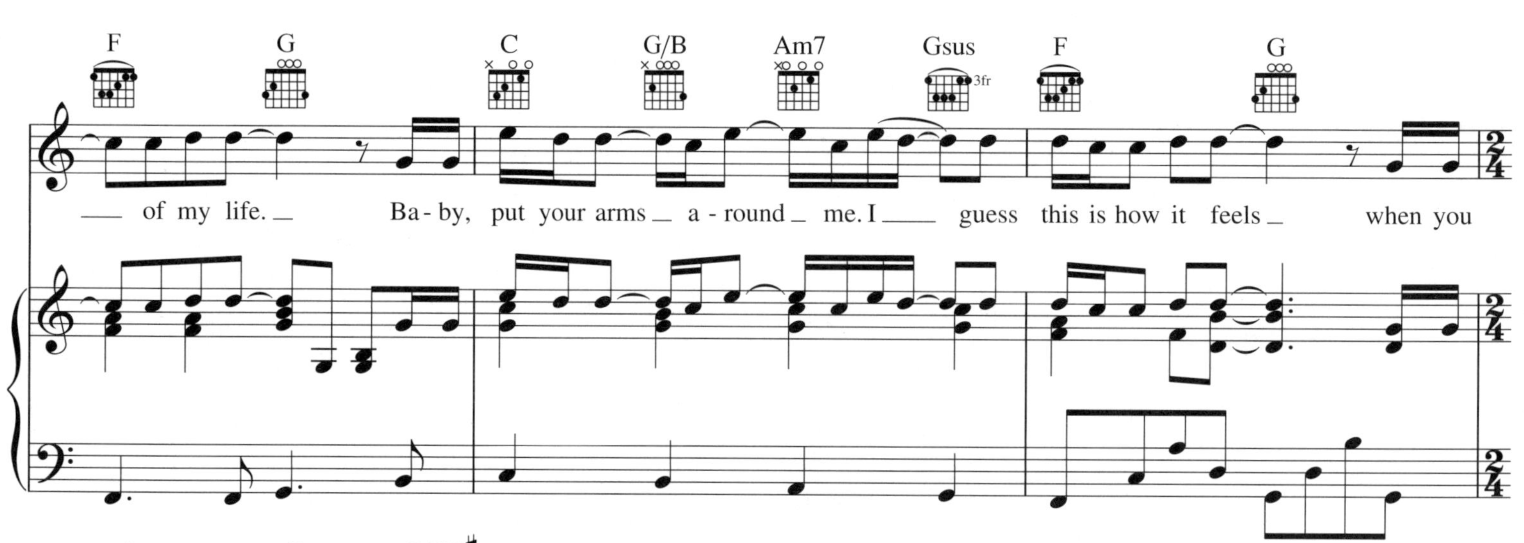
F
G
C
G/B
Am7
Gsus
F
G
of my life.
Ba - by, put your arms a - round me. I
guess this is how it feels
when you

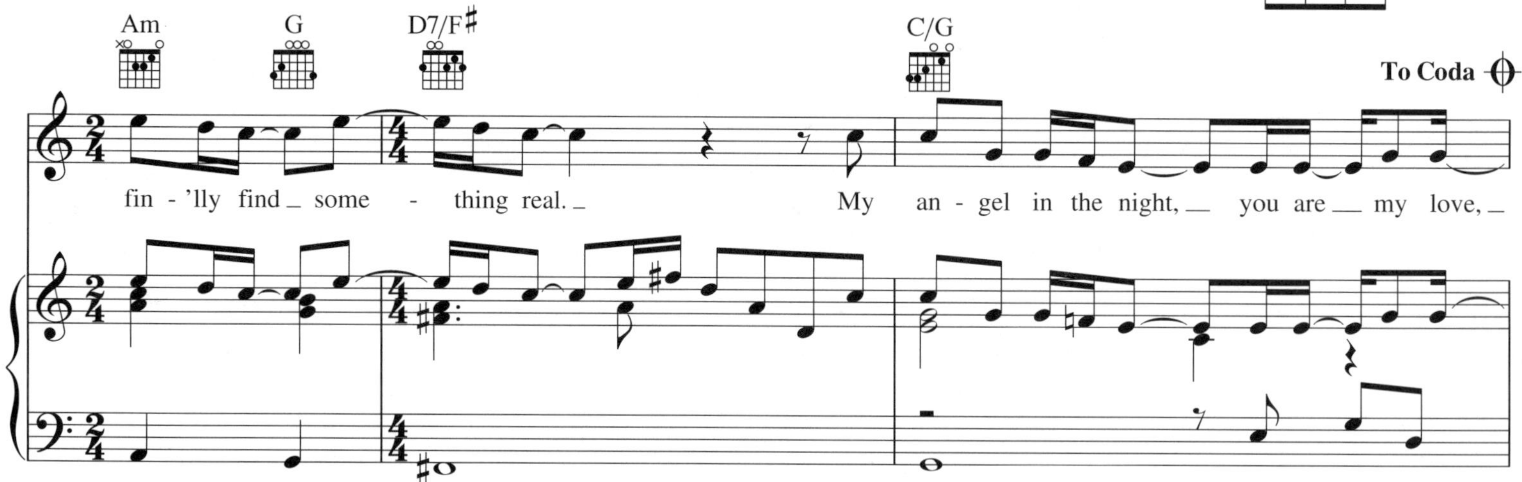
Am
G
D7/F♯
C/G
To Coda
fin - 'lly find some - thing real.
My an - gel in the night,
you are my love,

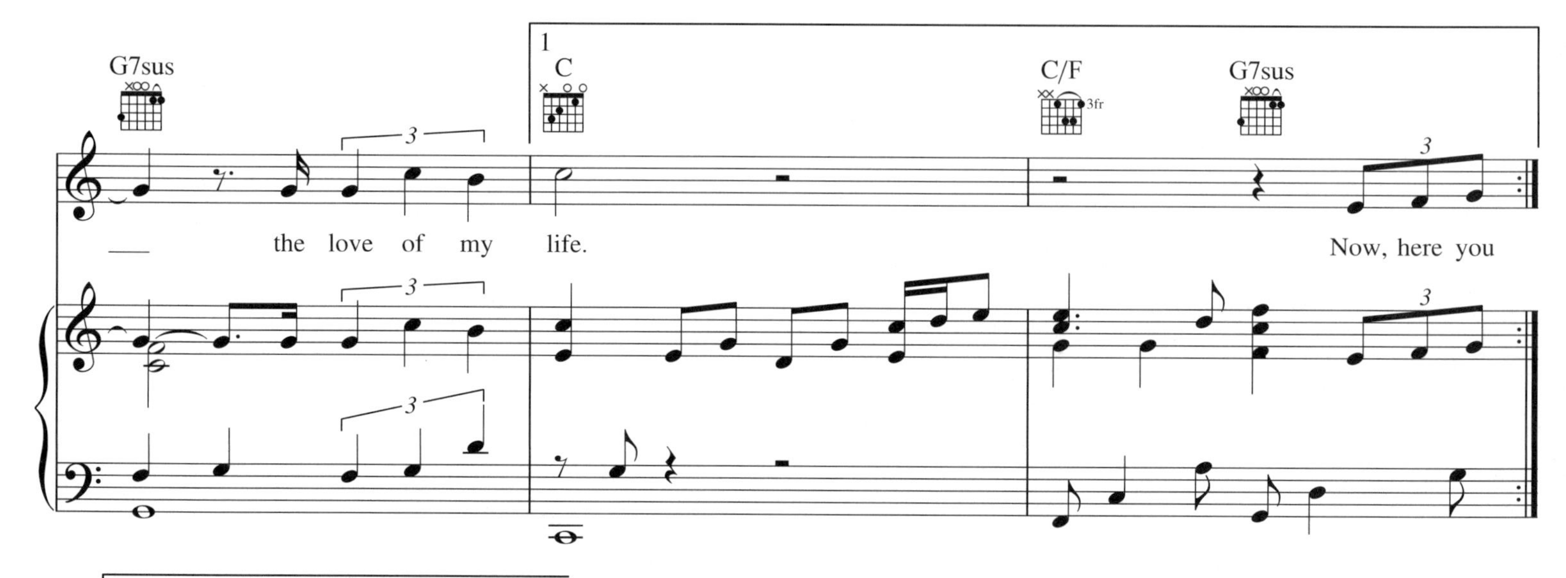
G7sus
1
C
C/F
G7sus
the love of my life.
Now, here you

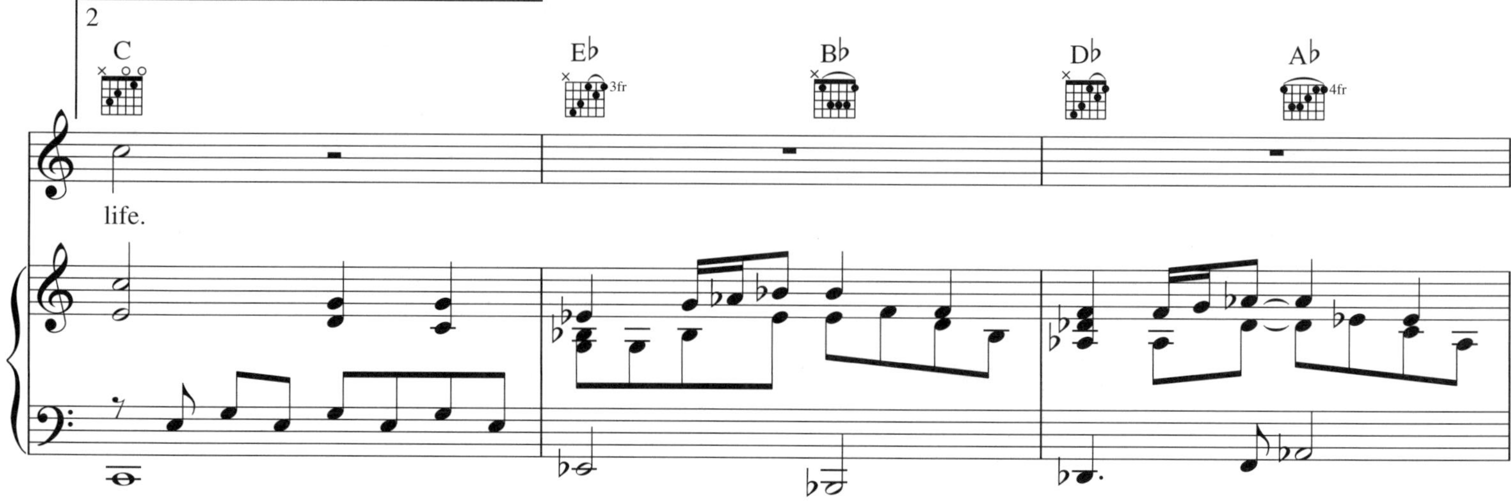
2
C
E♭
B♭
D♭
A♭
life.

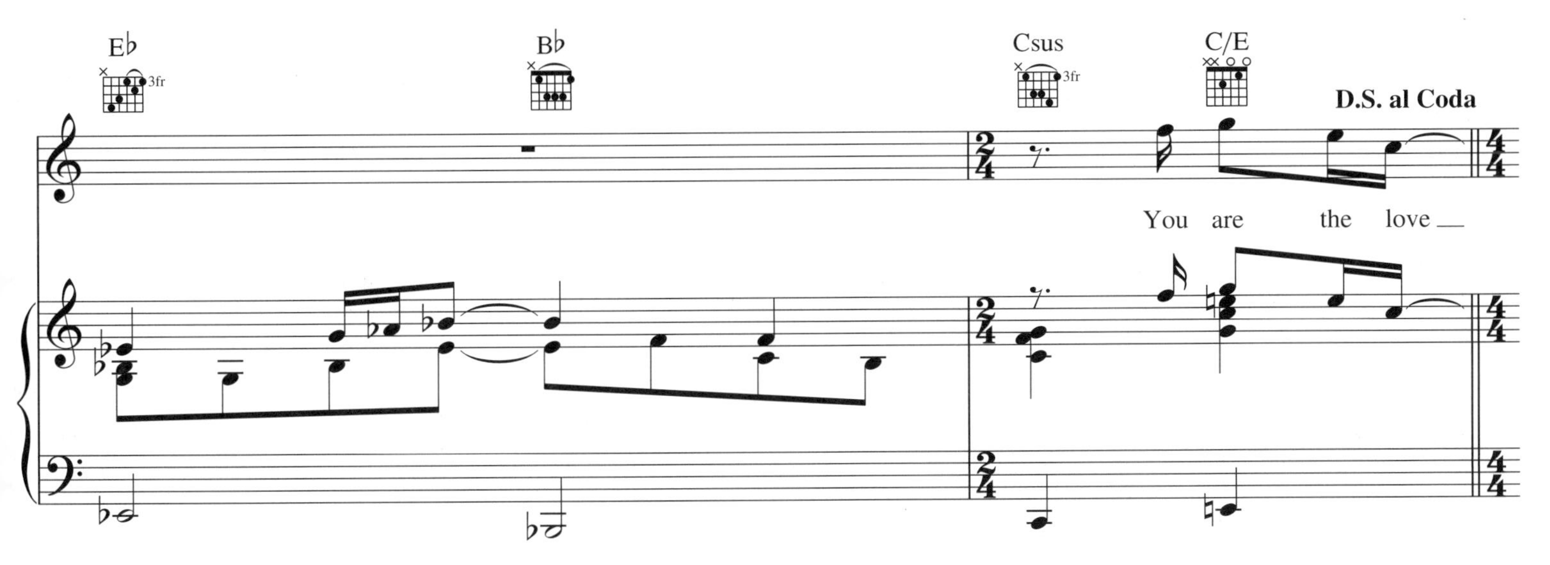
E♭
3fr
B♭
Csus
3fr
C/E
D.S. al Coda
You are the love

CODA
G7sus
Dm9
3fr
my an - gel in the night, you are my

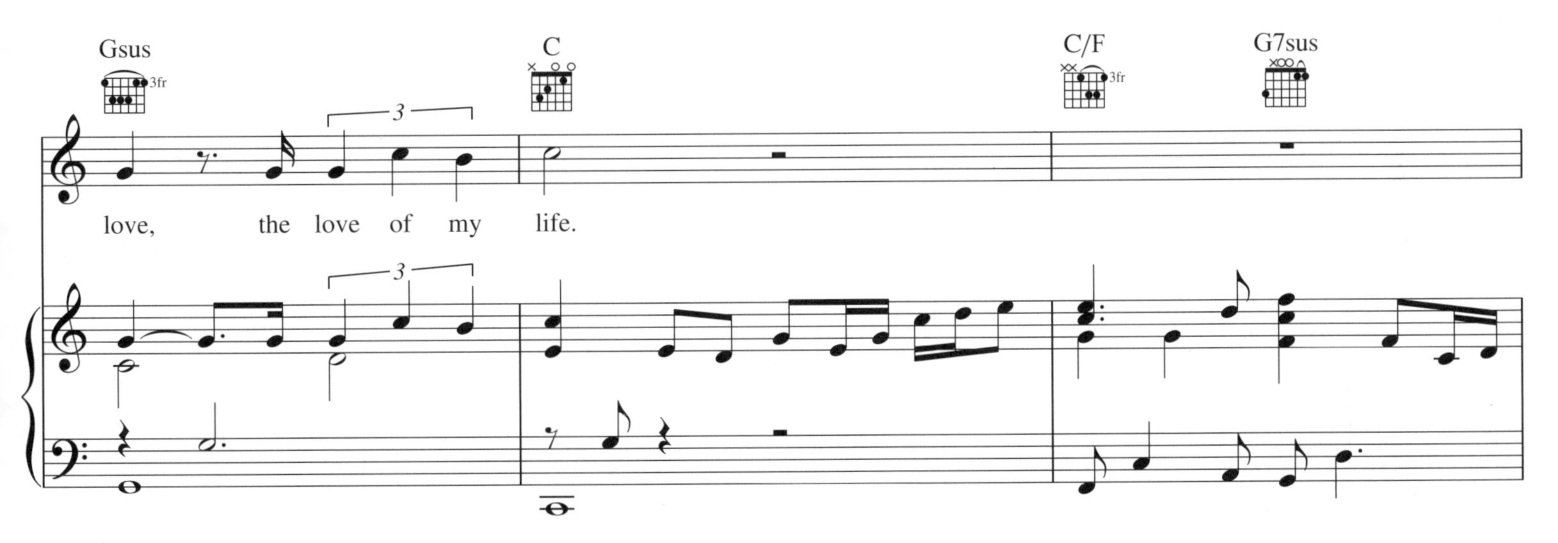
Gsus
3fr
C
C/F
3fr
G7sus
3
love, the love of my life.
3

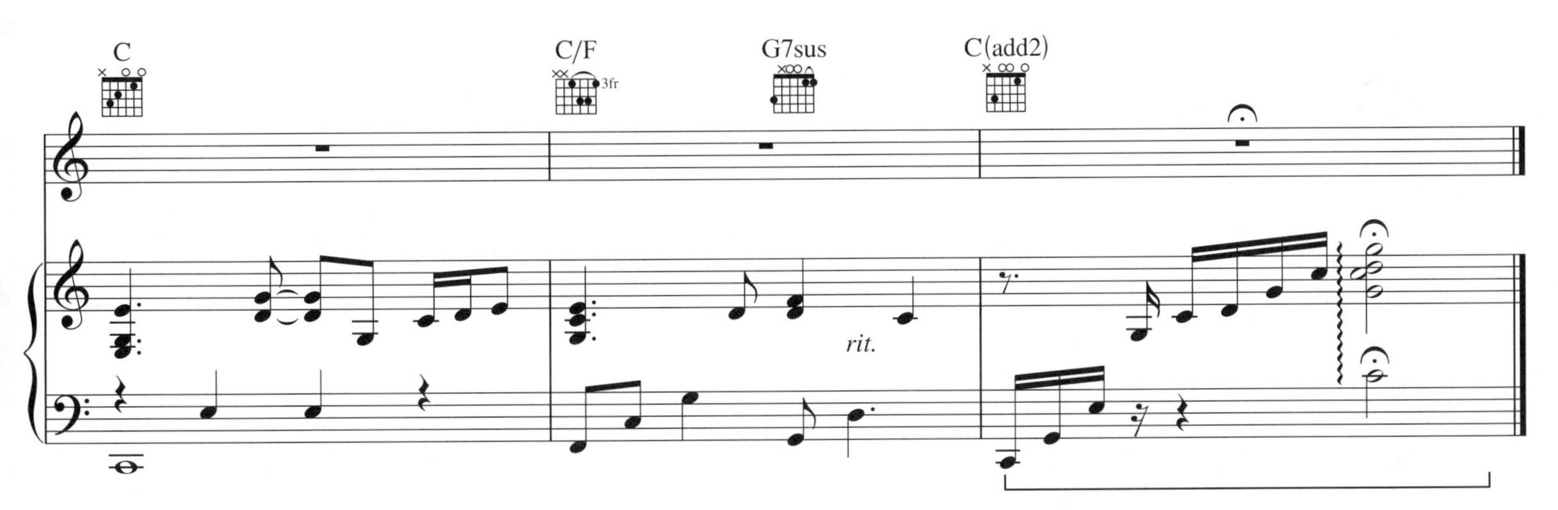
C
C/F
3fr
G7sus
C(add2)
rit.

A MOMENT LIKE THIS

Words and Music by JOHN REID
and JORGEN KJELL ELOFSSON

Moderately slow

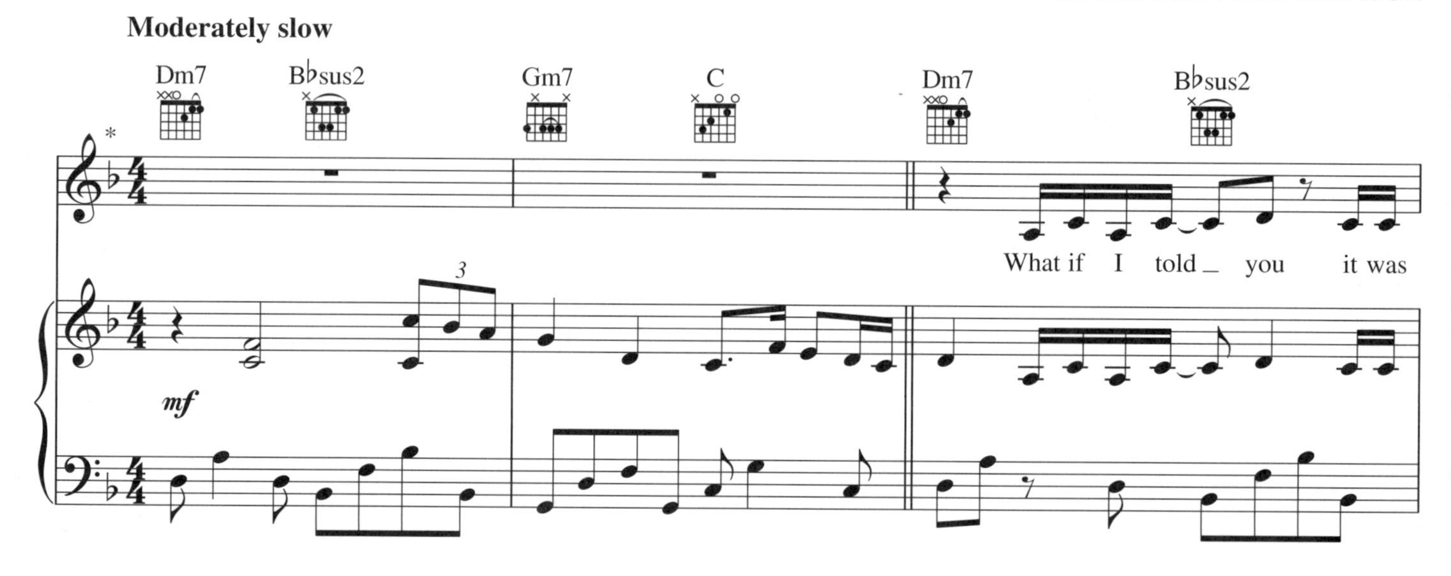

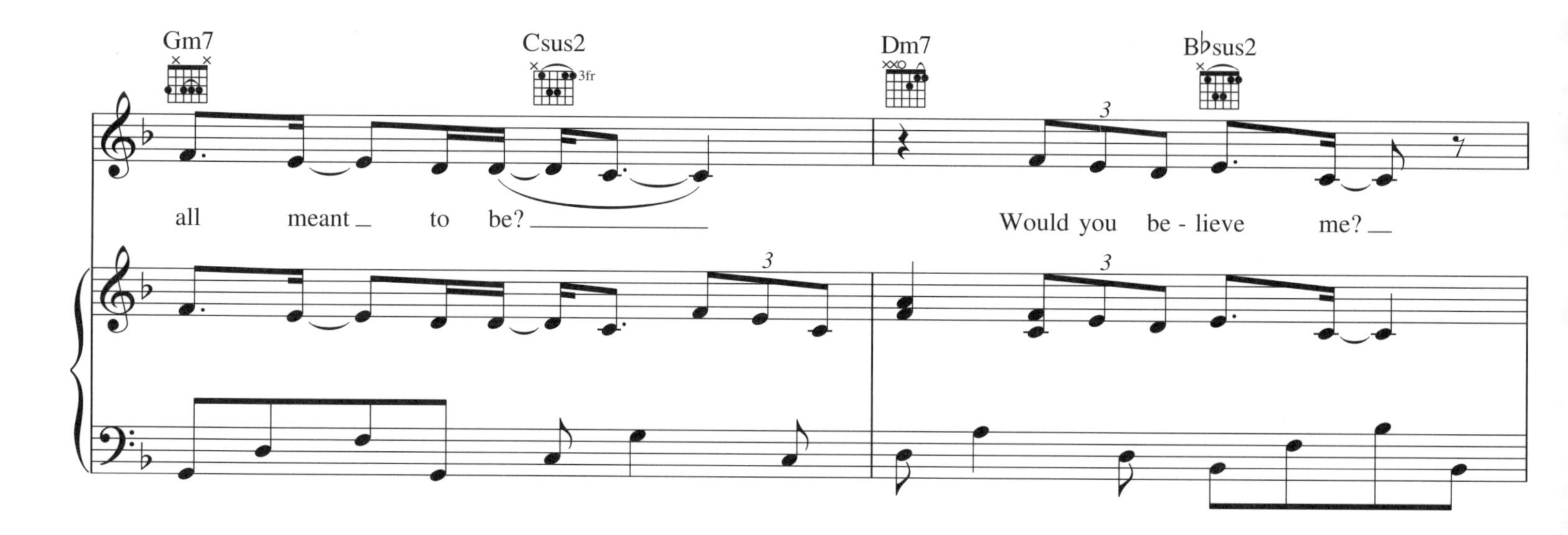

* *Recorded a half step lower.*

E♭(add2)
6fr
B♭(add2)
3fr
tell me that you don't think I'm cra - zy when I
Gm7
C
Dsus
tell you love has come here and now. A mo - ment like this.
G
D/F♯
C
D
Some peo - ple wait a life - time for a mo - ment like this.

G
D/F♯
C
D
Some peo - ple search for - ev - er for that one spe - cial kiss.

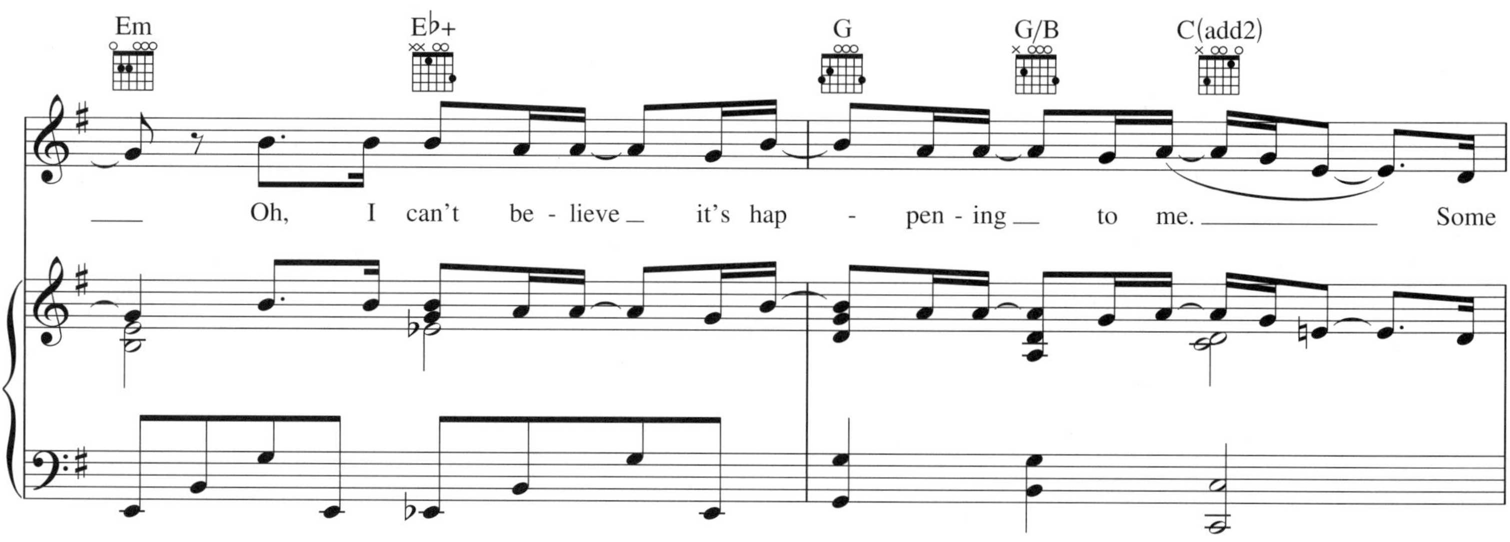
Em
E♭+
G
G/B
C(add2)
Oh, I can't be - lieve it's hap - pen - ing to me. Some

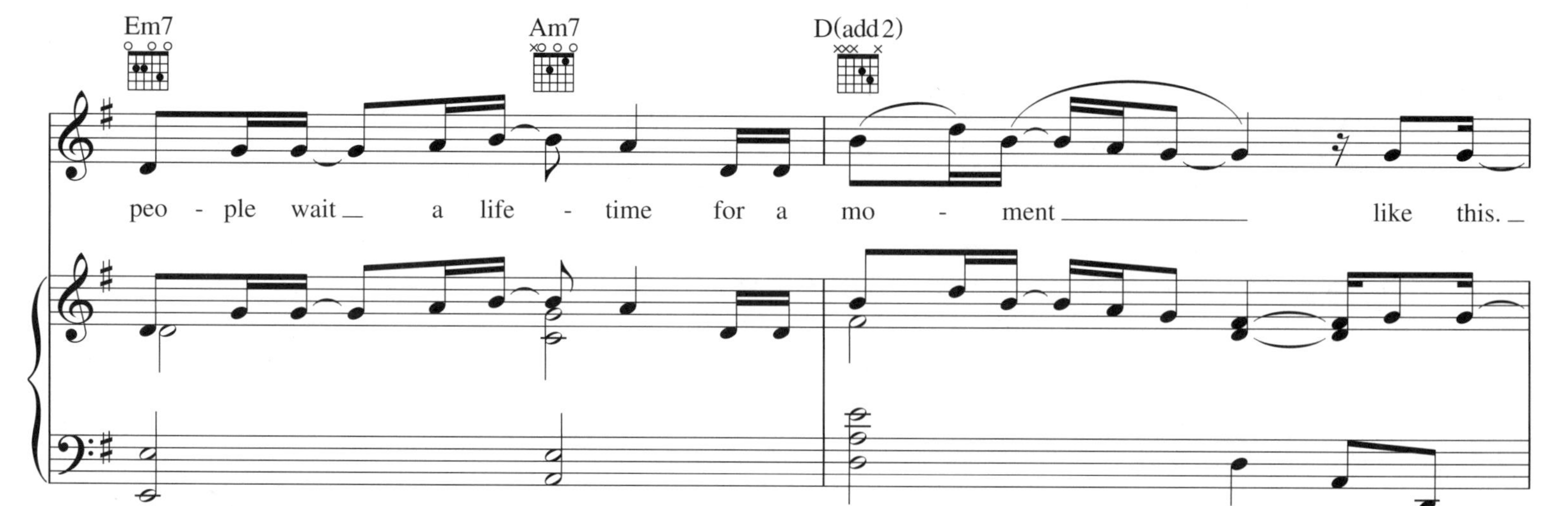
Em7
Am7
D(add2)
peo - ple wait a life - time for a mo - ment like this.

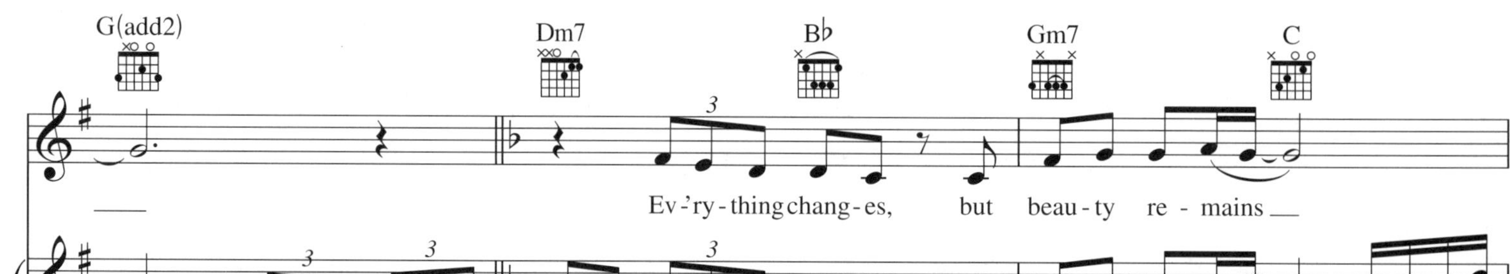

G(add2)
Dm7
B♭
Gm7
C
Ev-'ry-thing chang-es, but beau-ty re - mains

Dm7
B♭
Gm7
C
some - thing so ten - der I can't ex - plain.

Dm7
B♭
F/A
Gm7
Well, I may be dream - ing, but still lie a - wake.
E♭
3fr
B♭(add2)
3fr
Can't we make this dream last for - ev - er?
And I'll
Gm7
C
Dsus
cher - ish all the love we share.
A mo - ment like this.
G
D/F♯
C
D
Some peo - ple wait a life - time for a mo - ment like this.

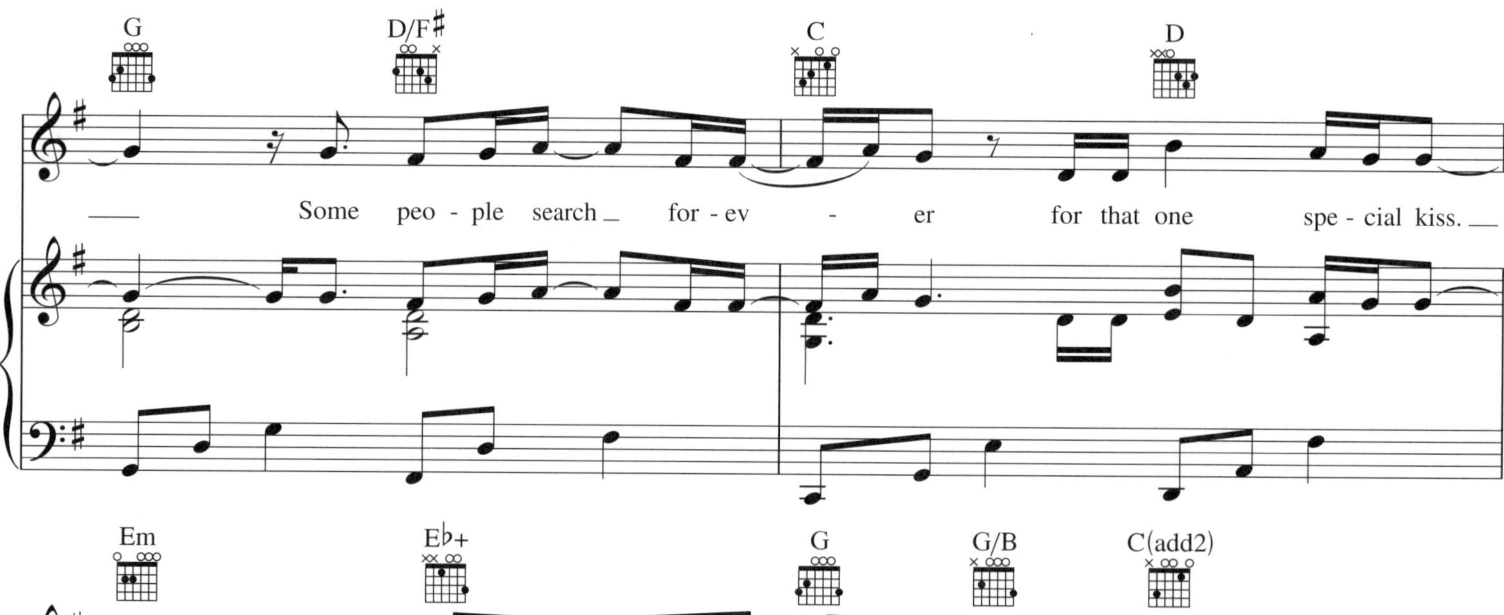
G
D/F♯
C
D
Some peo - ple search for - ev - er for that one spe - cial kiss.

Em
E♭+
G
G/B
C(add2)
Oh, I can't be - lieve it's hap - pen - ing to me. Some

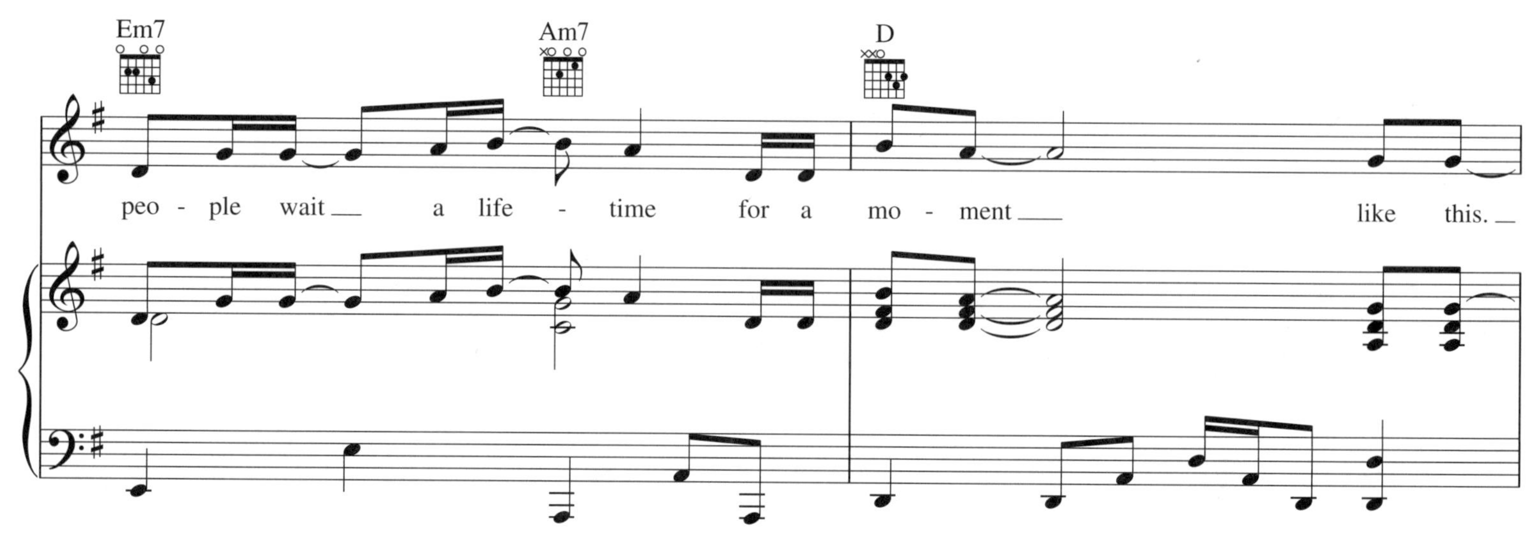
Em7
Am7
D
peo - ple wait a life - time for a mo - ment like this.

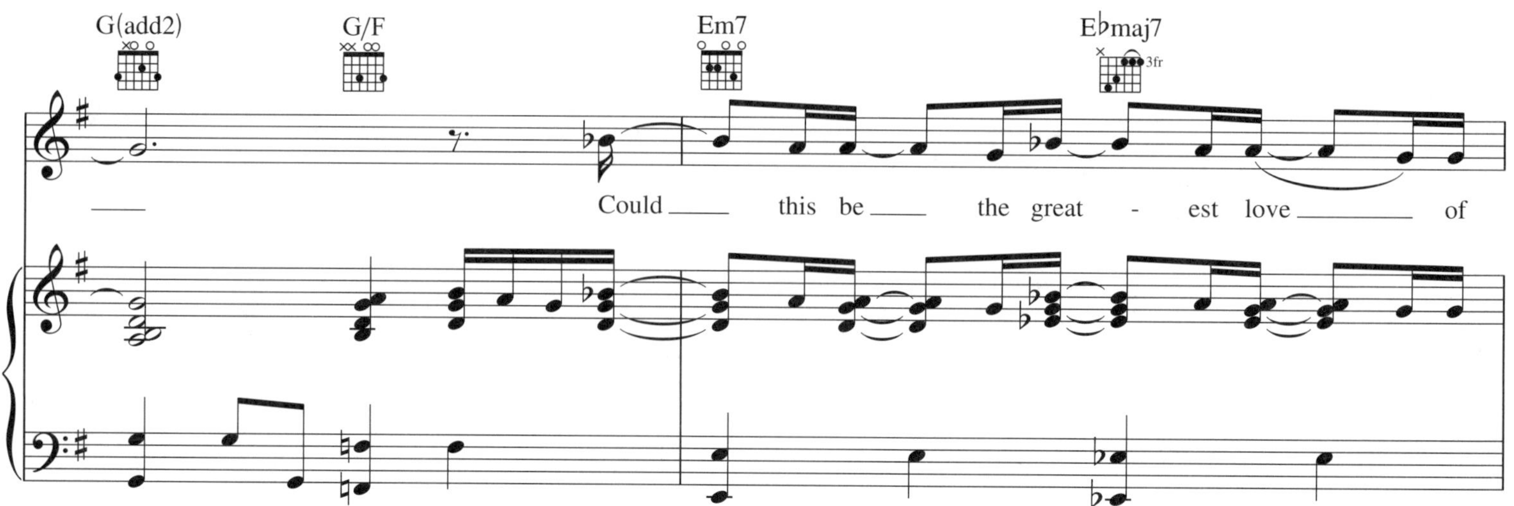
G(add2)
G/F
Em7
E♭maj7
3fr
Could this be the great - est love of

G
G/F
Em7
E♭maj7
3fr
all? I wan-na know that you will catch me when I fall,
Em7
E♭+
G
G/B
C(add2)
3
so let me tell you this: some
Em7
Am7
D(add2)
peo-ple wait a life - time for a mo-ment like this.
A
E/G♯
D
E
Some peo-ple wait a life - time for a mo - ment like this.

A
E/G♯
D
E
Some peo - ple search for - ev - er for that one spe - cial kiss.
F♯m
F+
A
A/C♯
D
Oh, I can't be - lieve it's hap - pen - ing to me.
Some
F♯m7
Bm
F♯m/E
E
A/E
peo - ple wait a life - time for a mo - ment like this.

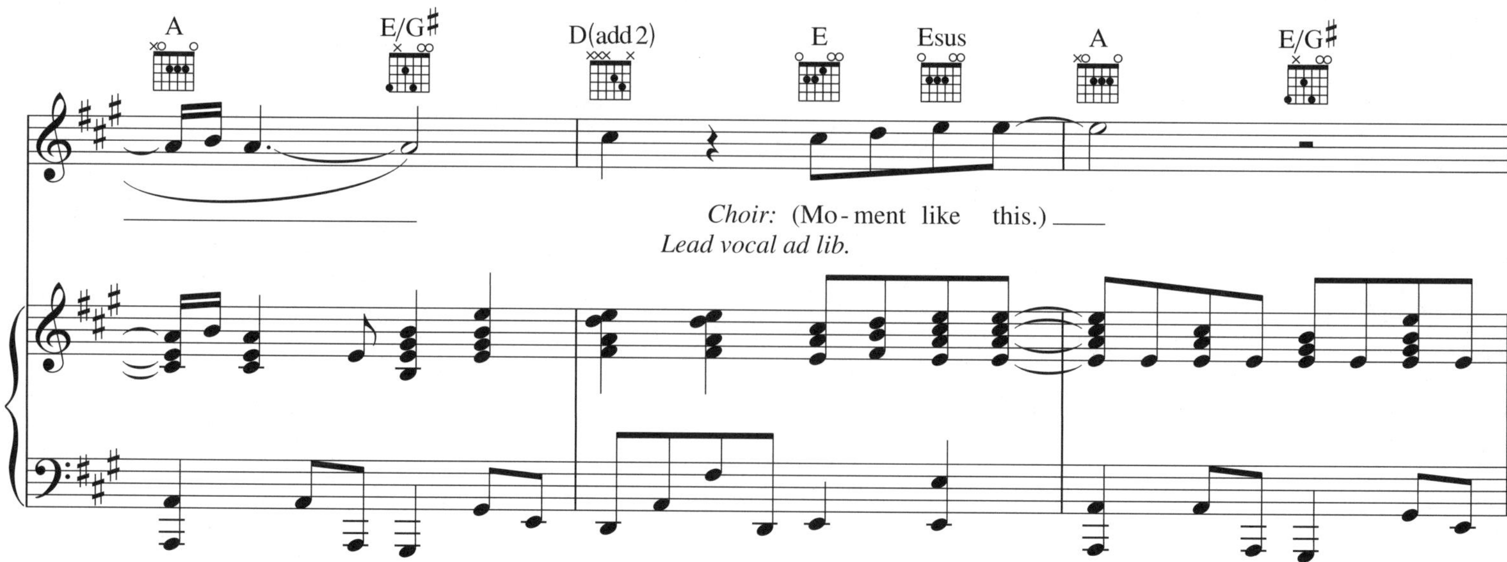
A
E/G♯
D(add 2)
E
Esus
A
E/G♯
Choir: (Mo - ment like this.)
Lead vocal ad lib.

D
Esus
E
F♯m
F+
Lead vocal:
(Mo - ment like.) Oh, I can't be - lieve it's hap -
A
A/C♯
D
F♯m7
Bm7
- pen - ing to me. Some peo - ple wait a life - time for a
E
A5
5fr
E/G♯
mo - ment like this,
D(add2)
E
A(add2)
oh, like this.
rit.

MY HEART WILL GO ON
(Love Theme from 'Titanic')
from the Paramount and Twentieth Century Fox Motion Picture TITANIC

Music by JAMES HORNER
Lyric by WILL JENNINGS

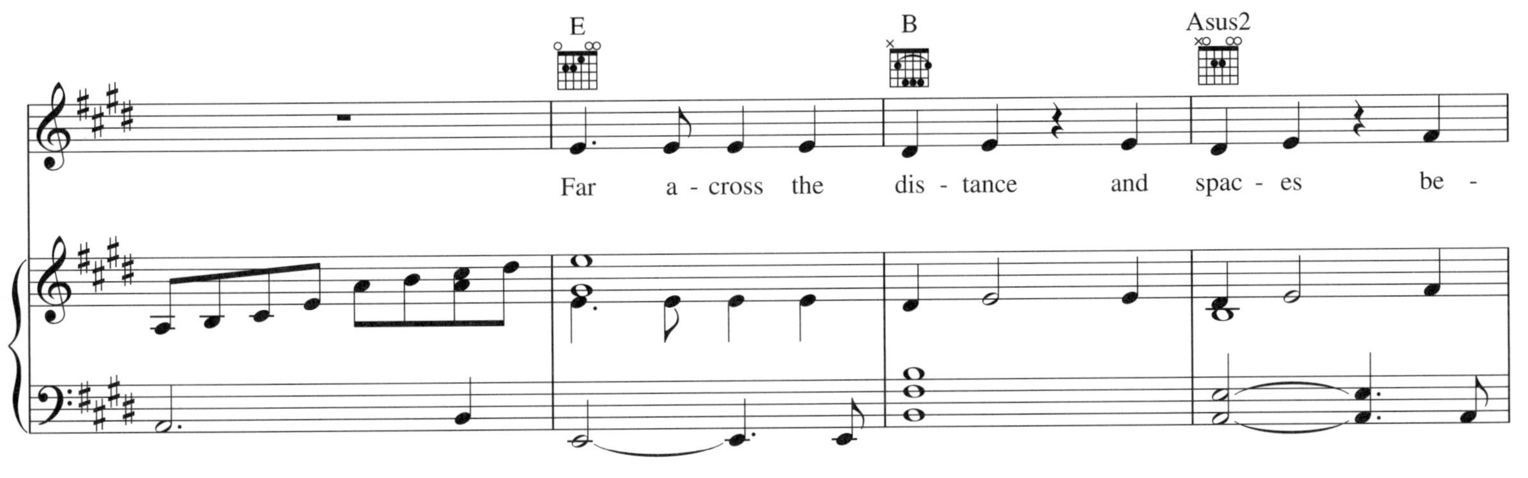
E
B
Asus2
Far a - cross the dis - tance and spac - es be -

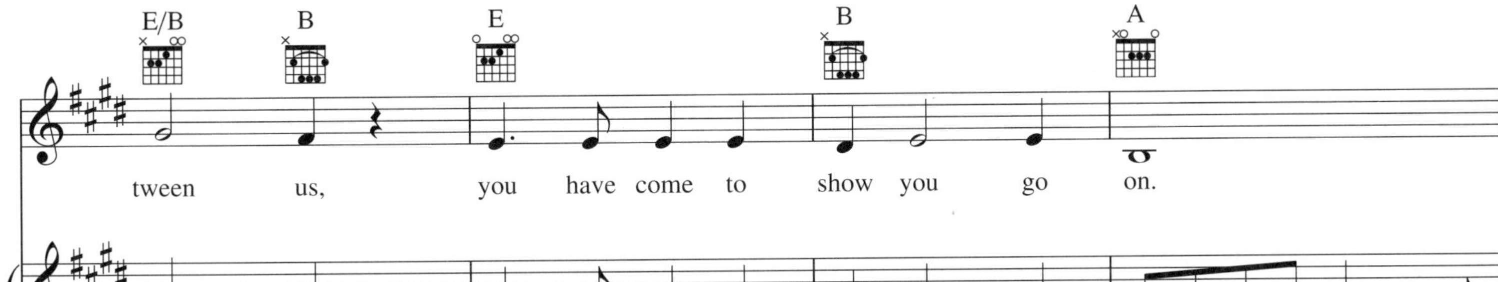
E/B
B
E
B
A
tween us, you have come to show you go on.

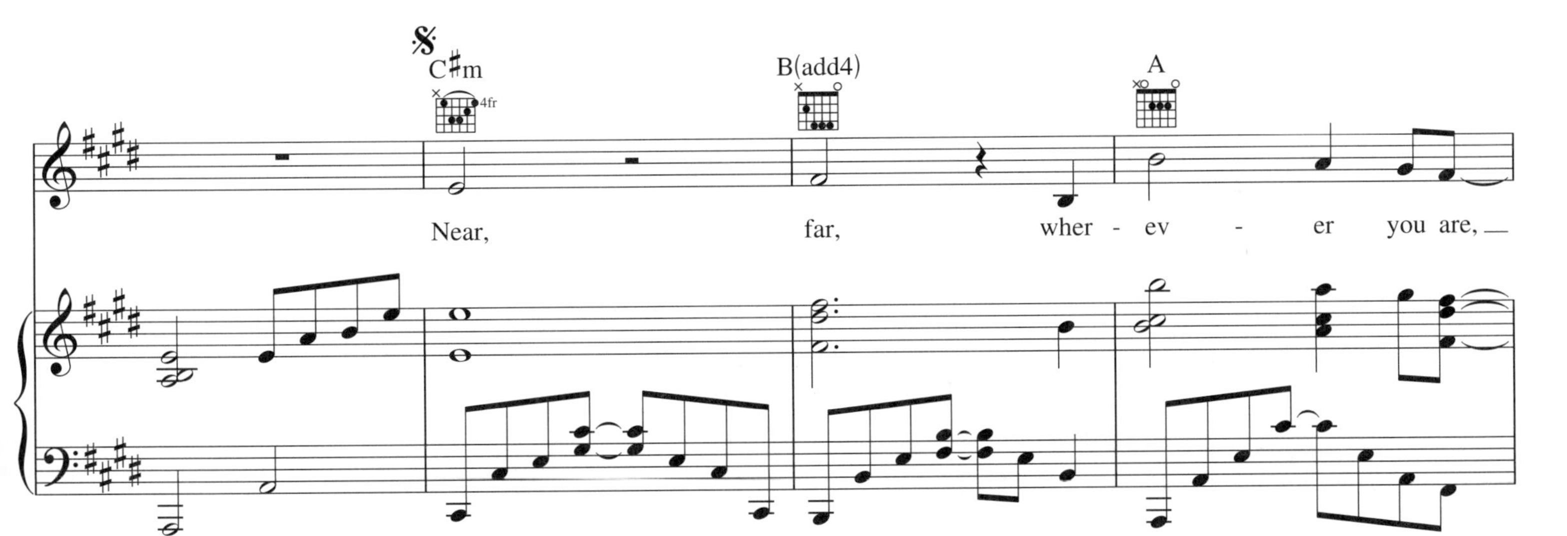
C♯m
4fr
B(add4)
A
Near, far, wher - ev - er you are,

B
C♯m
4fr
B(add9)
7fr
A
I be - lieve that the heart does go on.

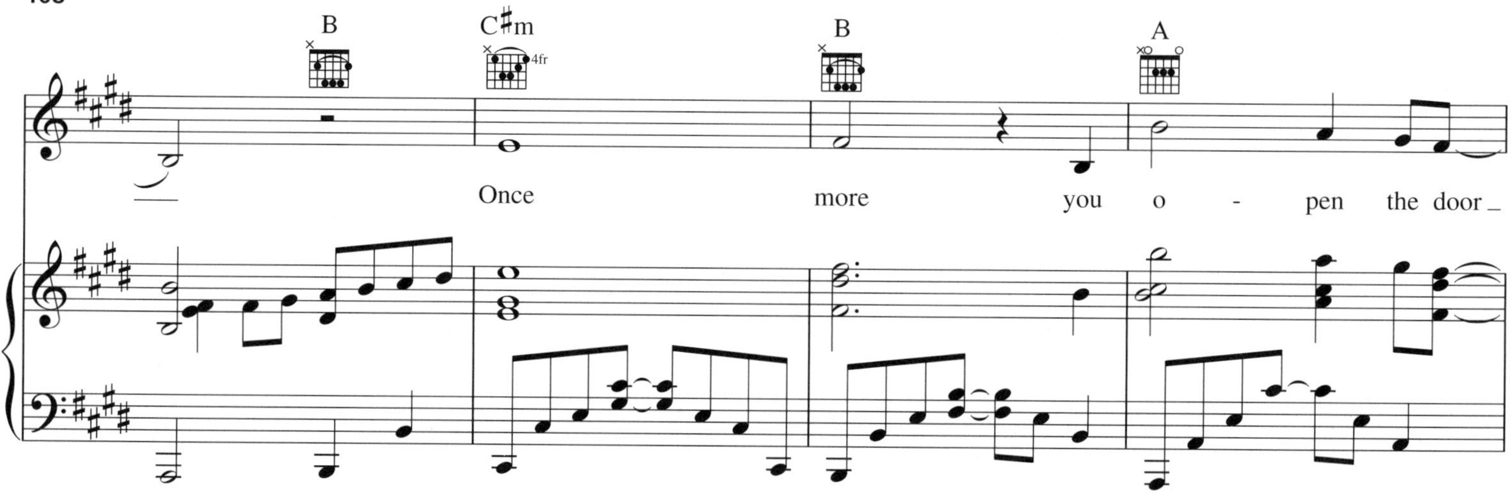
B
C♯m
4fr
B
A
Once more you o - pen the door

B
C♯m
4fr
G♯m
4fr
A
and you're here in my heart, and my heart will go

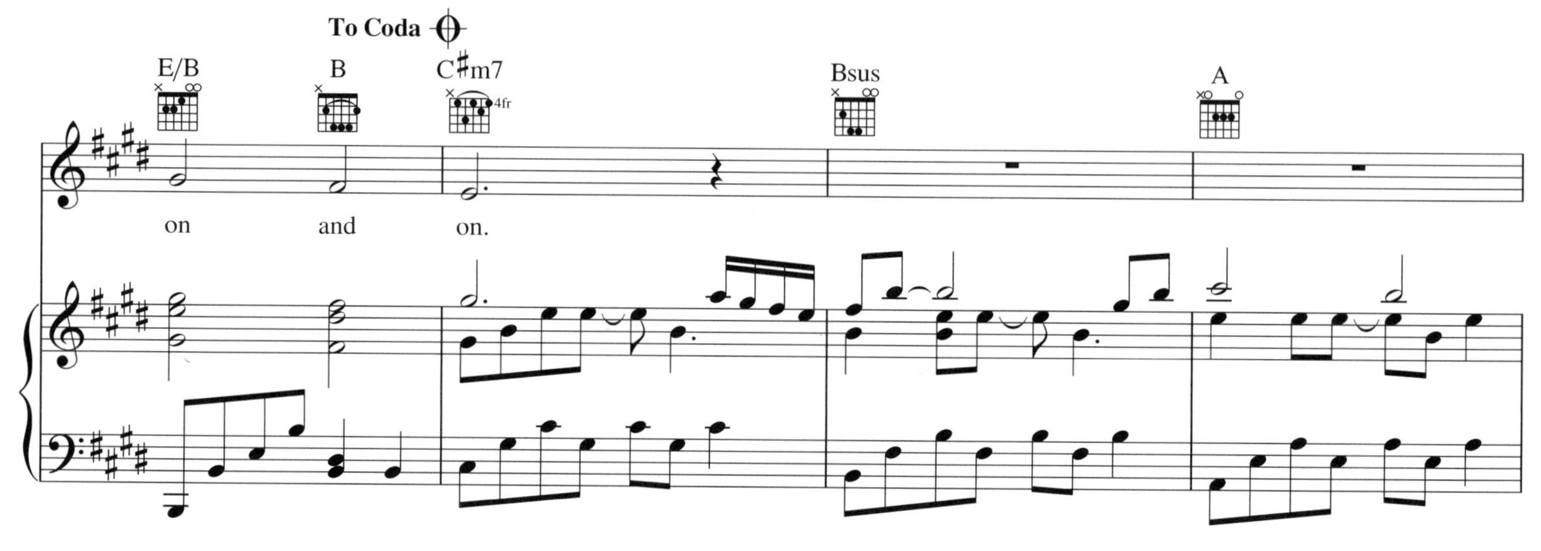
To Coda
E/B
B
C♯m7
4fr
Bsus
A
on and on.

Bsus
B
E
B
Asus2
Love can touch us one time and last for a

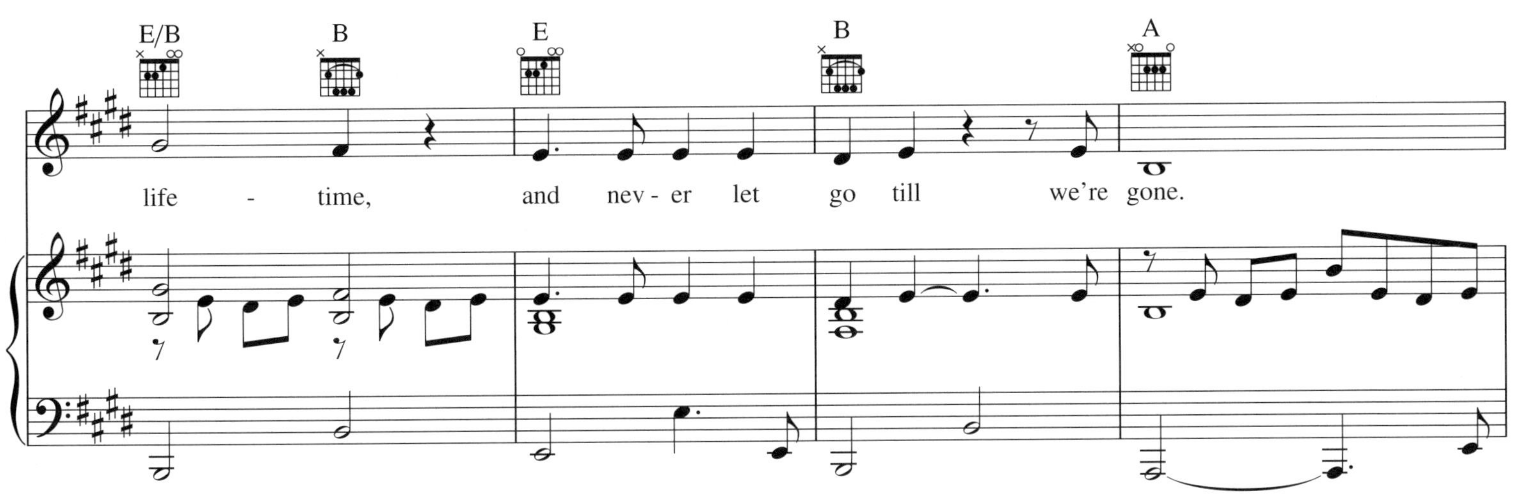
E/B
B
E
B
A
life - time, and nev - er let go till we're gone.

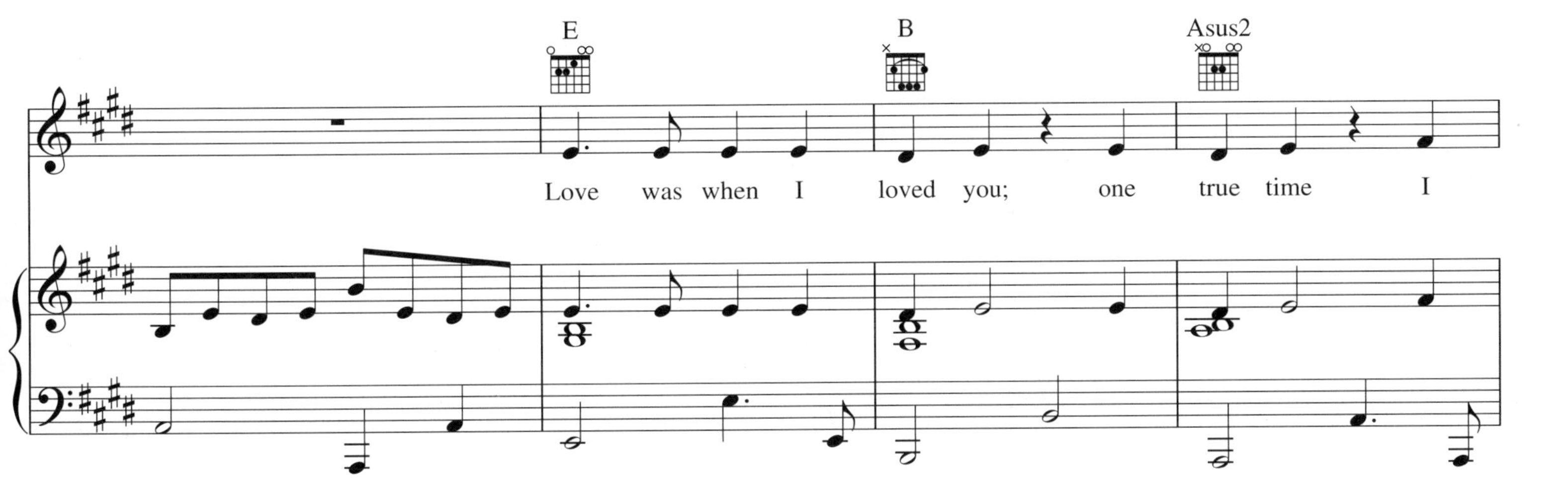
E
B
Asus2
Love was when I loved you; one true time I

E/B
G#7/B#
C#m
4fr
G#m
4fr
Asus2
hold to. In my life we'll al - ways go on.

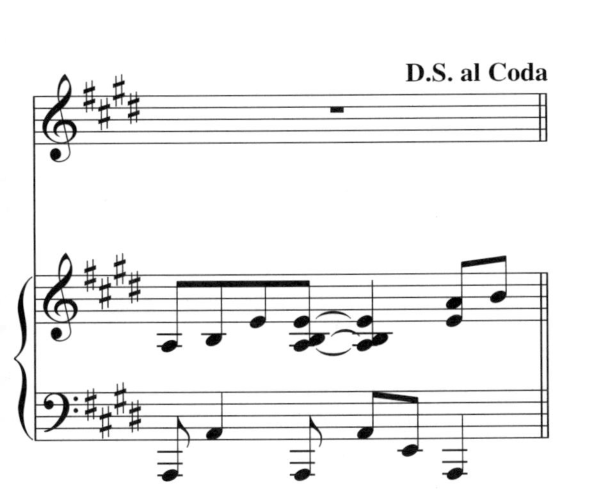
D.S. al Coda

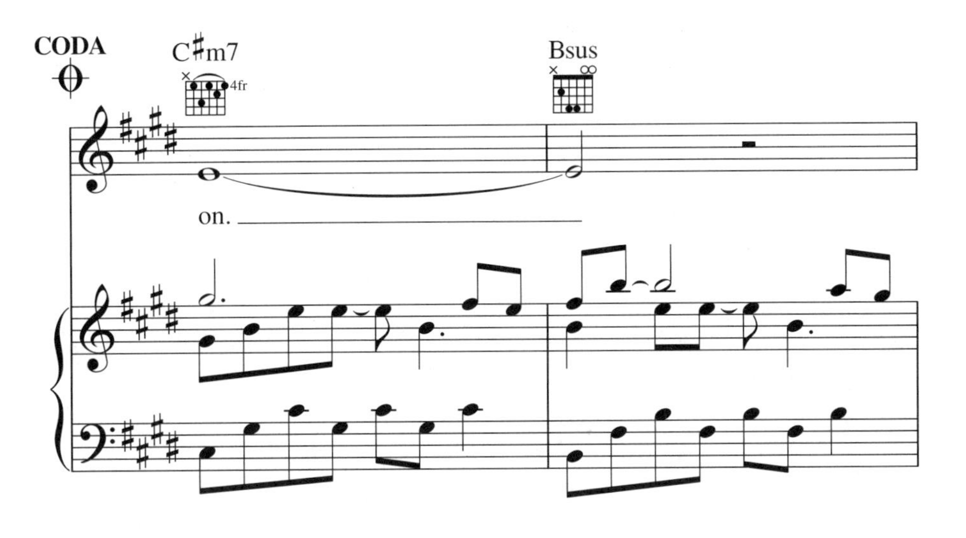
CODA
C#m7
4fr
Bsus
on.

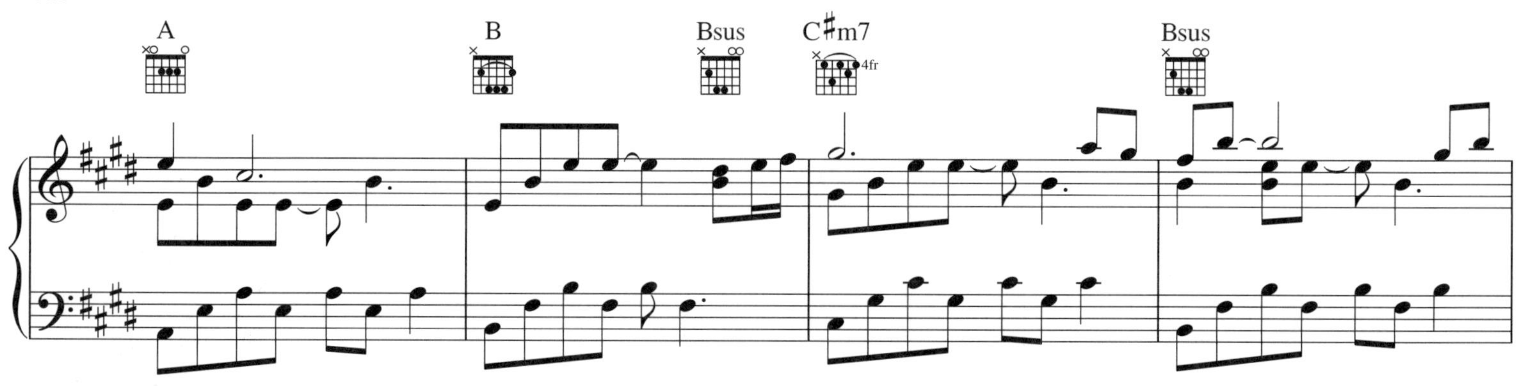
A
B
Bsus
C♯m7
4fr
Bsus

A
C♯m/G♯
4fr
G♯7/F♯
4fr
Fm
E♭
3fr
You're here, there's
f

D♭
E♭
3fr
Fm
E♭
3fr
noth - ing I fear and I know that my heart will go

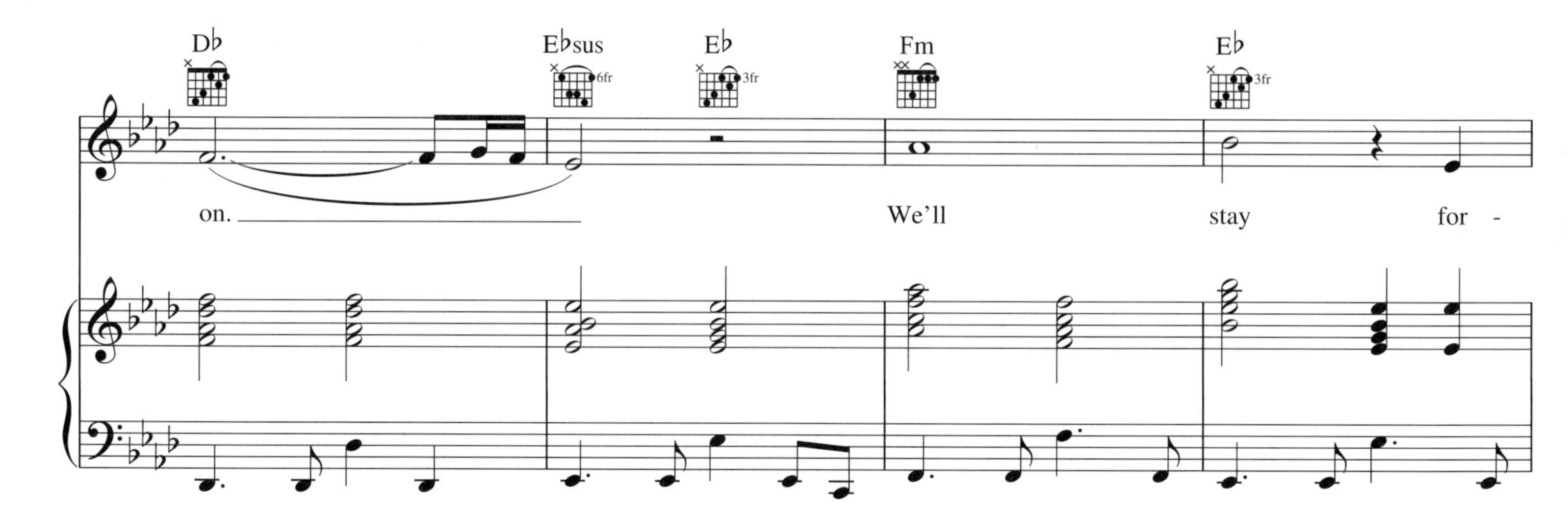
D♭
E♭sus
6fr
E♭
3fr
Fm
E♭
3fr
on. We'll stay for -

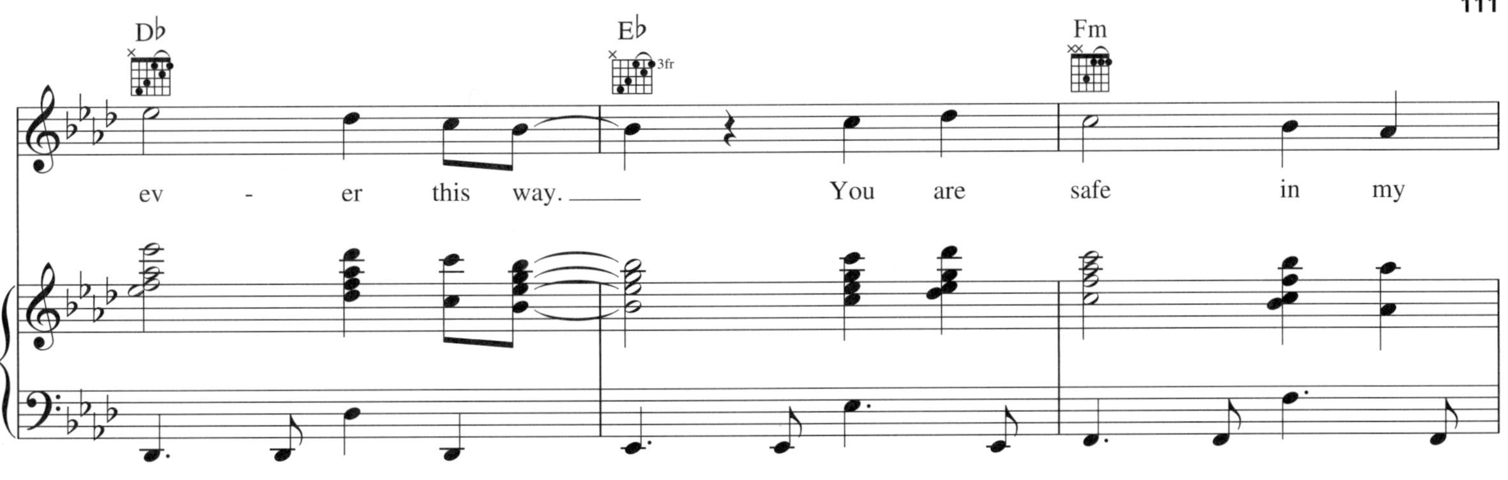
D♭
E♭
3fr
Fm
ev - er this way.
You are safe in my

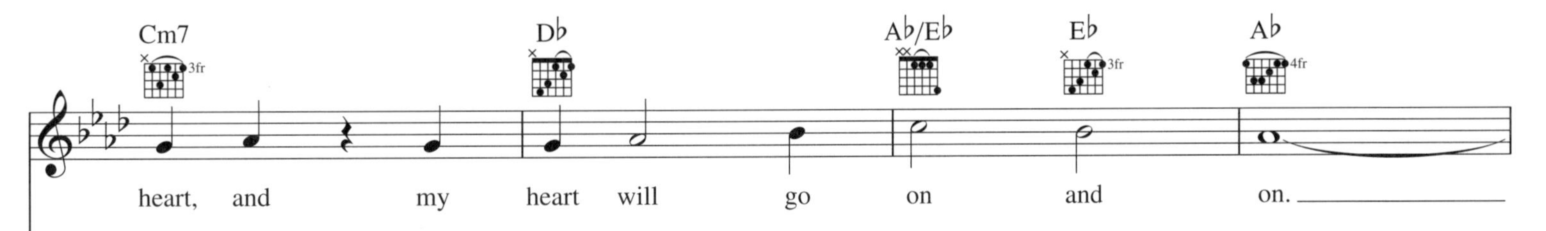
Cm7
3fr
D♭
A♭/E♭
E♭
3fr
A♭
4fr
heart, and my heart will go on and on.

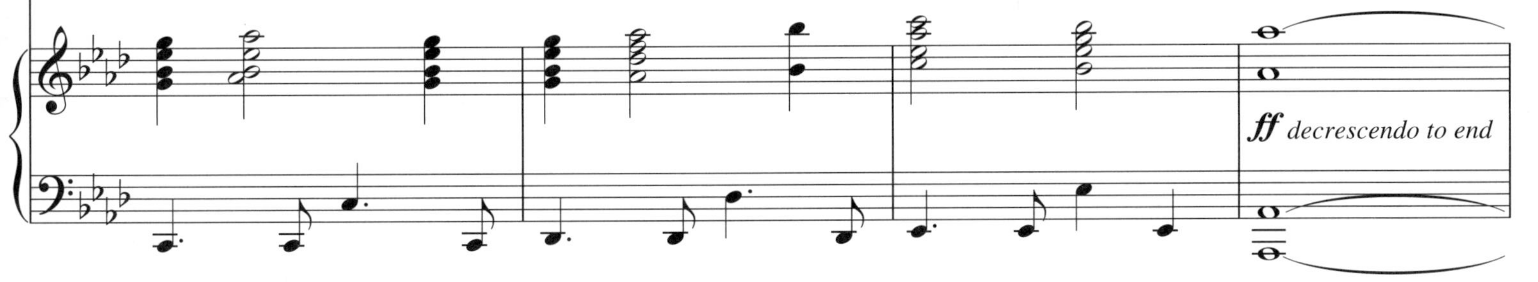
ff decrescendo to end

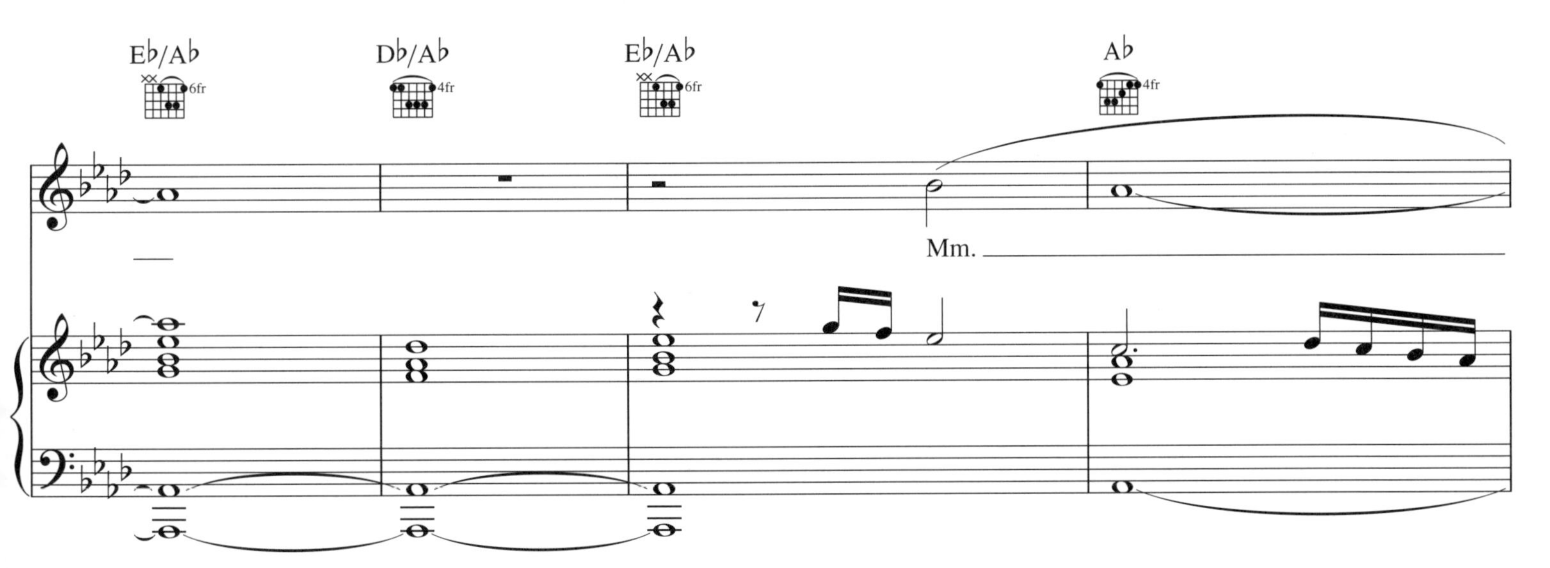
E♭/A♭
6fr
D♭/A♭
4fr
E♭/A♭
6fr
A♭
4fr
Mm.

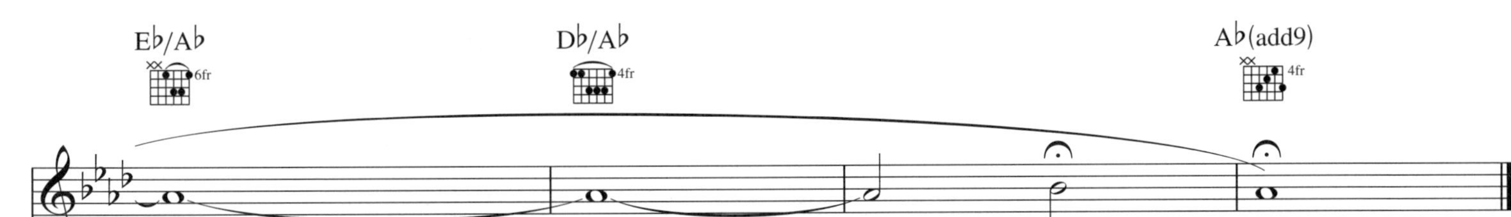
E♭/A♭
6fr
D♭/A♭
4fr
A♭(add9)
4fr

ONLY HOPE

from the Warner Bros. Motion Picture A WALK TO REMEMBER

Words and Music by
JONATHAN FOREMAN

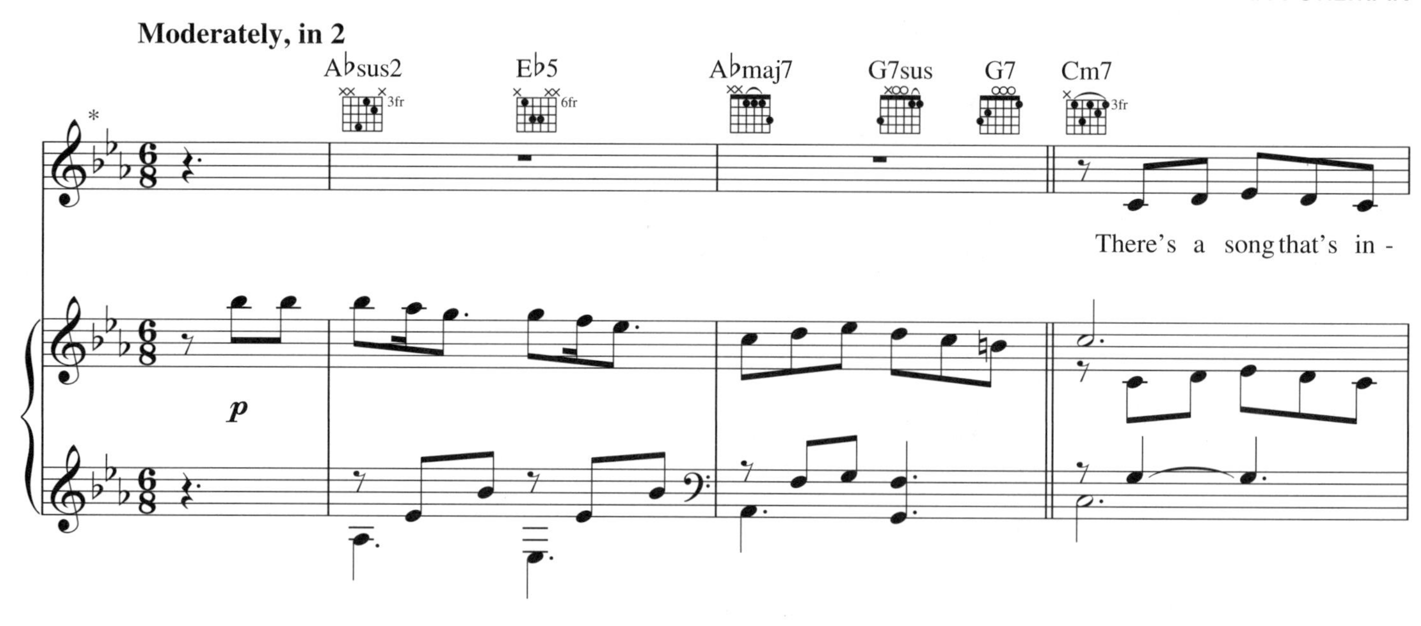

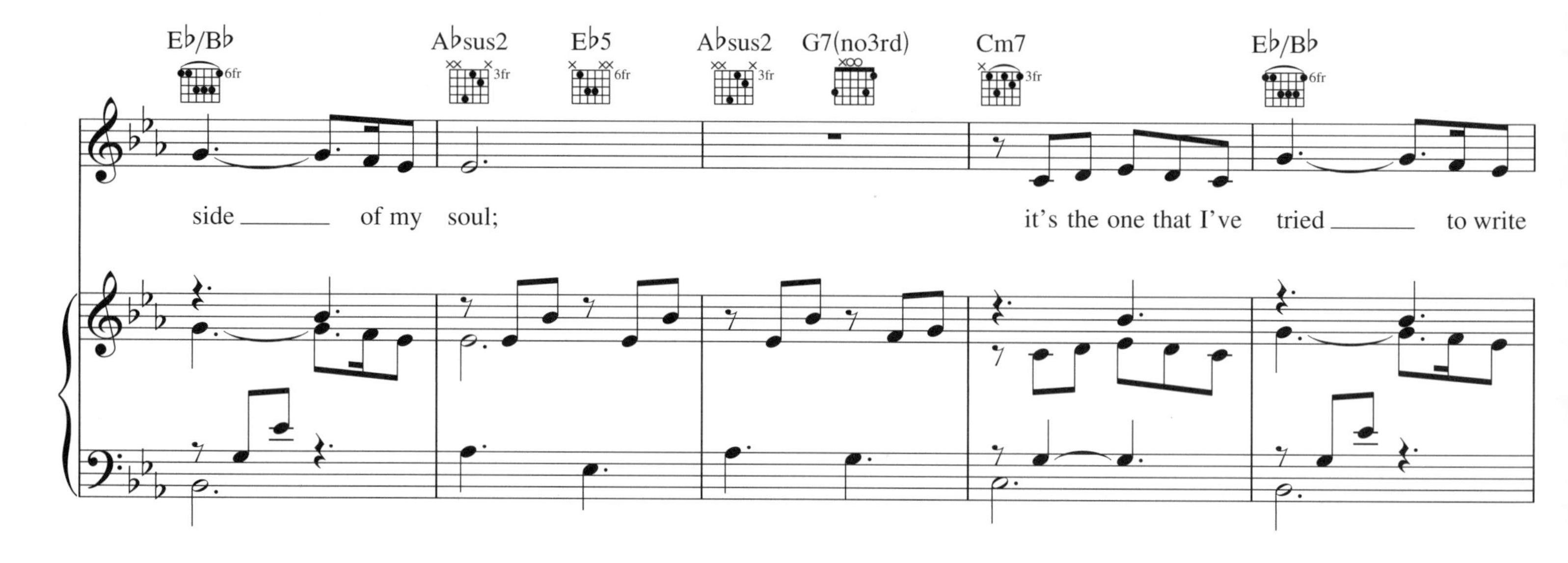

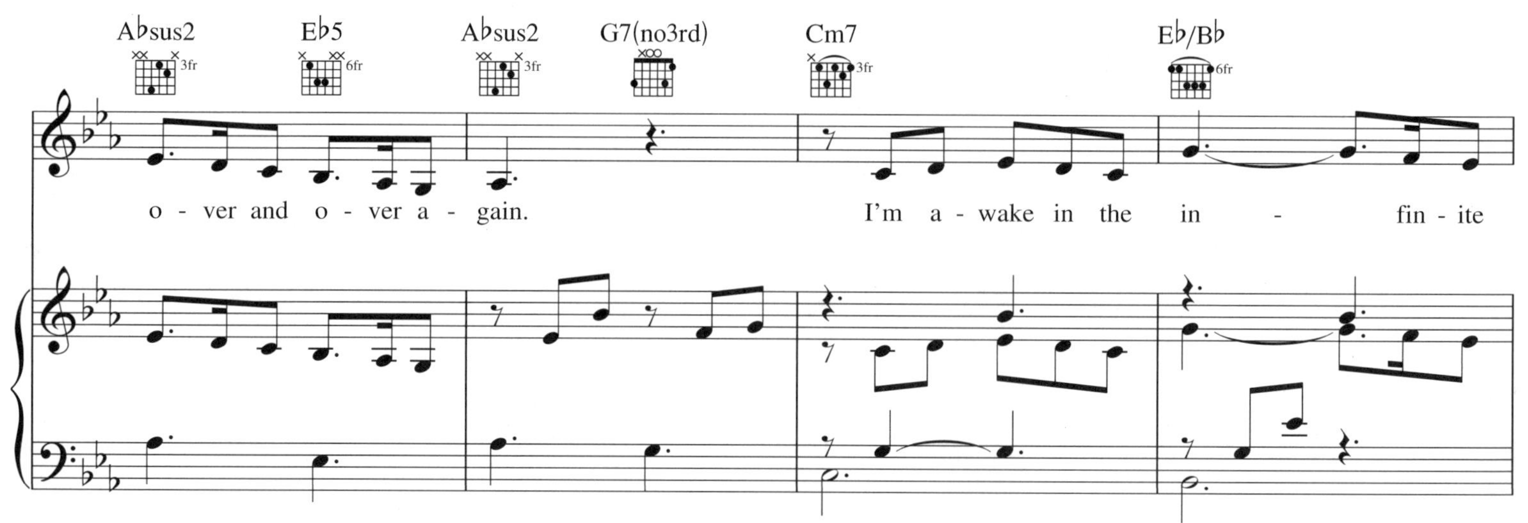

* Recorded a half step higher.

A♭sus2 E♭5 A♭sus2 G7(no3rd) Cm7 E♭/B♭
cold; but You sing to me o - ver and
A♭sus2 E♭5 A♭sus2 G7(no3rd) C5 Cmaj7(no3rd)
o - ver and o - ver a - gain. So I lay my head back
cresc.
mf
F(add9) C5 Cmaj7(no3rd)
down, and I lift my hands and
F(add9) G/A Am7 G/A Am7 F(add9) G/A Am7 G/A Am7
pray to be on - ly Yours, I pray to be on - ly Yours, I

A♭
A♭maj7
Fm6/A♭
Csus2
Cm7/E♭
know now You're my on - ly hope.
dim.
p
A♭maj7
G7sus
G7
Cm7
Cm7/B♭
Sing to me the song of the
When it feels like my dreams are so
mp
A♭sus2
E♭sus2
A♭sus2
G7(no3rd)
Cm7
Cm7/B♭
stars,
far,
of Your gal - ax - y danc - ing and
sing to me of the plans that you
A♭sus2
E♭sus2
1
A♭maj7
G7sus
G7
2
A♭maj7
G7sus
C5
laugh - ing and laugh - ing a - gain.
have for me o - ver a - gain.
So I lay my
cresc.
f

Cmaj7(no3rd)
F(add9)
G/F
F(add9)
C5
head back down, and I lift my
Cmaj7(no3rd)
F(add9)
G/A
Am7
G/A
Am7
F(add9)
hands and pray to be on - ly Yours, I pray to be
G/A
Am7
G/A
Am7
A♭
A♭maj7
Fm6/A♭
Csus2
on - ly Yours, I know now You're my on - ly hope.
dim.
p
B♭
Csus(add2)
Cm
B♭
I give You my des - ti - ny. I'm giv-ing You
cresc.
f

Csus(add2) Cm B♭ Csus(add2) G7/B Cm D7 D7/C
all of me. I want Your sym-pho-ny sing-ing in all that I
G/B G/A G F(add9) G F(add9) C/E
am. At the top of my lungs, I'm giv-ing it back.
Dm7(add4) G7sus C5 Cmaj7(no3rd) F(add9)
So I lay my head back down,
molto rit.
ff a tempo
G/F F(add9) C5 Cmaj7(no3rd) F(add9)
and I lift my hands and pray to be

G/A
Am7
G/A
Am7
F(add9)
on - ly Yours, I pray to be
on - ly Yours, I pray to be
Ab(add9)
Ab
Abmaj7
Fm6/Ab
Cm7
Cm7/Eb
on - ly Yours, I know now You're my on - ly hope.
dim.
p
Gm7(add4)
Csus2
Absus2
Eb5
G7sus
G7
Mm,
mm,
ooh.
rit.

SOMEWHERE OUT THERE

from AN AMERICAN TAIL

Music by BARRY MANN and JAMES HORNER
Lyrics by CYNTHIA WEIL

Moderately, with expression

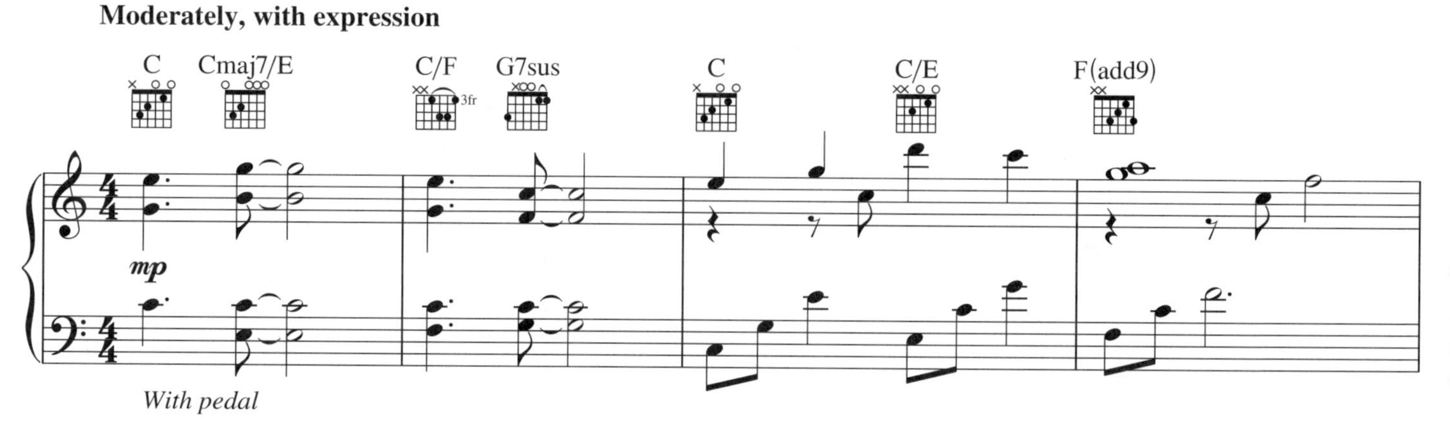

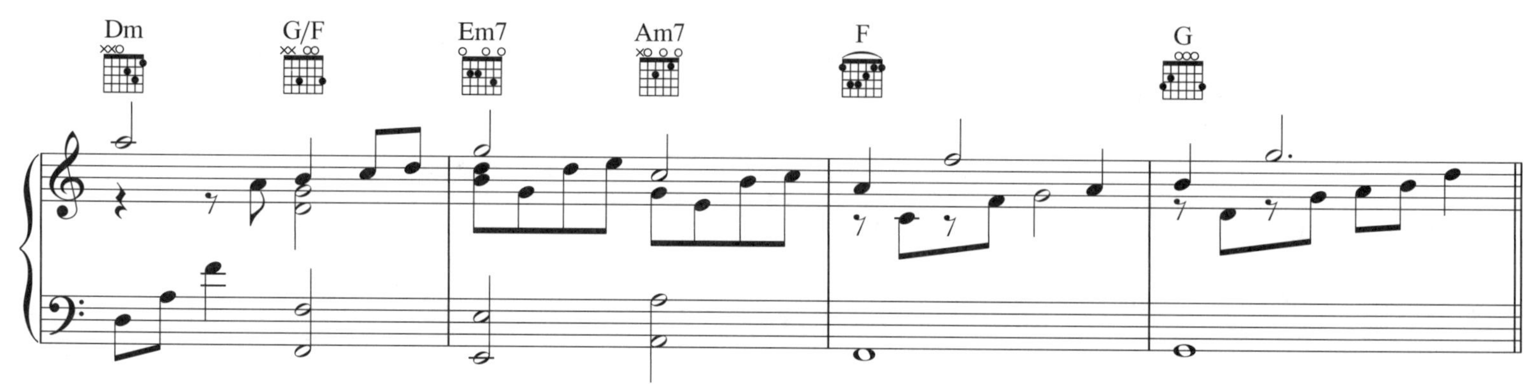

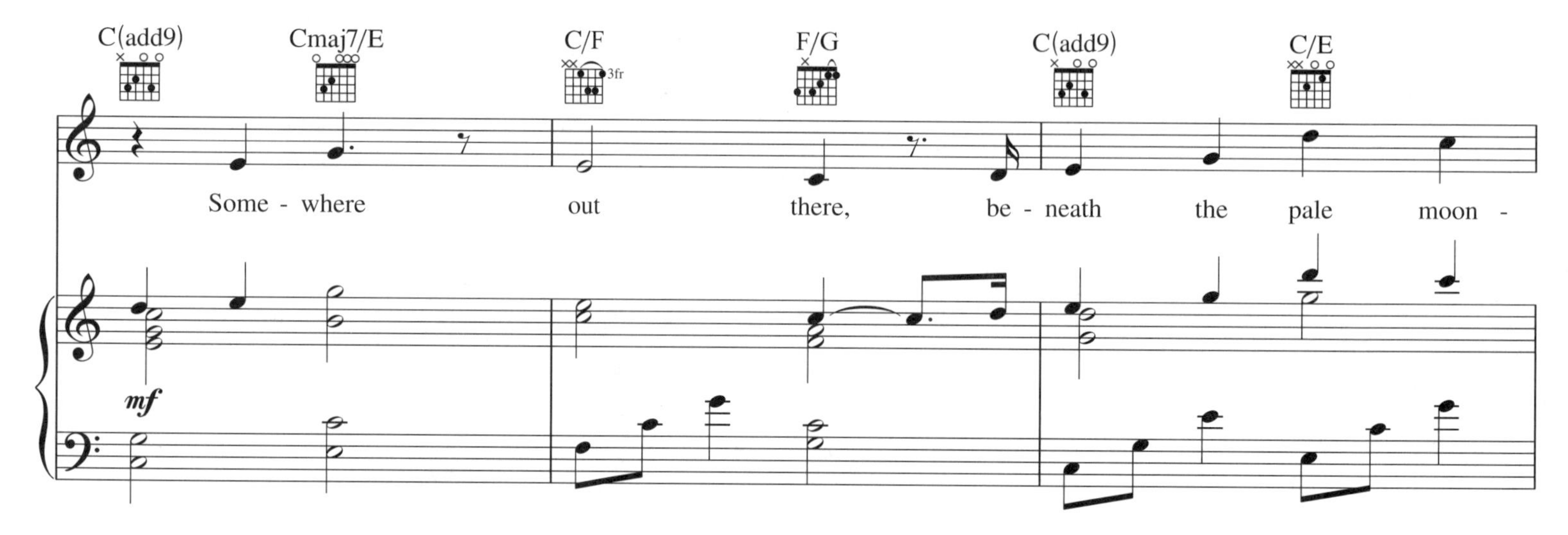

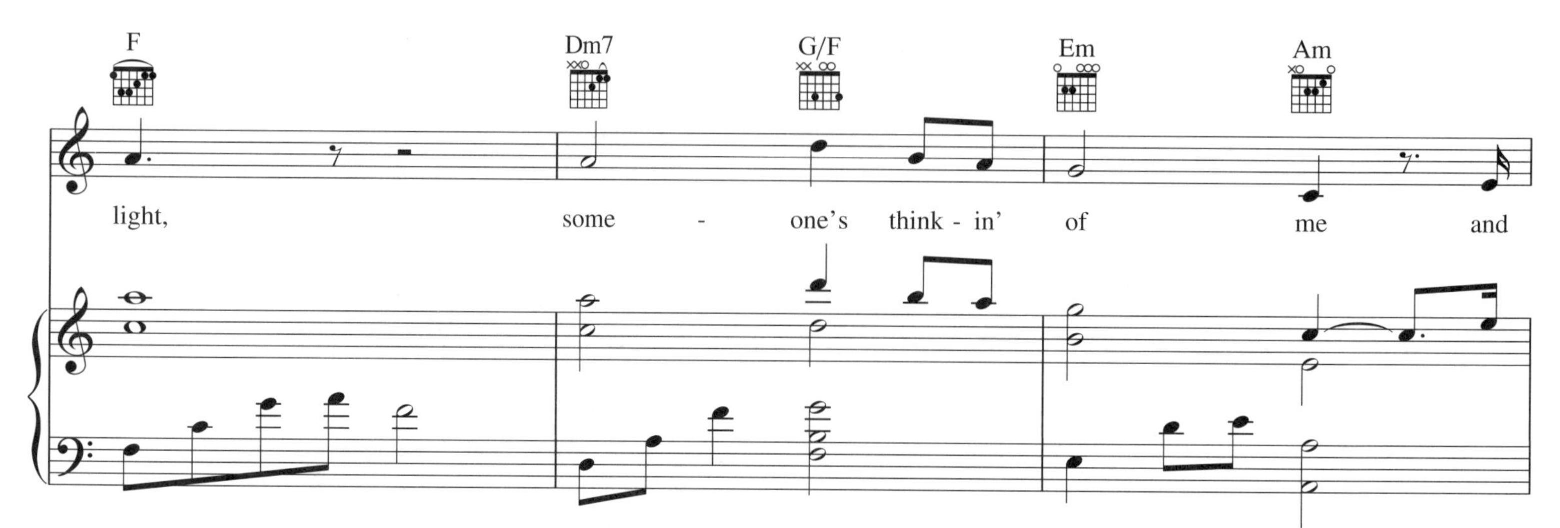

Dm7 C/E F Gsus G C(add9) Cmaj7/E
3fr
lov - ing me to - night. Some - where out

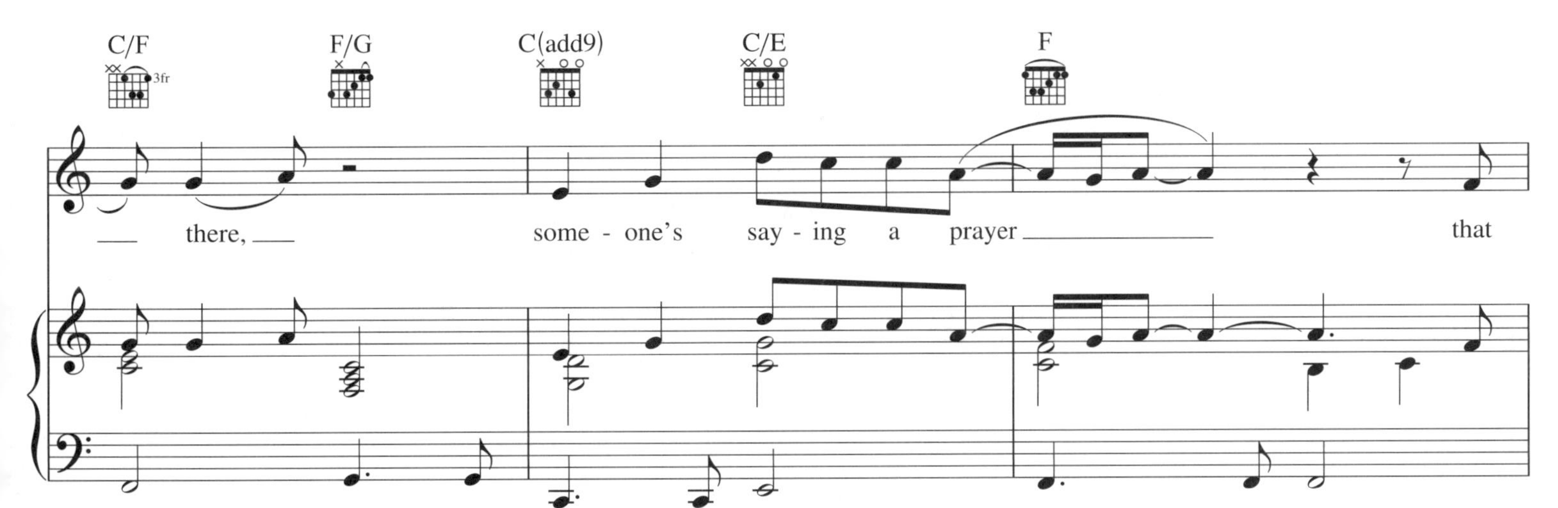
C/F F/G C(add9) C/E F
3fr
there, some - one's say - ing a prayer that

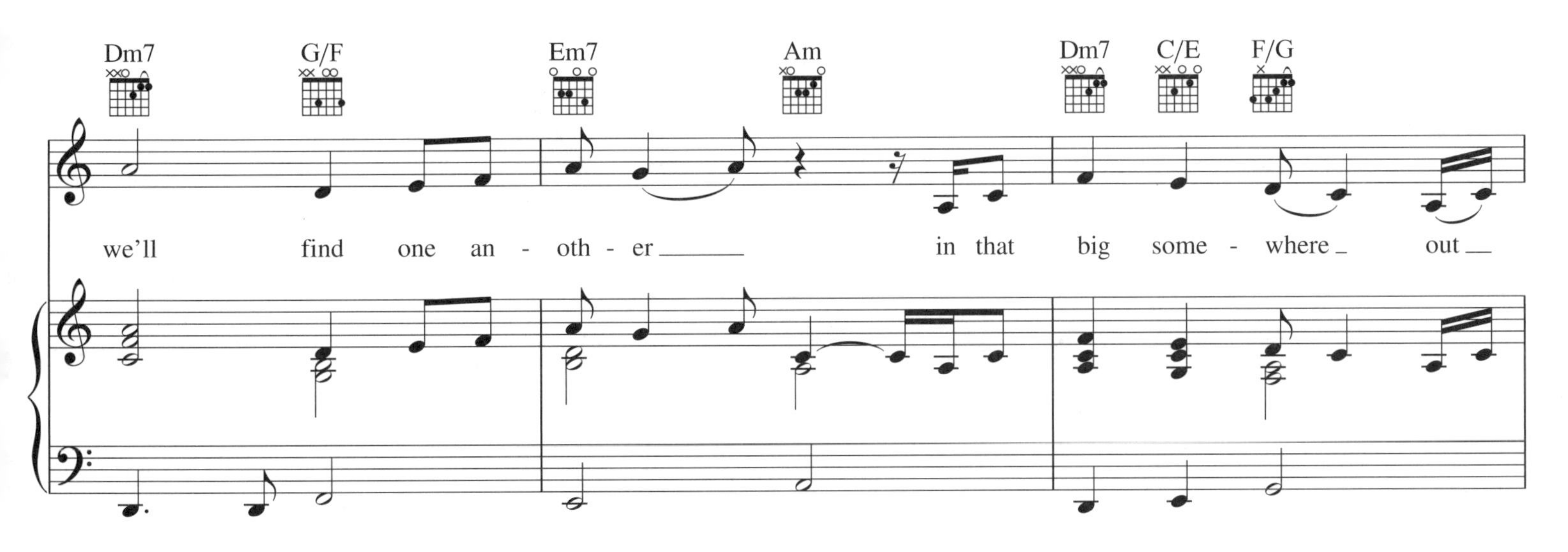
Dm7 G/F Em7 Am Dm7 C/E F/G
we'll find one an - oth - er in that big some - where out

C F G/F F G/F
there. And e - ven though I know how ver - y far a - part we are it

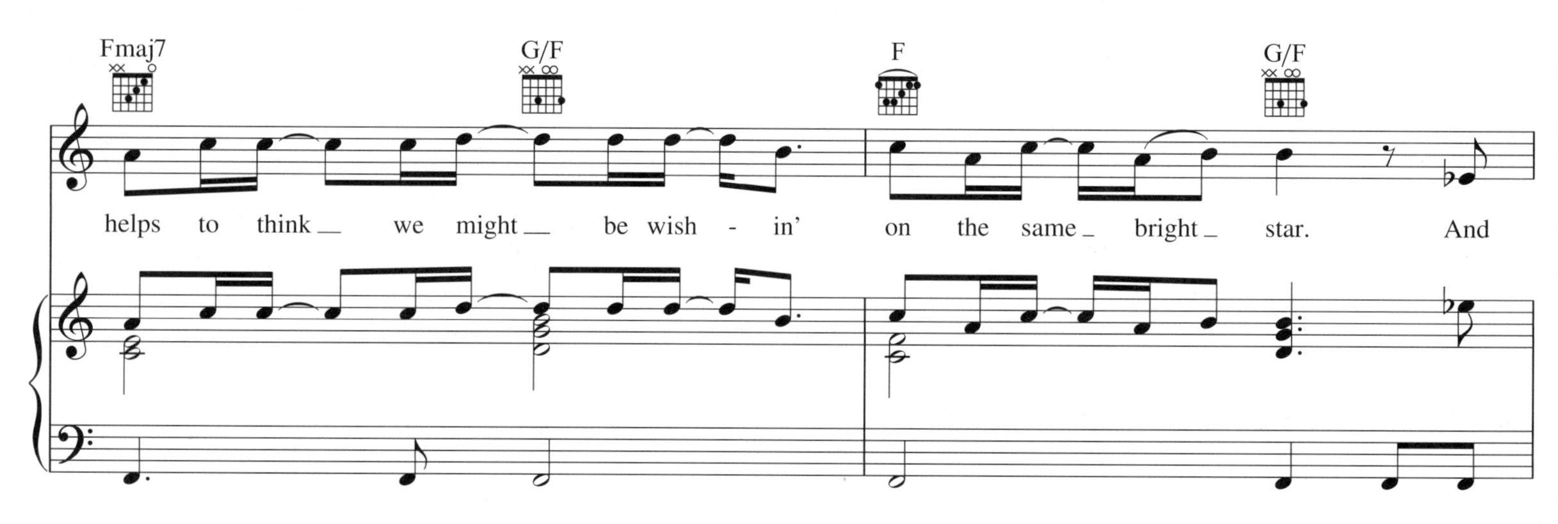
Fmaj7
G/F
F
G/F
helps to think we might be wish - in' on the same bright star. And

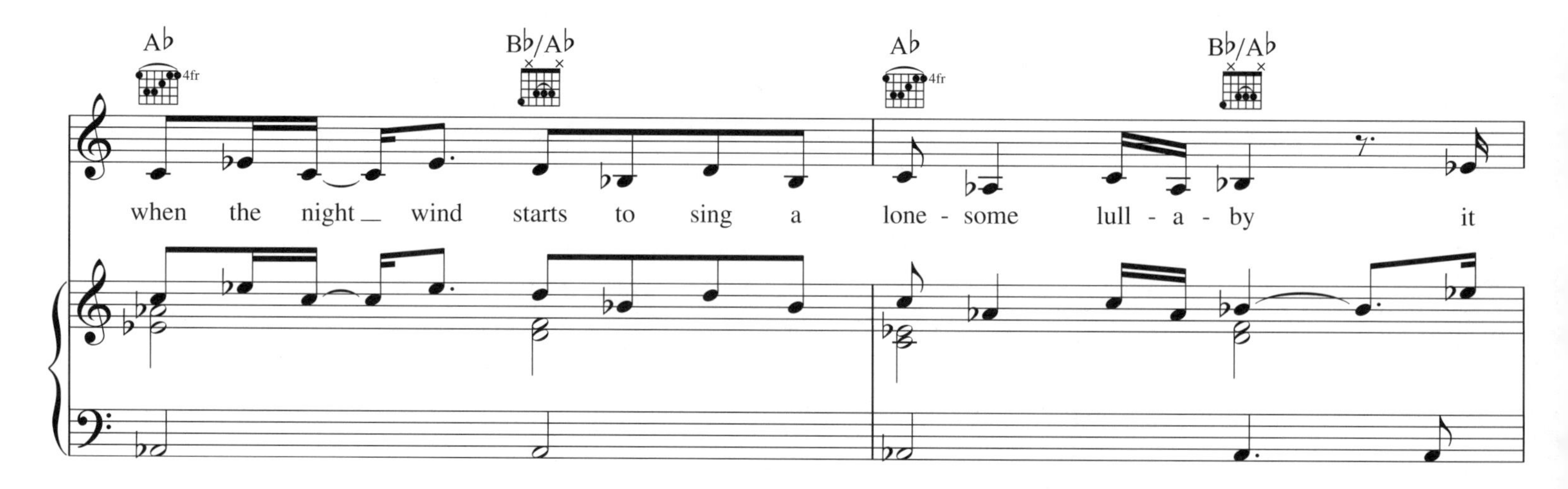
A♭
B♭/A♭
A♭
B♭/A♭
4fr
when the night wind starts to sing a lone - some lull - a - by it

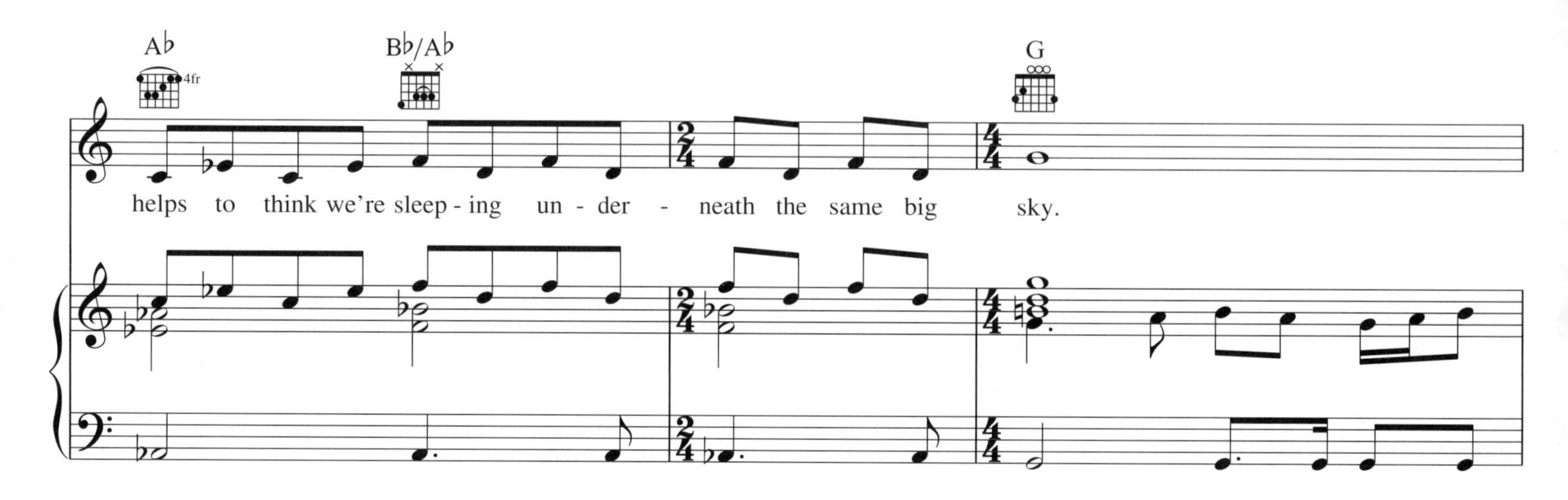
A♭
B♭/A♭
G
4fr
helps to think we're sleep - ing un - der - neath the same big sky.

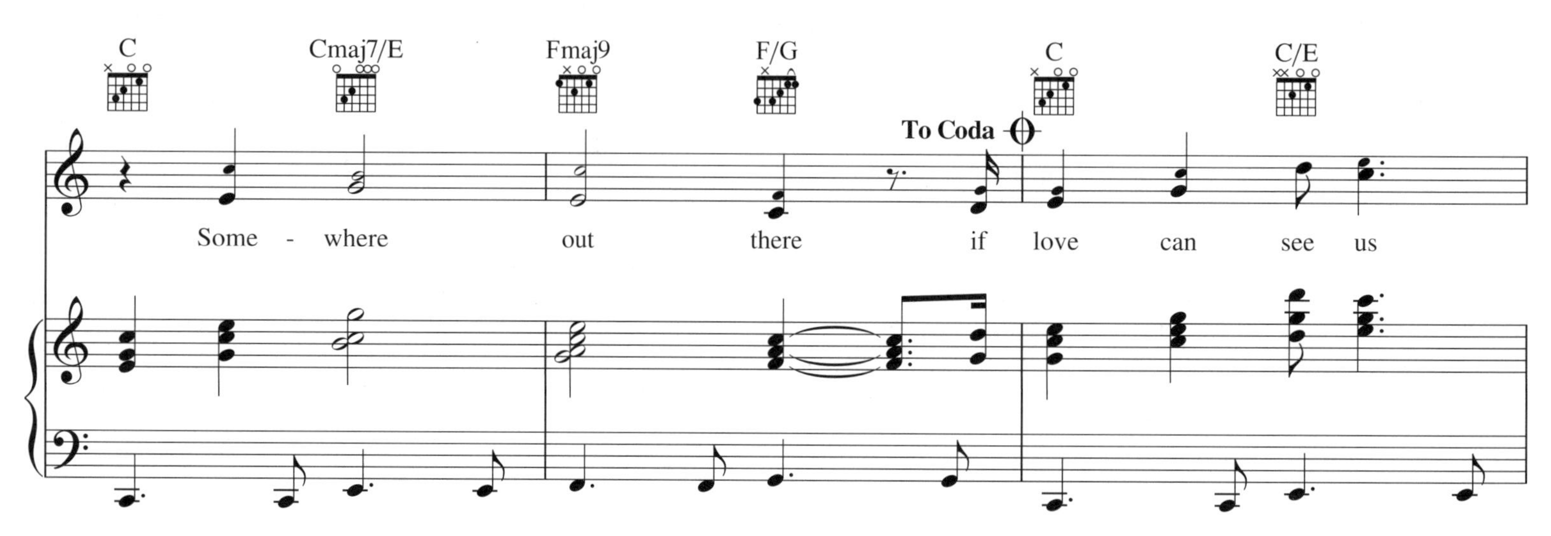
C
Cmaj7/E
Fmaj9
F/G
C
C/E
To Coda
Some - where out there if love can see us

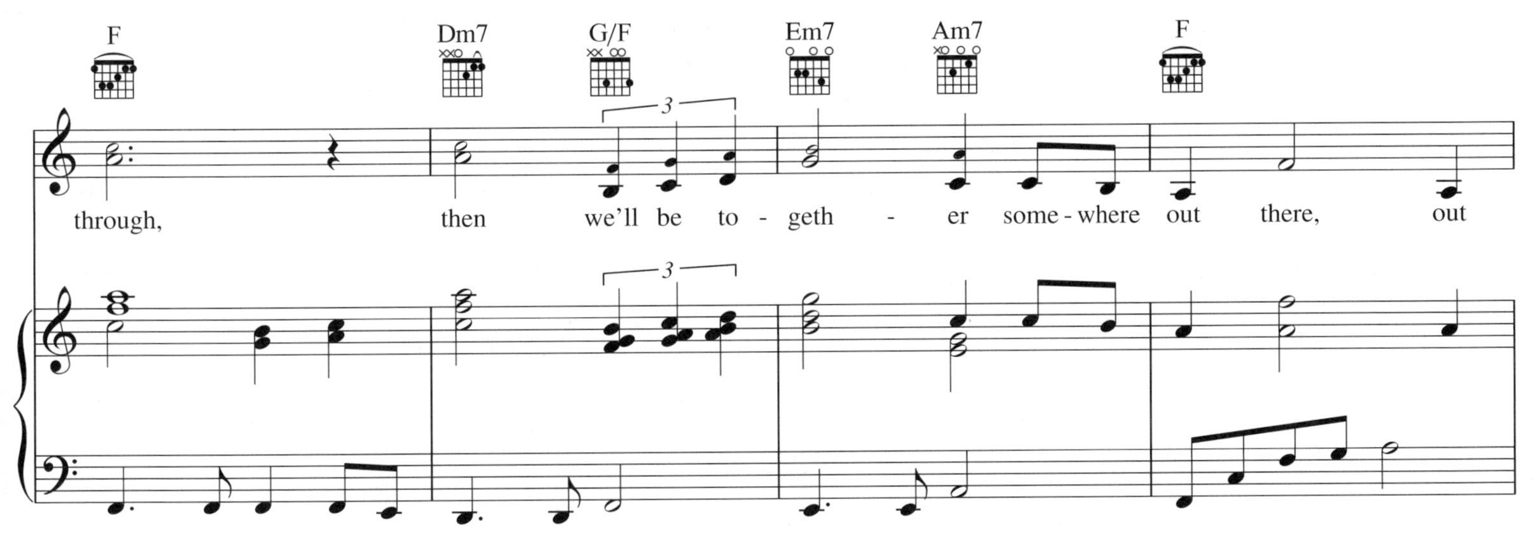
F
Dm7
G/F
Em7
Am7
F
3
through, then we'll be to - geth - er some - where out there, out
3

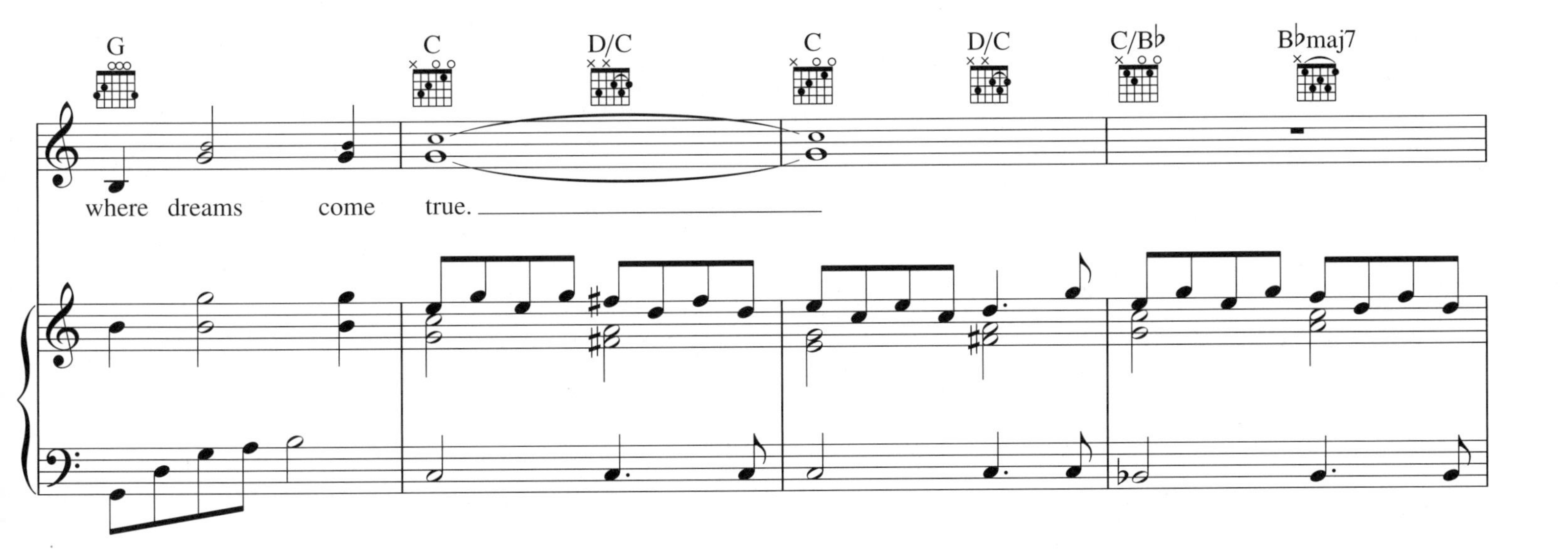
G
C
D/C
C
D/C
C/B♭
B♭maj7
where dreams come true.

Am/B♭
D/E
A
C♯m7
4fr

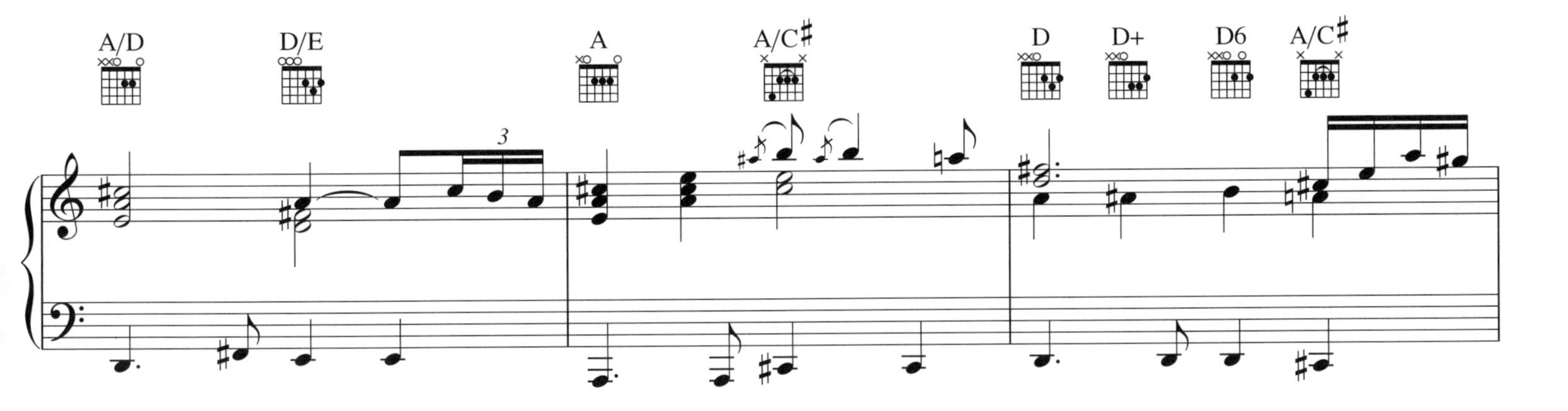
A/D
D/E
A
A/C♯
D
D+
D6
A/C♯
3

Bm7
Dmaj7
C♯m
4fr
F♯m7
Bm7
C♯m
4fr
D/E

A
D.S. al Coda
And

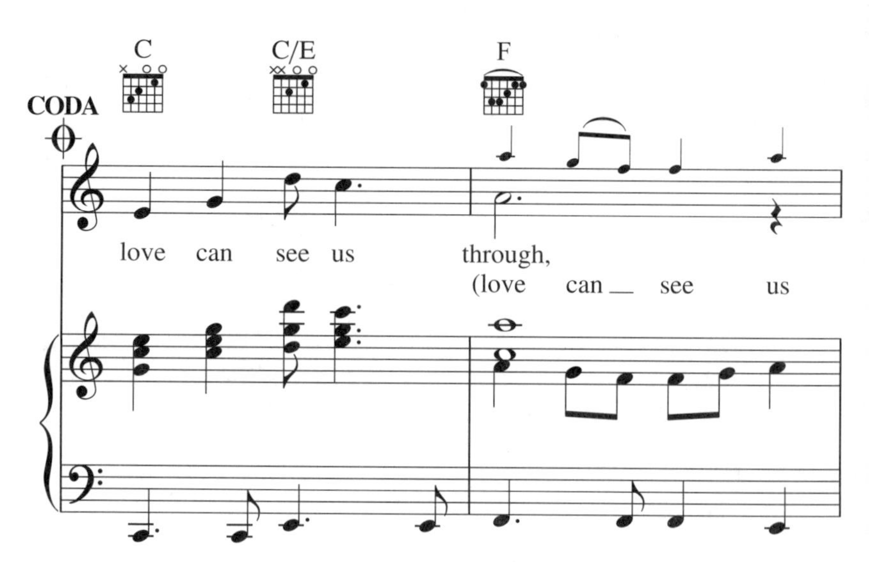
C
C/E
F
CODA
love can see us through,
(love can see us

Dm
G/F
Em7
Am
F
G
3
then we'll be to - geth - er some-where out there, out where dreams come
through)
3

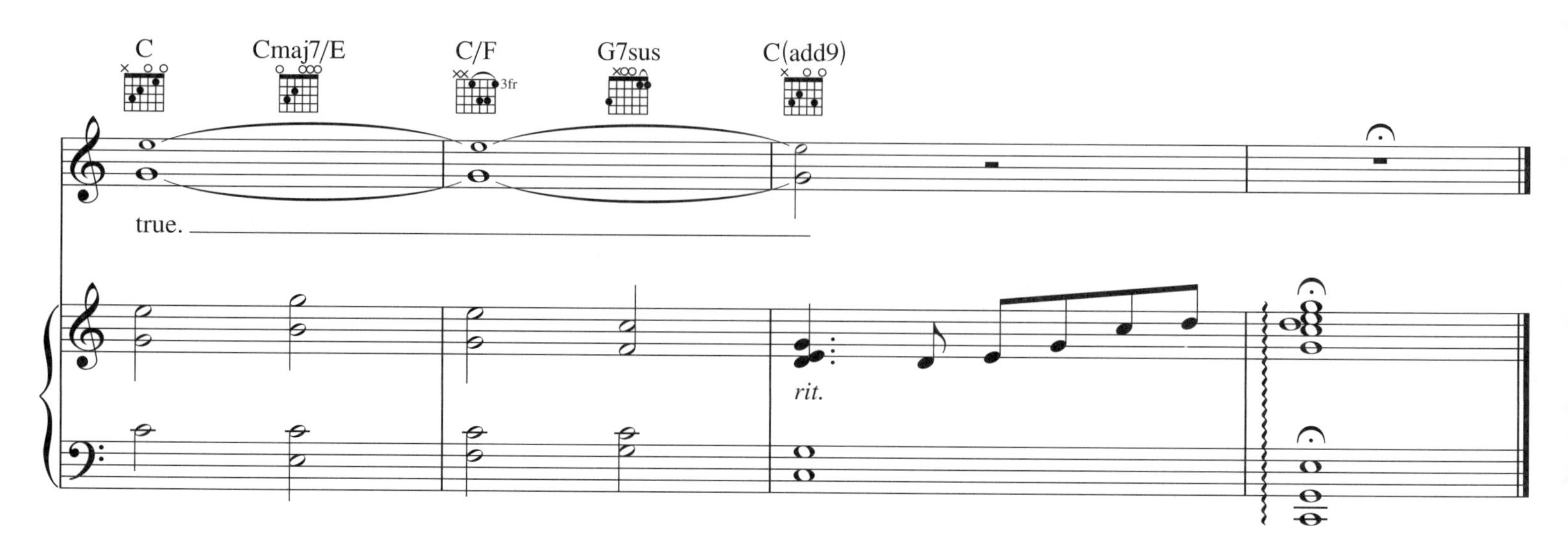
C
Cmaj7/E
C/F
3fr
G7sus
C(add9)
true.
rit.

THAT'S WHAT LOVE IS FOR

Words and Music by MARK MUELLER,
MICHAEL OMARTIAN and AMY GRANT

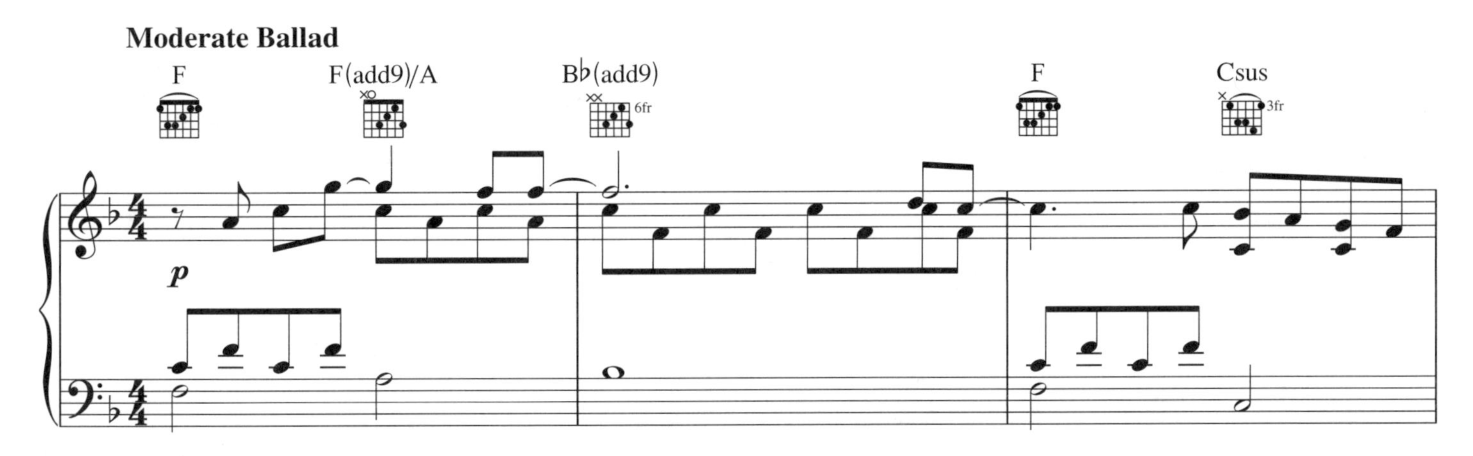

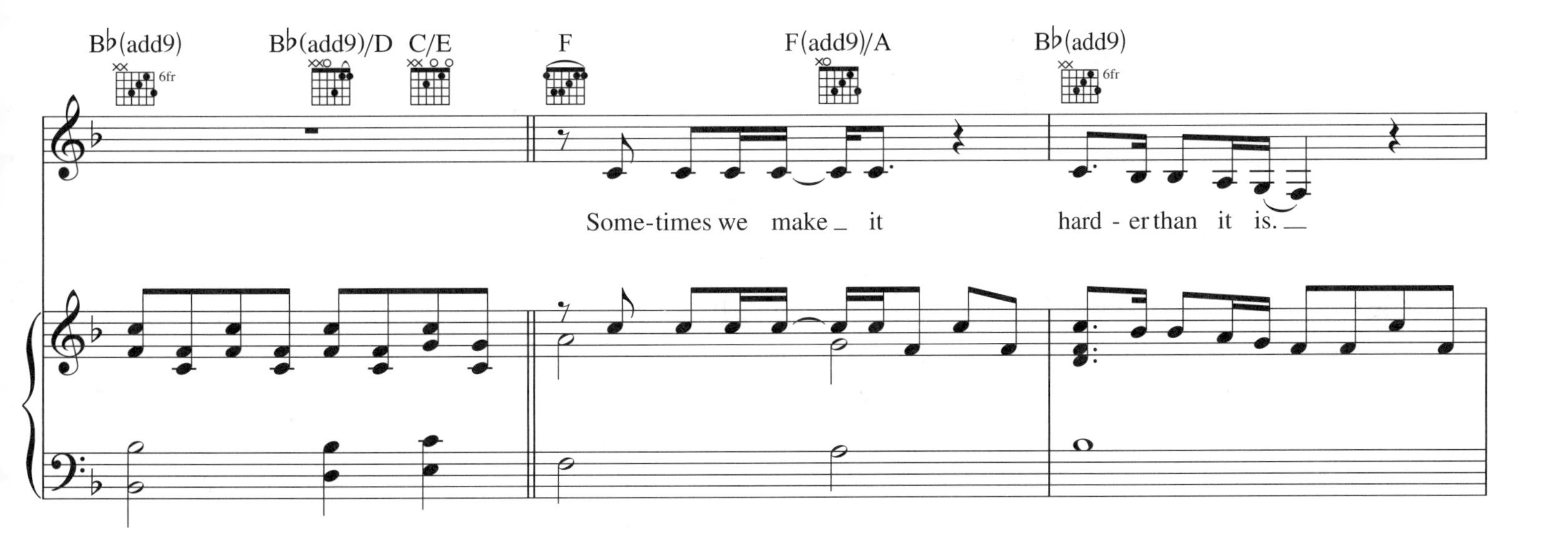

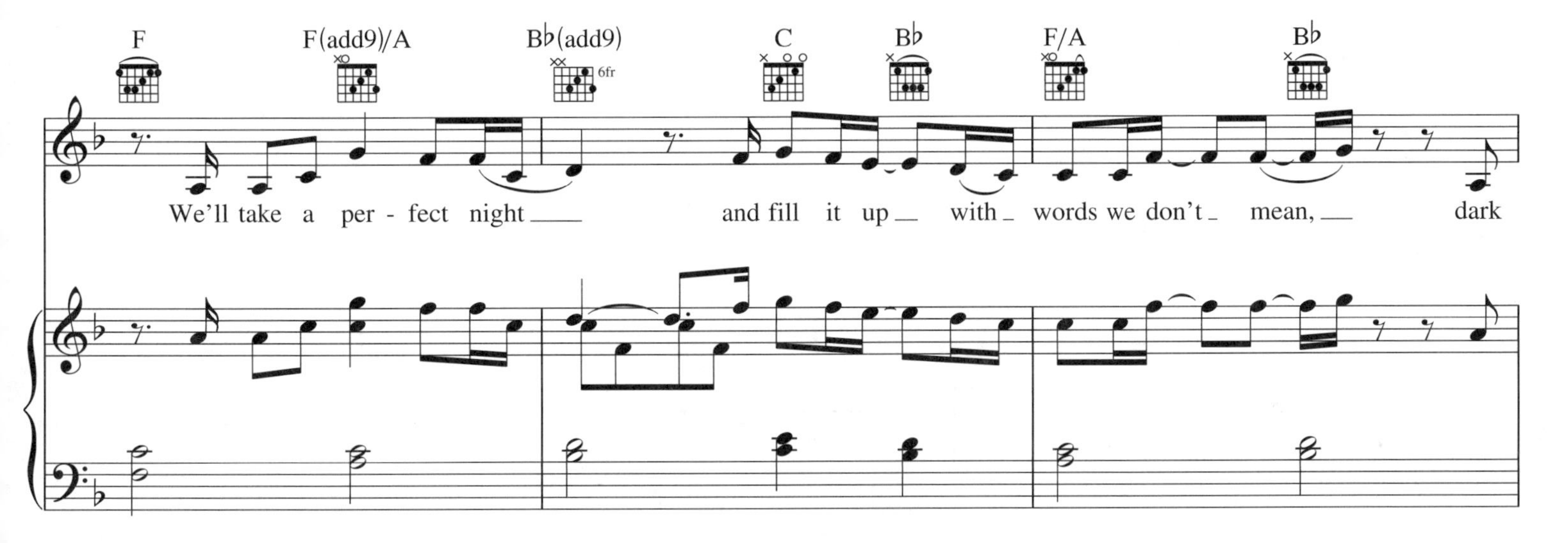

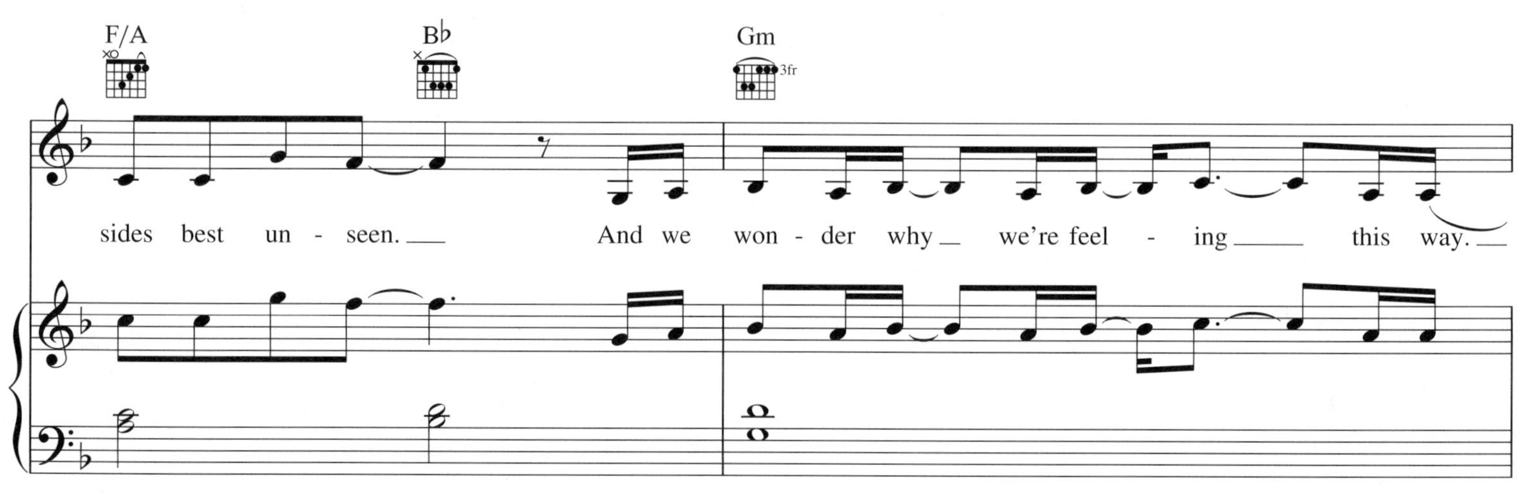
F/A
B♭
Gm
sides best un - seen.
And we won - der why we're feel - ing this way.

C
B♭(add9)
C
F
F(add9)/A
B♭(add9)
Some-times I won - der if we real - ly feel the same.
Some-times I see you and you don't know I am there,
F
F(add9)/A
B♭(add9)
C
B♭(add9)
Why we can be un - kind, ques - tion - ing the strong-
and I'm washed a - way by e - mo - tions I hold
F(add9)/A
B♭(add9)
F(add9)/A
B♭(add9)
- est of hearts. That's when we must start be -
deep down in - side, get - ting strong - er with time. It's

Gm7(add4)
F(add9)/A
B♭(add9)
6fr
B♭/D
C/E
liev - ing in the one thing that has got - ten us this far.
liv - ing through the fi - re and hold - ing on we find:
D(add9)
Gmaj7
A
G/B
A/C♯
D(add9)
G
Bm
That's what love is for. To help us through it. That's what love is for.
A/C♯
G
A
G/B
A/C♯
Noth-ing else can do it. Melt our de - fens - es, bring us
Gmaj7/B
A/C♯
B♭
C
back to our sens - es, give us strength to try once more. Ba -

B♭/D
C/E
1
D
D(add9)/F♯
G(add9)
B♭/D
C/E
- by, that's what love is for.
2
D(add9)
D(add9)/F♯
G(add9)
Bm
A
D(add9)
D(add9)/F♯
Guitar solo - ad lib.
G(add9)
B♭
C
F(add9)
F(add9)/A
B♭
B♭/D
C
Solo ends
Be -
Gm7
F/A
B♭
B♭/D
C/E
liev - ing in the one thing that has got - ten us this far.

E♭
A♭
B♭
A♭/C
B♭/D
3fr
4fr
3fr
That's what love is for.
To help us through it.

E♭
A♭
B♭/D
A♭(add9)
B♭
3fr
4fr
4fr
That's what love is for.
Noth-ing else can do it.

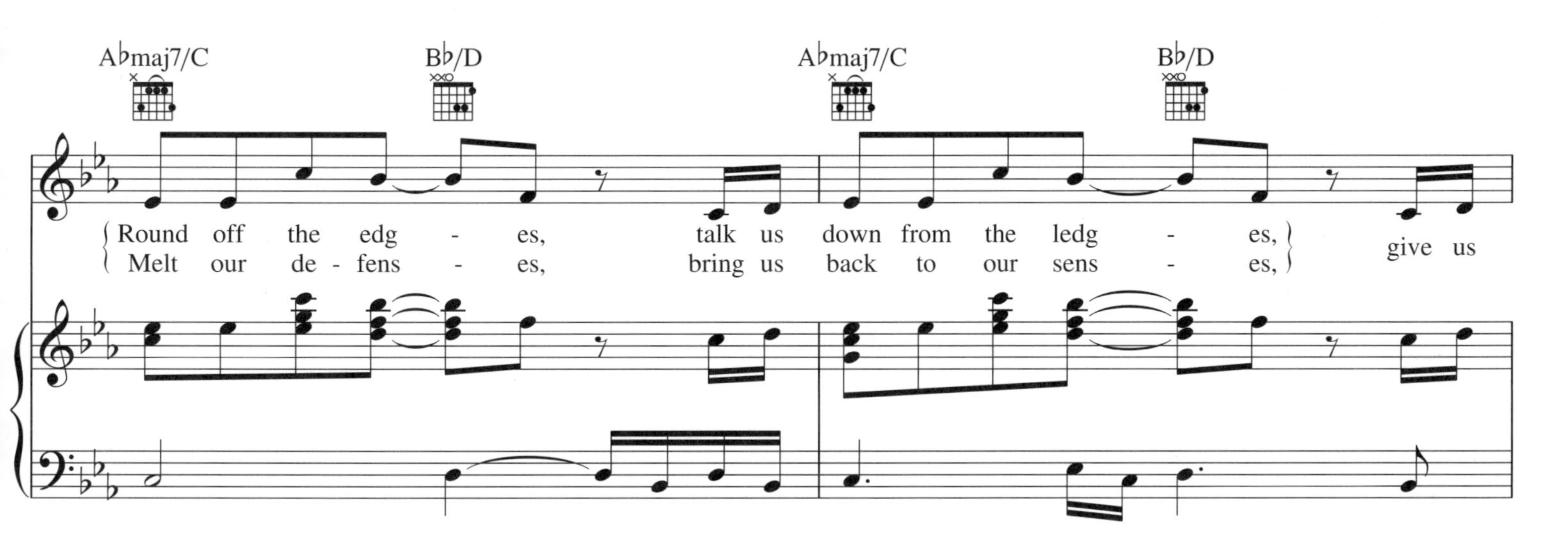
A♭maj7/C
B♭/D
A♭maj7/C
B♭/D
Round off the edg - es, talk us down from the ledg - es,
Melt our de - fens - es, bring us back to our sens - es,
give us

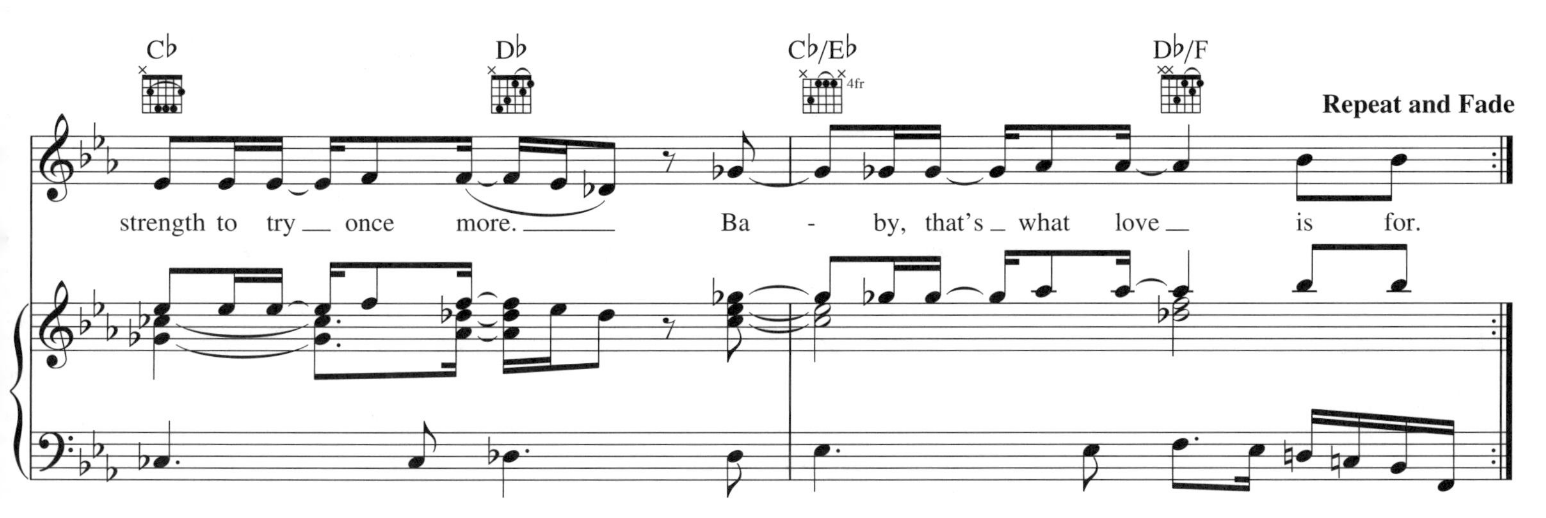
C♭
D♭
C♭/E♭
D♭/F
4fr
Repeat and Fade
strength to try once more.
Ba - by, that's what love is for.

UP TO THE MOUNTAIN
(MLK Song)

Words and Music by
PATTY GRIFFIN

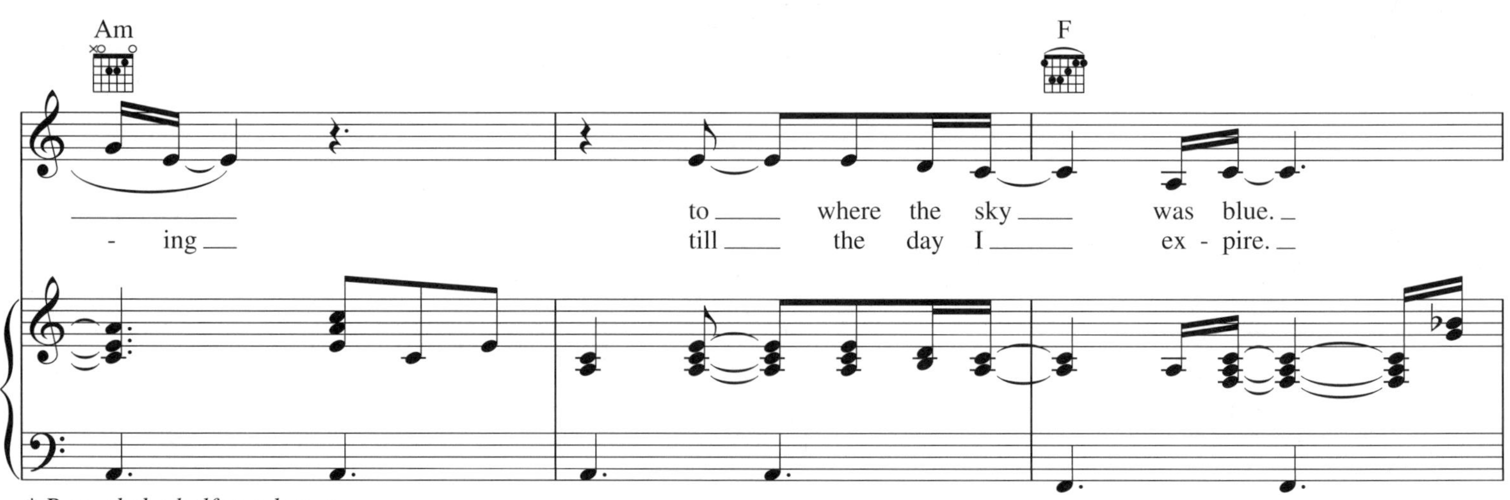

* Recorded a half step lower.

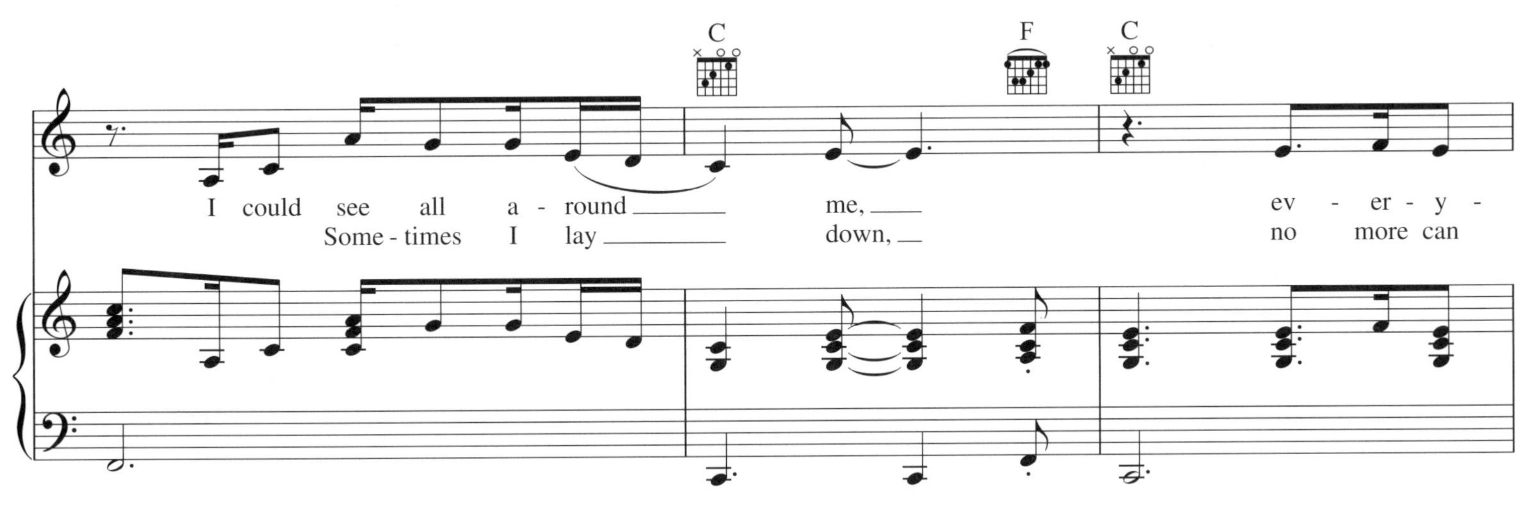
C
F
C
I could see all a - round me,
ev - er - y -
Some - times I lay down,
no more can

G
C/G
G
Am
3
where,
I could see all a - round me,
I do.
But then I go on a - gain

F
C
F/C
3
ev - er - y - where.
be - cause You ask me to.
3

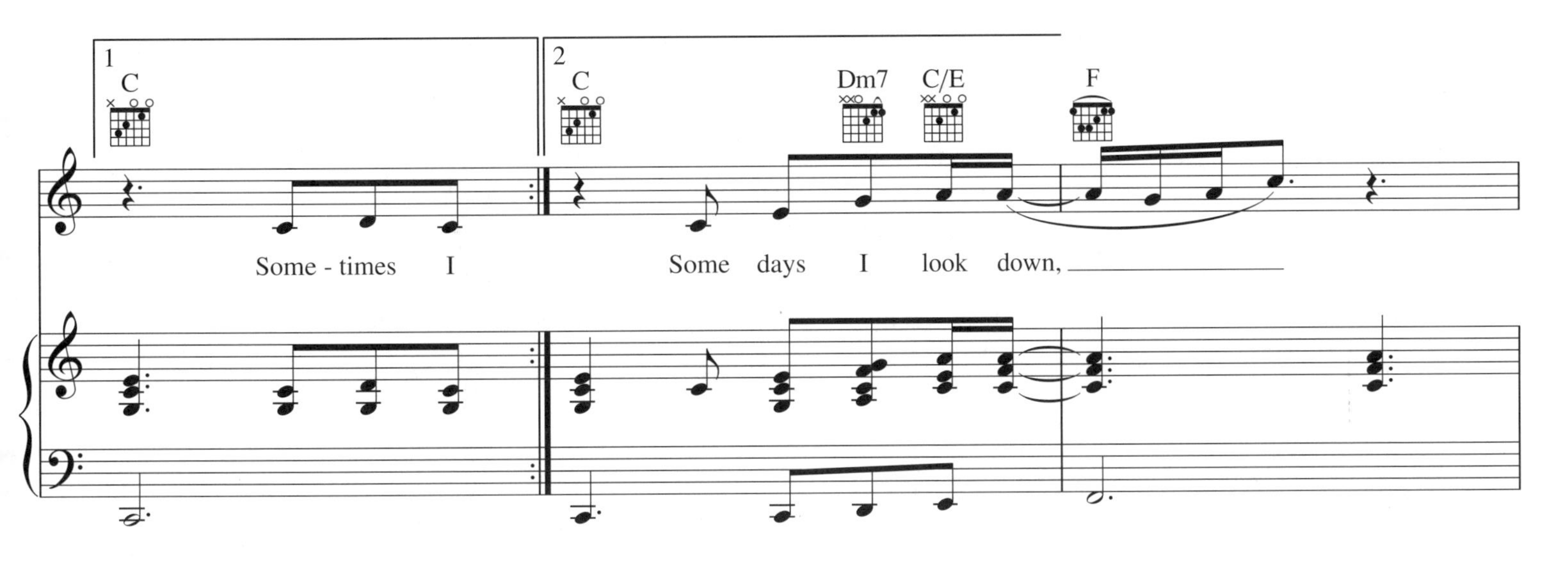
1
C
2
C
Dm7
C/E
F
Some - times I
Some days I look down,

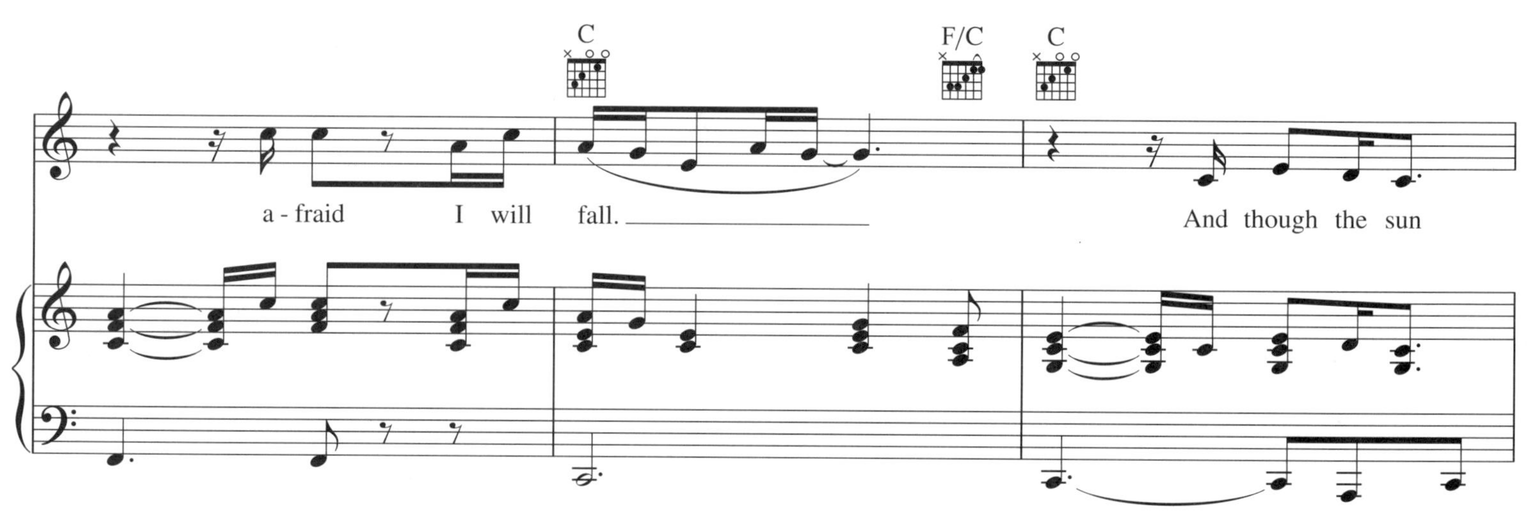
C
F/C
C
a - fraid I will fall.
And though the sun

Dm7
G
Am/G
shines,
I see noth - ing at all.

G
F
G
Then I hear Your sweet voice, oh, oh, oh, come and then go,

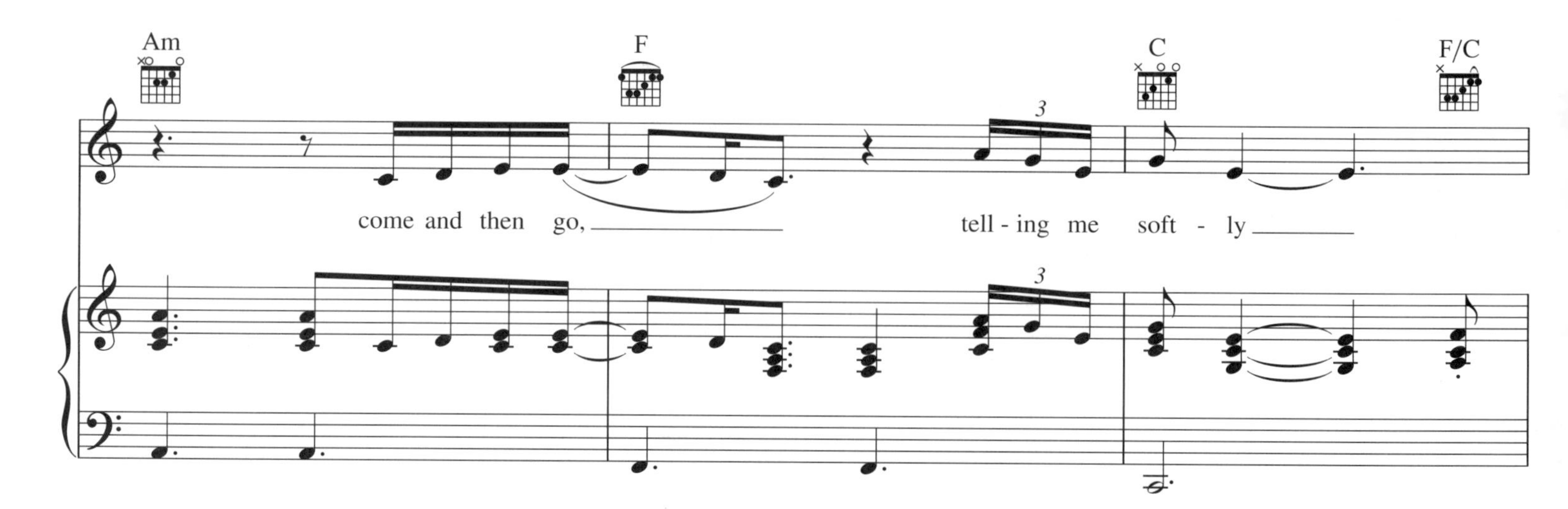
Am
F
C
F/C
come and then go,
tell - ing me soft - ly

C
G
You love me so.
The peace - ful

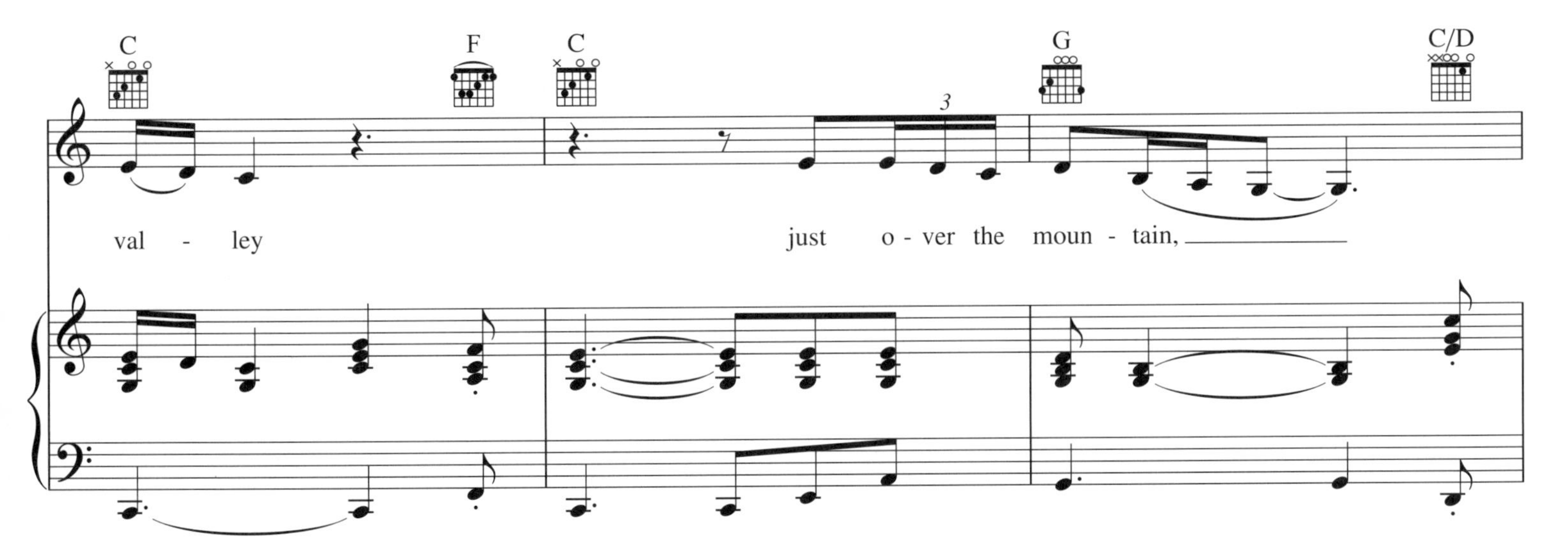
C
F
C
G
C/D
3
val - ley
just o - ver the moun - tain,

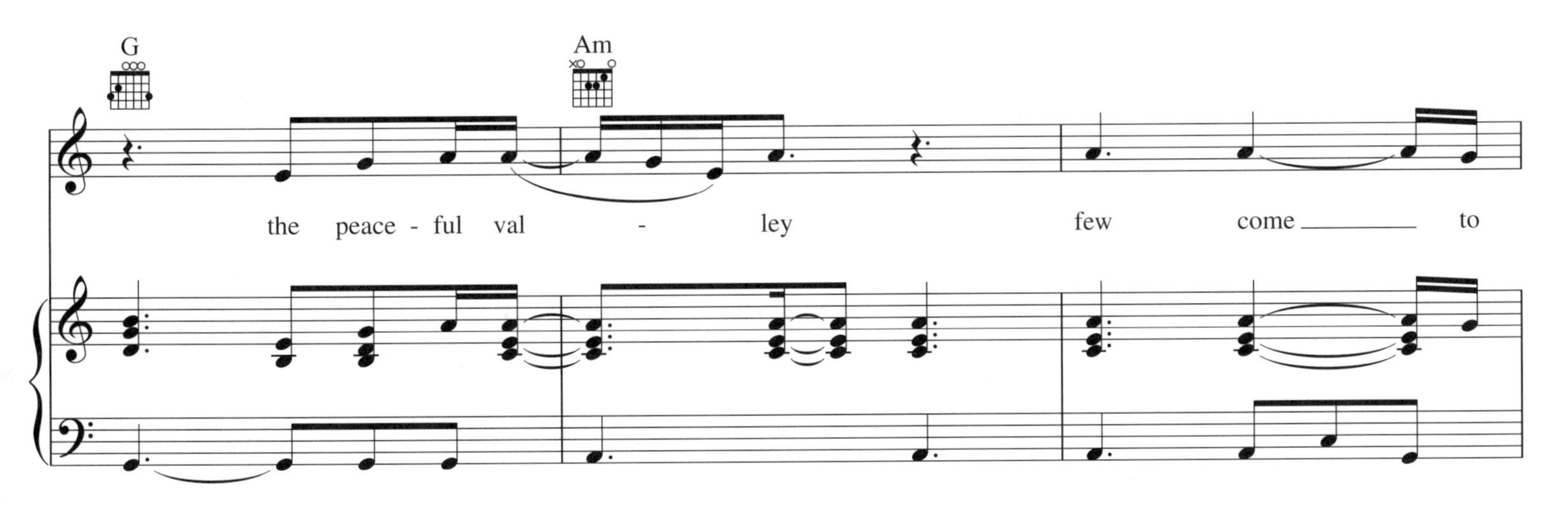
G
Am
the peace - ful val - ley
few come to

F
C
F
know.
I may nev - er get there

C
G
ev - er in this life - time,
but soon -

Am
F
Am
- er or lat - er,
it's there I will go.

F
C
G
Soon-er or lat - er,
it's there

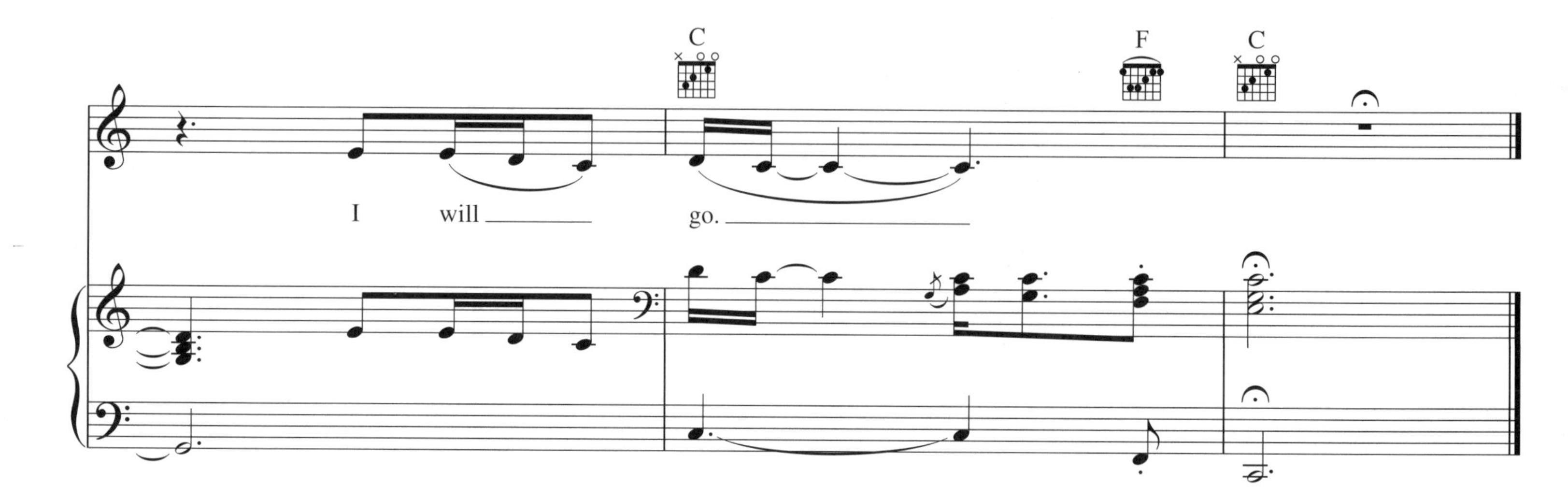
C
F
C
I will go.

THERE YOU'LL BE

from Touchstone Pictures'/Jerry Bruckheimer Films' PEARL HARBOR

Words and Music by
DIANE WARREN

Eb/G
Db
Dbsus2
Ab/C
Gb/Bb
Ab/C
Db
Eb
look and see your face.
owe so much to you.
You were right there for me.
Fm
Cm/Eb
Dbmaj7
Db6
Cm7
Ab/C
In my dreams I'll al - ways see you soar a - bove the sky.
Fm
Cm/Eb
Dbmaj7
Eb
In my heart there'll al - ways be a place for you, for all my life.
1
Ab
Eb/G
Fm
Cm/Eb
I'll keep a part of you with me, and ev -

D♭
A♭/C
B♭m7
A♭sus
A♭
B♭m
A♭/C
- 'ry - where I am, there you'll be, and ev -

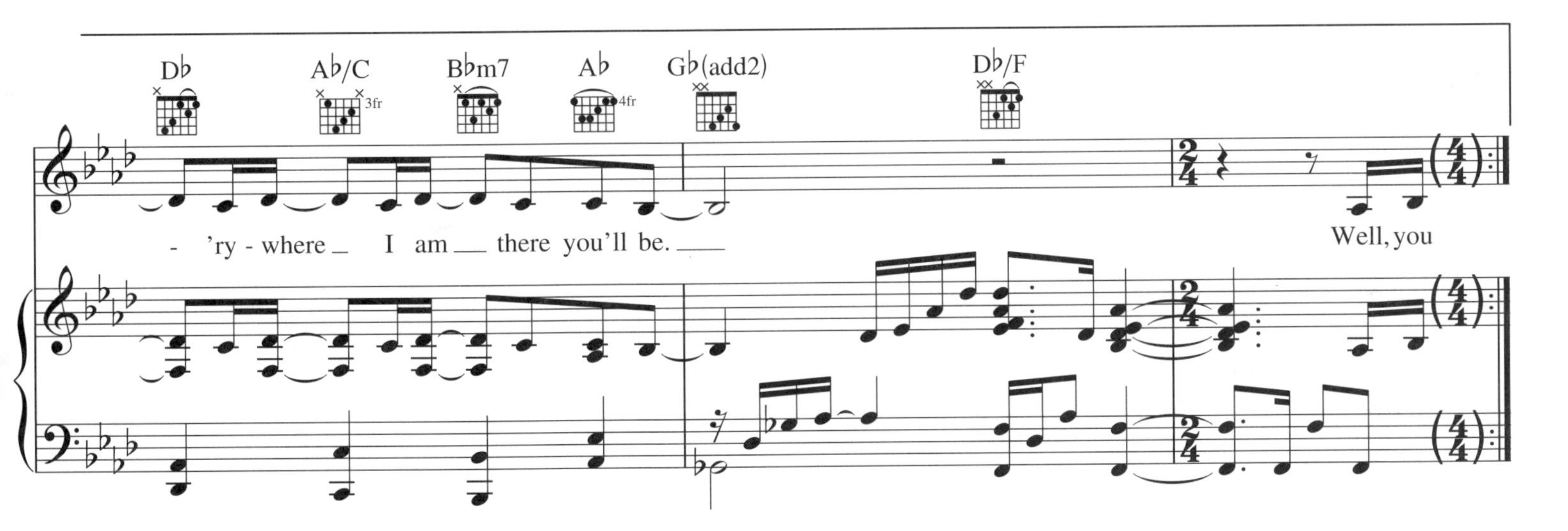

D♭
A♭/C
B♭m7
A♭
G♭(add2)
D♭/F
- 'ry - where I am there you'll be. Well, you

2
A♭
E♭/G
Fm
E♭6
I'll keep a part of you with me, and ev -

D♭
A♭/C
B♭m7
E♭
A♭
- 'ry - where I am, there you'll be. 'Cause I al-ways saw in you my light,

D♭/F
E♭/G
A♭
E♭
A♭
Fm7
D♭maj7
my strength, and I wan-na thank you now for all the ways

D♭(add2)
A♭/C
B♭m7
A♭/C
D♭(add2)
you were right there for me. You were right there for me, for

E♭
Fm
Cm/E♭
al - ways. In my dreams I'll al - ways see you

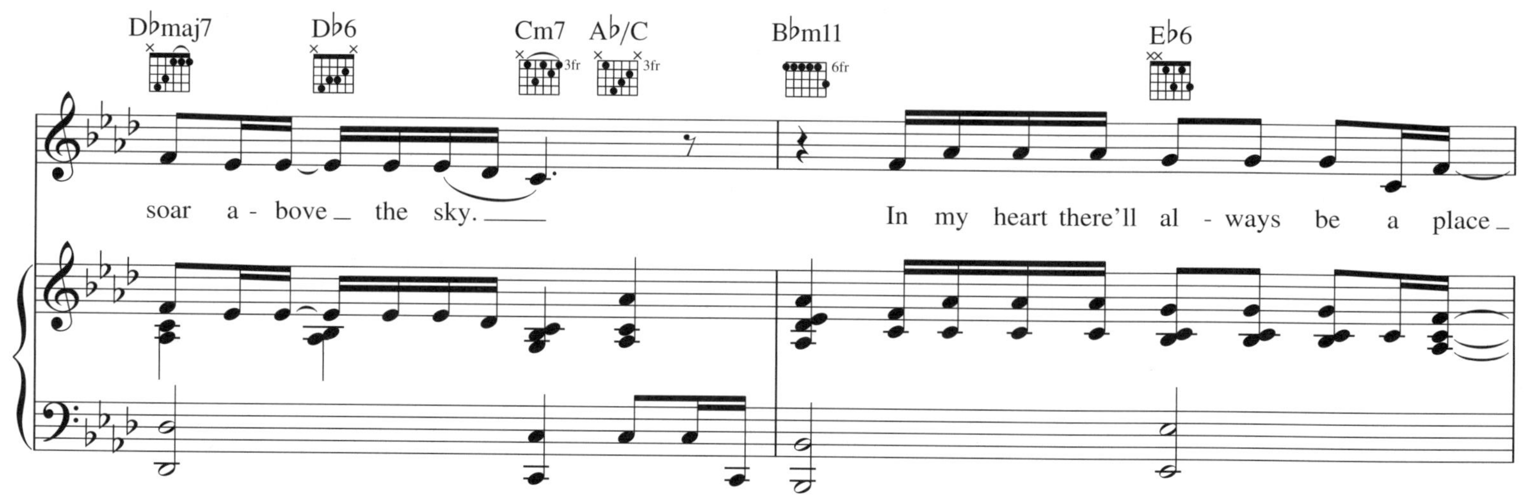

D♭maj7
D♭6
Cm7
A♭/C
B♭m11
E♭6
soar a - bove the sky. In my heart there'll al - ways be a place

D♭maj7
A♭
E♭/G
for you for all my life. I'll keep a part

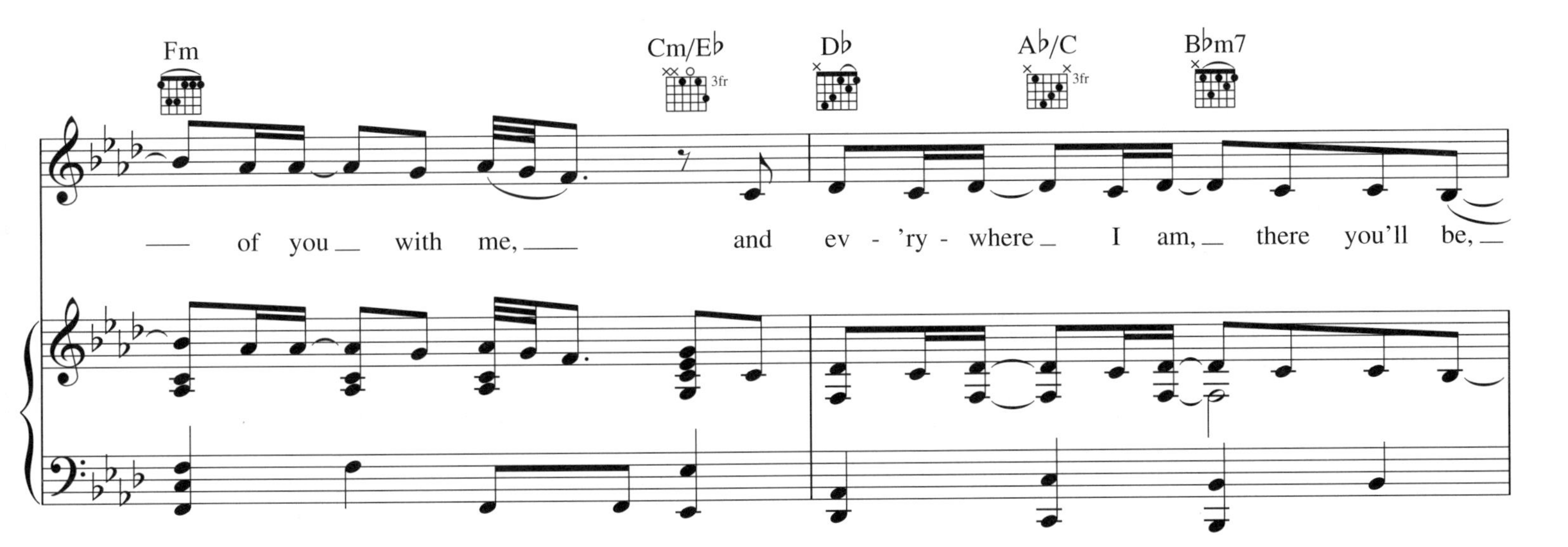

Fm
Cm/E♭
D♭
A♭/C
B♭m7
of you with me, and ev - 'ry - where I am, there you'll be,

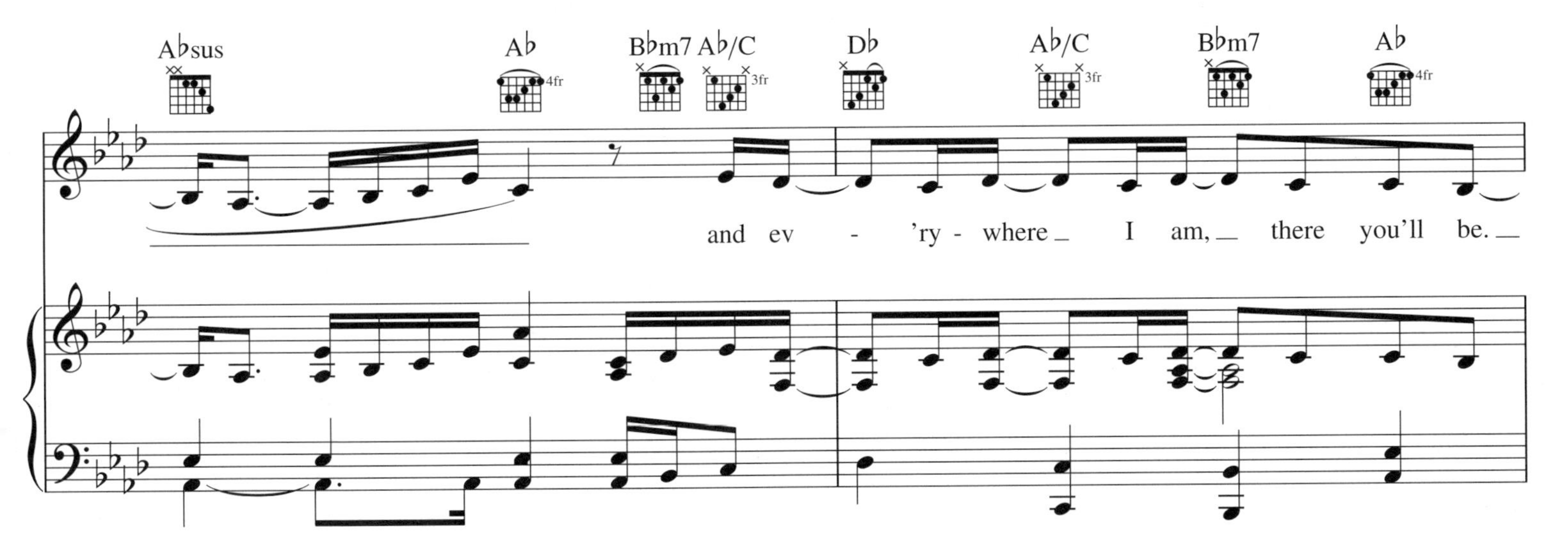

A♭sus
A♭
B♭m7
A♭/C
D♭
A♭/C
B♭m7
A♭
and ev - 'ry - where I am, there you'll be.

Freely
G♭maj9♯11
A♭(add2)
There you'll be.

WAY UP THERE

Words and Music by
TENA CLARK

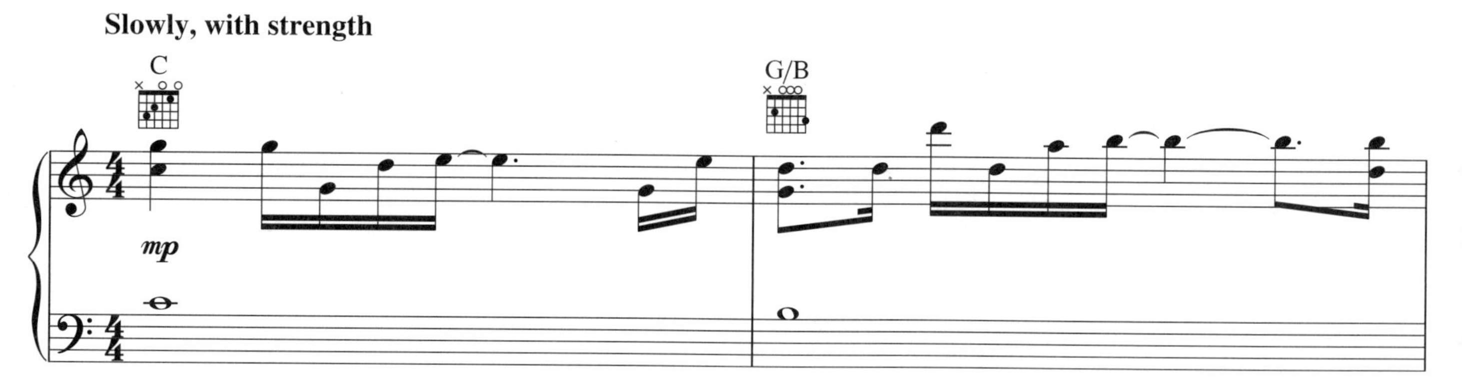

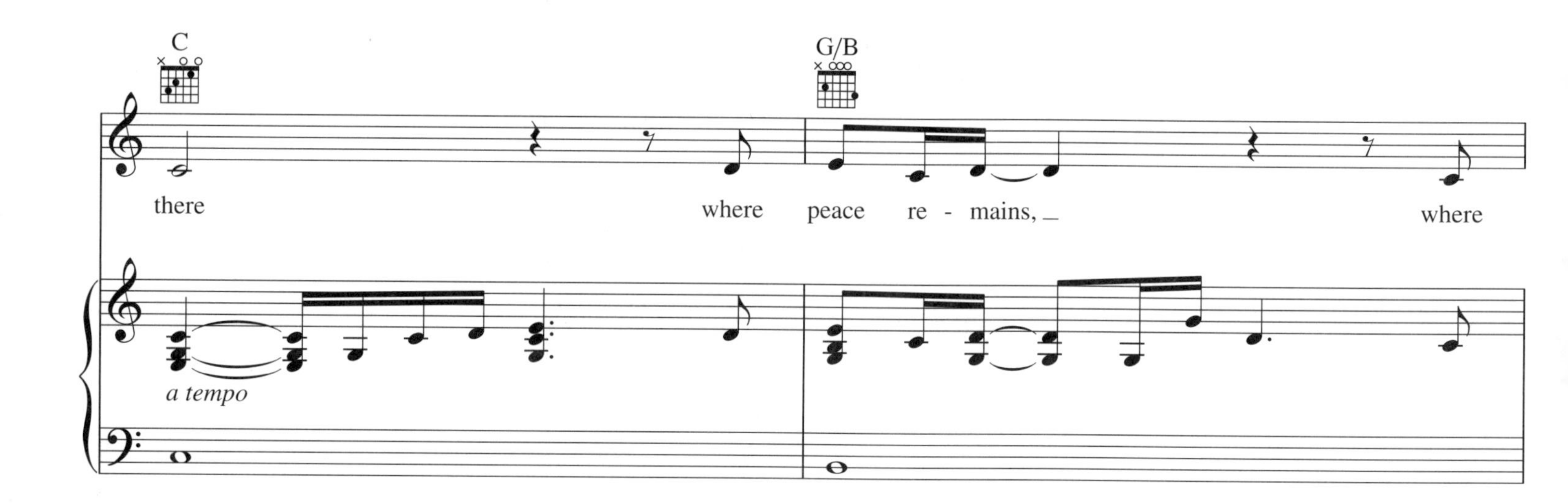

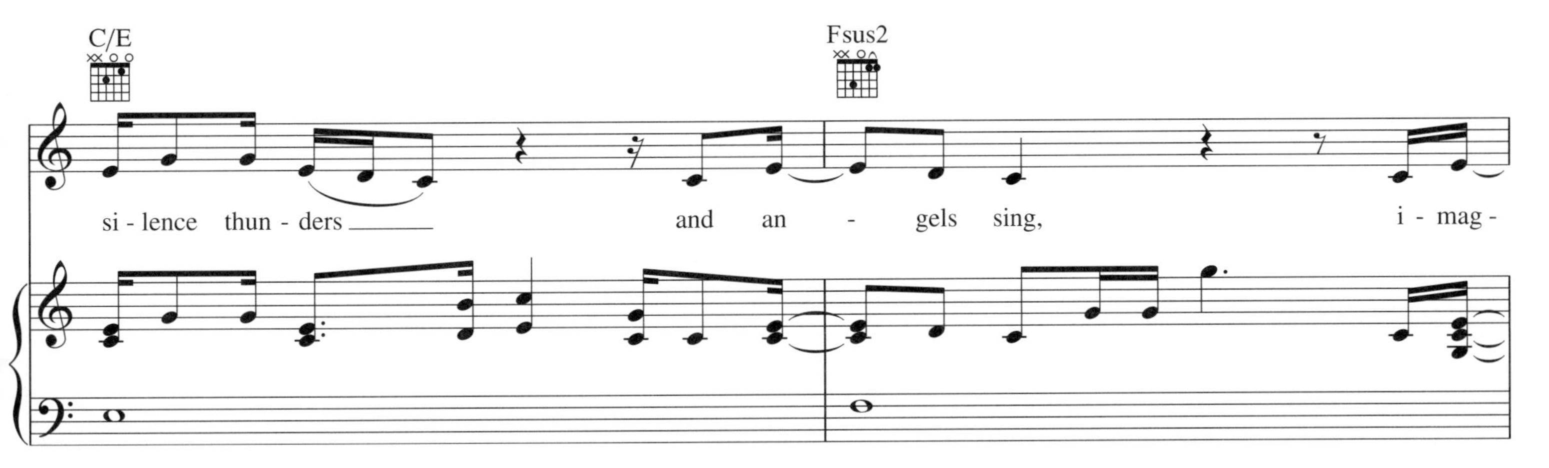

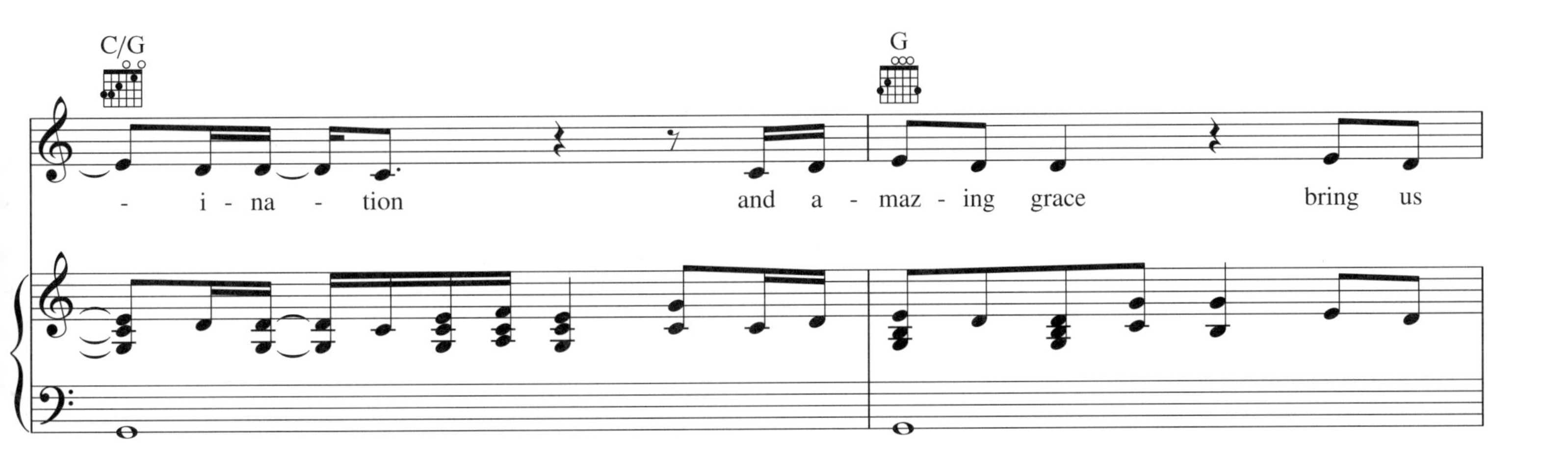

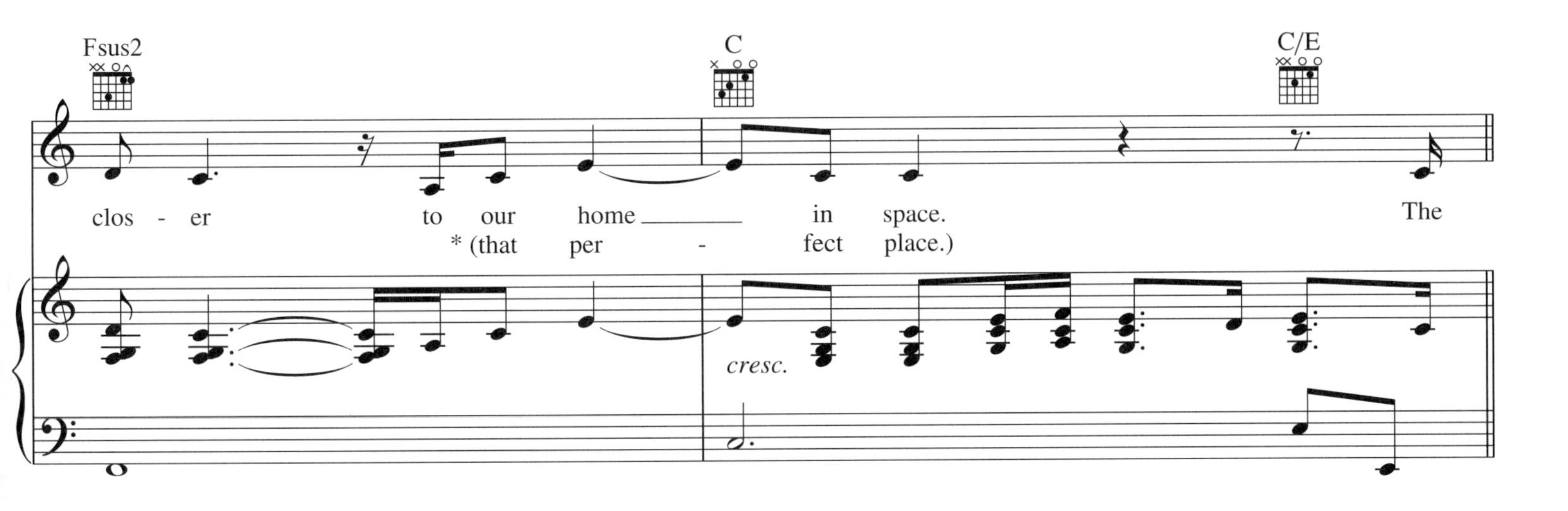

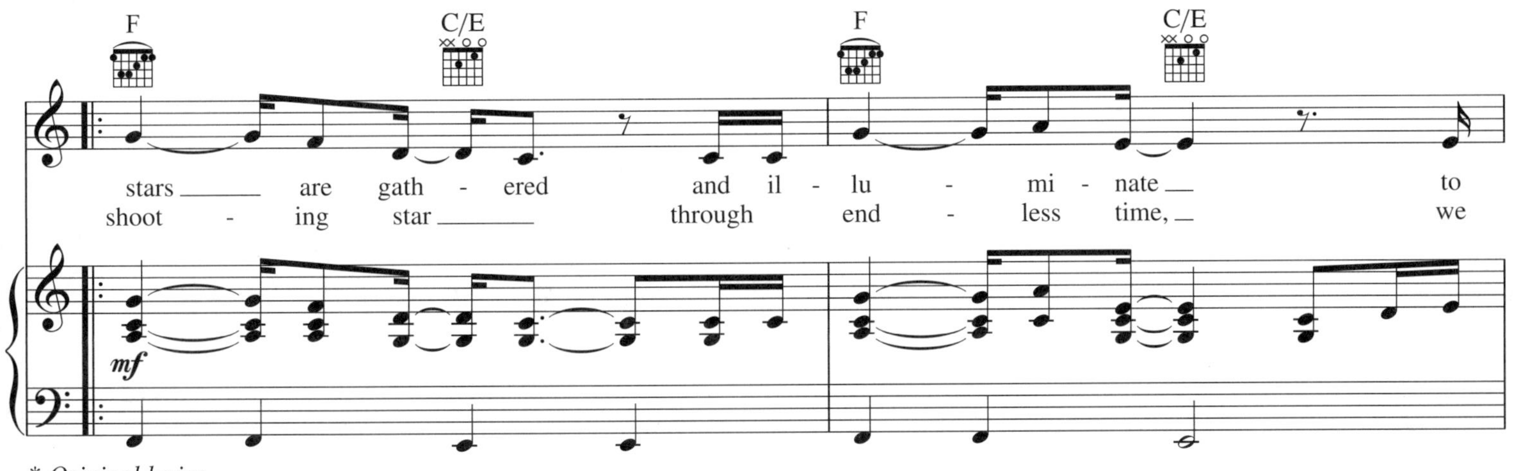

* *Original lyrics*

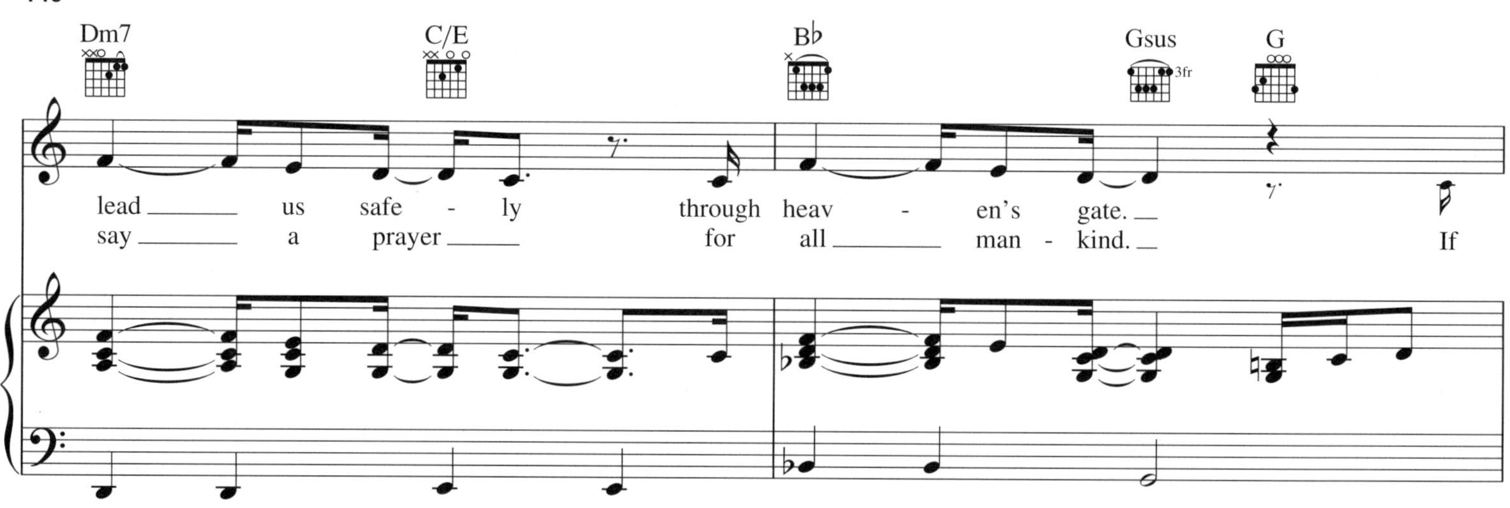
Dm7
C/E
B♭
Gsus
3fr
G
lead us safe - ly through heav - en's gate.
say a prayer for all man - kind. If

F
C/E
F
C/E
We look be - hind us at the won - der of the earth,
we could on - ly see through that ti - ny win - dow,

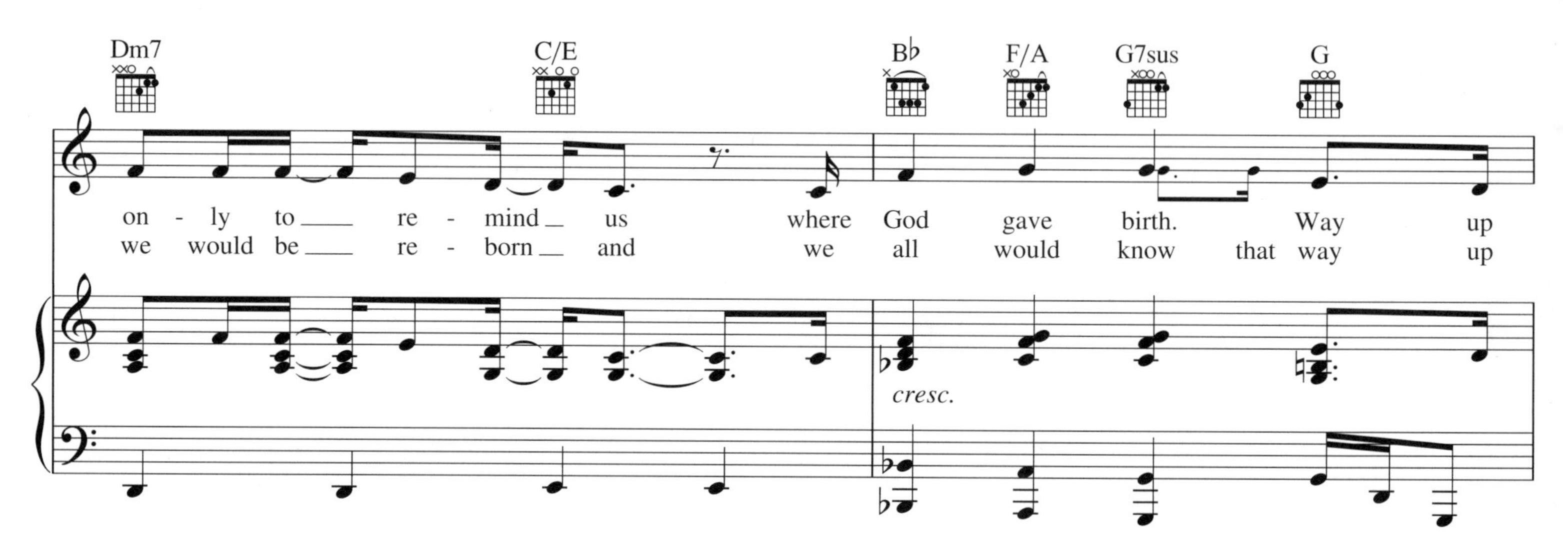
Dm7
C/E
B♭
F/A
G7sus
G
on - ly to re - mind us where God gave birth. Way up
we would be re - born and we all would know that way up
cresc.

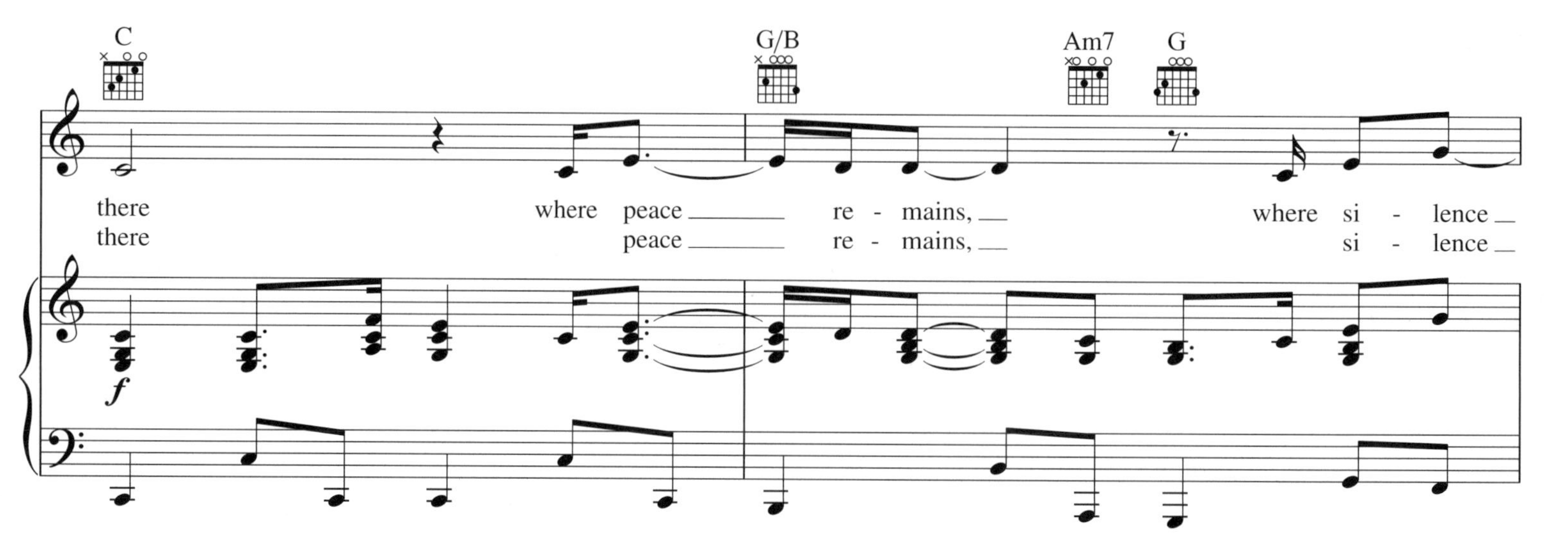
C
G/B
Am7
G
there where peace re - mains, where si - lence
there peace re - mains, si - lence
f

C/E
F
thun - ders and an - gels sing,
thun - ders and an - gels sing,
i - mag - i - na -
C/G
G
- tion and a - maz - ing grace bring us clos -
F
1
C
- er to our home in space. Like a
(that per - fect place.)
dim.
2
C
B♭
F
space. We are
place.)

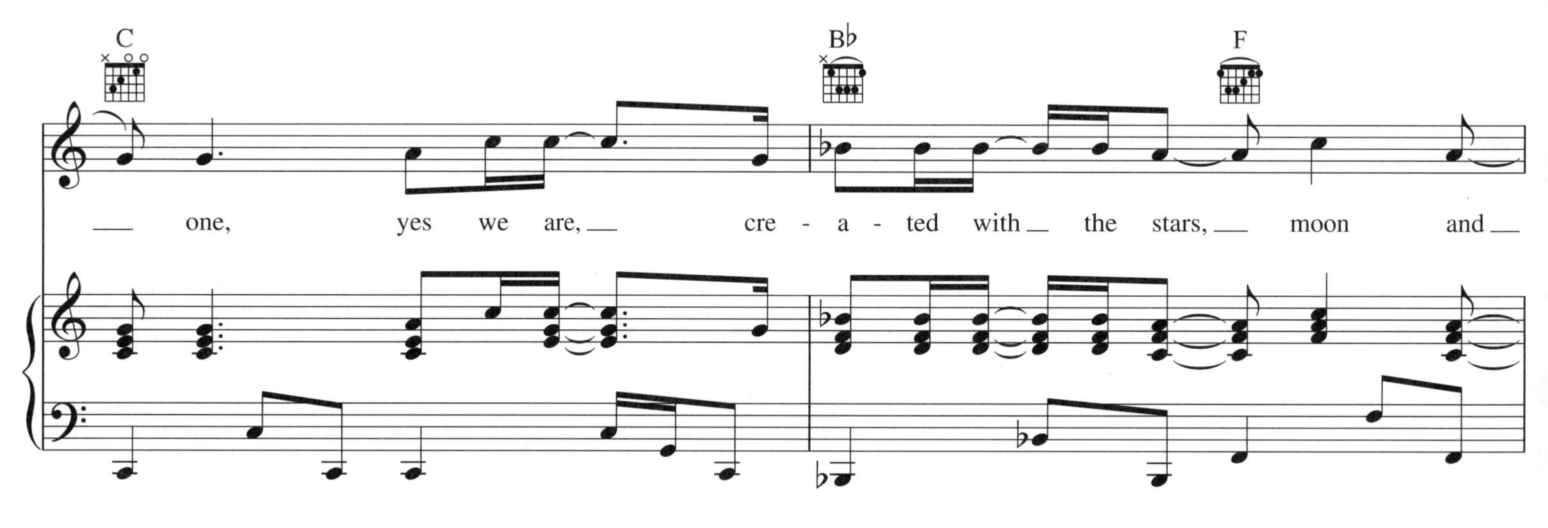
C
B♭
F
one, yes we are, cre - a - ted with the stars, moon and

C
G/B
Am
G
sun. Ev - 'ry wom - an, ev - 'ry child and

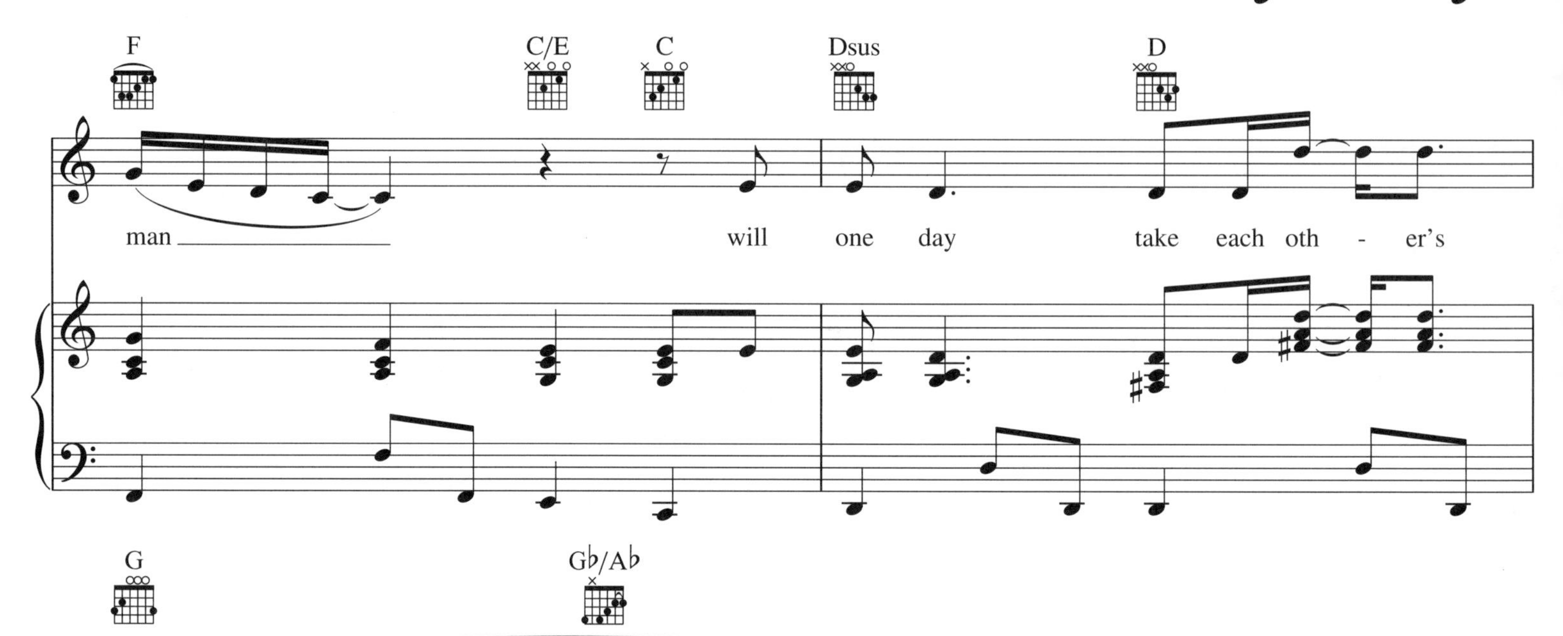
F
C/E
C
Dsus
D
man will one day take each oth - er's

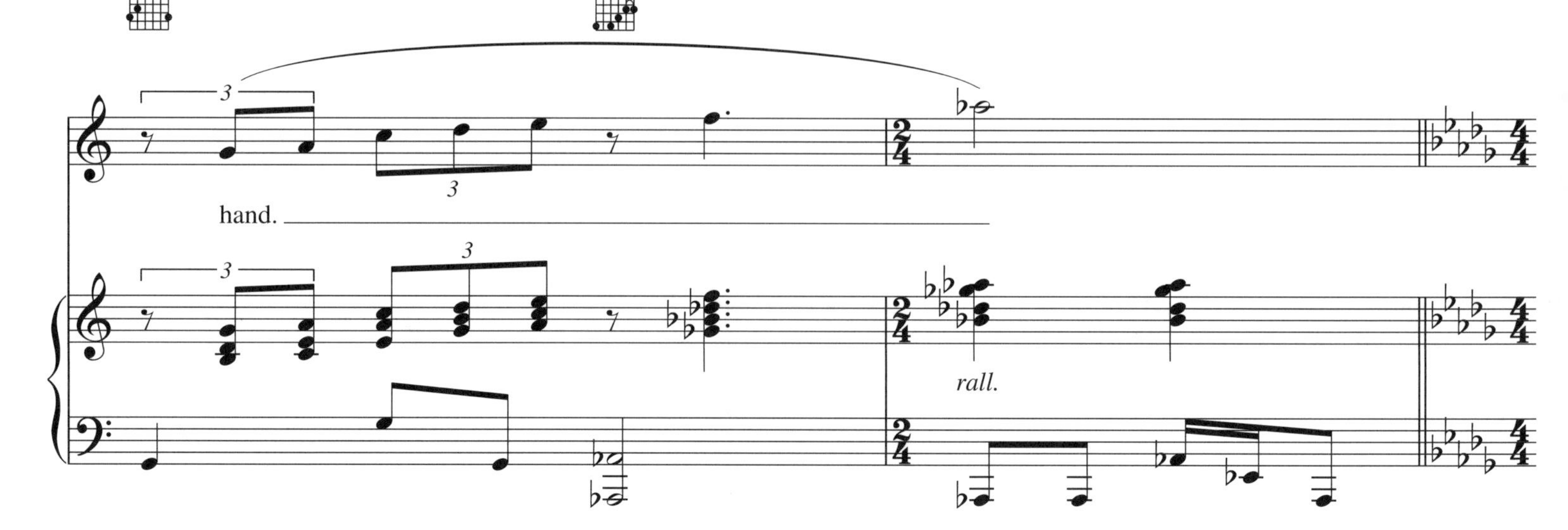
G
G♭/A♭
hand.
rall.

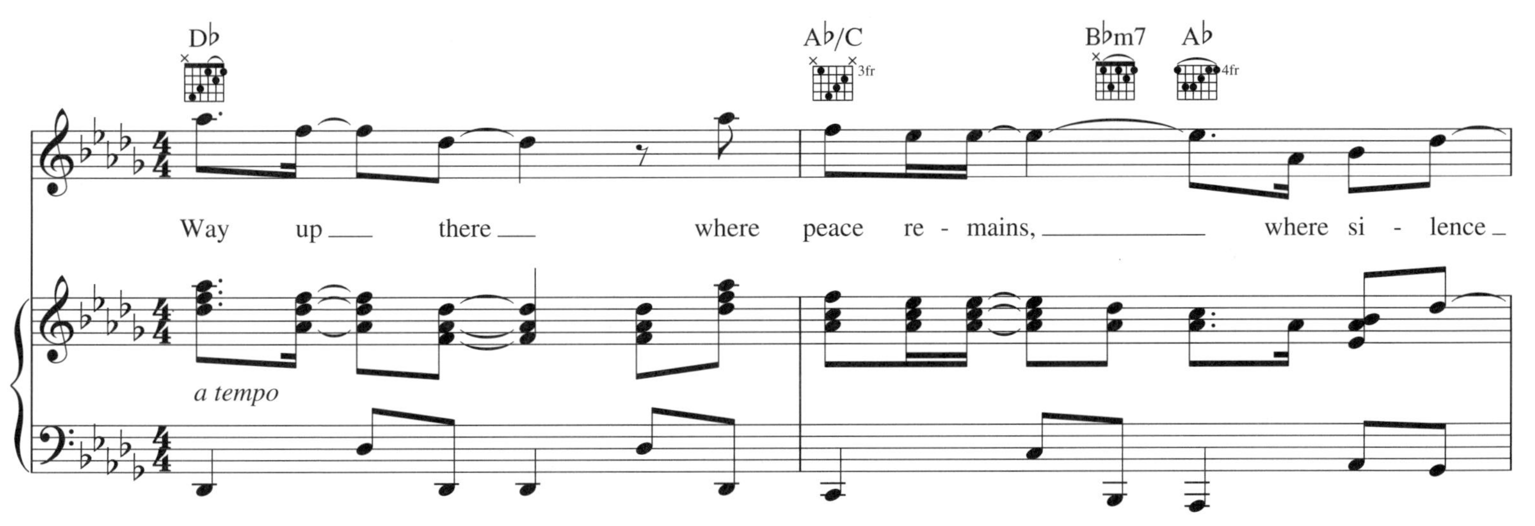
D♭
A♭/C
3fr
B♭m7
A♭
4fr
Way up there where peace remains, where silence
a tempo

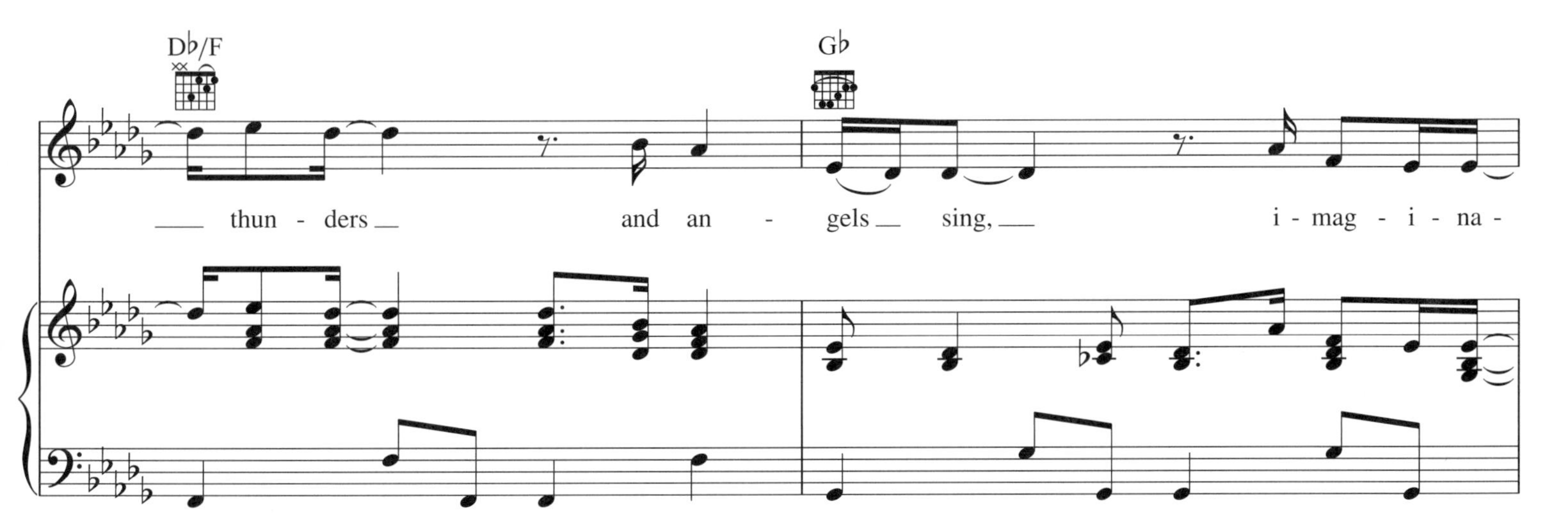
D♭/F
G♭
thunders and angels sing, imagina-

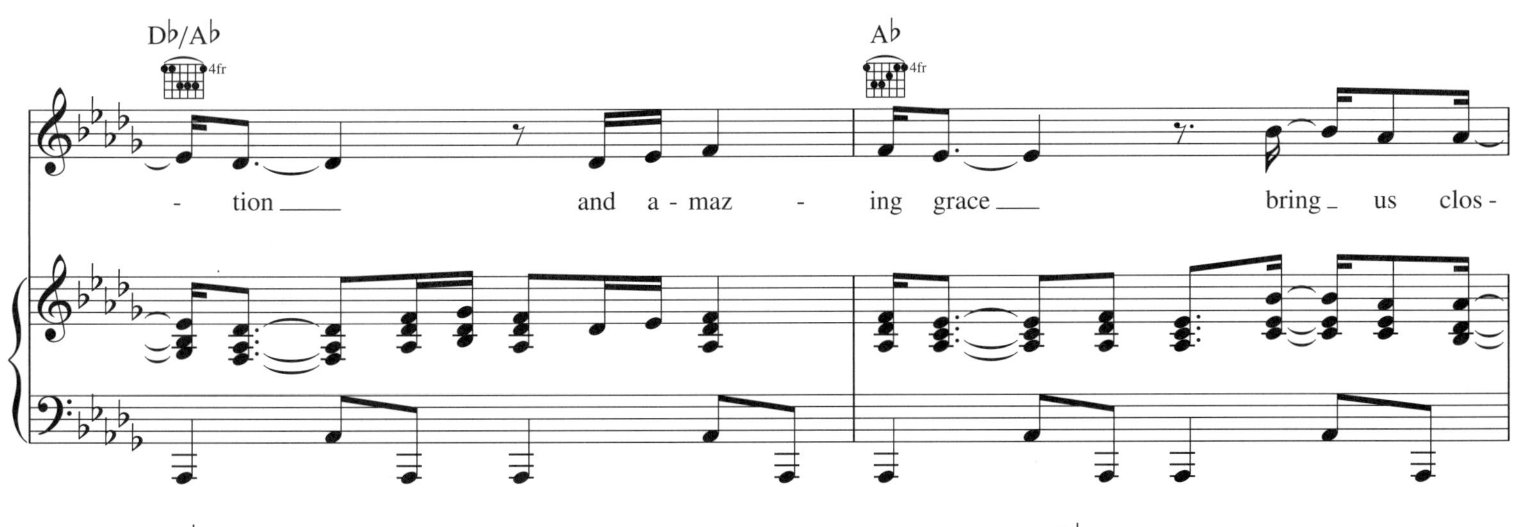
D♭/A♭
4fr
A♭
4fr
- tion and amazing grace bring us clos-

G♭
D♭
- er to our home in space.
(that perfect place.)
dim.
mp

YOU LIGHT UP MY LIFE

Words and Music by
JOSEPH BROOKS

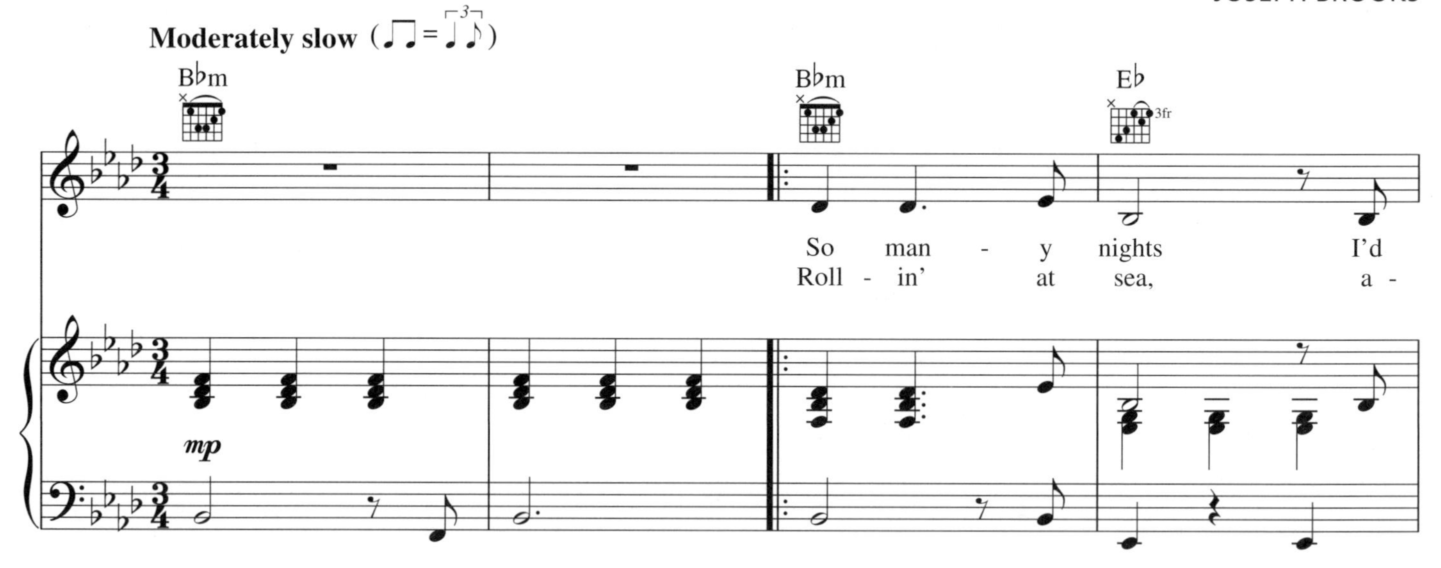

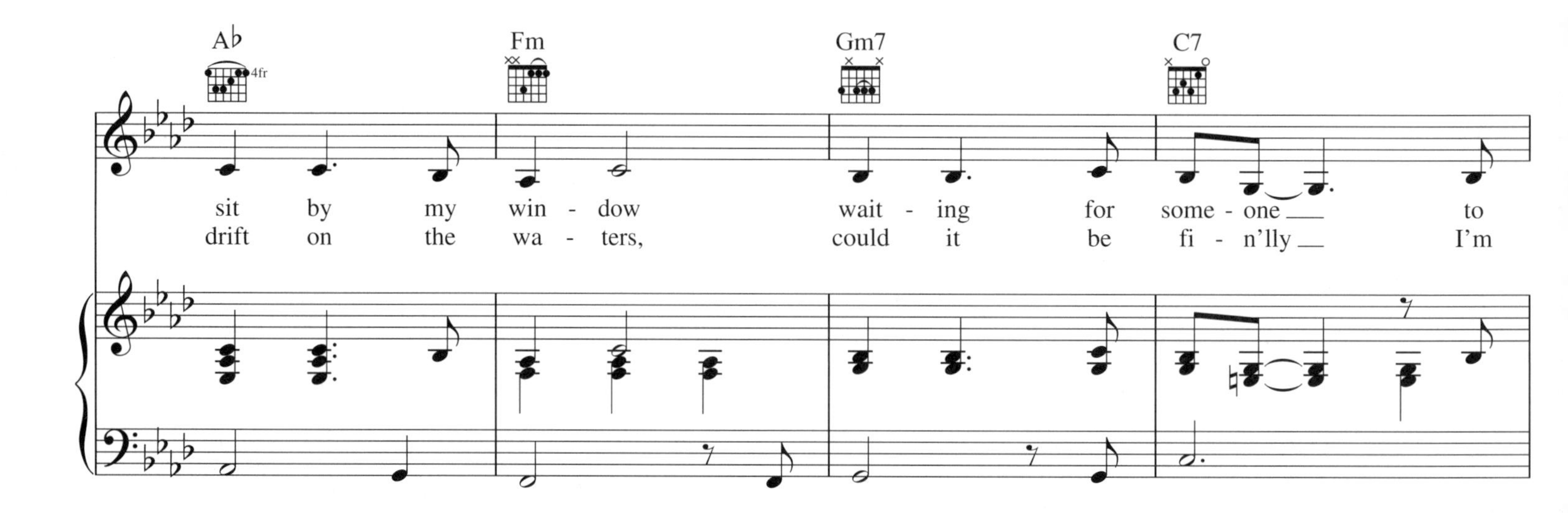

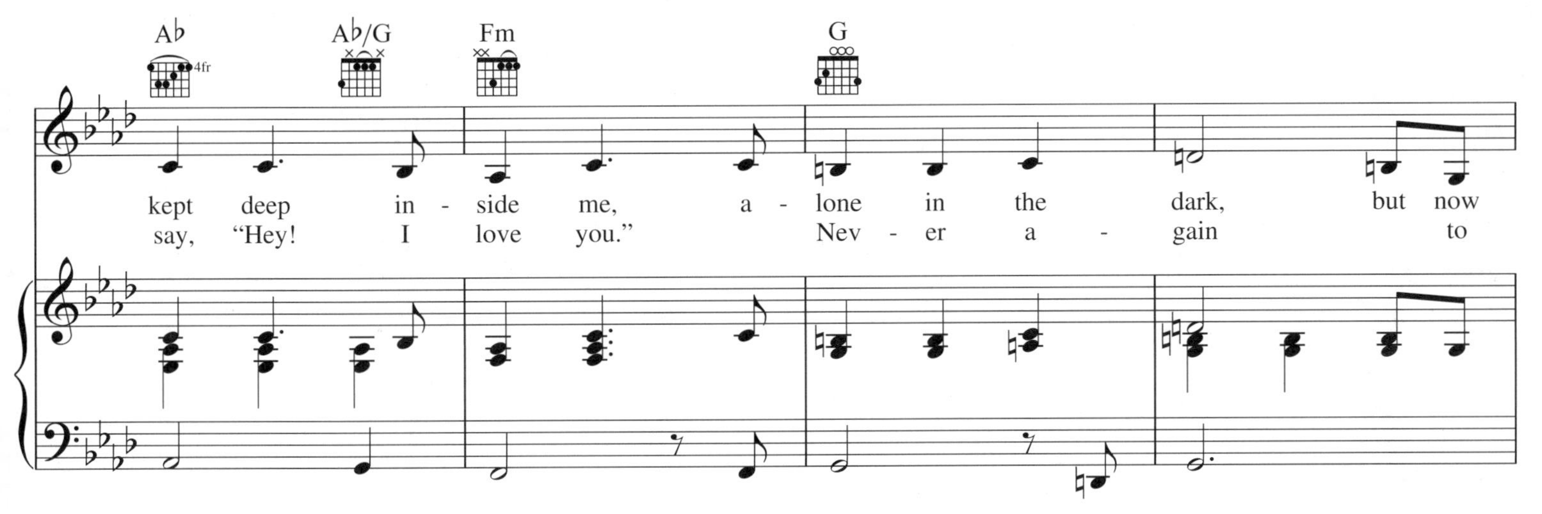
A♭
4fr
A♭/G
Fm
G
kept deep in - side me, a - lone in the dark, but now
say, "Hey! I love you." Nev - er a - gain to

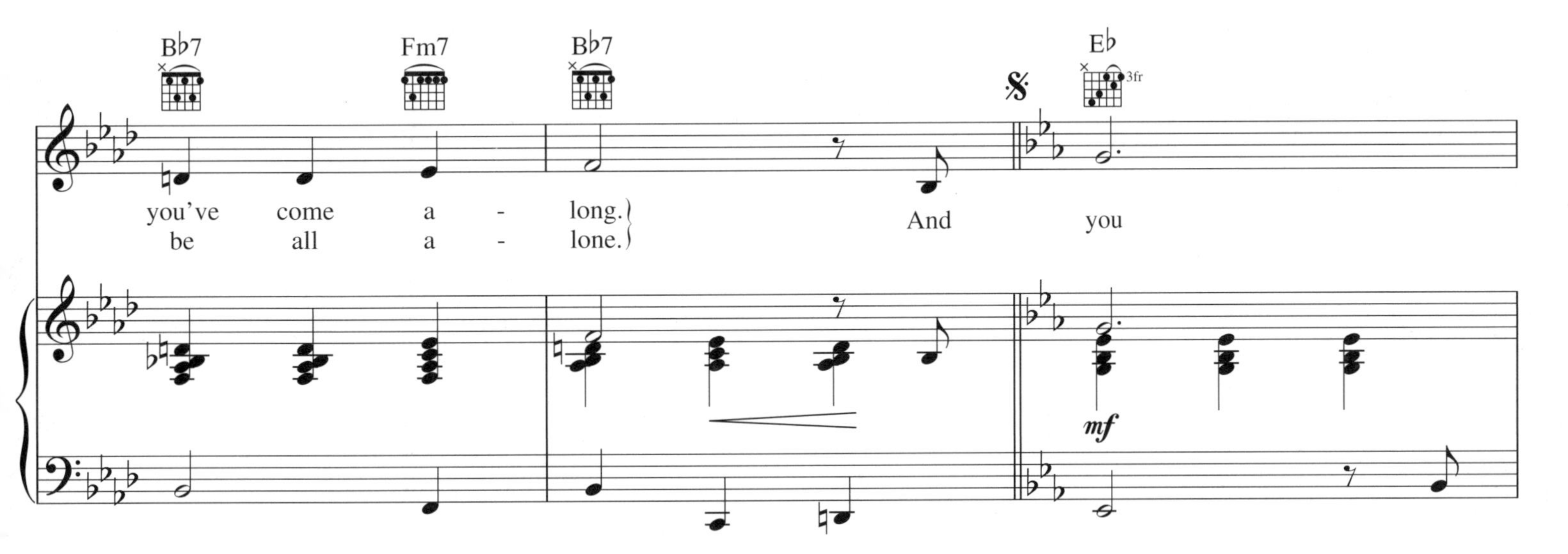
B♭7
Fm7
B♭7
E♭
3fr
you've come a - long.
be all a - lone.
And you
mf

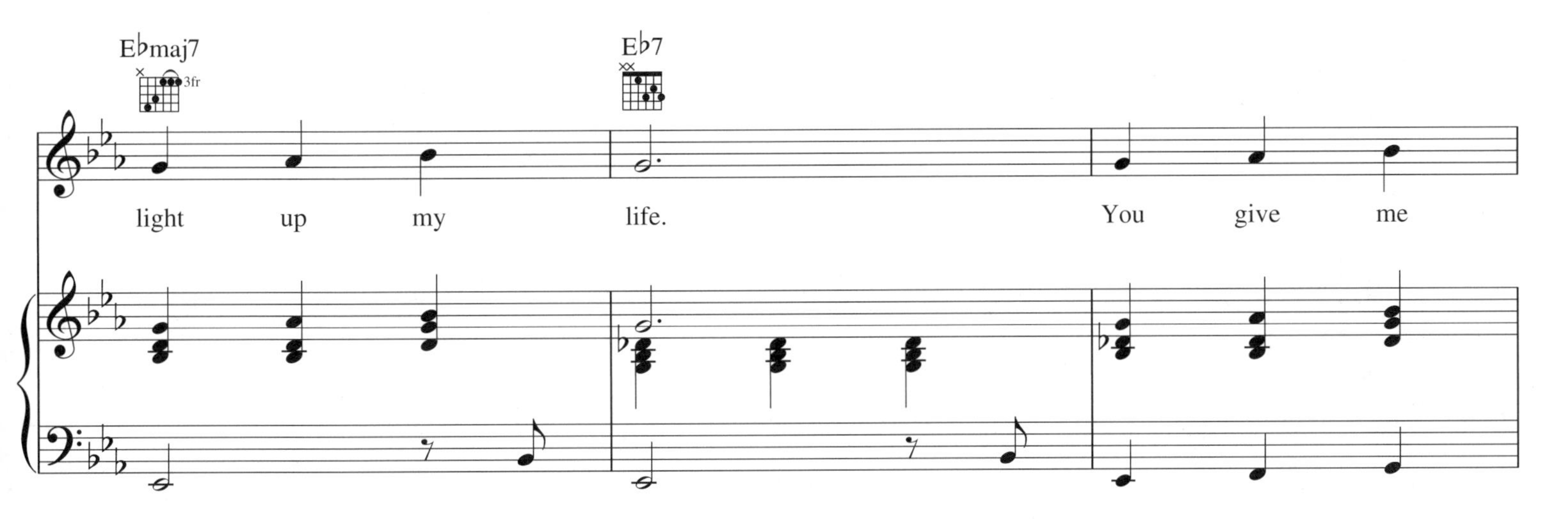
E♭maj7
3fr
E♭7
light up my life. You give me

C7
Fm
hope to car - ry on. You

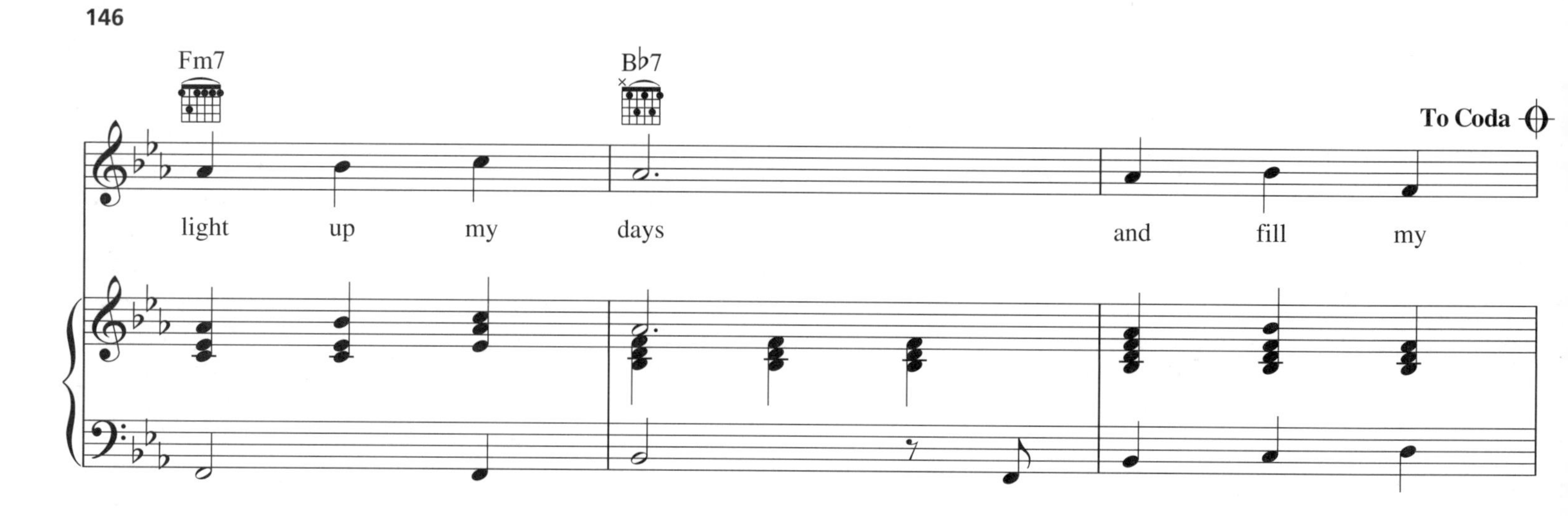
Fm7
B♭7
To Coda
light up my days and fill my

1
E♭
B♭/D
Cm
Fm
B♭7
3fr
nights with song.

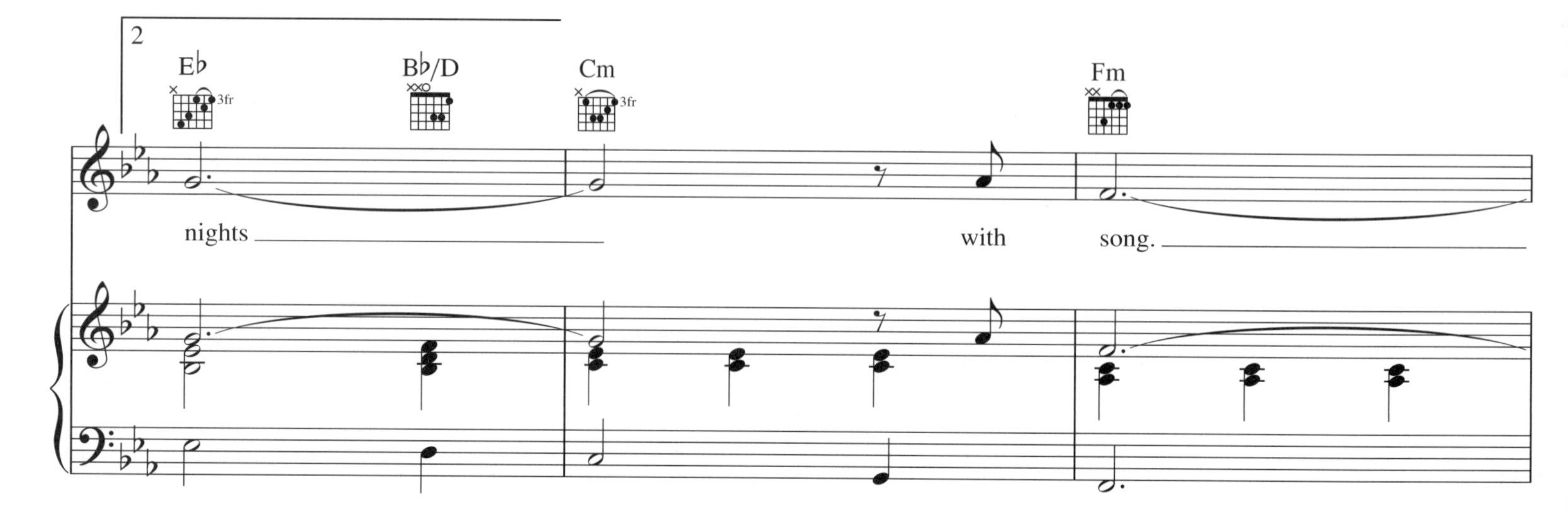
2
E♭
B♭/D
Cm
Fm
3fr
nights with song.

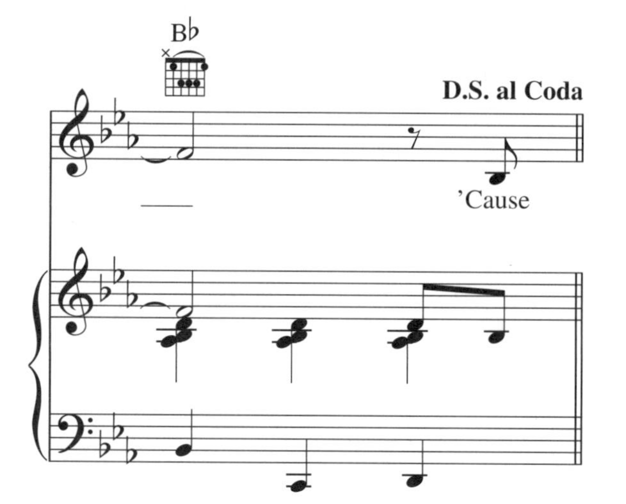
B♭
D.S. al Coda
'Cause

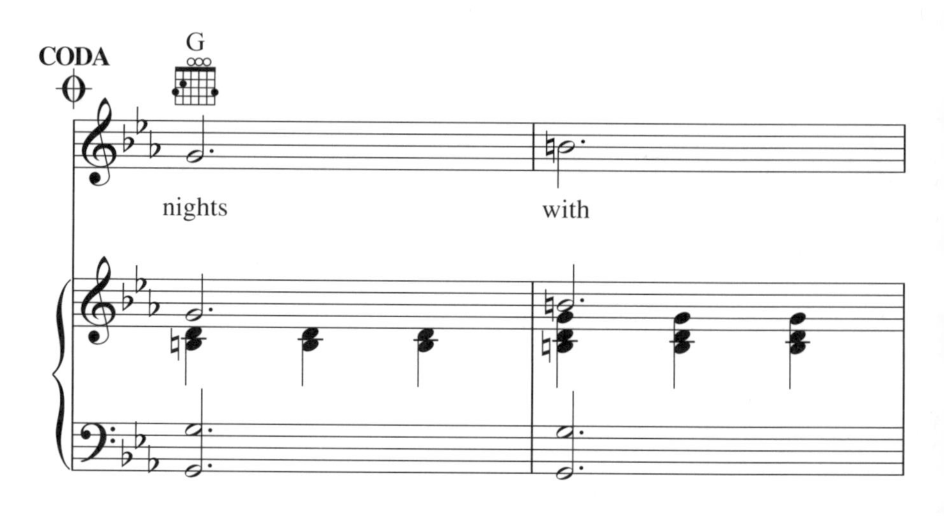
CODA
G
nights with

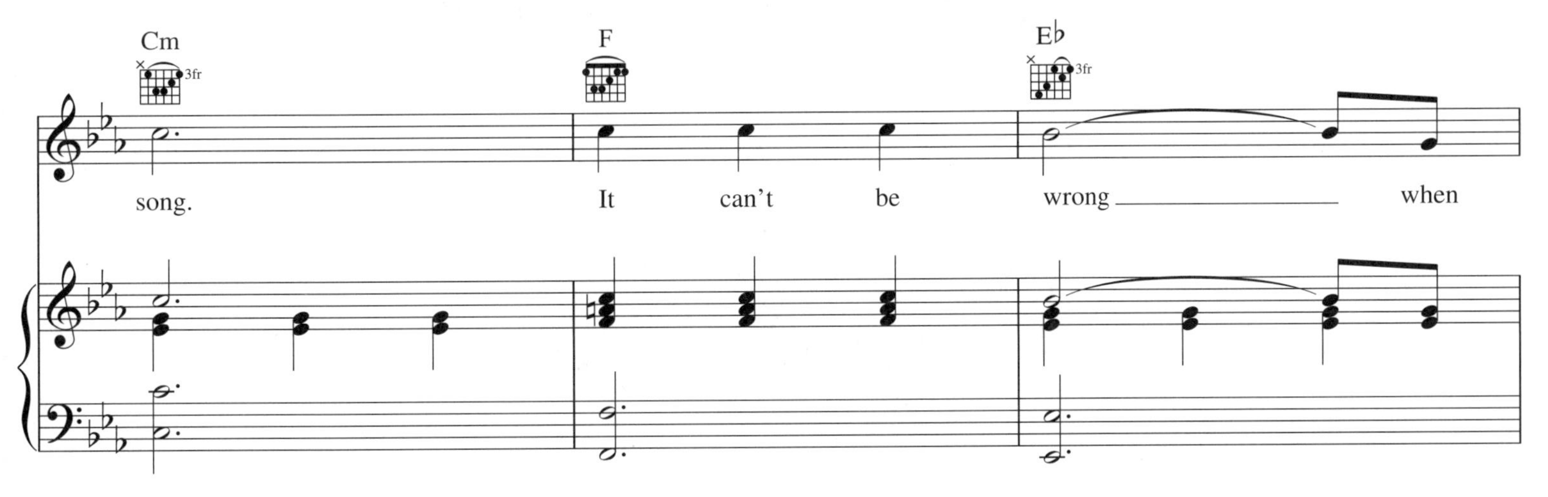
Cm
3fr
F
E♭
3fr
song.
It can't be wrong
when

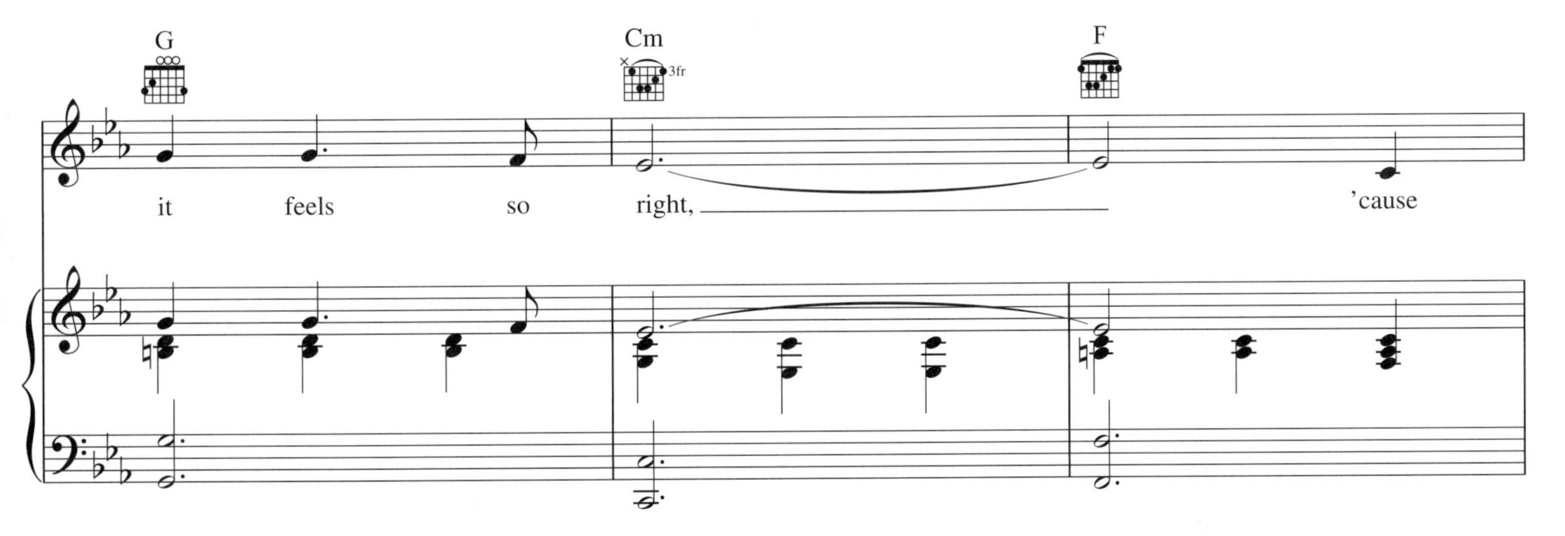
G
Cm
3fr
F
it feels so right,
'cause

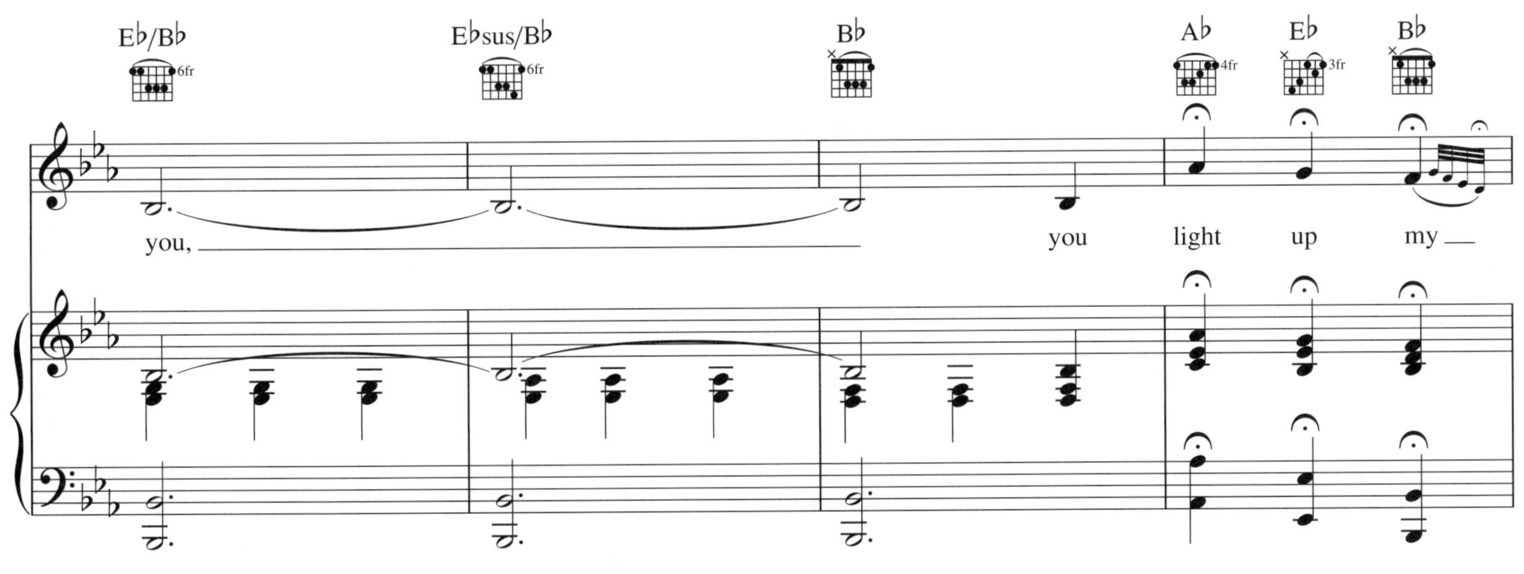
E♭/B♭
6fr
E♭sus/B♭
6fr
B♭
A♭
4fr
E♭
3fr
B♭
you,
you light up my

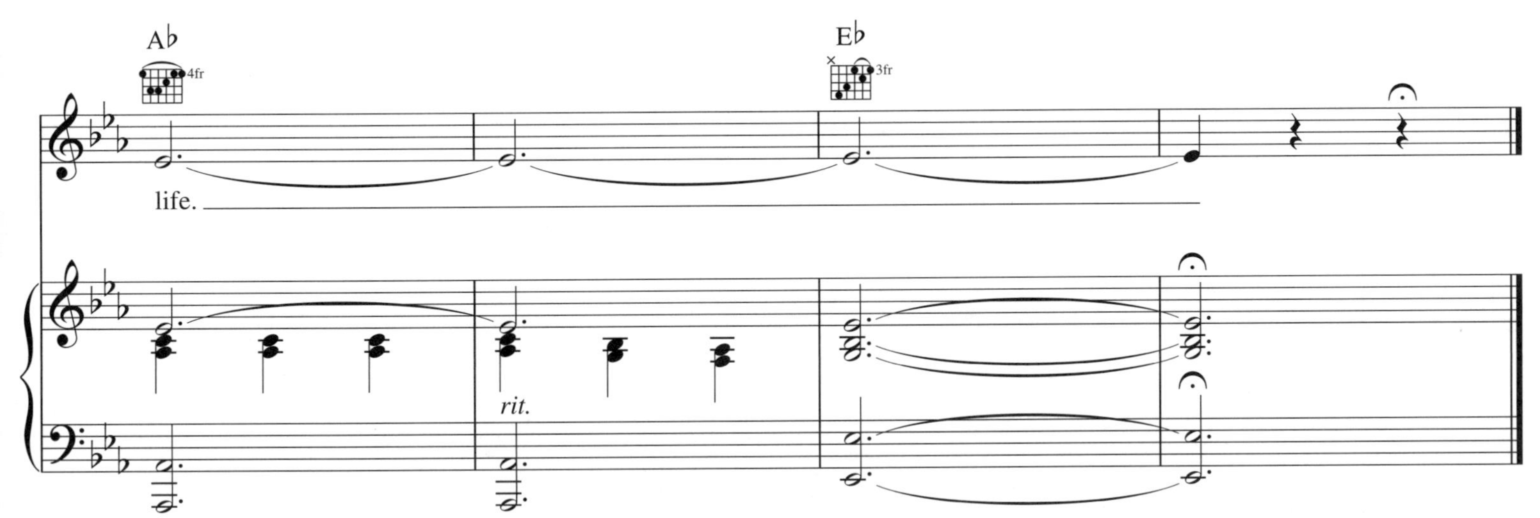
A♭
4fr
E♭
3fr
life.
rit.

YOU RAISE ME UP

Words and Music by BRENDAN GRAHAM
and ROLF LOVLAND

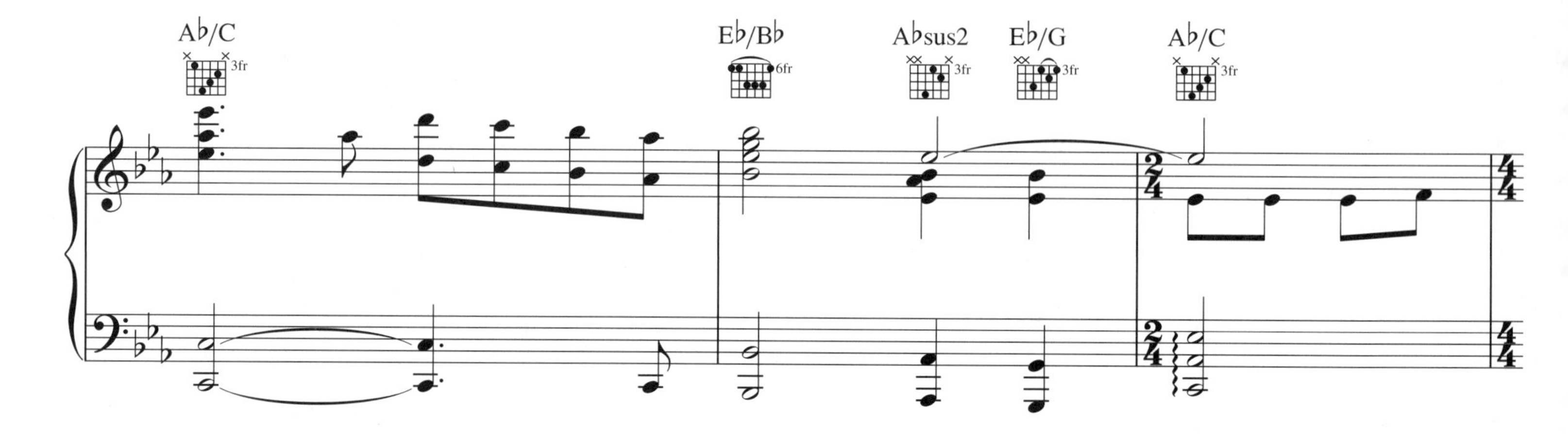

E♭5
E♭sus
E♭5
When I am down and oh, my soul's so wea - ry, when trou - bles
E♭/G
A♭sus2
B♭(add4)
A♭(add2)
A♭
come and my heart burdened be, then I am still and wait here in the
E♭(add2)/G
E♭/G
A♭
E♭
B♭7/E♭
E♭
si - lence un-til you come and sit a while with me. You raise me
Cm
A♭
E♭/G
B♭/D
Cm
A♭
up so I can stand on moun - tains. You raise me up to walk on storm - y

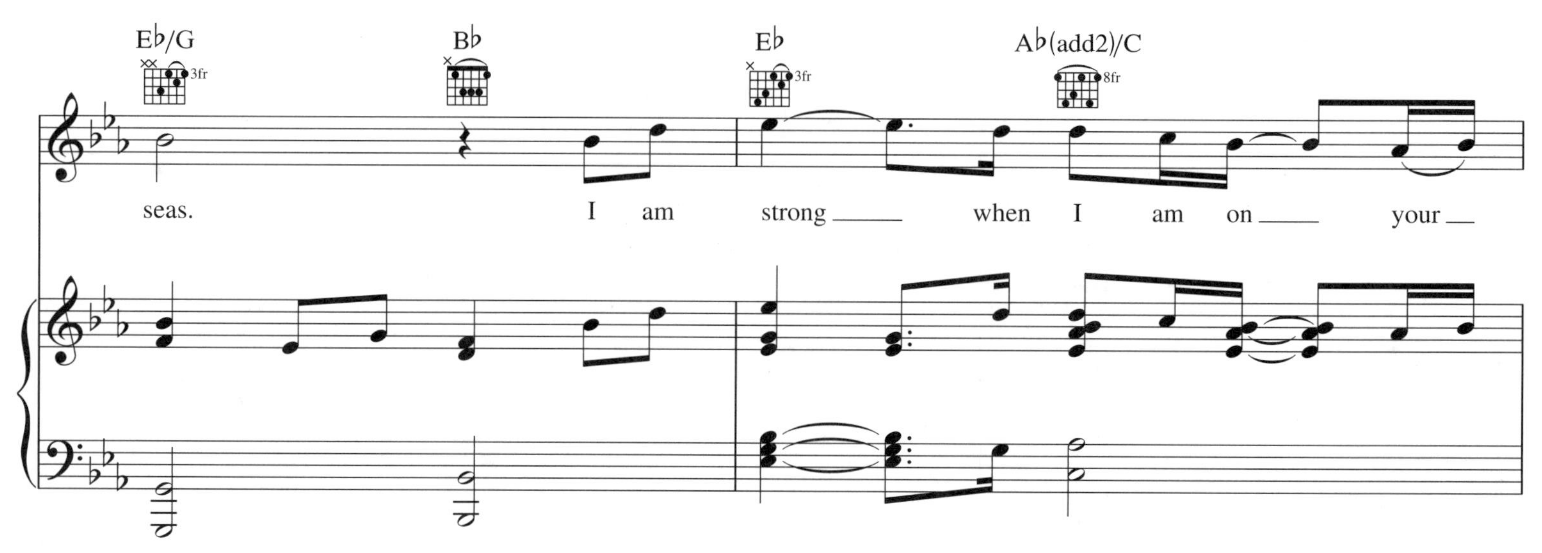
E♭/G
B♭
E♭
A♭(add2)/C
3fr
3fr
8fr
seas. I am strong when I am on your

E♭/B♭
E♭/G
A♭
E♭/B♭
B♭7
E♭
6fr
3fr
4fr
6fr
3fr
shoul - ders. You raise me up to more than I can be.

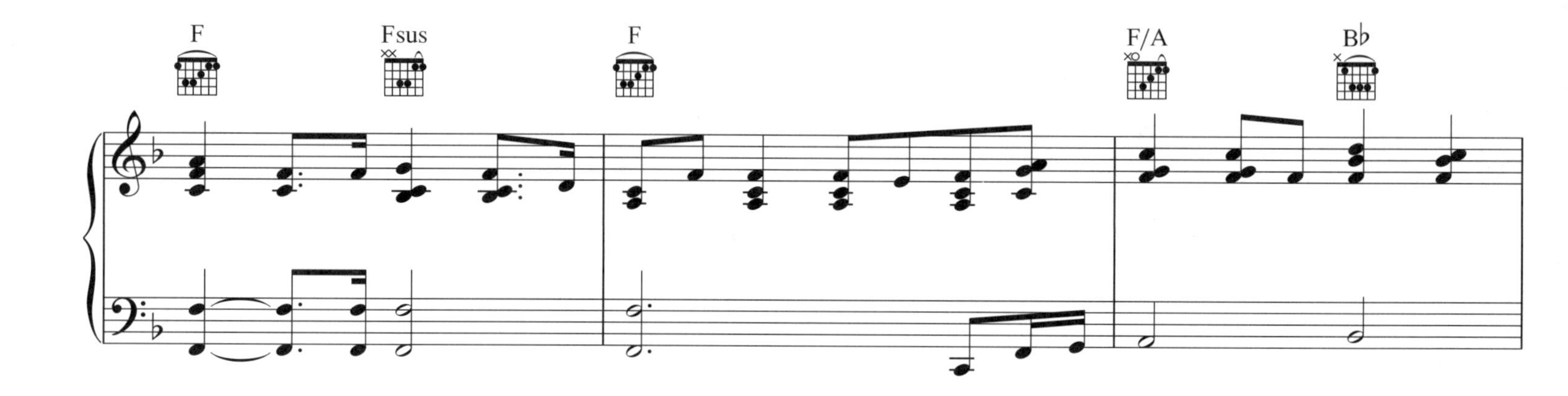
F
Fsus
F
F/A
B♭

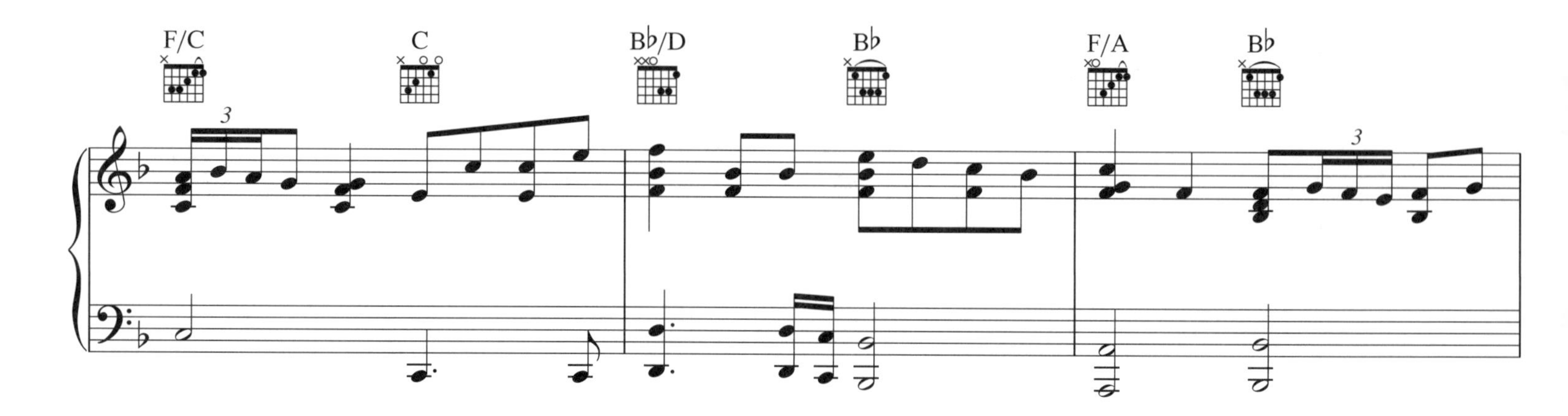
F/C
C
B♭/D
B♭
F/A
B♭
3
3

F/C
C7sus
F
C/E
Dm
C/B♭
B♭
You raise me up so I can stand on

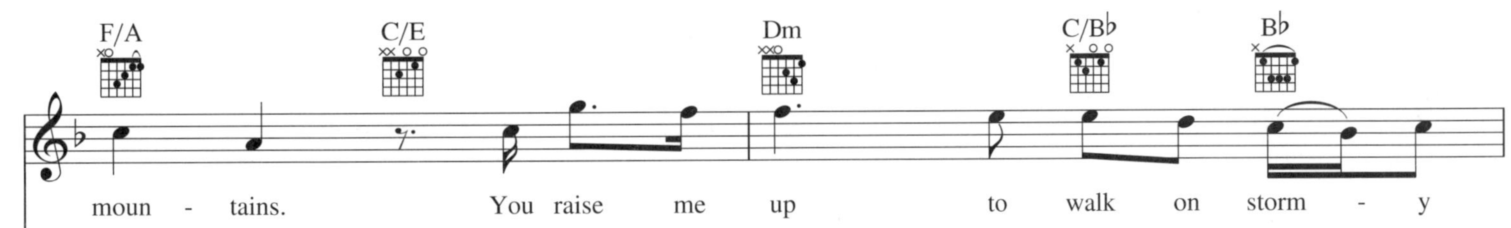
F/A
C/E
Dm
C/B♭
B♭
moun - tains. You raise me up to walk on storm - y

F/C
Csus
3fr
C
F
seas. I am strong when I am on your

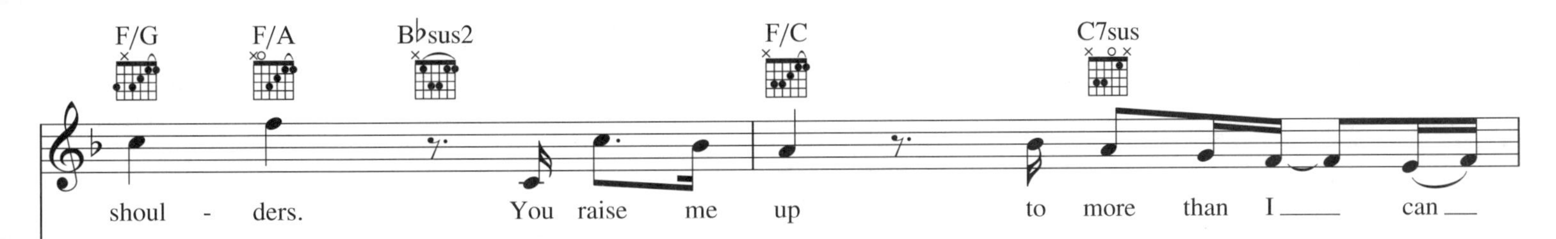
F/G
F/A
B♭sus2
F/C
C7sus
shoul - ders. You raise me up to more than I can

F
B♭/F
Gm/F
F
E♭m
6fr
D♭/C♭
C♭
be. You raise me up so I can stand _ on

G♭/B♭
6fr
D♭/F
E♭m
6fr
C♭
moun - tains. You raise me up to walk on storm - y

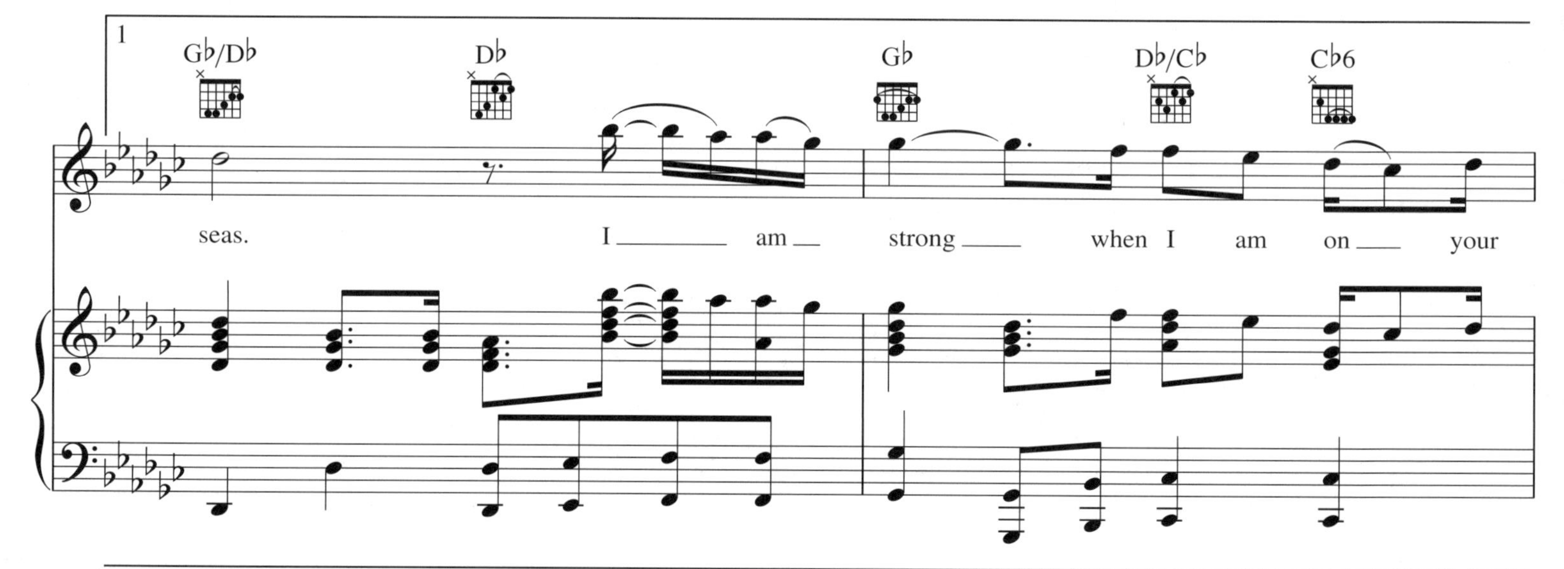
1
G♭/D♭
D♭
G♭
D♭/C♭
C♭6
seas. I ___ am ___ strong ___ when I am on ___ your

G♭
C♭/E♭
4fr
G♭/D♭
D♭7sus
4fr
D♭7
4fr
shoul - ders. You raise me up to more than I ___ can

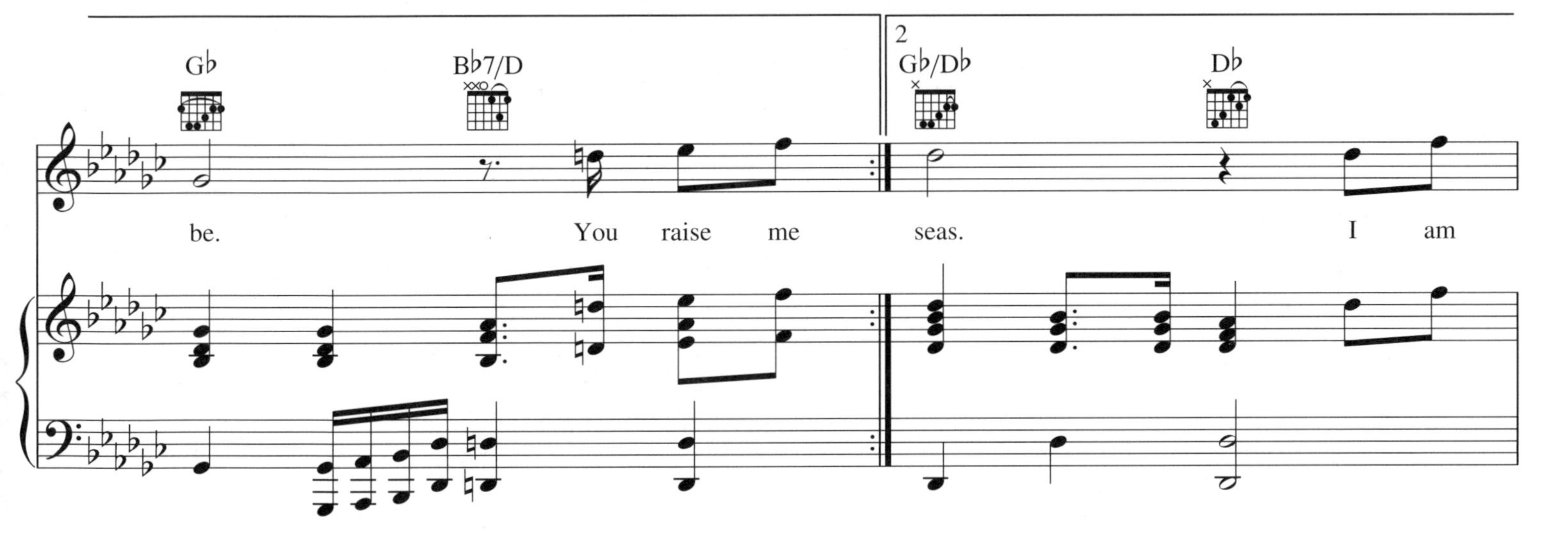
G♭
B♭7/D
2
G♭/D♭
D♭
be. You raise me seas. I am

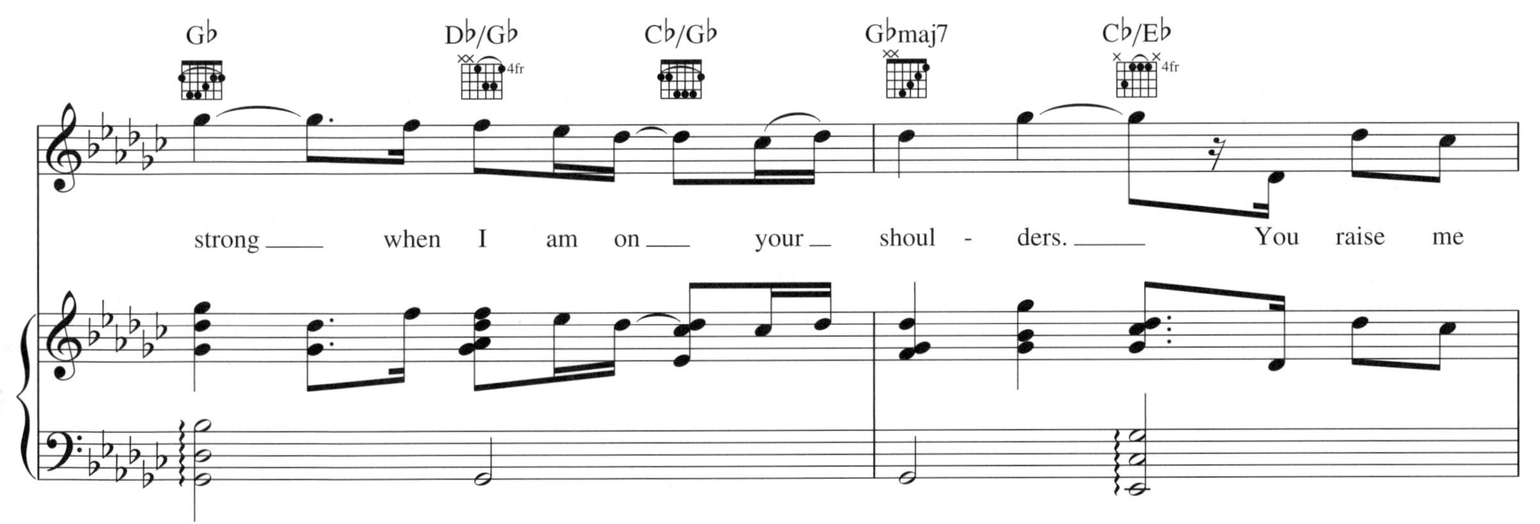
G♭
D♭/G♭
4fr
C♭/G♭
G♭maj7
C♭/E♭
4fr
strong when I am on your shoul - ders. You raise me

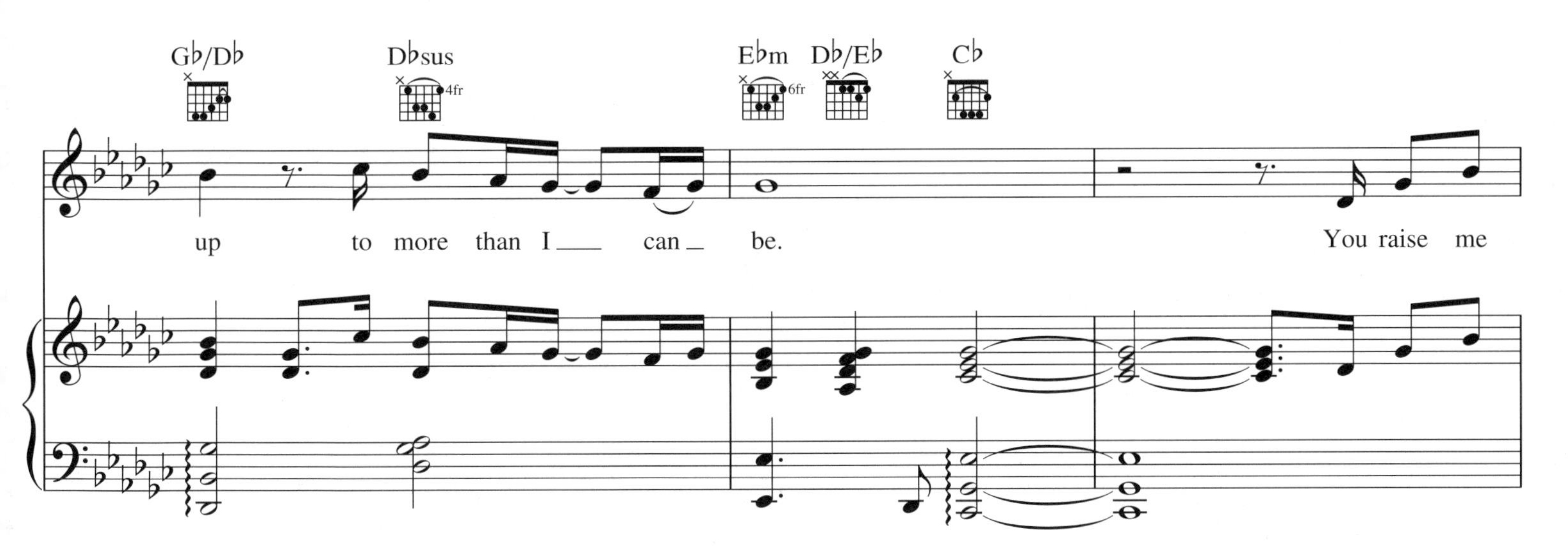
G♭/D♭
D♭sus
4fr
E♭m
6fr
D♭/E♭
C♭
up to more than I can be. You raise me

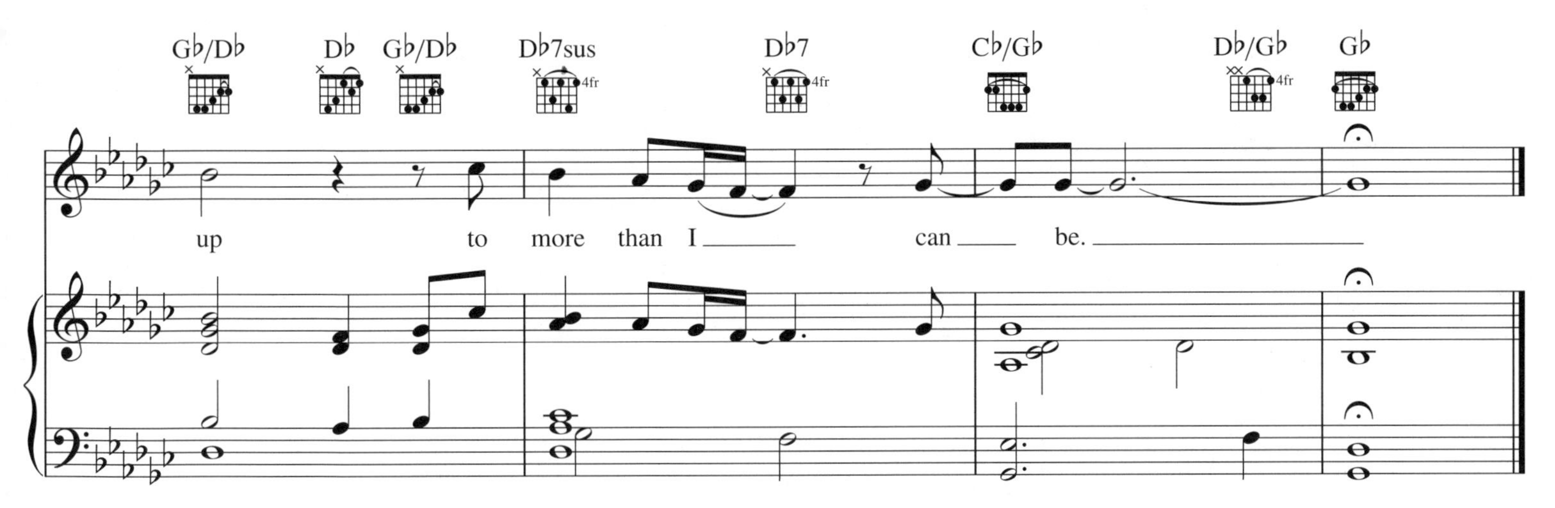
G♭/D♭
D♭
G♭/D♭
D♭7sus
4fr
D♭7
4fr
C♭/G♭
D♭/G♭
4fr
G♭
up to more than I can be.

WHEN YOU BELIEVE
(From The Prince Of Egypt)
from THE PRINCE OF EGYPT

Words and Music by STEPHEN SCHWARTZ
with Additional Music by BABYFACE

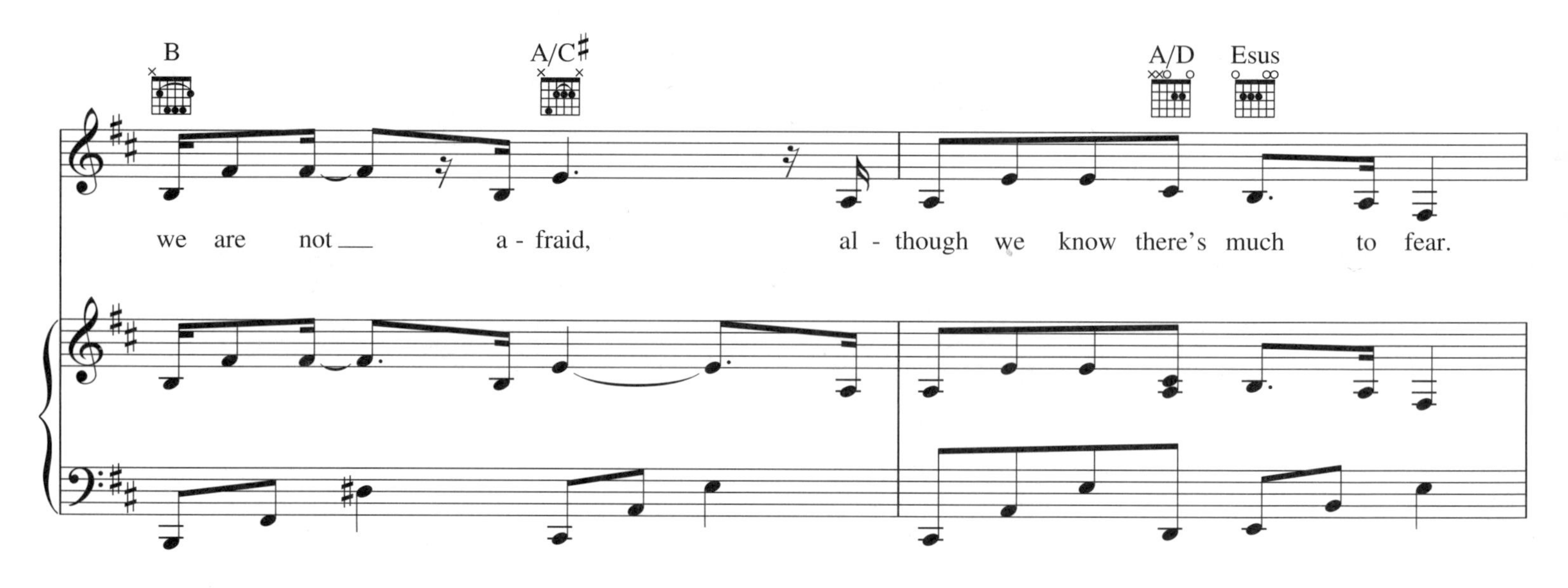

G
D/F♯
Em7
A/C♯
3
We were mov-ing moun - tains long _ be-fore we knew we could. ___
D
A/C♯
Bm
F♯m/A
There can be mir - a-cles, _ when you be - lieve. ___ Though hope is frail, it's
Gmaj7
F♯m/A
Em/A
D
A/C♯
hard to kill. Who knows what mir - a - cles _ you can a - chieve? ___
Bm
F♯m7
Gmaj7
Em7
A
When you be-lieve, some-how you will. You will when _ you _ be-lieve. _

Bm
A
In this time of fear, when
mf

F♯m7
Bm
Gmaj9
prayer so of - ten proves in vain, hope seems like the sum - mer birds, too

Em7
F♯m7
B
A/C♯
swift - ly flown a - way. Yet now I'm stand - ing here, my

A/D
Esus
G
D/F♯
heart so full I can't ex - plain, seek - ing faith and speak - ing words I

Em7
A/C♯
E
never thought I'd say:
There can be miracles,
B/D♯
C♯m
G♯m/B
Amaj7
G♯m/B
F♯m/B
4fr
when you believe.
(When you believe.)
Though hope is frail, it's hard to kill.
E
B/D♯
Who knows what miracles you can achieve?
(You can achieve?)
C♯m
G♯m7
Amaj7
G♯m7
When you believe, somehow you will.

F♯m7
E
B/D♯
4fr
E
C♯m7
4fr
You will when you be - lieve.
Amaj9
Bsus
2fr
B/A
A/C♯
B/D♯
4fr
They don't al - ways hap - pen when you ask.
Esus
E
B/D♯
4fr
C♯m7
4fr
A/C♯
B/D♯
4fr
And it's eas - y to give in to your fear.
Esus
E
F♯m7
E/G♯
Asus2
But when you're blind - ed by your pain, can't see

B
C♯m7
4fr
3
your way clear through the rain, a small but still re-sil - ient voice says
A/B
G♯m/B
F♯m/B
F♯
C♯/E♯
help is ver - y near. There can be mir - a - cles, when you be - lieve.
cresc.
rit.
f a tempo
D♯m
A♯m/C♯
Bmaj7
G♯m/C♯
6fr
Though hope is frail, it's hard to kill. Who knows what mir - a - cles
D♯m
F♯/A♯
you can a - chieve? When you be - lieve, some - how you will,

D♯m
F♯/A♯
G♯m7
C♯
D♯m
C♯6
now you will. You will when you be - lieve.
Bmaj7
N.C.
You will when you, you will when you be -
mf
F♯
D♯m
F♯
lieve, just be- lieve, just be-
mp
D♯m
F♯
lieve. You will when you be - lieve.